THE CAMBRIDGE COMPANION TO
BRITISH THEATRE, 1730–1830

This *Companion* offers a wide-ranging and innovative guide to one of the most exciting and important periods in British theatrical history. The scope of the volume extends from the age of Garrick to the Romantic transformation of acting inaugurated by Edmund Kean. The book brings together cutting-edge scholarship from leading international scholars in the long eighteenth century, offering lively and original insights into the world of the stage, its most influential playwrights and the professional lives of celebrated performers such as James Quin, George Anne Bellamy, John Philip Kemble, Dora Jordan, Fanny Abington and Sarah Siddons. The volume includes essential chapters about eighteenth-century acting, production and audiences, important surveys of key theatrical forms such as tragedy, comedy, melodrama and pantomime as well as a range of thematic essays on subjects such as private theatricals, 'black' theatre and the representation of empire.

JANE MOODY is a Professor in the Department of English and Related Literature at the University of York.

DANIEL O'QUINN is an Associate Professor in the School of English and Theatre Studies at the University Guelph.

D0221958

THE CAMBRIDGE COMPANION TO
BRITISH THEATRE, 1730–1830

EDITED BY
JANE MOODY

and

DANIEL O'QUINN

CAMBRIDGE
UNIVERSITY PRESS

CAMBRIDGE UNIVERSITY PRESS
Cambridge, New York, Melbourne, Madrid, Cape Town, Singapore, São Paulo

Cambridge University Press
The Edinburgh Building, Cambridge CB2 8RU, UK

Published in the United States of America by Cambridge University Press, New York

www.cambridge.org
Information on this title: www.cambridge.org/9780521617772

First published 2007

Printed in the United Kingdom at the University Press, Cambridge

A catalogue record for this publication is available from the British Library

ISBN 978-0-521-85237-1 hardback
ISBN 978-0-521-61777-2 paperback

CONTENTS

ILLUSTRATIONS

CONTRIBUTORS

MISTY G. ANDERSON is an Associate Professor of English at the University of Tennessee. She is the author of *Female Playwrights and Eighteenth-Century Comedy: Negotiating Marriage on the London Stage* (Palgrave, 2002) and the current co-editor of the journal *Restoration*.

JACKY BRATTON is a Research Professor in the Department of Theatre at Royal Holloway College, University of London. She is the author of numerous books and essays on the nineteenth-century stage and nineteenth-century popular culture. Her most recent book, *New Readings in Theatre History* was published by Cambridge University Press in 2003.

CHRISTOPHER BAUGH is Professor in the School of Performance and Cultural Industries, University of Leeds. He has written widely on the history of scenography in the eighteenth and nineteenth centuries and is a practising scenographer. His most recent book, *Theatre, Performance and Technology* (Palgrave, 2005) examines the development of scenography in the twentieth century.

MICHAEL BURDEN, who is director of New Chamber Opera, is Dean and Fellow in Opera Studies at New College, University of Oxford and Reader in Music. He has published numerous articles on opera, staging, and music theatre, is Associate Editor for eighteenth-century music subjects for the Dictionary of National Biography, and has editing interests in seventeenth- and eighteenth-century Italian and English music. He is currently completing a volume for Yale University Press on the staging of opera in London from 1660 to 1860.

HELEN M. BURKE is an Associate Professor of English at Florida State University. She is the author of *Riotous Performances: The Struggle for Hegemony in the Irish Theatre, 1712–1784* (University of Notre Dame, 2003), and has written a number of articles on Irish and English theatre in the eighteenth century.

JULIE A. CARLSON is Professor of English at University of California, Santa Barbara. She is author of *In the Theatre of Romanticism: Coleridge, Nationalism, Women*

(Cambridge University Press, 1994), editor of a special issue of *South Atlantic Quarterly* entitled 'Domestic/Tragedy' (1998), and has written numerous articles on Romantic drama and theatre. Her most recent book is *England's First Family of Writers: Mary Wollstonecraft, William Godwin, Mary Shelley* (Johns Hopkins University Press, 2007).

JIM DAVIS is Professor and Chair of Theatre Studies at the University of Warwick. He is the author of several books and articles on eighteenth- and nineteenth-century theatre including the recent co-authored study, *Reflecting the Audience: London Theatregoing, 1840–1880* (University of Iowa Press, 2001).

LISA A. FREEMAN is an Associate Professor of English at the University of Illinois, Chicago. She is the author of *Character's Theater: Genre and Identity on the Eighteenth-Century English Stage* (University of Pennsylvania Press, 2002). She is currently at work on a book-length study titled *Antitheatricality and the Body Public: From the Renaissance to the NEA*.

JANE MOODY is a Professor in the Department of English and Related Literature at the University of York. She is the author of *Illegitimate Theatre in London, 1770–1840* (Cambridge University Press, 2000), co-editor of *Theatre and Celebrity in Britain, 1660–2000* (Palgrave, 2005), and has written a number of essays on the history of British theatre in the eighteenth and nineteenth centuries.

JONATHAN MULROONEY is Assistant Professor of English at the College of the Holy Cross. His interests include Romantic-period public culture, William Hazlitt and John Keats. His essays have appeared in *Studies in the Novel*, *Nineteenth-Century Contexts* and *Studies in Romanticism*. He is currently completing a book entitled *Romanticism and the Subject of Theater*, which explores the relation between theatrical experience and lyric poetry in early nineteenth-century Britain.

JOHN O'BRIEN is Associate Professor of English at the University of Virginia. He is the author of *Harlequin Britain: Pantomime and Entertainment, 1690–1760* (Johns Hopkins University Press, 2004) and edited the Broadview Literary Texts edition of Susanna Centlivre's 1714 play *The Wonder: A Woman Keeps a Secret*.

DANIEL O'QUINN is an Associate Professor in the School of English and Theatre Studies at the University of Guelph. He is the author of *Staging Governance: Theatrical Imperialism in London, 1770–1800* (Johns Hopkins University Press, 2005). His articles on the intersection of sexuality, race and British culture have appeared in journals including *Theatre Journal*, *Romantic Praxis*, *ELH*, *Texas Studies in Literature and Language*, *Studies in Romanticism*, *European Romantic Review*, *Literature Compass* and *October*. He is currently editing the *Travels of Mirza Abu Taleb Khan* for Broadview Press and working on a project on late eighteenth-century political performance.

LAURA ROSENTHAL teaches in the Department of English at the University of Maryland. She is the author of *Playwrights and Plagiarists in Early Modern England: Gender, Authorship, Literary Property* (Cornell University Press, 1996) and a number of articles on Restoration and eighteenth-century theatre. Her book *Infamous Commerce: Prostitution in Eighteenth-Century British Literature and Culture* was published by Cornell in 2006.

GILLIAN RUSSELL is Reader in the School of Humanities, Australian National University, Canberra. She is the author of *The Theatres of War: Performance, Politics and Society, 1793–1815* (Oxford, 1995) and co-editor of *Romantic Sociability: Social Networks and Literature Culture in Britain, 1770–1840* (Cambridge, 2002).

SUSAN STAVES is Emeritus Professor in the Department of English and American Literature at Brandeis University. She has published over forty books and articles on Restoration and eighteenth-century literary, historical and legal subjects. Her most recent book is *A Literary History of Women's Writing in Britain, 1660–1789* (Cambridge University Press, 2006).

KRISTINA STRAUB is Professor of Literary and Cultural Studies at Carnegie Mellon. She has written books and articles on the eighteenth-century English novel and on theatre, as well as essays on feminist theory. She is editor of a collection of essays on gender ambiguity and has contributed to a number of teaching and scholarly editions of eighteenth-century British novels and plays.

PETER THOMSON is Emeritus Professor of Drama at the University of Exeter. He has written books on Shakespeare and Brecht, *On Actors and Acting* (University of Exeter Press, 2000) and was General Editor of the three-volume *Cambridge History of British Theatre* (2004).

PREFACE

This *Companion* explores one of the most exciting and important periods in British theatre history, from the age of Garrick to the Romantic transformation of acting pioneered by Edmund Kean. Designed for readers wishing to learn more about the players, playwrights and theatre of this period, the volume acts as a bridge between the *Cambridge Companion to English Restoration Theatre*, edited by Deborah Payne Fisk, and the *Cambridge Companion to Edwardian and Victorian Theatre*, edited by Kerry Powell.

A few plays from the eighteenth-century stage, including Goldsmith's *She Stoops to Conquer* and Sheridan's *The School for Scandal*, are immediately familiar to the modern playgoer. Names of celebrated performers such as David Garrick, Frances Abington, John Philip Kemble, Dora Jordan and Sarah Siddons may also strike a recognisable chord. In towns and cities, the passer-by glimpses the rich architectural heritage of the period's theatre in the facades and interiors of Britain's metropolitan and provincial playhouses. For many decades, however, these legacies have suffered from critical distortions and relative scholarly neglect. Perhaps because theatre was both insistently topical and deeply connected to the conditions and controversies of eighteenth-century social and political life, the plays of this period have not always fared well among critics focusing solely on dramatic literature. But it was precisely these close relationships between audiences, performances and institutions which helped to make British theatre an important site for political, social and cultural debate.

The period covered by this *Companion* corresponds to the emergence and institutionalization of commercial entertainment across the British Isles as well as important developments in the nature of and audiences for print culture. Indeed, the dynamic interactions between performance and print in eighteenth-century Britain helped to generate many features of what we now recognise as mass culture. Nowhere is this phenomenon more evident than in the complex history of theatrical celebrity charted in many of the essays in this volume. At the same time, the symbiotic relationships between theatre, newspapers and the graphic arts helped to broaden the social interactions taking place in and around metropolitan and provincial theatres. In turn, this extension of sociability sparked the emergence of cultural media which commented on and also attempted to regulate the relationship between audiences, plays and theatrical institutions. This is a period characterised by various kinds of theatrical censorship as well as some direct and indirect forms of resistance to censorship. Sometimes, the theatre itself became a site of violence: a telling indication of just how risky the enterprise of performance could be. And the eighteenth century is also the historical moment when British theatre goes global, both in the sense of being exported around the world and in the sense of starting to represent the emerging British empire.

Over the last two decades, a critical transformation has taken place which offers the opportunity to enlarge our knowledge and to provide a richer context for eighteenth-century British theatre. Moreover, the issues arising from these performances have become important beyond the immediate fields of theatre history and theatrical criticism, for they now speak to some of the most pressing concerns of historical and cultural studies. Significantly, this transformation has shaped the contemporary theatrical repertoire as well as the terms of academic debate. Dramatists have even made eighteenth-century theatre the subject of new plays: April de Angelis's comedy, *A Laughing Matter*, revisits the witty and scandalous world of the London stage; Timberlake Wertenbaker's haunting drama, *Our Country's Good*, explores the politics of colonialism through the lens of George Farquhar's *The Recruiting Officer* as the play is rehearsed by convicts in eighteenth-century Australia. Over the last few years, many performances of eighteenth-century plays by amateurs and by professionals have also taken place in the UK, in Italy and in North America.

New approaches have provided the critical foundation for these performances. In a variety of ways, the 'new' theatre history highlights the importance of institutions, lives and careers which earlier scholarship tended to ignore or marginalise: the wide-ranging contribution of women, as playwrights, as actresses and as spectators, is one telling example. Studies of the 'minor' playhouses have altered our understanding of theatrical institutions in this period; discussions about the export of British plays to the colonies have encouraged scholars to think in new ways about performance as a colonial enterprise. Critical interest in the geographies of theatrical production complements a growing fascination with the dramaturgy and significance of illegitimate theatrical forms such as melodrama and pantomime. What links this burgeoning interdisciplinary field is a preoccupation with the power of the British stage as a political, social and cultural institution at the heart of the nation.

By reflecting and extending these interests, this *Companion* aims to change the historiographic lens through which we look at performers, playwrights and theatres in eighteenth-century Britain. Given the century of theatrical history under discussion here, coverage is necessarily selective: authors have been chosen for their expertise in a particular area and encouraged to tease out relationships between the performance of specific plays and broader social and political concerns. Throughout, our aim has been to strike a balance between providing fresh perspectives on well-known plays and introducing less familiar writers and performances alongside critical questions which will stimulate future research and debate.

The Chronology at the front of the book provides a historical framework for individual chapters and draws attention to the various contexts which shaped theatrical production. The opening section of the volume contains essays which introduce the period's performances and celebrated players as well as highlighting the circulation of plays and players around the nation. Part II, 'Genres' focuses on the major genres of comedy, tragedy, melodrama and pantomime, offering broad insights into the operation of dramatic conventions and presenting a wide range of plays from the period. The third section, entitled 'Identities', contains a group of case studies which investigate the operation of class, gender and race on the eighteenth-century stage. Part IV, 'Places of Performance' extends the introductory discussion of theatrical geography to particular sites and arenas of dramatic production. This section includes a chapter on the position of Dublin in the circulation of British and Irish drama and an essay exploring dramatisations of colony and empire. The final part of the book contains a bibliographic essay together with a bibliography for the volume.

This book is the fruit of a transatlantic editorial collaboration between the UK and Canada and we are glad to acknowledge help and encouragement from friends and family on both sides of the Atlantic. The contributors to this volume are scattered all over the English-speaking world and approach the period's theatre from a wide range of critical positions. They have been an inspiration and we offer warm thanks for their patience, efficiency and good humour. Our editor at Cambridge, Vicki Cooper, has supported the project from the beginning: we have greatly appreciated her advice and expertise. We have been fortunate, too, in our two editorial assistants, Vike Plock (at the University of York) and Heather Davis (at the University of Guelph). Their precision and attention to detail has helped in many ways to smooth the progress of this book: in particular we would like to thank Vike for her meticulous work in preparing the volume for publication and Heather for the valuable research she did in drafting the Chronology. The F. R. Leavis Fund in the Department of English and Related Literature at the University of

York kindly provided financial support for this editorial assistance. The project has also benefited from support given by the School of English and Theatre Studies at the University of Guelph and the Social Sciences and Humanities Research Council of Canada.

The experience of producing this volume has reminded us of the intellectual debts we owe to scholars of earlier generations and to colleagues and students across the world who share a fascination with the world of eighteenth-century and Romantic theatre. We are grateful for their knowledge and insight and hope that this *Companion* will mark a new stage in our collaborative conversations.

ABBREVIATIONS

A	Adelphi
C	Coburg
CG	Covent Garden
DL	Drury Lane
EOH	English Opera House (later Lyceum)
GF	Goodman's Fields
HM	Little Theatre in the Haymarket
LIF	Lincoln's Inn Fields
O	Olympic
OP	Old Price riots
P	Pavilion
RC	Royal Circus (later Surrey)
S	Surrey
SA	Smock Alley Dublin
SP	Sans Pareil
SW	Sadler's Wells

Please note that the date given alongside the abbreviation corresponds to the first performance of the play, unless otherwise stated in the text.

CHRONOLOGY

Chronology of dates 1730–1830

	Historical Events	Theatrical Performances in London	Theatrical Events in London	Theatrical Performances and Events outside London	Related Publications	Births/Deaths
1730		Fielding, *The Author's Farce* & *Tom Thumb* (HM)	Debut of Charke at Drury Lane			
1731	Second Treaty of Vienna	Lillo, *The London Merchant* (DL); T. Cibber, Coffey and Mottley, *The Devil to Pay* (DL)	Giffard becomes proprietor of Goodman's Fields			Cowper b.
1732		John Kelly, *The Married Philosopher* (LIF); Fielding, *The Covent-Garden Tragedy*	Rich opens Covent Garden	Voltaire, *Zaïre* (Paris)		Cumberland b.; Colman (Elder) b.; Gay d.
1733	Defeat of Walpole's Excise Bill; Family Compact between France and Spain	Gay, *Achilles* (CG)	T. Cibber leads actors to secede from Drury Lane			
1734		Fielding, *The Intriguing Chambermaid* (DL); Carey, *Chrononhotonthologos* (HM)	C. Fleetwood becomes proprietor of Drury Lane		A. Hill, *The Prompter*; Theobald's edition of Shakespeare	
1735		Handel, *Alcina* (CG)	Barnard's Bill, intended to limit number of playhouses, introduced and defeated		Voltaire, *La Mort de César*	
1736	Porteous riots in Edinburgh	Fielding, *Pasquin* (HM); Lillo, *Fatal Curiosity* (HM)	Fielding becomes manager of Little Theatre in Haymarket	Opening of New Smock Alley Theatre in Dublin; theatre built in Charleston, South		

	Political events	Drama	Theatre	Music and other events	Publications	Births and deaths
1737	Queen Caroline dies; Commons debates over war with Spain	Fielding, *The Historical Register* (HM); Fielding, *Eurydice* (HM); Carey, *The Dragon of Wantley* (HM)	Riots at Drury Lane over footmen's right to upper gallery; Stage Licensing Act		Wesley, *Psalms and Hymns*	Abington b.
1738	John Wesley converts, begins Methodist movement	Lillo, *Marina* (CG)	Riot against French troupe at Little Theatre in Haymarket			
1739	England declares war on Spain	Mallet, *Mustapha* (DL)	Brooke's *Gustavus Vasa* and Thomson's *Edward and Eleanora* denied licences			Lillo d.; Kelly b.; Wilkinson b.
1740	Holy Roman Emperor Charles VI dies; Irish famine	Garrick, *Lethe* (DL)	Giffard's company holds 'concerts' at Goodman's Fields; London debut of Woffington		C. Cibber, *Apology*	
1741	War of the Austrian Succession	Theobald, *The Happy Captive* (HM)	Macklin plays Shylock at Drury Lane; debut of Garrick at Ipswich and later at GF			
1742	Walpole resigns	Fielding, *Miss Lucy in Town* (DL)	Giffard's company moves to Lincoln's Inn Fields	First performance of Handel's *Messiah* (Dublin)		
1743	Henry Pelham becomes Prime Minister; Treaty of Worms signed	Fielding, *The Wedding Day* (DL); Handel, *Messiah* (CG)	Actors' strike at Drury Lane			Carey d.; Cowley b.
1744	France declares war on England	Havard, *Regulus* (DL); Ralph, *The Astrologer* (DL)	Audience riots at Drury Lane; debut of Bellamy	Debut of Barry (SA); *Gustavus Vasa* performed (SA); new theatre in York opens	Garrick, *Essay on Acting*	

Chronology of dates *1730–1830* (cont.)

	Historical Events	Theatrical Performances in London	Theatrical Events in London	Theatrical Performances and Events outside London	Related Publications	Births/Deaths
1745	Walpole dies; Jacobite Rebellion	Thomson, *Tancred and Sigismunda* (DL)	Lacy becomes manager of Drury Lane		Goldoni writes *Il Servitore di due padroni*	H. More b.; C. Dibdin b.; Holcroft b.
1746	Battle of Culloden	Macklin, *Henry VII; or, The Popish Imposter* (DL) & *A Will or No Will* (DL)	Barry appears at Drury Lane		A. Hill's *Essay on the Art of Acting*	
1747		Garrick, *Miss in Her Teens* (CG); Hoadly, *The Suspicious Husband* (CG); Handel, *Judas Maccabeus* (CG)	Foote, *The Diversions of the Morning* (HM); Garrick and Lacy become joint patentees and co-managers at Drury Lane		Foote, *A Treatise on the Passions* and *The Roman and English Comedy Consider'd*	
1748	War of Austrian Succession ends	Moore, *The Foundling* (DL)				Thomson d.
1749		Johnson, *Irene* (DL)	Riot at Little Haymarket	Debut of Griffith (SA)	Fielding, *Tom Jones*	
1750		Whitehead, *The Roman Father* (DL)	Barry leaves Drury Lane for Covent Garden	L. Hallam opens season at Williamsburg, Virginia with *The Merchant of Venice*		
1751		Moore, *Gil Blas* (DL); Thomson and Mallet, *Alfred* (DL); A. Hill, *Zara* (CG)	Quin retires			R. B. Sheridan b.

Year	Historical events	Drama	Theatre / legislation	Stage events	Criticism	Births / deaths
1752	Benjamin Franklin proves lightning is electricity	Foote, *Taste* (DL)	Disorderly Houses Act allows magistrates in London to regulate theatres such as SW.	Opening of Nassau Street Playhouse in New York		Burney b.
1753	Marriage Act	Moore, *The Gamester* (DL); Glover, *Boadicea* (DL)			Hogarth, *Analysis of Beauty*	Inchbald b.
1754	French and Indian war begins in North America	Whitehead, *Creüsa Queen of Athens* (DL)		*Mahomet* riot in Dublin		Fielding d.
1755		Mallet and Arne, *Britannia* (DL)	Anti-French riots over Noverre's ballet *The Chinese Festival* at Drury Lane	Lessing, *Miss Sara Sampson* (Leipzig)	Johnson, *Dictionary*; Pickering, *Reflections upon Theatrical Expression in Tragedy*	Siddons b.
1756	England declares war on France, formally beginning the Seven Years' War	Murphy, *The Apprentice* (DL); Murphy, *The Englishman Returned from Paris* (DL)		Home, *Douglas* (Edinburgh)		
1757	Thomas Pelham becomes Prime Minister	Smollett, *The Reprisal*; Foote, *The Author* (DL); Garrick, *The Male Coquette* (DL)			Diderot, *Le Fils Naturel*; Hume, 'Of Tragedy'	J. P. Kemble b.; Moore d.; C. Cibber d.
1758	Battle of the Bay of Bengal	Home, *Agis* (DL); Dodsley, *Cleone* (CG)		Opening of theatre in Norwich	Diderot, 'Discours sur la poésie dramatique'; Rousseau, *Lettre à d'Alembert*	

Chronology of dates 1730–1830 (cont.)

	Historical Events	Theatrical Performances in London	Theatrical Events in London	Theatrical Performances and Events outside London	Related Publications	Births/Deaths
1759	Wolfe takes Quebec	Murphy, *The Orphan of China* (DL); Townley, *High Life below Stairs* (DL); Macklin, *Love à la Mode* (DL)	Closure of footmen's Gallery (DL); Macklin returns to DL	Comédie Française clears spectators from stage	Sterne, *Tristram Shandy*, vols 1 and 2	Handel d.; Farren b.
1760	George II dies, George III accedes	Murphy, *The Way to Keep Him* (DL); Foote, *The Minor* (DL); Colman (Elder), *Polly Honeycombe* (DL)		Foote, *The Minor* (Crow Street, Dublin)	Lloyd, *The Actor*	Charke d.; Woffington d.
1761	Pitt (the Elder) resigns	Macklin, *The Married Libertine* (CG); Murphy, *The Citizen* (DL)		Goldoni becomes resident playwright at the Théâtre Italien in Paris	Churchill, *The Rosciad*	Kotzebue b.; Jordan b.; Rich d.
1762	War with Spain; Bute becomes Prime Minister	Arne, *Artaxerxes* (CG); Bickerstaffe, *Love in a Village* (CG); Foote, *The Orators* (HM)	Garrick clears spectators from stage at Drury Lane			Baillie b.; Colman (the Younger) b.; Starke b. (c.)
1763	Peace of Paris	F. Sheridan, *The Discovery* (DL); Foote, *The Mayor of Garratt* (HM)	Half-price riots at DL & CG			
1764		Foote, *The Patron* (HM)		Opening of theatre in Glasgow	Walpole, *The Castle of Otranto*	Morton b.; Reynolds b.
1765	Stamp Act passed	Bickerstaffe, *The Maid of the Mill* (CG); Clive, *The Faithful Irishwoman* (DL)	Garrick concludes two year tour of Europe		Johnson's edition of Shakespeare	
1766	Stamp Act repealed	Colman (Elder) and Garrick, *The Clandestine Marriage* (DL)	Foote gains patent for Little Haymarket; Barry re-engaged by Garrick	Opening of South Street Theatre in Philadelphia; Bristol Theatre gains	Lessing, *Laoköon*	Quin d.; F. Sheridan d.; S. Cibber d.

Year		Drama	Theatre		Arts and letters	Births/deaths
1767	Townshend Acts	Colman (the Elder), *The English Merchant* (DL)		Edinburgh Theatre granted patent		Fawcett b.
1768	Royal Academy founded	Kelly, *False Delicacy* (DL); Goldsmith, *The Good Natur'd Man* (CG); Bickerstaffe, *The Padlock* (DL)		Bath & Norwich Theatres granted patents	Sterne, *Sentimental Journey*; Lessing, *Hamburgische Dramaturgie*	
1769	Captain Cook arrives in Tahiti	Griffith, *The School for Rakes* (DL); Home, *The Fatal Discovery* (DL)	Stratford Jubilee marks Shakespeare bicentenary	Theatre at York granted patent	Montagu's essay on Shakespeare	
1770	Boston massacre	Kelly, *A Word to the Wise* (DL); Macklin's *The Man of the World* denied licence		Wilkinson becomes manager of York circuit	Rousseau, *Pygmalion*	Wordsworth b.
1771		Cumberland, *The West Indian* (DL)		Liverpool Theatre gains patent		T. Dibdin b.
1772	Somerset case makes forced removal of slaves from England illegal	Murphy, *The Grecian Daughter* (DL); Foote, *The Nabob* (HM)	Loutherbourg engaged at Drury Lane; opening of EOH (Lyceum)			Coleridge b.
1773	Boston tea riots; Hastings becomes Governor General in India	Foote, *Piety in Pattens* (HM); Goldsmith, *She Stoops to Conquer* (CG); Kelly, *The School for Wives* (DL)	Macklin plays Macbeth in Scottish Highland dress		Goethe, *Götz von Berlichingen*; Goldsmith publishes essay on laughing & sentimental comedy	Pixérécourt b.
1774	Abolition of perpetual copyright	Colman (the Elder), *The Man of Business* (CG); Foote, *The Cozeners* (HM)		More, *The Inflexible Captive* (Bath)		Goldsmith d.
1775	War against America begins	R. B. Sheridan, *The Rivals* (CG); Garrick, *Bon Ton* (DL); Bickerstaffe, *The Sultan* (DL)	Unsuccessful debut of Siddons at Drury Lane	Beaumarchais, *Le Barbier de Séville* (Paris); Manchester Theatre gains patent	Griffith's essay on Shakespeare	Lamb b.; Lewis b.; C. Kemble b.

Chronology of dates 1730–1830 (cont.)

	Historical Events	Theatrical Performances in London	Theatrical Events in London	Theatrical Performances and Events outside London	Related Publications	Births/Deaths
1776	Declaration of Independence in America	Cowley, *The Runaway* (DL)	Garrick retires; R. B. Sheridan becomes manager of Drury Lane		Smith, *The Wealth of Nations*	
1777	British army surrenders to Americans at Saratoga	R. B. Sheridan, *The School for Scandal* (DL); More, *Percy* (CG); Jackman, *All the World's a Stage* (1777)	Debut of Henderson at Haymarket			Barry d.; Kelly d.; Foote d.; Ireland b.
1778	Catholic Relief Act	C. Dibdin, *Poor Vulcan!* (CG)	Farren joins Drury Lane company	Washington orders troops to perform Addison's *Cato* at Valley Forge; Bristol Theatre gains patent	Burney, *Evelina*	Arne d.; Hazlitt b.; Grimaldi b.; Townley d.
1779	War with Spain	C. Dibdin, *The Touchstone* (CG); R. B. Sheridan, *The Critic* (DL); Griffith, *The Times* (DL)	Yates speaks Sheridan's 'Monody to the Memory of Mr. Garrick'	Chester Theatre gains patent	Burney, *The Witlings*	Garrick d.
1780	Gordon Riots	Cowley, *The Belle's Strategem* (CG)			Holcroft, *Alwyn; or, The Gentleman Comedian*	Kenney b.
1781	American War of Independence ends	Macklin, *The Man of the World* (CG); Holcroft, *Duplicity* (CG)	Loutherbourg builds *Eidophusikon*		Schiller, *Die Räuber* published	Lessing d.
1782	Peace talks in Paris between Britain and America	Cowley, *Which is the Man?* (CG)	CG enlarged; opening of RC; Siddons returns to Drury Lane	Pit is seated at Comédie Française	More, *Sacred Dramas*	Pocock b.

1783	Fox introduces India Bill; Treaty of Versailles; Pitt (the Younger) becomes Prime Minister	Cowley, *A Bold Stroke for a Husband* (CG)	London debut of J. P. Kemble at DL			
1784	Pitt's India Act	Inchbald, *The Mogul Tale* (HM)	Handel commemorations	Beaumarchais, *Le Mariage de Figaro* (Paris)		Knowles b.
1785	Resignation of Warren Hastings	Inchbald, *I'll Tell You What* (HM); Loutherbourg and O'Keeffe, *Omai* (CG)	Siddons plays Lady Macbeth for first time; Jordan engaged at Drury Lane		Whately's essay on Shakespeare	Whitehead d.; Glover d.; Clive d.
1786		Burgoyne, *The Heiress* (DL)		Mozart, *The Marriage of Figaro* (Vienna); Irish Stage Act	J. P. Kemble, *Macbeth Reconsidered*	Poole b.
1787	Formation of society for abolition of slave trade; Warren Hastings impeached	Inchbald, *Such Things Are* (CG); Colman (the Younger), *Inkle and Yarico* (HM)	Royalty Theatre opens in defiance of patentees	Mozart, *Don Giovanni* (Prague); Smock Alley closes	Schiller, *Don Carlos*	E. Kean b.; Mitford b.
1788	George III suffers mental collapse	Wallace, *The Ton* (CG); Starke, *The Sword of Peace* (HM)	J. P. Kemble becomes manager of Drury Lane; Astley's Amphitheatre opens	Enabling Act or Theatre Representations Act paves way for licensing of theatres in provinces	Goethe, *Egmont*	Byron b.
1789	Fall of the Bastille; declaration of Rights of Man	Reynolds, *The Dramatist* (CG)	Macklin retires; Colman the Younger becomes manager of HM	*The Recruiting Officer* performed at Port Jackson, Australia; Yearsley, *Earl Goodwin* (Bath)	Boydell's Shakespeare Gallery opens; Kotzebue, *Menschenhass und Reue*	
1790	Habeas Corpus suspended in Britain	Starke, *The Widow of Malabar* (CG)	Debut of Munden at CG	Stanley, *Elmira* (Norwich)	Burke, *Reflections*; Kotzebue, *Das Kind der Liebe*	

Chronology of dates *1730–1830* (cont.)

	Historical Events	Theatrical Performances in London	Theatrical Events in London	Theatrical Performances and Events outside London	Related Publications	Births/Deaths
1791	Louis XVI captured	O'Keeffe, *Wild Oats* (CG); Cowley, *A Day in Turkey* (CG)		Goethe becomes director at Weimar Theatre; Mozart, *Die Zauberflöte* (Vienna)	Paine, *Rights of Man*; Inchbald, *A Simple Story*; Boswell, *The Life of Johnson*	Milman b.
1792	France declares itself a republic; Hastings acquitted	Holcroft, *The Road to Ruin* (CG); Cumberland's *Richard the Second* denied licence	Covent Garden reopens after renovations		Wollstonecraft, *Vindication*	P. B. Shelley b.; Goldoni d.; Burgoyne d.; Fitzball b.
1793	Louis XVI and Marie Antoinette executed; France declares war on Britain	Inchbald, *Every One Has His Fault* (CG)			Godwin, *Political Justice*	Hemans b.; Griffith d.; Macready b.
1794	Robespierre executed; treason trials in London	Holcroft, *Love's Frailties* (CG); Cumberland, *The Jew* (DL); J. P. Kemble, *Lodoiska* (DL)	Debut of C. Kemble; Drury Lane reopens after renovations		Coleridge & Southey, *The Fall of Robespierre*; Southey writes *Wat Tyler*	Colman (the Elder) d.; Moncrieff b.
1795	Bonaparte enters Italy; Pitt passes 'Two Acts' against treasonable conspiracy & assembly	Reynolds, *Speculation* (CG)	Kemble and Sheridan's production of *Venice Preserv'd* closed due to political unrest; Thelwall's lectures on theatre	Wallace, *Whim* refused licence (Margate)	Burke, *Letters on a Regicide Peace*	Keats b.; Boswell d.

1796	Spain declares war on Britain	Holcroft, *The Man of Ten Thousand* (DL); Colman (the Younger), *The Iron Chest* (DL); Ireland, *Vortigern* (DL); Holcroft, *The Force of Ridicule* (DL)		Inchbald, *Nature and Art*; Planché b.
1797	Spithead and Nore mutinies	Lewis, *The Castle Spectre* (DL)	Etienne Robertson presents *Phantasmagorie* (Paris)	Wordsworth sends *The Borderers* to CG; Coleridge sends *Osorio* to DL; Kotzebue publishes *Die Spanier in Peru*; Macklin d.
1798	Irish Rebellion; Battle of the Nile	Colman (the Younger), *Blue-Beard* (DL); Holcroft, *Knave or Not?* (DL) and *He's Much to Blame* (CG); Benjamin Thompson, *The Stranger* (DL), adapted from Kotzebue, *Menschenhass und Reue*; Inchbald, *Lovers' Vows* (CG), adapted from Kotzebue, *Das Kind der Liebe*	Pixérécourt, *Victor* (Paris)	Canning, Ellis and Frere, *The Rovers*; Wordsworth and Coleridge, *Lyrical Ballads*; Baillie, *Plays on the Passions*, vol. 1.
1799	Bonaparte becomes Consul; Six Acts passed; defeat of Tipu Sultan at Mysore	R. B. Sheridan, *Pizarro* (DL), adapted from Kotzebue, *Die Spanier in Peru*		

Chronology of dates 1730–1830 (cont.)

	Historical Events	Theatrical Performances in London	Theatrical Events in London	Theatrical Performances and Events outside London	Related Publications	Births/Deaths
1800		Morton, *Speed the Plough* (CG); Baillie, *De Monfort* (DL); Fawcett, *Obi* (HM); Godwin, *Antonio* (DL)		Schiller, *Maria Stuart* (Weimar); Pixérécourt, *Coelina* (Paris)	More's *Strictures* attacks contemporary drama; Thompson, *The German Theatre*	Cowper d.
1801	Act of Union with Ireland; Pitt (the Younger) resigns	Holcroft, *Deaf and Dumb* (DL); Lewis, *Adelmorn the Outlaw* (DL)	Paul de Philipstal opens first *Phantasmagoria* at the Lyceum	Schiller, *Die Jungfrau von Orleans* (Weimar)		
1802	Peace of Amiens	Holcroft, *A Tale of Mystery* (CG), adapted from Pixérécourt, *Coelina*			Baillie, *Plays on the Passions*, vol. 2	Hugo b.; Buckstone b.
1803	Britain declares war on France	Colman (the Younger), *John Bull* (CG); Lewis, *The Captive* (CG); Kenney, *Raising the Wind* (CG)	J. P. Kemble becomes manager of CG	Glasgow Theatre gains patent; A. W. Schlegel's adaptation of Euripides' *Ion* (Weimar)	James Winston, *The Theatric Tourist*	Jerrold b.; Wilkinson d.
1804	Napoleon crowned emperor; Pitt (the Younger) becomes Prime Minister again	T. Dibdin, *Valentine and Orson* (SW)		Theatrical censorship re-established in Paris	Baillie, *Miscellaneous Plays*	Schiller d.
1805	Battle of Trafalgar		Master Betty craze; debut of Liston at Haymarket			Murphy d.

1806	Pitt (the Younger) dies; Holy Roman Empire formally dissolved	Lamb, *Mr H.* (DL); T. Dibdin, *Harlequin and Mother Goose* (CG)	Debut of Grimaldi at CG; opening of SP and Olympic Pavilion			
1807	Abolition of slave trade in England; beginning of Peninsular War	Godwin, *Faulkner* (DL) and *Furibond; or, Harlequin Negro* (DL)		Eight theatres in Paris gain patents; Birmingham Theatre receives patent	C. and M. Lamb, *Tales from Shakespeare*	Aldridge b.
1808	France invades Spain; Convention of Cintra	Colman (the Younger), *The Africans* (HM)	Covent Garden destroyed by fire	A. W. Schlegel's lectures on dramatic art and literature	Goethe, *Faust*, part 1; founding of *Examiner*; Lamb, *Specimens of the English Dramatic Poets*	Home d.
1809	British expedition to Walcheren; proposals for Parliamentary reform defeated in London	Dibdin, *The Wild Man* (SW); Dimond, *The Foundling of the Forest* (HM); Hook, *Killing No Murder* (HM)	Drury Lane destroyed by fire; Covent Garden re-opens; Old Price riots	W. Scott purchases share in Edinburgh Theatre		F. Kemble b.; Cowley d.; Holcroft d.
1810	Riots in London in support of Parliamentary reform	Pocock, *Hit or Miss* (L); Rhodes, *Bombastes Furioso* (HM)	G. F. Cooke leaves for America	Baillie, *The Family Legend* (Edinburgh)		
1811	Regency begins; Luddite attacks	Poole, *Hamlet Travestie* (New Theatre, later Regency); Lewis, *Timour the Tartar* (CG)	Third Theatre Bill	Coleridge lecturing on Shakespeare	Lamb, 'On the Tragedies of Shakespeare'	Cumberland d.
1812	United States declares war on Britain; Napoleon enters Moscow; food riots in various English cities	T. Dibdin, *Harlequin and Humpo* (DL)	Drury Lane re-opens; Siddons retires		Baillie, *Plays on the Passions*, vol. 3.	Dickens b.

Chronology of dates 1730–1830 (cont.)

	Historical Events	Theatrical Performances in London	Theatrical Events in London	Theatrical Performances and Events outside London	Related Publications	Births/Deaths
1813	French defeated at Leipzig	Coleridge, *Remorse* (DL); Pocock, *The Miller and his Men* (CG)		Byron appointed to subcommittee of DL; opening of Chowringhee Theatre in Calcutta		Wagner b.
1814	Napoleon defeated and exiled to Elba; Peace of Ghent establishes peace between Britain and the US	Baillie, *The Family Legend* (DL)	Debut of E. Kean as Shylock at Drury Lane; debut of O'Neill; Jordan retires		Austen, *Mansfield Park*	C. Dibdin d.
1815	Battle of Waterloo; Second Peace of Paris			Baillie, *The Beacon* (Edinburgh); Knowles, *Caius Gracchus* (Belfast)	J. H. L. Hunt, *The Descent of Liberty*	
1816	Spa Fields riots in London	Maturin, *Bertram* (DL); Morton, *The Slave* (CG); Milman, *Fazio* (S)	Debut of Macready at CG		Hazlitt, *Memoirs of Holcroft*	R. B. Sheridan d.; Jordan d.
1817	Prince Regent attacked by demonstrators in London; Habeas Corpus suspended in Britain	Moncrieff, *Giovanni in London* (O)	Kean and Booth in rival performances of Shakespeare in London; J. P. Kemble retires; DL & CG install gas lighting		Southey, *Wat Tyler*; Hazlitt, *Characters of Shakespeare's Plays*; Coleridge, *Biographia Literaria*; Byron, *Manfred*	

Year						
1818	Mathews performs his *Mail Coach Adventures* (EOH); Moncrieff, *Rochester* (O)	Opening of Coburg Theatre	Pocock's *Rob Roy* (Edinburgh); opening of New Montreal Theatre in Quebec	Bowdler, *Family Shakespeare*; Hazlitt, *A View of the English Stage*	Lewis d.
1819	Peterloo massacre, Manchester	Maturin, *Fredolfo* (CG); Mathews, *Trip to Paris* (EOH)	O'Neill retires; SP renamed Adelphi		Byron's *Don Juan*; Cantos I and II; W. Scott's essay on Drama; P. B. Shelley, *The Cenci*	Kotzebue d.
1820	George IV accedes; Cato St. conspiracy;	Moncrieff, *The Lear of Private Life* (C); Knowles, *Virginius* (CG); Planché, *Vampyre* (EOH)		Knowles, *Virginius* (Glasgow); E. Kean performs at New York	P. B. Shelley, *Prometheus Unbound.*	Boucicault b.
1821	War of Greek Independence begins; death of Napoleon; Queen Caroline dies	Byron, *Marino Faliero* (DL); Moncrieff, *Tom and Jerry* (A)	Opening of New Haymarket	African Grove Theater founded in New York	Malone's edition of Shakespeare; Shelley writes *A Defence of Poetry*; Byron publishes *Marino Faliero, Sardanapalus, The Two Foscari & Cain*	Keats d. Inchbald d.
1822	Greek independence proclaimed	T. Dibdin, *The Pirate* (S)		Paris Opera begins to use gas lighting	Lamb, 'On the Artificial Comedy of the Last Century'	P. B. Shelley d.
1823	Monroe Doctrine promulgated in America	Payne, *Clari* (CG); various plays based on Shelley's *Frankenstein*; Moncrieff, *The Cataract of the Ganges* (DL); Felicia Hemans, *The Vespers of Palermo* (CG)	C. Kemble's revival of *King John*			J. P. Kemble d.

Chronology of dates 1730–1830 (cont.)

	Historical Events	Theatrical Performances in London	Theatrical Events in London	Theatrical Performances and Events outside London	Related Publications	Births/Deaths
1824	First Burmese War	Mathews's Trip to America (EOH)	Grimaldi retires; Munden retires		Byron, The Deformed Transformed	Byron d.
1825		Knowles, William Tell (DL); Poole, Paul Pry (HM); Fitzball, The Pilot (A)	London debut of Aldridge		Egan, The Life of an Actor; Hazlitt, The Spirit of the Age	
1826		Buckstone, Luke the Labourer (A); Mitford, Foscari (CG); Fitzball, The Flying Dutchman (A)				
1827	Turks take Athens		Debut of C. Kean; English actors visit Paris		Hugo's preface to Cromwell rejects neoclassical conventions	
1828	Wellington becomes Prime Minister	Mitford, Rienzi (DL)				Ibsen b.
1829	Catholic Emancipation Act	Jerrold, Black-Ey'd Susan (S)	Debut of Fanny Kemble in role of Juliet			Farren d.; T. W. Robertson b.
1830	Revolution in Paris; death of George IV and accession of William IV	Jerrold, The Mutiny at the Nore (P)	Vestris becomes manager of Olympic	Byron, Werner (Bath); Hugo's Hernani begins fight between neoclassicists and Romantics (Paris)		Hazlitt d.

PART I

Performance

I

PETER THOMSON

Acting and actors from Garrick to Kean

Garrick flourished during the years when educated Englishmen (and a few privileged English women) were admiring their own enlightenment at the same time as they debated issues of 'proper' public conduct. He both encouraged and benefited from a new, quasi-philosophical interest in actors as exemplars of controlled behaviour. Some measure of self-admiration is essential to any actor's wellbeing, and Garrick, despite his constant fear of ridicule, had plenty of it; a current of concern with how he 'looks' runs through his voluminous correspondence. His career marks a transition from an insistently aural theatre, represented by the sonorous James Quin (1693–1766), to a primarily visual one.

The demand for looking-glasses boomed during the final decades of the eighteenth century,[1] indicative both of an increase in self-awareness and of 'the new prominence of beauty as a social and political category'.[2] The idea of the spectator as detached observer and connoisseur, boosted by Addison and Steele's launching of *The Spectator* in 1711, was not swept away, but it was subjected to pressure by the contradictory cult of sensibility. Laurence Sterne's sentimental traveller carries with him everywhere 'the interest ... which men of a certain turn of mind take ... in their own sensations'.[3] *A Sentimental Journey* was the publishing highlight of 1768, and not all its readers were alert to the wicked innocence of its irony. Hugh Kelly's *False Delicacy*, puffed into popularity that same year at Drury Lane by Garrick's publicity machine, imported 'sentiment', in the form of exaggerated altruism, to the theatre without a hint of irony. The play was an invitation to actors to parade fine feeling, to display the appropriate vocal and bodily expression of it – in other words, to offer themselves as a mirror image for the men and women in the audience whose gentility was best evidenced by their feeling for others. In the sentimental comedies and tragedies of the period from 1759 (the year in which the first two volumes of Sterne's *Tristram Shandy* were published) to 1789, actors embodied and empowered that significant proportion of the public who took an interest in their own sensations.

If we are to understand the vehemence with which debates on theatre and morality were being conducted, we need to recognise the peculiar delight that people took in the spectacle of fellow human beings – or themselves – in benevolent action during the years immediately preceding the French Revolution. 'Let us never forget', says Harley, the eponymous hero of Henry Mackenzie's pseudo-novel *The Man of Feeling* (1771), 'that we are all relations.'[4] This is a book, improbably successful on first publication, in which homage to Sterne unintentionally reaches the level of parody. It features a Miss Walton, for whom 'humanity was a feeling, not a principle' (p. 9), and even a dog of feeling, appropriately named Trusty, which 'gave a short howl and died' when its master was evicted by a landlord 'who did not choose to have any farm under £300 a year value on his estate' (pp. 61–2). The vogue for *The Man of Feeling* was matched in the theatre by Richard Cumberland's *The West Indian*, staged at Drury Lane in 1771 with Thomas King (1730–1805) in the title role of Belcour. King was a versatile comedian, but ill-equipped to play the dashingly insouciant prodigal son in whom the audience must perceive 'through the veil of some irregularities, a heart beaming with benevolence and animated nature.'[5] For one thing, King was too old for the part and, according to Mrs Inchbald, 'looked to be so'. What Betterton could get away with at the beginning of the century was no longer so readily acceptable after the Garrick reformation, which had placed acting, particularly comic acting, in closer touch with 'real life'.[6]

In an age inclined to make a virtue of sentiment, theatrical connoisseurs were subjected to ridicule. In Sterne's view, 'the whole set of 'em are so hung round and *befetished* with the bobs and trinkets of criticism . . . that a work of genius had better go to the devil at once, than stand to be tricked and tortured to death by 'em.' He takes as his exemplar the connoisseur who answers the question, 'how did *Garrick* speak the soliloquy last night?', like this:

> Oh, against all rule, my Lord, – most ungrammatically! betwixt the substantive and the adjective, which should agree together in *number, case* and *gender*, he made a breach thus, – stopping, as if the point wanted settling; – and betwixt the nominative case, which your lordship knows should govern the verb, he suspended his voice in the epilogue a dozen times, three seconds and three fifths by a stop-watch, my Lord, each time.

To which Sterne's narratorial voice responds:

> Admirable grammarian! – But in suspending his voice – was the sense suspended likewise? Did no expression of attitude or countenance fill up the chasm? – Was the eye silent? Did you narrowly look? – I look'd only at the stop-watch, my Lord. – Excellent observer!![7]

Sterne was already indebted to Garrick for introductions to literary society in London before Volume 3 of *Tristram Shandy*, from which this passage is quoted, was published in 1761, and would be further indebted to him for a loan of £20 the following year, sufficient to enable him to visit Paris, where he wrote to his benefactor on 10 April 1762: 'You are much talked of here, and much expected, as soon as the peace will let you – These last two days you have happened to engross the whole conversation of two great houses where I was at dinner.'[8] But, even allowing for bias and flattery, both as narrator and letter-writer Sterne's observations provide an important commentary on Garrick's style and status.

Garrick's acting antagonised many connoisseurs of the 'old' school, more because of what he did with his voice than what he did with his body. When he made his London debut as Richard III in 1741 – in the comparatively safe playground of an unfashionable 'illegitimate' theatre – he knew the risk he was taking. It was an extraordinarily lively theatrical year, during which green-room orthodoxy – the unrecorded gossip of backstage aficionados – was to be disturbed. The issue, fundamentally a matter of morality, was villainy. In February 1741, Charles Macklin (1699–1797) had offered to the Drury Lane audience, without the sanction of his fellow-actors, a Shylock who was *not* a comic grotesque. He had made regular visits to London's Jewish quarter and read Josephus's *History of the Jews*, and he invested Shylock with a pathos that owed more to observation and study than to stage tradition. Garrick, formally in trade as a wine merchant, spent off-duty time with Macklin and was impressed by his revisionary approach to rhetoric: first practise the lines as you would speak them in normal conversation, was Macklin's advice, and only then elevate them for performance. There is a case to be made for Macklin as the first active professional to envisage a systematic training for actors, one which he was himself too quarrelsome to sustain, and Alan S. Downer has gone so far as to propose that 'what Macklin taught, Garrick tricked up for popular consumption'.[9] What is certain is that the Richard III Garrick presented to the audiences who flocked to Goodman's Fields in October 1741 was received by them as a 'real' villain. But the furore inspired by Garrick's performance had more to it than that. For both its attackers and its defenders the theatre was a testing ground for moral progress. If Garrick's villainy as Richard was real, it was also irresistibly charming. The moral ambiguity of such an apparent contradiction inflamed debate. The argument that theatre deludes met the counter-argument that theatre reiterates the worldly need to distinguish between appearance and reality. Through the eighteenth-century quest for self-knowledge the fluid interplay of actor and role came to be thematised. The actor under pressure from the text was comparable to the quester for virtue under pressure from circumstance. The personal status of Garrick, during his thirty-year management of Drury Lane (1747–1776), was rarely absent from such fundamental enquiries, many of which centred on the exercise and control of the passions.

By the time Garrick took to the stage, it had become axiomatic that tragic acting was the domain of the passions. There was certainly some kind of gestural code to assist in 'the just delineation of the passions',[10] though we know neither how rigorously it was adhered to by the actors nor how confidently it was read by the spectators. Insofar as the tragic actor was expected to represent humanity under the pressure of extreme emotion, though, the more significant point is Macklin's: '[i]f the actor has not a philosophical knowledge of the passions, it is impossible for him to imitate them with fidelity'.[11] Of what might 'a philosophical knowledge of the passions' have consisted? For Descartes, writing in the mid-seventeenth century, the passions were perceptions, sentiments or emotions of the soul which were caused, sustained and strengthened by some circumstantial agitation, and most eighteenth-century theories were variations or elaborations on this Cartesian theme. In proposing that the soul's passion is communicated through the body as an action, Descartes was unwittingly accommodating Hamlet's advice to the players. Properly disciplined, the tragic actor verified Descartes, and the capacity of the body to express the mind (or soul) was an eighteenth-century commonplace, encapsulated with casual flair by Sterne: '[a] man's body and his mind, with the utmost reverence to both I speak it, are exactly like a jerkin, and a jerkin's lining; – rumple the one, – you rumple the other'.[12] But it does not follow that the rumpling of the lining will accurately echo the rumpling of the jerkin. It will certainly not do so, Sterne goes on, 'when you are so fortunate a fellow, as to have had your jerkin made of a gum-taffeta, and the body-lining to it, of a sarcenet or thin persian'. It is the special skill of the (great) actor to communicate through the body, by way of the 'sympathetic imagination', the condition of the mind. The commonplace injunction to actors was to 'learn to FEEL', and the common assumption that 'No actor pleases that is not *possess'd*'.[13]

So far so good; but bodily expressiveness is insufficient if the voice is dissonant. Garrick's characteristic pauses were carefully studied, both to ensure that each passion was fully established and to make the most of his eventually celebrated skill in executing rapid transitions from one passion to another within a single speech. The shift was already in progress during the 'three seconds and three fifths' (more likely one and a half seconds) of silence, and it was in the facial features that the transition was most vividly signalled. The 'scientific' interest in physiognomy was well established by the time Lavater wrote his famous *Essays* (1789–1798). Applied to the passions, it merited the title of 'pathognomy'. Garrick's extraordinary mobility of face, which was the despair of many portrait artists and the basis of his best-known party trick, amazed and thrilled audiences. It provided Denis Diderot with confirmation of his argument that actors can communicate passions without feeling them:

> Garrick will put his head between two folding doors, and in the course of five or six seconds his expression will change successively from wild delight to tempe-rate pleasure, from this to tranquility, from tranquility to surprise, from sur-prise to blank astonishment, from that to sorrow, from sorrow to the air of one overwhelmed, from that to fright, from fright to horror, from horror to despair, and thence he will go up again to the point from which he started. Can his soul have experienced all these feelings, and played this kind of scale in concert with his face?[14]

Diderot's concern was not simply with acting, nor simply with contra-dicting the followers of Horace who argued that an actor must truly experi-ence the emotions he is portraying if he is to move his audience, but philosophically with actors as exemplars of human complexity. The admira-tion felt for Garrick in France (and reported by Sterne in 1762) was unadult-erated by the petty rivalries and professional jealousies that threatened to blight his life in London. The vital truth about Garrick is that his social and cultural impact was not confined to the theatre. His legendary energy, scarcely containable on stage, was given free rein elsewhere. Even Dr Johnson, often critical of his former pupil, credited him with being 'the cheer-fullest man of his age'.[15] The flavour of Garrick is neatly captured in an anecdote recorded by William Hazlitt in his 1826 essay, 'Of Persons One Would Wish to Have Seen':

> Once at a splendid dinner party at Lord –'s, they suddenly missed Garrick, and could not imagine what was become of him, till they were drawn to the window by the convulsive screams and peals of laughter of a young negro boy, who was rolling on the ground in an ecstasy of delight to see Garrick mimicking a turkey-cock in the court-yard, with his coat-tail stuck out behind, and in a seeming flutter of feathered rage and pride.[16]

It is of no importance whether such an incident ever took place. It gives us Garrick, hobnobbing with the aristocracy but taking time out to reduce a houseboy to helpless laughter, and it introduces us to the fact that Garrick, almost uniquely in an age of increasing specialisation, was at home in both tragedy and comedy. Attempts retrospectively to establish a theory of acting that determined his performances in either genre are doomed to failure. He was a showman, one of those rare stars who, even when following fashion, gave the appearance of leading it. The various manuals that appeared in the wake of Aaron Hill's *Essay on the Art of Acting* (1746) are more detailed, but rarely more informative, than Robert Lloyd's *The Actor* (1760), which is itself little more than a consensual poetic homage to Garrick. For contemporaries, he maintained the appropriate balance between understanding and the finer sensibility that is the essential characteristic of the great actor; the sensibility, that is, that enables him to feel and to communicate the passions (and/or humours) that the playwright aims to excite.

If tragedy was the domain of the passions, comedy was the domain of the humours. It was a distinction that Garrick endorsed, though with the slippage inevitable in an actor who never systematically theorised his practice. Critical of the rigidity of French tragic actors, he could persuade himself that 'there must be *comedy* in the perfect actor of tragedy', a fruitful insight not easily reconciled with his doctrinaire insistence that the passions have no place in comedy nor laughter in tragedy.[17] It was generally accepted in the eighteenth-century theatre that the humours, unlike the passions, are constitutional, and constitutionally unique to each individual. It was of the actor of comedy, rather than tragedy, that Macklin was thinking when he answered the question 'what is character?' with, 'the alphabet will tell you. It is that which is distinguished by its own marks from every other thing of its kind.'[18] Comic actors could meet the expectations of playwrights by displaying the warring humours that brought the characters into conflict. Passions, by contrast, are subject to human control, and defenders of the high moral purpose of the theatre could argue that tragic actors exemplified for theatregoers the perils of unrestrained passion. In 'high' comedy, though – the kind that Garrick played – there should always be restraint:

> Familiar nature forms thy only rule,
> From Ranger's rake to Drugger's vacant fool.
> With powers so pliant, and so various blest,
> That what we see the last, we like the best.
> Not idly pleas'd, at judgment's dear expence,
> But burst outrageous with the laugh of sense.[19]

As caricature for Hogarth stood below character, below comedy was farce, but it was the stageworthiness of eighteenth-century farces that provided comic actors with their most reliable showground.[20] Garrick wrote and acted in them. It is only the snobbery of literary tradition that has shackled him, whose genius was for comedy, in the ranks of tragic actors.

Actors of tragedy

Despite the pre-eminence it accorded to tragedy, the eighteenth century produced none that has held its place in the national repertoire. Even those that shone briefly were modelled on the poetic drama of a bygone era. For the most part, then, tragic actors made their reputations in a language that was not of the age, and in plays that had been beaten into shape – 'reformed' – by journeymen dramaturgs. By the end of the century, not least because of Garrick's enthusiastic endorsement, Shakespeare's supremacy was undisputed, and this has caused some distortion in the historical assessment of tragic acting. The hierarchy established by the brief stage histories that preface many editions of Shakespeare has left its imprint. Garrick features, along with John Philip Kemble and Edmund Kean, but actresses of the period, other than Sarah Siddons as Lady Macbeth, are largely ignored. Susanna Cibber (1714–1766) and the versatile Hannah Pritchard (1711–1768) supported Garrick in many of his most celebrated tragic roles, and Mary Ann Yates (c.1729–1787) was chosen above any of her male colleagues to speak Sheridan's 'Monody to the Memory of Mr. Garrick' at Drury Lane in March 1779. The neglect of Yates is symptomatic of the insistently masculine and misleadingly 'Shakespearean' reading of Garrick's period of management. She tends to be mentioned, when mentioned at all, in the list of capricious women with whom the beleaguered manager was forced to negotiate; but caprice may be no more than the male interpretation of legitimate assertiveness.[21] Historically speaking, it is Yates's misfortune to have been a great performer in small plays – as the Duchess in Robert Jephson's *Braganza* (DL, 1775), as Margaret of Anjou in Thomas Franklin's *The Earl of Warwick* (DL, 1766) and in the title role of Richard Glover's *Medea* (DL, 1761). What signifies here is the eagerness of playwrights, from Nicholas Rowe in the early eighteenth century to Percy Bysshe Shelley one hundred years later, to provide material for powerfully affecting actresses. Sarah Siddons was only one among many performers to assert, by their own example if rarely by their own precept, the rights of women. Even so, the Siddons phenomenon demands attention.

The Kemble dynasty was a force in the London theatre for more than fifty years. Sarah (1755–1831) was the eldest child of theatrical parents. Her mother, also Sarah, was the daughter of a provincial theatre manager, and evidently the impetus behind her husband's following his father-in-law into management. The strength and the independence of the female line, from mother to daughter to daughter's niece, famous in her own right as Fanny Kemble (1809–1893), are striking. Striking, too, is the provincial apprenticeship served by Sarah Siddons and the most famous of her siblings, John Philip

Kemble (1757–1823). We should be wary of assumptions that the provinces were the preserve of coarse acting throughout this period, though it is probably true that the style of performance encouraged in the intimate Georgian theatres outside the capital was ill-suited to the challenge of playing at the constantly enlarging patent theatres of London. Certainly Siddons floundered on her metropolitan debut in 1775. But, seven years later, the actress returned triumphant, now the mother of four young children and the chief breadwinner in a family shadowily served by her ineffectual husband.

The private lives of actresses were hungrily probed by gossip-mongers, and it is not the least of Siddons's achievements to have kept scandal at bay for most of her unquiet life. She came to represent, for two generations, the pain and dignity of womanhood, for the most part in non-Shakespearean roles: Isabella in Garrick's version of Southerne's *The Fatal Marriage*, Belvidera in Otway's *Venice Preserv'd*, Lady Randolph in Home's *Douglas*, Calista in Rowe's *The Fair Penitent*, the title role in Rowe's *Jane Shore*. It was not until 1785 that she first played Lady Macbeth in London. This was her most celebrated role, but not her favourite. She found the part, in accordance with contemporary critical views, too masculine, and her 'possession' of it (in the imagination as much as the memory of the immediately succeeding generations of theatregoers) is the chief reason for her curiously abiding asexual image. Siddons was, in fact, acutely conscious of her femininity. From preference, as Jan MacDonald has argued, 'she "performed" herself as a good mother before her audiences to excuse her "unwomanly" ambition as an actress in the public sphere.'[22] It was, then, an accident of history that Siddons became associated in the public mind with the Burkean sublime. The sublime, in Uvedale Price's paraphrase, 'produces astonishment by stretching the nervous fibres beyond their normal tone',[23] and this is an apt enough description of the Siddons effect. For Burke, the distinguishing feature of the sublime is that we submit to it, as Hazlitt clearly did to Siddons:

> She raised Tragedy to the skies, or brought it down from thence ... she was not less than a goddess, or than a prophetess inspired by the gods ... She was Tragedy personified. She was the stateliest ornament of the public mind.[24]

This, from one of the most acute theatrical observers of any age, is not criticism but surrender, and it speaks for Siddons's thirty-year reign (1782–1812) as Queen of Tragedy. Joshua Reynolds, painting her as the Tragic Muse in 1784, translates her into an image of the sublime. Even Gainsborough's society portrait of 1785, whilst not disguising the length of the nose, offers an image of serene elegance. For a more astringent analysis, it would be hard to better Shearer West, for whom 'Siddons's perfectionism did not consist so much in knowing the character intimately as acquainting herself with the picturesque possibilities of the passions expressed by that character'.[25]

Shearer West's informed linking of acting with easel art, in the case of Siddons with the grand manner of historical painting, is an essential guide to our understanding of the eighteenth-century stage. Garrick, a friend of artists and a judicious collector of their work, had done much to stimulate the connection, and it was almost inevitable that the idea of himself caught on canvas at a dramatic high point would infiltrate his performances.[26] Siddons, monotonously reviewed as if she were a work of art, carried the process to its limit. In later years the self-image stultified. Trapped in her own formidable legend, she used grandeur to protect herself on stage and off it. There is a well-attested anecdote which suggests that she may have lost the ability to hear, but not to see, herself. The year was 1802, and Siddons was embarking on a money-making tour of Irish theatres with Patty Wilkinson, daughter of the indefatigable manager of the York circuit of theatres, as her companion. On the way through Wales they stopped at Penmaen-Mawr to admire the landscape:

> A lady, within hearing of us, was in such ecstacies, that she exclaimed, 'This awful scenery makes me feel as if I were only a worm, or a grain of dust, on the face of the earth.' Mrs. Siddons turned round and said, 'I feel very differently.'[27]

The Tragic Muse had pronounced. Did 'Mrs. Siddons' agree with her?

John Philip Kemble's theatrical scars were always more visible than his sister's. For a man so long engaged in management, he remained oddly isolated from most of his theatrical colleagues. His Catholicism may have been a contributory factor, but his major crises, culminating in 1809 with the debacle of the Old Price riots at Covent Garden, were the result of an inability – or stubbornly conservative refusal – to recognise the shift in political conscious-ness consequent on the French Revolution. To rid himself of the Catholic taint of Jacobitism, he made a spectacle of his Hanoverian monarchism. The Prince Regent, whilst welcoming Kemble into his Whiggish circle, would sometimes entertain his 'court' by mimicking him, making a feature of Kemble's famously pedantic pronunciation, but after his accession as George IV, he would remember him as 'one of my earliest friends'.

The point here is that Siddons and Kemble were able to take advantage of the access to high society that had been opened up by Garrick, but that they did so at the cost of their relationship with their fellow-actors. Often mis-judged by his contemporaries, Kemble has been historically frozen in mis-judgment. He is the 'cold' actor, surrounded on one side by the heat of Garrick and on the other by the fire of Edmund Kean. Thomas Lawrence's grandiose portraits of Kemble advertise the statuesque splendour of his style, particularly in the Roman roles (Cato, Brutus, Coriolanus) that he made his own. There he is, and there he stays, aloof beside a plinth. It is an image, almost, of the beleaguered condition of the patent theatres as the London of the 1790s and after was enjoying an 'entertainment boom',[28] and there is no doubt that Kemble, even without the Old Price riots, embodied what Jane Moody has called 'the hidden relationship between the patent institution and the state'.[29] It is true that Kemble took tragedy immensely seriously, but there is a clear distinction between his youthful performances, marked by athleticism and rapid transitions, and those of his maturity, when he was contending with asthma. His reputation as 'the greatest English classical actor'[30] derives from his nineteenth-century performances and records his systematic search for the *ruling passion* of the tragic roles he chose to play. Modern commentators rarely mention his gothic repertoire – Penruddock in Cumberland's *The Wheel of Fortune* (1795), Octavian in George Colman the Younger's *The Mountaineers* (1793), the title role in Benjamin Thompson's *The Stranger* (1798), in which, according to James Boaden, 'he bore a living death about him'.[31] It was in such *avant-la-lettre* melodramas that Kemble tingled the nerves of excitable audiences.

The London debut of Edmund Kean (1787–1833) in 1814 ruined Kemble's last active years. 'We wish we had never seen Mr. Kean', wrote Hazlitt in the *Examiner* on 27 October 1816. 'He has destroyed the Kemble religion and it is the religion in which we were brought up.' By now, melodrama – an egalitarian genre in inherent opposition to hierarchical tragedy – was dominant in the British theatre, and it was Kean's natural inclination (or limitation) to turn tragedies into melodramas that captured the spirit of the age. It was his intensity that thrilled Regency audiences. Inner fury, amounting frequently to paranoia, fuelled his finest performances and made them dangerous to a degree unrivalled on the English stage. Kean's staple repertoire of great Shakespearean roles was small, and confined to those most readily susceptible to melodramatic treatment – Shylock, Richard III, Othello – and a dispassionate analysis of his turbulent career would reveal that he sank as often as he soared. But it is not easy to remain dispassionate in the face of charisma. Where Kemble aimed to build a character towards a coherent resolution, Kean set his sights on the intermittent peaks and was prepared to coast between them:

> Who can ever forget the exquisite grace with which he leaned against the side-scene while Anne was railing at him, and the chuckling mirth of his 'Poor fool! what pains she takes to damn herself!'. It was thoroughly feline – terrible yet beautiful.[32]

Kean was the supreme exploiter of 'points' – those passages of a play that could be enlivened by eye-catching stage business, much of it traditional, and for which the actor would be rewarded by ritually repeated rounds of applause. Our problem is that the Kean of history can no longer be detached from the Kean of legend. He was a genius; he was a drunkard; his rise from poverty justified the age's preoccupation with individualism; his fall was a cautionary tale on that very preoccupation. Three years after Kean's death, Alexandre Dumas *père* chose him as the subject of a play, *Kean; or, Disorder and Genius*, in which he was to embody the rebellious spirit of romanticism. The embodiment has been historically persuasive, but Kean's contemporaries were more inclined to read him as an overreacher in that seedbed of overreaching, the theatre. It was left to his son Charles to live his father down in the very different atmosphere of the Victorian stage, on which gentlemanly melodrama would be securely elided with tragedy.

Actors of comedy

The last great eighteenth-century actor to emulate Garrick's effectiveness in both tragedy and comedy, John Henderson, died untimely in 1785, leaving John Kemble free to compete for the crown of tragedy, with Siddons already in place as his consort. Comedy was less monarchic. Comic actors generally stuck to their own lines of business: the fop was in transition to the dandy (this was James Dodd's property at Drury Lane); old men came in various shapes (and Richard Yates could adapt himself to most of them); Irishmen turned up in the most unlikely places, because there was always a popular Irish actor to play them; and there were specialists, too, in the gentlemanly line. Eccentric soloists like Samuel Foote (1720–1777) and Charles Mathews (1776–1835) are harder to categorise. Henry Woodward (1717–1777) should be better remembered, not only because he was a versatile comedian (charming as Mercutio, a brilliantly eccentric Bobadil in a revival of Ben Jonson's *Every Man In His Humour*), but also as the finest Harlequin of his time, often in his own pantomimes. His *Queen Mab* and *The Genii* were, by a considerable margin, the most frequently performed dramatic pieces during Garrick's management of Drury Lane. John Bannister (1760–1836) provides a fascinating index to the shifts in British taste during his lifetime, an actor who eased himself from buffoonery into gentlemanly roles and could dapple laughter with pathos.[33] Low comedians, descendants of the Elizabethan clown and fairground buffoon and ancestors of stand-up, had a life below stairs in comedy and often a place of their own in farce. Charles Lamb has assured a place in posterity for one of the best of the face-pullers ('muggers'), Joseph Munden (1758–1832) – inheritor of the Thomas Weston tradition which built up laughter by being apparently unaware of it – but there were many others, of whom the finest was certainly John Liston

(1776–1846).[34] 'His dancing', wrote Hazlitt, 'is equal to the discovery of a sixth sense, which is certainly different from *common* sense.'[35] Liston's painstaking attention to costume was designed to enhance the grotesque floppiness of his body: he would stuff his enormous bottom into overtight trousers, bend over away from the audience and look quizzically under his outstretched arm at the convulsed audience. His gift was the seriousness with which he played the fool. In the endlessly interfering title role of John Poole's *Paul Pry* (1825), he had the distinction of adding the catchphrase, 'I hope I don't intrude', to the discourse of at least two generations. Interestingly, though, most of the real stars of comedy in this period were women.

Frances Abington (1737–1815), a thorn in Garrick's side but indispensable at Drury Lane, rose from poverty to become a trendsetter in female fashion. The 'Abington cap' was briefly in vogue, and the loose, flowing gowns – almost negligées – that she modelled, more durably so. Joshua Reynolds's portrait of her as Miss Prue in Congreve's *Love for Love*, more even than his better known *Mrs. Abington as the Comic Muse*, captures her playing the coquette with the artist and, through him, with us who view. To borrow a distinction from Meyer Schapiro, this is a portrait whose sitter says 'I' rather than allowing the artist to say 'she'.[36] As a result, the viewer becomes 'you' in much the same way as Abington's audience did during an aside or one of the many flirtatious epilogues in which she specialised. She was the inevitable choice for Sheridan's Lady Teazle in the premiere of *The School for Scandal* (1777), but she was forty by then, and made acutely conscious of her age when, in 1778, Sheridan brought the much younger Elizabeth Farren (1759–1829) into his Drury Lane company. Abington's way with competition had always been to defeat it, but Farren was her nemesis. It was mostly pique, disguised as a dispute over salary (she was rich enough to live comfortably after her retirement in 1790), that drove her to forsake Drury Lane for Covent Garden in 1782.

It was not unknown for aristocratic patronesses to nurture the careers of young actresses. The Countess of Burlington had sponsored and chaperoned the dancer Eva Maria Veigel on her London debut, prior to her meeting with and eventual marriage to David Garrick. The celebrated Duchess of Devonshire had sponsored, but *not* chaperoned, Mary Robinson (1758–1800) in 1776, introducing her to four of the men she slept with, Charles James Fox, Lord George Cavendish, Lord Cholmondeley and the playwright Sheridan, though Robinson's more notorious liaison with the youthful Prince of Wales was independently negotiated.[37] It seems probable that the interest taken by the Duchess of Leinster in Elizabeth Farren similarly mixed generosity with an element of procurement. The Duchess was Fox's aunt, and knew his proclivities. She was on the fringes of the free-living

1. Joshua Reynolds, *Mrs Frances Abington as 'Miss Prue'* in Congreve's *Love for Love*.

Devonshire House set, to which her brother, the immensely wealthy Duke of Richmond, belonged, and she may have shared the view of concupiscent aristocrats that actresses were fair game. But if Elizabeth Farren was a fortune hunter, she went far more prudently about it than Mary Robinson. Fox was not the only suitor whose advances she rejected. For a while, at least, she concentrated on a stage career, in which, from the outset, she was perceived as Abington's rival in the portrayal of society ladies. In time, she inherited Lady Teazle. Tall, slim, blue-eyed and fine-featured, Farren only half-unwittingly encouraged the tendency of later eighteenth-century spectatorship to spill over into scopophilia. Her power over the audience was matched by the audience's power over her.

Lawrence's fine portrait of 1789 catches Farren at the height of her social and theatrical success. It was exhibited at the Royal Academy in 1790 alongside the same artist's commissioned portrait of Queen Charlotte. By then Farren's (possibly platonic) friendship with the Earl of Derby was public knowledge. It had been cemented during the amateur theatricals at the home of the Duke of Richmond in 1787 and 1788, which she had been invited to supervise. The Earl lived separately from his wife, who had shocked society by defecting to the Duke of Dorset, and had formally asked, in the watchful presence of her upwardly aspiring widowed mother, to become Farren's 'protector' in 1785. Since he was unprepared to divorce his wife, Farren declined. But it was Derby who persuaded Richmond to employ her. The implications are worth exploring. The Duke of Richmond had, in 1780 and while the Gordon Riots were raging outside, introduced a bill in the House of Lords proposing annual parliamentary elections and the extension of the franchise to all males over twenty-one. He was, then, more than fifty years ahead of the democratic game, and a political wildcard. But he was also the uncle of Charles James Fox and a power in the land.

On 19 April 1787, the House of Commons postponed a debate on the national budget because it was the opening night of the Richmond House theatricals.[38] The audience for the play – Arthur Murphy's *The Way to Keep Him* – included both Pitt and Fox, inveterate political enemies, as well as the Prince of Wales, the Duke and Duchess of Cumberland, General Burgoyne (who had composed the epilogue) and such theatrical luminaries as the Sheridans, Mrs Garrick and John Philip Kemble. The Earl of Derby took the leading role of Lovemore. This was heady company for a mere actress, and it says much for Farren that she was able to hold her own in it. There is no way of knowing how, or even whether, she discussed politics there, but according to Henry Meister, who met her at Richmond House, 'What will make you downright in love with her, is that they tell me she is as declared a democrat as the noble lord her sweetheart.'[39] Democrat or not, Farren married the Earl in 1797, six weeks after the death of his first wife, having made her farewell appearance – as Lady Teazle – to a packed auditorium at Drury Lane. For more than thirty years, almost until her death, she was known as the gracious hostess of the Earl's seat at Knowsley House.

Actresses who married (or nearly married) into the aristocracy were not usually so fortunate. Dora Jordan (1761–1816), who had ten children by the Duke of Clarence, the future William IV, between 1794 and 1807, and who was married to him in all but name, was fobbed off with an allowance in 1811 when the Duke's affection waned. As an actor in comedy, she had been idolised nationwide, as a mistress to royalty she was still acceptable, at the end she was shuffled into obscurity.[40] Even people who acknowledged acting as a profession found it hard to place actors within the class system. Garrick, Henderson and Spranger Barry were buried in Westminster Abbey, but that did nothing to resolve the status of their fellows. Were they to be ranked with artisans or with the bourgeoisie? The victory of the Old Price rioters over Kemble seemed to prove that performers were servants of the public, but there was so much troubling of the social status quo in the years between the French Revolution and the Reform Act of 1832 that even servitude had become ambiguous. Successful actors – stars – could, anyway, command salaries greater than a lawyer's, and boost them with lucrative provincial tours, or with longer summer engagements at the Haymarket or out of town.

Recent studies have confirmed that, despite the efforts of successive Examiners of Plays in the Lord Chamberlain's office, the theatre was much more politically engaged than used to be thought. High society – the old political elite – could not hope to maintain control, even of the two patent theatres, whose capacity had risen to above 3000 by the new century. Playing to distant audiences in vast spaces did not encourage subtlety, but it put a premium on scenery. In Garrick's Drury Lane, actors' salaries accounted for nearly two thirds of the annual expenditure; by 1800 the ratio had dropped to one third. Like figures in picturesque painting, actors stood out against spectacular backdrops. It was only with the advance of lighting technology that the next major development in acting would occur, when performers began to work among the scenery rather than in front of it. Actors were the speaking parts of moving pictures, and the handbooks (if they read them) continued to advise them to visit galleries for inspiration – from history painting for tragedy, from genre painting for comedy. And, of course, to practise in front of a mirror. There were, after all, plenty of them about.

NOTES

1. Russian mirrors, many of them manufactured in Prince Potemkin's factories, were particularly in vogue. See Simon Sebag Montefiore, *The Life of Potemkin*, London: Weidenfeld and Nicolson, 2000, p. 300.

2. Julia Swindells, *Glorious Causes: the Grand Theatre of Political Change, 1789–1833*, Oxford: Oxford University Press, 2001, p. 115n.

3. Laurence Sterne, *A Sentimental Journey*, ed. Ian Jack, Oxford and New York: Oxford University Press, 1968, p. 14.

4. Henry Mackenzie, *The Man of Feeling*, New York: Norton, 1958, p. 68.

5. The quotation is from the play's penultimate speech. See Elizabeth Inchbald's *The British Theatre; or a Collection of Plays which are acted at the Theatres Royal ... with biographical and critical remarks by Mrs Inchbald*, 25 vols., London: Longman & Co., 1808, vol. XVIII.

6. Betterton was in his sixties when he created the part of Valentine in Congreve's *Love for Love* (1695), and it was the part he chose for his farewell performance in 1709. King was not much over forty when he played Belcour.

7. Laurence Sterne, *The Life and Opinions of Tristram Shandy, Gentleman*, ed. Ian Campbell Ross, Oxford and New York: Oxford University Press, 1983, pp. 143–4.

8. Quoted in George Winchester Stone, Jr. and George M. Kahrl, *David Garrick: A Critical Biography*, Carbondale, IL: Southern Illinois University Press, 1979, p. 297.

9. Alan S. Downer, 'Nature to Advantage Dressed: Eighteenth-Century Acting', in *Restoration Drama: Modern Essays in Criticism*, ed. John Loftis, New York: Oxford University Press, 1966, pp. 328–71, 343.

10. See George Taylor, '"The Just Delineation of the Passions": Theories of Acting in the Age of Garrick', in *Essays on the Eighteenth-Century English Stage*, eds. Kenneth Richards and Peter Thomson, London: Methuen, 1972, pp. 51–72. See further, Joseph Roach, *The Player's Passion: Studies in the Science of Acting*, London: Associated University Presses, 1985.

11. Quoted in Taylor, '"Just Delineation"', p. 57.

12. Sterne, *Tristram Shandy*, p. 127.

13. The quotations are from Robert Lloyd's poetic essay, *The Actor*, London: R. & J. Dodsley, 1760.

14. This passage from Diderot's *The Paradox of Acting* is quoted at a crucial point in Richard Sennett's illuminating *The Fall of Public Man*, New York: Norton, 1986, p. 112.

15. James Boswell, *The Life of Samuel Johnson*, ed. R. W. Chapman, Oxford and New York: Oxford University Press, 1970, p. 1021.

16. *Complete Works of William Hazlitt*, ed. P. P. Howe, 21 vols., London: J. M. Dent, 1930–4, vol. XVII, pp. 122–34, 130.

17. *The Letters of David Garrick*, eds. David M. Little and George M. Kahrl, 3 vols., Cambridge, MA: Harvard University Press, 1963, vol. II, p. 478.

18. J. T. Kirkman, *Memoirs of the Life of Charles Macklin*, 2 vols., London: Lackington & Co., 1799, vol. I, p. 66.

19. Robert Lloyd's *The Actor* (1760). Ranger was Garrick's role in Benjamin Hoadly's *The Suspicious Husband*, and he played Abel Drugger in his own version of Ben Jonson's *The Alchemist*.

20. Viewing farce as an inferior genre, the best playwrights tended to smuggle their often-satirical short afterpieces into the repertoire as 'comedies'. Samuel Foote's *The Author* (DL, 1757) characteristically defies easy classification. But 'farce' is the best single-word description of such plays as George Colman the Elder's *Polly Honeycombe* (DL, 1760), *The Musical Lady* (DL, 1762) and *The Spleen* (DL, 1762), Arthur Murphy's *The Citizen* (DL, 1761) and *Three Weeks after Marriage* (CG, 1776) and David Garrick's *The Lying Valet* (GF, 1741), *Miss in Her Teens* (CG, 1747) and *Bon Ton* (DL, 1775).

21. For a fuller picture of Mary Ann Yates's authority and initiative, see the account of her partnership with Frances Brooke in the management of the King's Theatre in Ian Woodfield, *Opera and Drama in Eighteenth-Century London: The King's Theatre, Garrick, and the Business of Performance*, Cambridge: Cambridge University Press, 2001. For the immensely impressive print of her as Medea, see Peter Thomson, *On Actors and Acting*, Exeter: University of Exeter Press, 2000, p. 106.

22. Jan MacDonald, 'Sarah Siddons performs maternity', in *Extraordinary Actors*, eds. Jane Milling and Martin Banham, Exeter: University of Exeter Press, 2004, pp. 57–70, 58.

23. Uvedale Price, *An Essay on the Picturesque as compared with the Sublime and the Beautiful . . .*, 3 vols., London: Edward Orme, 1810, vol. I, 68.

24. 'Mrs. Siddons', in *Complete Works of William Hazlitt*, vol. V, p. 312.

25. Shearer West, *The Image of the Actor: Verbal and Visual Representation in the Age of Garrick and Kemble*, New York: St. Martin's Press, 1991, pp. 106–18.

26. See further, Thomson, *On Actors*, pp. 79–96.
27. Michael Kelly, *Reminiscences*, ed. Roger Fiske, Oxford: Oxford University Press, 1975, p. 295.
28. See Jacky Bratton's illuminating *New Readings in Theatre History*, Cambridge: Cambridge University Press, 2003, pp. 17–66, 40.
29. Jane Moody, *Illegitimate Theatre in London, 1770–1840*, Cambridge: Cambridge University Press, 2000, p. 62.
30. Peter Holland on Kemble, in *The Cambridge Guide to World Theatre*, ed. Martin Banham, Cambridge: Cambridge University Press, 1988, p. 547.
31. James Boaden, *Memoirs of the Life of John Philip Kemble*, 2 vols., London: Longman & Co., 1825, vol. II, p. 215.
32. George Henry Lewes, *On Actors and the Art of Acting*, London: Smith, Elder & Co., 1875, p. 10.
33. Trained as an artist, and the life-long friend of Thomas Rowlandson, Bannister is in urgent need of reassessment. As things stand, he labours to be heard through the obsequiousness of John Adolphus's *Memoirs of John Bannister, Comedian*, 2 vols., London: R. Bentley, 1839.
34. Liston's acting is judiciously analysed in Jim Davis's *John Liston, Comedian*, London: Society for Theatre Research, 1985.
35. Cited in Davis, *John Liston*, p. 17.
36. Meyer Schapiro, *Words and Pictures: On the Literal and the Symbolic in the Illustration of a Text*, The Hague and Paris: Mouton, 1973, p. 39.
37. Mary Robinson's *Memoirs* were posthumously published in 1801. In them, she dramatises herself as a sentimental heroine, the victim of her own sensibility, rather than the actress-courtesan she undoubtedly was for a time.
38. See Sybil Rosenfeld, *Temples of Thespis: Some Private Theatres and Theatricals in England and Wales, 1700–1820*, London: Society for Theatre Research, 1978, pp. 34–52.
39. Henry Meister, *Letters Written During a Residence in England*, London: Longman & Rees, 1799, p. 202.
40. The best account of Dora Jordan's life is Claire Tomalin's *Mrs Jordan's Profession: The Actress and the Prince*, New York: Knopf, 1995.

2

JANE MOODY

Dictating to the empire: performance and theatrical geography in eighteenth-century Britain

London has dominated the historiography of the British stage in the long eighteenth century. Our theatrical histories are intensely, avowedly metropolitan; moreover, they focus almost exclusively on the playwrights, performers and managers associated with the London patent theatres, Drury Lane and Covent Garden. By comparison with discussions about *literary* production in provincial cities, performance outside London has received little attention.[1] When the provinces do emerge from the theatrical shadows, it is all too often as the places from which great performers such as David Garrick and Sarah Siddons escaped for the bright lights and fame of the London stage. One of the major aims of this essay is to challenge the marginal position of provincial theatres.

The need to question what Loren Kruger has called 'the habitual assumption of metropolitan authority in London' is fundamental to the redefinition of British theatre history currently taking place.[2] Joseph Roach's groundbreaking account of 'circum-Atlantic' performances between London and New Orleans highlighted the way in which performances cut across national borders; the last decade has also seen a resurgence of interest in Irish and Scottish theatre and a new emphasis on dramatic 'micro-history'.[3] My own essay sets out in a different direction with the aim of producing a more comprehensive interpretation of Britain's theatrical geography. The focus of this argument is designed to reveal the circulation of performers and plots between metropolitan and provincial theatres, the varied forms of artistic innovation taking place beyond the capital and the important role of provincial stages in the business of imagining the nation.

The habit of mocking provincial theatre and regarding its performances as below cultural notice is a phenomenon of the mid and late eighteenth century. During this period, the provincial performer – usually represented as a disreputable 'strolling' player moving from place to place – appears in various media as the subject of embarrassment, laughter and disdain. Memoirs of celebrated performers skate over their subjects' provincial engagements and make comic, sometimes pejorative allusions to the impoverished lives of itinerant actors; sometimes the provincial player also becomes a laughing stock on the metropolitan stage.

Perhaps the best example of this figure is the character of Sylvester Daggerwood in George Colman's occasional piece, *New Hay at the Old Market* (HM, 1795). In this entertaining skit, the unkempt actor-manager of the Dunstable company comes to London seeking an engagement at the Haymarket Theatre, then run by Colman himself. Fustian, an aspiring playwright, finds him asleep, dreaming in Shakespearean quotations. As so often, the performance of Shakespeare serves to highlight the laughable usurpation of legitimate theatre by an unlettered provincial vagabond, acting *Hamlet* 'before twelve tallow candles in the country'. When he awakes, Daggerwood describes theatrical commerce in Dunstable ('eight shillings a week, four bits of candle, one wife, three shirts, and nine children') and describes his performances 'to an overflowing and brilliant barn – house, I mean – with unbounded and universal applause.'[4]

New Hay creates laughter from various kinds of migration and displacement: even Molly, the young broom sweeper is fresh from the country, hence her naive fears about the 'mortal frightful' straw figure of Apollo up in the flies. Clearly, Daggerwood's commercial value lies in the farcical contrast he provides to the comic sophistication of Colman's company. But is Colman's determination to satirise provincial theatre also an indication of its growing popularity? And what made Sylvester Daggerwood such an engaging character at theatres outside London, where he even became the star of a dramatic sequel?

To understand the invention and after-life of Sylvester Daggerwood, we need to explore a remarkable institutional change taking place in late eighteenth-century culture: the creation of provincial Theatres Royal. The emergence of these playhouses produced new audiences, both local and national, engaged talented actors from across the country, and staged original plays and fresh adaptations, as well as the latest hits from London. Britain's changing theatrical geography, I shall suggest, has major consequences for our understanding of dramatic authorship, spectatorship and performance.

My argument investigates a series of theatrical exchanges between London and the provinces. The first part explores the prologue Garrick wrote for the opening of the Bristol Theatre; in the second, I revisit a trope of metropolitan theatre history – Sarah Siddons's engagement by the manager of Drury Lane – in order to reassess her early provincial career. This section of the essay reveals that provincial theatres staged a variety of new plays by local authors and highlights the implications of this phenomenon, especially for the interpretation of women's playwriting. The essay then discusses the theatrical market outside London, considering the tension between pressures for integration into the metropolitan economy and desires for cultural independence. Finally, I turn to a specific series of performances: Charles Mathews's famous *At Homes*. Here, one of the most celebrated actors of the period converts the comic materials from a provincial show into a series of trans-national entertainments whose characters crossed boundaries between regions, nations and cultures.

1. Garrick's Bristol prologue

In the spring of 1766, David Garrick travelled to Bristol in order to see the newly completed theatre in King Street. Frustrated by the inconvenient position of the existing playhouse at Jacob's Well, a group of merchants had decided to build a theatre in the centre of the city. What better way for the managers to demonstrate their cultural ambition – and to mitigate the hostility of local Quakers, Methodists and tradesmen – than by a visit from the nation's most celebrated performer? The publicity stunt paid off. According to local versifiers, a delighted Garrick '[p]ronounced the Fabric elegantly neat, / Fit school for Genius, and the Muses' Seat'.[5]

Emboldened by this praise, John Arthur and William Powell invited Garrick to write a prologue or epilogue for the theatre's opening night. Perhaps they mentioned the publication of pamphlets and angry letters against the King Street venture; maybe the managers discussed their plans to perform Congreve's *The Conscious Lovers* and Arthur Murphy's farce, *The Citizen* – two plays which confidently promote the values of modern commerce – on the opening night. Certainly Garrick knew that the King Street Theatre possessed no legal authority to perform plays, and that the managers would circumvent this obstacle by advertising the evening's entertainment with 'a Concert of Music, with a Specimen of Rhetoric to be exhibited gratis'. As we shall see, Garrick's paratexts seek to encapsulate the position of the Bristol theatre in the local and colonial economy.

Not surprisingly, Garrick's addresses counter moral and religious objections to the King Street Theatre. Provincial players, he suggests, are 'harmless' descendants of the fool whom every king needs to have in his court. Garrick even devises a ludicrous character to embody this hostility: a puritan rises from her stays to declare her hatred for 'wicked Plays' and insists that '. . . seeing Plays is dealing with the Devil!' In a letter, Garrick advised Arthur to play for laughs here, explaining that he must 'mimic the *Prude* drawing up herself and speaking affectedly'.[6] At the same time, Garrick's texts set out to legitimise the King Street Theatre by creating an analogy between theatrical and colonial commerce. Like the city's merchants, the men who 'traffic in

Dramatic ware' will bring treasures from distant worlds, extending Bristol's name, wealth and fame '[f]rom East to West'.[7] Performance is imagined here as a form of colonial merchandise. Though a full discussion of this metaphor lies beyond the remit of my essay, the ideological terms of Garrick's 'licence' for the Bristol theatre are curiously prophetic.

The triumphant opening of the King Street playhouse was not an isolated event. Increasing civic pride, together with a surge in prosperity at mid-century, provided the impetus for a wave of theatre building. New playhouses opened in many towns and cities including Bath (1750), Norwich (1758), Glasgow (1764) and Manchester (1774). None of these theatres, however, possessed a licence. Between the Licensing Act of 1737 and the late 1760s, provincial stages were compelled to operate in a twilight zone, relying on the toleration of local magistrates and the enthusiasm of city corporations for entertainments which promoted civic sociability and attracted genteel visitors.

The catalyst for institutional change came in 1766 when the mischievous actor Samuel Foote received a royal patent for summer performances at the Haymarket Theatre. Provincial towns and cities, eager to prove the wealth and gentility of their inhabitants (and to steal a march on their rivals), decided to ask Parliament for similar privileges. Their petitions defined the provincial theatres as sites of urban citizenship and polite sociability. According to these gentlemen, manufacturers, traders and city corporations, provincial theatres produced instructive, 'rational' amusements which promoted virtue and patriotism. Members of Parliament also began to acknowledge that provincial theatres could preserve, rather than undermine, order and good government. It seems likely that these campaigns benefited from pervasive fears about the spread of Methodism: provincial theatregoing was being identified as a civic prophylactic against religious fervour. In 1767, Edinburgh became the first city to be granted a Theatre Royal. Despite opposition in several cities, others soon followed, including Bath and Norwich (1768), York and Hull (1769), Liverpool (1771), Manchester (1775), Chester (1777), Bristol (1778), Margate (1786) and Newcastle (1787). The acquisition of these patents marked a transformation in the moral and political status of provincial theatre.

In London too, the late eighteenth century was a period of major theatrical expansion. The Theatre Representations Act (1788) allowed magistrates to license performances for a period of sixty days, provided that the playhouse lay beyond the boundaries of Westminster. Theatrical entrepreneurs throughout Britain soon realised that the legislative mood was changing. That year, Philip Astley's Amphitheatre opened on the south bank of the Thames, attracting thousands of spectators to its circus performances and military spectacles; nearby, Astley's rival Charles Hughes built the Royal Circus, a playhouse later famous for dramatising novels by Walter Scott. Within two decades, new theatres even began to open within Westminster. In 1806, to the consternation of the patent managers, the Lord Chamberlain granted licences to the Sans Pareil (later renamed the Adelphi) and the Olympic Pavilion, both in the immediate vicinity of Covent Garden and Drury Lane.

The 'minor' playhouses ostensibly occupied a lowly position in the London theatre. Their licences limited performances to music, pantomime, spectacle, burletta and other illegitimate forms. Crucially, these theatres were forbidden to stage 'legitimate drama' (i.e. plays such as tragedies and comedies featuring spoken dialogue). Sometimes, daring managers found a way of avoiding this prohibition, as in 1787 when John Palmer opened the Royalty Theatre in the liberty of Tower Hamlets with a performance of *As You Like It*, but the patentees soon crushed these acts of defiance. However, the minor theatres had more success in circumventing the monopoly when they began to disguise plays by Shakespeare and other stock dramatists under illegitimate labels such as melodrama or burletta. By the 1810s, the campaign against the monopoly began to gather theatrical steam, fuelled by the notorious production of gothic spectacles such as *Timour the Tartar* at the patent houses. The appearance of Astley's horses at Covent Garden seemed to prove the irresistible rise of illegitimate theatre. Managers at the Surrey and the Coburg now started to justify their illicit performances by pointing out that Drury Lane and Covent Garden had abandoned the legitimate repertoire. Critics, playwrights, actors and spectators started to take up positions in this lively, often comic dispute over the definition and ownership of legitimate drama. For several decades, the two sides waged theatrical warfare on stage, in newspapers and periodicals, in the courts and even in Parliament until the monopoly was finally abolished in 1843.[8]

Though the Act of 1788 acted as a green light for the construction and renovation of theatres throughout Britain, the institutional position of the provincial theatres was, for a variety of reasons, distinctive. For a start, these stages were simply too remote to pose a commercial threat to the patent managers. Indeed, the metropolitan and provincial houses benefited from a degree of integration: in the summer season, when Drury Lane and Covent Garden were closed, London actors usually took engagements in towns such as Bath, Norwich and Margate. The frequent appearance of performers from the metropolis encouraged the depiction of provincial theatres as satellites of the dramatic capital. Forms of patronage also differentiate the provinces from theatres in London. By contrast with the minor theatres, provincial playhouses enjoyed generous financial support from gentlemen, merchants and members of the aristocracy. As we shall see, this patronage powerfully shaped the economy and repertoire of these stages.

The granting of letters patent was a moment of symbolic as well as practical significance. At York, Tate Wilkinson proudly commissioned a copy of the King's arms, as well as splashing out on fresh scenes and costumes. 'I was high in public favour', he remembered, 'and do not remember any season from that period to this when the theatre was so regularly and fashionably attended'.[9] During a prologue spoken at Windsor, a man came onto the stage exhibiting the licence to perform and 'the sanction of our good King's name'.[10] The royal patents came to define the watershed between a time of '[c]ontraband mummeries and unlicens'd plays' and a new age of polite entertainment outside London.

The Theatres Royal now became a cultural magnet in the local and national economy: wealthy spectators wanted to take out subscriptions for the season and to 'bespeak' performances; the demise of the old sharing system and the introduction of actors' salaries helped to attract a higher calibre of performers; the increasing respectability of provincial theatres encouraged local authors to try their hand at writing plays.[11] In the next section of this essay, I explore a series of questions about dramatic authorship in the provinces through the lens of Sarah Siddons's early career.

2. Sarah Siddons, female Hamlets and provincial drama

On 31 July 1775, Garrick wrote to his friend 'Parson' Henry Bate, editor of the *Morning Post*, 'If You pass by Cheltenham in Your Way to Worcester, I wish you see an Actress there, a Mrs *Siddon's* . . . if she seems in Your Eyes worthy of being transplanted, pray desire to know upon what conditions She would make ye Tryal'.[12] In this letter, Garrick acts another role in Britain's provincial theatres, this time as the director of Drury Lane's theatrical 'intelligence'. That summer, Garrick was so determined to discover more about Siddons's acting that he also penned a letter to his friend John Moody, an Irish comedian then engaged at Liverpool, requesting similar information. A few days later, Bate wrote with a positive report, reassuring Garrick that the actress 'had contracted no strolling habits, w[hich] have so often been the tone of many a theatrical genius'.[13] It was precisely the lack of those declamatory vulgarities associated with itinerant performance which made Siddons such a valuable commodity. The conditions for her 'transplantation' – note the colonial connotations of Garrick's language, as if Siddons was to be settled in another country – were already propitious.

As Bates explained, Covent Garden had sent its own spies to watch Siddons, now 'entrench'd near the place' and tellingly imagined by Bates as the 'Mohawks'. The rhetoric here is revealing. This is an imperial campaign, involving 'military stratagems' and the 'siege' of a provincial 'garrison': a garrison which, as Bate brutally points out, must exhibit its star to best advantage or else 'fall by famine'.[14] Little more than a month had passed, of course, since British forces had seized the Charleston peninsula at the Battle of Bunker Hill and suffered heavy losses; Garrick's pursuit of Siddons takes place in the wings of, and by analogy with, the theatre of war in America. In Cheltenham, however, the victory of the colonisers was never in doubt. By the end of December, Siddons had left Roger Kemble's company of comedians and opened as Portia in *The Merchant of Venice*.

Like Garrick and Bates, theatre historians have often regarded the provincial theatre as a site of aesthetic vulgarity ('strolling habits') and financial desperation (the prospect of falling 'by famine').[15] But one of Siddons's roles helps to provide evidence for a different model of Britain's theatrical geography. Having observed that Siddons has been performing a 'great number of characters' in the provinces, Bate informs Garrick that she has 'a very good breeches figure' and mischievously continues, 'nay beware yourself *Great Little* Man, for she plays Hamlet to the satisfaction of the Worcestershire Critics'.[16] How naïve and ignorant these spectators must have been, Bate suggests, to accept Siddons's Hamlet as a substitute for Garrick's celebrated performances at Drury Lane. But his joke unwittingly directs us to some performances which flout the terms of metropolitan theatrical history.

During the 1770s, Siddons was playing Hamlet in major cities such as Bristol (where her husband played Guildenstern), Manchester and Liverpool. More than twenty years later, dressed in a long, black-fringed cloak, she played the role in Dublin, where audiences marvelled at her skills in the fencing match with Laertes, for which she had received tuition from her alleged lover, the French maestro, Philemon Galindo. These performances suggest that the provinces sometimes resembled dramatic 'liberties' where theatrical experiments or distinctive forms of cultural commentary could take place. In his biography, James Boaden quickly passes over Siddons's provincial Hamlet, remarking with undisguised condescension, 'I do not imagine on our larger stages, upon which the performer walks so much, that Mrs. Siddons was ever desired in that or any other *male* character …'.[17] But whether she was 'desired' in this role was really a question of the patriarchal control of Shakespearean property. When Siddons was first engaged at Drury Lane, the part of Hamlet belonged to Garrick; the season after her return to London, her brother, John Philip Kemble, made his debut in the role. Though Jane Powell had played Hamlet at Drury Lane in 1796 and received applause for her representation of melancholy passion, Siddons had good reason not to follow her lead in challenging the metropolitan ownership of Hamlet by men.

In the eyes of spectators in Manchester or in Dublin, Siddons's Hamlet was not a breach of propriety but a sensation. Her performances, like those of other female Hamlets in this period, are a sign of the liberties occasionally taken by the provinces: the freedom of these stages from, or simply their ignorance of, the conventions of Drury Lane and Covent Garden. In the provinces, Siddons presented audiences with a new interpretation of Shakespeare's hero, an interpretation which highlighted both the character's passionate energy and his desolate grief. And Siddons's decision to play Hamlet in Dublin at the height of her fame constitutes an implicit declaration that the cultural authority of Britain's 'Tragic Muse' now extended to the portrayal of Shakespearean heroes.

If, as we have seen, the provincial stages promoted female Hamlets, did these theatres also provide a more hospitable space than London for women's playwriting? Again, Siddons's career offers some intriguing clues. In 1778, the young actress accepted an engagement at the Orchard Street Theatre in Bath. For the next four years, she performed both in Bath and also at Bristol: the company travelled backwards and forwards between the two theatres in a stage coach designed for the purpose by the manager, John Palmer. During this period, as Ellen Donkin notes, the Orchard Street theatre performed an increasing number of plays by women playwrights.[18] Though Donkin suggests that Garrick's retirement offers the most plausible explanation for this phenomenon, it seems more likely that Siddons's presence acted as a catalyst for the creation and production of drama by women.

Siddons's arrival quickly transformed the stock repertoire at Bath. Tragedies, formerly performed only on Thursdays – when the fashionable had once preferred to attend the Cotillon balls – became all the rage amongst genteel spectators. Audiences marvelled at the 'complicated agony' of Siddons's Calista in Rowe's *Jane Shore* and her 'magic delicacy' in Otway's *Venice Preserv'd* as Belvidera; many of her most celebrated stock roles were wronged women and victims of illicit love, riven by pride and shame.[19] Siddons also took leading roles in new plays by women, including the role of Elwina in her friend Hannah More's tragedy, *Percy* (first performed at Covent Garden in 1777) and Cecilia in Sophia Lee's comedy, *The Chapter of Accidents* (first performed at the Haymarket in 1780). Critics and spectators were intrigued by the idea of Siddons as the champion of women's writing: letters printed in local newspapers gave high praise to her portrayal of Cecilia, and sales of the play text jumped sharply.

As Jacky Bratton has pointed out, we need to be more alert to the ways in which theatre women create and transmit 'cultural capital'.[20] Sarah Siddons's performances changed the conventions surrounding the writing

2. Tragedies in the Bath repertoire, from the Bath Theatre Royal stock book of 1778.

and representation of tragic heroines. There are evocative signs of this transmission in Joanna Baillie's work: the pious, austere and resolute Jane in *De Monfort* is unquestionably a Siddonian creation. But the influence of Siddons's performances on playwrights living or spending a season in Bath is not yet understood: we need to know more about her friendships with dramatists such as Sophia Lee (whose father managed the Bath Theatre and whose mother was an actress), Frances Burney and Hannah More. At the end of the 1780s, the character of Emma in Ann Yearsley's political tragedy, *Earl Goodwin* (Bath, 1789) evokes and transforms the lineaments of Siddons's courageous, lofty heroines. Other tragedies by local women included Catherine Metcalfe's *Julia de Roubigné* which was performed at Bath after the author's death in 1790. Significantly, both the prologue to Metcalfe's play and the preface to Yearsley's printed text intervene in contemporary debates about the status and definition of tragedy: Siddons's cultural authority seems to have encouraged a number of women to defy convention and write for the tragic market.

Performance, I have argued, sometimes leaves behind tantalising traces of women's dramatic 'authorship'.[21] We might imagine Siddons in Bath and Bristol as a shadow playwright, a figure behind the scenes, an agent in the provincial greenroom. On at least one occasion, however, Siddons did lay claim to the status of an author:

> Have I not raised some expectation here? –
> Wrote by herself? – What! – authoress and player?[22]

Critics then and now remember Siddons's farewell address of 1782 as the occasion when she exhibited her young children as the 'three reasons' for leaving the Bath stage. Significantly, however, this speech also marks the moment when she defines herself as a writer. By making this claim in Bath, Siddons reveals her sense of shared identity with local women writers, and her knowledge of the dynamic interdependence of dramatic authorship and theatrical performance.

My argument so far has questioned the presumption that provincial theatre represented a mere 'nursery' for the metropolis. So to what extent did these theatres pioneer new writing? Could successful plays transfer from the provinces to London? How effective was the system for the censorship of plays at the provincial Theatres Royal? Constraints of space in this essay prevent a comprehensive account of dramatic writing outside London. Any discussion of provincial authorship, however, will need to range across a number of (inevitably fluid) categories. These include, but are not limited to (a) plays performed only in a specific town or circuit: a large category including plays such as James Plumptre's comedy of feminine stratagem, *The Coventry Act* (Norwich, 1793) and melodramas by the Scottish playwright, Archibald McLaren; (b) plays performed in the provinces, having been 'rejected' by London theatres, for example Home's *Douglas* (Edinburgh, 1756) and Baillie's *Constantine Paleologus* (Liverpool, 1808); (c) plays which transfer from the provinces to the metropolis, including Frederic Reynolds's tragedy, *Werther* (Bath, 1785), Hannah More's *The Inflexible Captive* (Bath, 1774) and Hannah Brand's *Huniades; or, The Siege of Belgrade* (Norwich, 1791); (d) 'closet' plays (not performed, for a variety of reasons) including Edward Stanley's political tragedy, *Elmira: A Dramatick Poem* (published in Norwich, 1790).

The number and range of plays within these groups defy the assumptions of our metropolitan historiography. This experiment in theatrical 'devolution' also reveals the presence of intriguing connections between plays written in different cities. Historical tragedies such as *Earl Goodwin, Elmira* and *Huniades*, for example, strike up polemical conversations from the periphery about the politics of empire. Far from being passive mediators of metropolitan culture, the provincial stages authorised, modified and indeed challenged Britain's theatrical centre.

3. Provincial theatres, national markets

Despite these notable exceptions, hit plays such as Cumberland's *The West Indian*, Inchbald's *Such Things Are* and Sheridan's *The School for Scandal* represented the most valuable stock for provincial managers. It is notable that all these dramas explore characters who migrate from the colonies to Britain or vice versa. As in Calcutta or Philadelphia, provincial newspapers disseminated information about the latest London plays; increasingly, however, wealthy spectators in the provinces had seen these productions at first hand, on their visits to the capital. Managers promoted this new merchandise by writing self-aggrandising advertising which praised their own diligence and liberality in obtaining new plays for the city. Sometimes, the manager purchased the manuscript, or made an agreement to perform a new play 'for one night only'; on other occasions, a manager or group of players would go into the gallery of a London theatre and make a surreptitious transcription. Unauthorised performances regularly took place and several playwrights, notably the litigious Charles Macklin, threatened legal action against the offenders.

The major barrier facing provincial managers keen to introduce original plays was the audiences' suspicion that London plays must be superior to provincial drama. Prologues and epilogues attempt to dissolve this anxiety by reassuring spectators that 'Authors, as well as Actors here may spring, /If your applause but give their Genius wing.'[23] But provincial spectators preferred to rely on metropolitan judgments, silently waiting 'Till London Critics deemed the work as good'.[24] One important task of provincial prologues was to present the appearance of new plays as a sign of cultural prestige. Indeed, a feisty address for a play entitled *Caledonia; or, The Thistle and the Rose* (Edinburgh, 1812) even took a swipe at the patent houses, mocking the notion that the provincial stages were merely condemned '. . . to glean/The hasty droppings of the London Scene!'[25]

Newspapers and other forms of print culture publicised the fame of metropolitan performers across the nation. Provincial audiences were eager to convert this second-hand knowledge into the sensuous (and sometimes sensational) experience of watching celebrated actors in the flesh. Faster roads and the development of mail coaches made it possible for 'star' players, as they became known, to visit provincial theatres on short tours, 'for a few nights only': performers such as Dora Jordan, Sarah Siddons, John Philip Kemble, Edmund Kean and the child prodigy 'Master Betty' took away hundreds of pounds from a single engagement. Such 'expeditions' became the highlights of the cultural calendar: box offices were besieged, normal life all but suspended whilst provincial managers – who often charged 'London prices' for the week – made huge profits.

Some cities enjoyed distinct advantages on the touring circuit: York bene-fited from its position on the Great North Road; Bristol engaged players on their way to and from Dublin. Even Scotland, once almost as distant in the metropolitan imagination 'as the West Indies', according to Tate Wilkinson, could now be reached in just a few days.[26] In 1770, the actor-manager Samuel Foote took his entire company to Edinburgh (a trip funded, iron-ically, by a loan from Garrick) and returned in triumph, claiming to have made a good profit. Though ultimately detrimental to the provincial thea-tres, the star system created a sense of shared experience amongst spectators who lived hundreds of miles apart. These circuits helped to form a national audience, bound together by the illusion of intimate acquaintance with the nation's most celebrated performers.

Provincial theatre enabled managers, performers, playwrights, critics and spectators to rehearse the relationship – and sometimes the tensions – between civic, national and imperial identities. There are four main reasons why the theatre played such an influential role in this process. First, the promulgation of 'national character' had particular saliency in the provinces as a means of proving the theatre's utility against the virulent hostility of local Methodists and other antitheatrical groups. Secondly, the cultural identity of provincial performers was, in the eyes of the audience, strongly marked: 'natives' came from the immediate locality; 'exotics' or 'strangers', as they were called, from outside. The provincial theatre defined its identity both in relation to a specific town or city and within a national, and indeed colonial, system of theatrical recruitment and exchange. In an ironic reversal, new forms of citizenship began to be figured through the bodies of actors who, a few decades earlier, had been condemned as strolling players.

Thirdly, the geography of eighteenth-century drama represented a great variety of places both near and distant, from local sights (often featured in pantomimes) to military conflicts thousands of miles away. Stock plays provided managers with flexible scripts for the theatrical production of Britain's empire, allowing local spectators vicarious experiences of imperial citizenship.[27] Fourthly, the civic community of a provincial theatre was unusual both for its social heterogeneity and because of the degree of inter-action between cultural producers and consumers. Apart from disputes about particular plays, the sources of confrontation were surprisingly wide-ranging, from individual complaints about the 'getting up' of a siege to collec-tive demands in cities such as Liverpool for a metropolitan company. Whilst promising the integration of civic, national and imperial identities, provincial stages sometimes revealed the pressures and conflicts between them.

When James Winston, waxing eloquent about the Bath Theatre, imagines the playhouse being able to 'dictate' its theatrical character to 'the proud city of the Empire, nay, to the Christian world' he was not simply indulging a fantasy.[28] The late eighteenth century marked a new stage in the colonial circulation of British theatre. Plays introduce the strolling player as a mysterious and even heroic member of this colonial stage. A good example of such a character is Jack Rover, the benevolent hero of John O'Keeffe's comedy, *Wild Oats; or, The Strolling Gentlemen* (CG, 1791). Rover, inspired by 'a spark from Shakspeare's muse of fire', migrates from the Calcutta Theatre and joins a company of strolling players who work a circuit around Portsmouth and Winchester.[29] As Rover's migration suggests, the geographical boundaries of British theatre were changing rapidly. Many players, especially from the provincial theatres, decided to try their luck on American stages. As Tate Wilkinson pointed out, with an air of evident resignation, America was fast becoming 'the fashionable resort for country actors'.[30]

The loss of these talented players damaged both metropolitan and provincial companies.[31] In the short term, however, migration produced new transatlantic networks between provincial and colonial cities. Local newspapers published triumphant reports about the commercial success of the Philadelphia or New York stages, using correspondence sent between emigrant players and their families as their source of information.[32] These accounts did indeed allow spectators to imagine provincial theatre as a form of merchandise which, as Garrick had promised, would extend the city's fame '[f]rom East to West'.

Audiences and managers, however, wanted to assert a degree of independence from the theatrical capital. In Bristol, for example, audiences liked to dispute the judgments of London spectators. At Manchester the flamboyant manager, James Whitley, encouraged spectators to judge plays for themselves, even if that meant rejecting the cultural verdicts of London or Dublin. Given the city's rising fame in science and in commerce, why could not Manchester '... vie/For Judgment, and the Powers to descry/Comedians Faults, or their Perfections own'?[33] On some occasions, the managers at Manchester risked controversy by sailing close to the political wind. In 1777, the theatre craftily adapted an old play in order to capitalise on the recent excitement surrounding the Duchess of Kingston's sensational trial for bigamy. The production of Alexander Fyfe's *The Royal Martyr*, starring Sarah Siddons as Lady Fairfax and Elizabeth Inchbald as the Queen, promised that the trial of Charles I would feature 'a representation of the Scaffolding which was erected for the Reception of Peers, Peeresses, Ambassadors, etc., at the State Trial of her Grace the Duchess of Kingston'.[34] Whereas the Lord Chamberlain had refused to license *The Trip to Calais* (Samuel Foote's satirical skit about the Duchess),[35] the

Manchester Theatre avoided the Lord Chamberlain's authority by staging a historical tragedy with a topical slant. In the 1780s, Manchester continued to produce plays with topical and political inflections, including a contentious revival of *Robinson Crusoe* (1785) involving 'a Representation (in Miniature) of the Procession for the Repeal of the Fustian Tax'.

In Scotland, the tensions between integration and the desire for a distinct cultural identity were particularly complex and intense. Performance often promulgated the benefits of union with England and – sometimes within the same bill of fare – promoted the values of cultural nationalism. Members of the Kemble dynasty, including Sarah Siddons, became leading protagonists in this political history. When Siddons came to Edinburgh for the first time in 1784, one of the roles she played was that of Lady Randolph in Home's *Douglas*. By this time, of course, Home's play had become inseparable from the idea of a Scottish theatre. The 'return' of Lady Randolph, a character now identified with Britain's most famous actress, was an act freighted with symbolic value, a gesture akin to a form of cultural restitution. The control of Edinburgh's Theatre Royal by English actor-managers such as Stephen Kemble, the crucial position of Edinburgh and Glasgow on the circuits of English stars and the rich, conflicting representations of Scotland by Scottish, English and Irish playwrights, all disturb the boundaries of metropolitan theatrical histories. Moreover, it was the Theatre Royal at Edinburgh which implicitly disputed the claims of Drury Lane and Covent Garden to exclusive possession of Britain's 'national drama' by proceeding to invent and publicise a national drama of its own.

The ubiquity of patronage in the provincial economy acted both as a catalyst for integration and as a lever for local interference. Actors' memoirs frequently recall the awkward and sometimes humiliating tradition of calling on prominent spectators to 'bespeak' a play. In return for their money, patrons – including freemasons, resident and visiting members of the gentry and aristocracy, and elite women – selected their chosen play from the company's stock book. These patrons also acted as dramatic censors. At York, the redoubtable Lady Bingley and her friends sent a deputation of gentlemen to demand the withdrawal of Vanbrugh's comedy, *The Provoked Wife*, on the grounds of indecency. The manager was forced to order fresh playbills, explaining that the play had been altered 'at the universal desire of persons of distinction'.[36] At Liverpool, Southerne's *Oronooko* (a tragedy about a royal slave) was withdrawn from the repertoire, apparently at the instigation of the slave merchants.[37] As these examples demonstrate, patronage at the provincial theatres produced idiosyncratic and insidious forms of censorship.

Military personnel represented influential patrons, for many provincial theatres were located in garrison towns and at major ports. Officers bespoke large numbers of plays (especially dramas such as *The Recruiting Officer*) and they also supplied the theatre with military supernumeraries: English crew members for a performance of Smollett's *The Reprisal; or, The Tars of Old England* (DL, 1757) at Portsmouth; Highland guards for the premiere of Baillie's *The Family Legend* (Edinburgh, 1810). Through these acts of co-operation, the business of theatre and the prosecution of imperial warfare became a seamless national project. As we have seen, managers liked to depict themselves as military commanders who mobilised 'recruits' or 'soldiers' and set out to 'take possession' of towns occupied by enemy 'troops' (rival companies). These playful associations acquired a new significance when provincial theatres put soldiers and sailors on stage. Actors and military personnel now became members of the same national 'company', playing for and on behalf of the nation. Such productions explicitly identified the theatre's cultural work with the production, defence and expansion of the imperial state.

The final section of this essay recapitulates many of the themes explored so far: the migration of plots and performers, the equivocal status of the strolling player, networks between provincial and colonial cities, and representations of national and imperial identity. Again, one of Britain's leading actors – the comic performer, Charles Mathews – takes centre stage. But in this case, we shall be exploring the migration of a performance from the provinces to the metropolis and from London to America. In these acts of migration, new ways of staging modern British identities emerged.

4. Charles Mathews and Britain's colonial stage

Charles Mathews's *Mail Coach Adventures* became one of the sensations of 1817. More than sixty thousand fashionable spectators flocked to the English Opera House to watch Mathews's virtuosic impersonations of odd and eccentric characters, assembled in a mail-coach which departs from Piccadilly. Mathews went on to create a series of solo performances showcasing his extraordinary skills in ventriloquism. These included the *Trip to Paris* (1819) and, following his celebrated tour of Philadelphia, New York and Boston, the *Trip to America* (1824).

Mathews's 'At Homes', as these entertainments became known, mark the translation to the metropolis (and subsequently to America) of a provincial show. In 1798, the York actor-manager Tate Wilkinson had engaged Mathews as successor to the low comedian, John Emery. The time he spent at York shaped Mathews's career in a variety of ways: many of the absurd legal cases featured in his shows were based on trials he attended at the York Assizes. It was in Yorkshire, too, that Mathews tried out a one-man show about the experiences of an itinerant actor entitled *Rambles in Yorkshire* (Hull, 1808). Some years later, the *Rambles* would metamorphose into the *Mail Coach Adventures*, an entertainment exploring the accents, impressions and prejudices of miscellaneous characters who are 'out of their element': in transit between different parts of Britain and even between nations. To the recognised subgenre of the provincial 'Budget' pioneered by actors such as John Bannister, Mathews had brought his own unique combination of psychological insight and self-conscious absurdity.

Mathews's choice of a mail coach as his theatrical vehicle was an apposite one: after all, it was a savvy actor-manager who had invented this machine for transporting his performers between Bath and Bristol. But in Mathews's hands, the mail coach is a vehicle for reconstructing the modern nation on stage. In the mail coach, everyone is on the move: the Yorkshireman Zachary Flail sings a song about a countryman going to London; in another song metropolitan physicians travel to Yorkshire to attend a gouty Earl. Ironically, the 'At Homes' exhibit the excitements, aspirations and confusions of characters who are, by definition, away from home. What fascinates Mathews is not so much the experience of travel and migration as its effects on the construction of national and imperial identities.

In 1822–3, Mathews's fascination with geographical and social mobility took a transatlantic turn. During this season, he made a very profitable tour of America, performing his comic impersonations of John Bull to packed houses in Baltimore, New York, Boston and Philadelphia, and gathering accents, anecdotes and vignettes about America for his next show. From the ingredients of a provincial budget, Mathews began to create a new kind of trans-national entertainment. Soon after his return, the *Trip to America* (1824) opened in front of excited crowds at the English Opera House. Mathews recounted his journey along the eastern seaboard, accompanied by a witty young spendthrift, Jack Topham, who has been sent to America to be out of harm's way, and his irrepressible cousin, Barnaby Brag. At various points, the *Trip* explores the tendency of Britons to caricature and misunderstand American attitudes and values; at the same time, Mathews highlights examples of racial intolerance. Through vividly drawn characters such as the steady, respectable Mr Pennington, who quietly objects to the misrepresentation of his country by English tourists ('They give mortal wounds with the pen, which go deeper, and reach further than the sword'); the stolid English farmer John Houghton (who still thinks there is no place like England and sings an 'Illinois Inventory' designed to discourage his countrymen from considering emigration); and the pathetic *emigré*, M. Mallet (whose poignant efforts to extract his daughter's letter from the Boston Post Office are frustrated by confusion over the pronunciation of his name), Mathews explores the ideals and contradictions involved in the making of American identity.

Significantly, Mathews chooses to highlight rather than to ignore America's position as Britain's former colony. His journey takes him to Bunker Hill, site of the confrontation between British and American forces in 1775 (where, as the actor explains, graffiti writers have inscribed facetious comments on the monuments), and to Providence (where the commemorative dinner features a chauvinistic and bloodthirsty 'Ode to General Jackson'). It is crucial to realise that Mathews is playing both British and American parts in this entertainment: a single actor quite literally embodies the opposing forces in a war which had split Britain's empire. In Mathews's one-man entertainment, impersonation provides the conditions for a post-colonial dialogue between two nations.[38]

In at least one episode, however, the liberal opinions of the *Trip* are compromised by more rebarbative points of view. Mathews's shows often featured impersonations of performers both famous and anonymous. His imitations of provincial players fizz with humorous double entendre, as in the *Mail Coach Adventures* which depicts two provincial managers requesting the loan of props and characters including 'two or three virgins', 'genteel assassins', a 'calm sea' and a coffin. Despite obvious points in common, Mathews's portrait of the provincial player differs from that of George Colman, not least because it respects the tenacity of these characters and their sheer capacity for commercial survival. What is more, Mathews presents the strolling player's itinerant life and many roles as a theatrical model for the experiences and conflicting identities of a colonial society. But when Mathews decided to impersonate an American actor in his *Trip to America*, he irrevocably damaged the forms of reconciliation which his show tried to encourage. As we shall see, his willingness to profit from mocking America's first black theatrical company anticipates the rise of minstrelsy.

On his visit to America, Mathews had attended performances at the African Theatre in New York starring James Hewlett; he also arranged to meet the actor in private. Given their acquaintance, Hewlett was horrified to discover from a newspaper report that the *Trip*'s characters included a 'Kentucky Roscius' who debated 'whether it is nobler in de mind to suffer, or tak'up arms against a sea of trouble, and by oppossum end 'em' (the pronunciation of which prompts the audience to demand a popular song, 'Opossum Up a Gum Tree').[39] From the striking habits of local allusion at the African Theatre and the performers' 'jazz-like' conflation of speeches from different Shakespearean plays, Mathews had created a ludicrous black-face performance.[40]

3. The Georgian Theatre Royal, Richmond, North Yorkshire.

In this impersonation, Mathews's stock-in-trade of accents, incongruous juxtapositions and odd characters acquires a disturbingly racist edge. As in Colman's *New Hay*, Mathews invokes Shakespeare's *Hamlet* to expose the risibility of a claim – in this case the claim of black actors – to the ownership of legitimate theatre. Unlike the other characters in the *Trip*, the Kentucky Roscius is a composite satire which denigrates an ethnic group utterly disenfranchised from American society and its theatrical institutions. Hewlett responded to reports about this performance by pursuing Mathews to England in the vain hope of extracting a confession. But he also wrote an eloquent public letter to Mathews, protesting against the injustice and cruelty of his insult to the African Theatre. Here, Hewlett sharply upbraids Mathews for ridiculing the accents of the players and 'the tincture' of their skin.[41] At the same time, he uses this public forum to establish the legitimate status of black Shakespeare. With the aid of some pointed references to *Othello*, the actor makes a powerful case that Shakespeare 'is *our* bard as well as yours'. Though no evidence exists that Mathews received Hewlett's letter, the *Trip to America* had inadvertently provoked a fundamental challenge to the terms – and the colour – of Britain's theatrical empire.

This essay has argued that British theatre history needs to escape from London. My argument has demonstrated the growth of the provincial theatres and their crucial position in the dramatic market. Throughout, I have empha-sised the circulation of plots and performers around and beyond the nation. The arguments mounted here cast new light on the theatrical past but also illuminate the state of British theatre at the beginning of the twenty-first century. In many towns and cities, tantalising traces of the eighteenth-century stage are still visible. In Richmond, North Yorkshire, the intimate Georgian theatre in which Elizabeth Inchbald and Edmund Kean performed has been restored to its original state with magnificent results. As in eighteenth-century Britain, the position of regional theatres has again become intertwined with broader initiatives to aid urban regeneration and civic renewal. In other ways, too, the theatrical world of Garrick, Siddons and Mathews resonates with contemporary British theatre: institutions such as the Royal Shakespeare Company represent the global, corporate successors to the strolling players and the spirit of 'fringe' theatre evokes the dramatic innovations which took place in eighteenth-century Britain beyond the walls of Drury Lane and Covent Garden. Having challenged the metropolitan bias of theatrical history, we can better understand the British theatre's pivotal role in interpreting and imagining the nation.

NOTES

1. Historians have recently begun to analyse British theatre as a stage for dis-courses of cultural nationalism. See further, Kathleen Wilson, 'Pacific Modernity: Theatre, Englishness, and the Arts of Discovery 1760–1800', in *The Age of Cultural Revolutions: Britain and France, 1750–1820*, eds. Colin Jones and Dror Wahrman, Berkeley, CA: University of California Press, 2002, pp. 62–93.
2. Loren Kruger, 'History Plays (in) Britain: Dramas, Nations, and Inventing the Present', in *Theorizing Practice: Redefining Theatre History*, ed. W. B. Worthen with Peter Holland, New York: Palgrave, 2003, pp. 151–76, 158.
3. Joseph Roach, *Cities of the Dead: Circum-Atlantic Performance*, New York: Columbia University Press, 1996. On Scottish and Irish theatre in this period see, inter alia, *A History of Scottish Theatre*, ed. Bill Findlay, Edinburgh: Polygon, 1998 and Christopher Morash, *A History of Irish Theatre, 1601–2000*, Cambridge: Cambridge University Press, 2002.
4. George Colman the Younger, *New Hay at the Old Market*, London: W. Woodfall, 1795, scene i, pp. 9–10.
5. See the extracts from *Felix Farley's Bristol Journal* reprinted in 'The Centenary of the Bristol Theatre', *Western Daily Press*, 30 May 1866.
6. Undated letter to John Arthur in *The Letters of David Garrick*, eds. David M. Little and George M. Kahrl, 3 vols., London: Oxford University Press, 1963, vol. II, pp. 513–14.
7. The prologue and epilogue are reprinted in Richard Jenkins, *Memoirs of the Bristol Stage*, Bristol, printed for the author, 1826, pp. 79ff. An anonymous pamphleteer ironically contested Garrick's terms, arguing that 'real Tradesmen

can't like the THEATRIC MERCHANTS!' [James Gough], *Bristol Theatre*, Bristol: S. Farley, 1766.

8. See further Jane Moody, *Illegitimate Theatre in London, 1770–1840*, Cambridge: Cambridge University Press, 2000.

9. Tate Wilkinson, *The Wandering Patentee; or, A History of the Yorkshire Theatres*, 4 vols., York: printed for the author, 1795, vol. I, p. 80.

10. Henry E. Huntington Library, Larpent MS 488.

11. Members of provincial companies, of course, had been writing plays for decades: the farces and ballad operas created by John Arthur and Joseph Yarrow for the York Theatre are good examples. Some of these plays are conveniently collected in Walter H. Rusbamen, (ed.), *York Ballad Operas and Yorkshiremen*, New York: Garland, 1974.

12. *Letters of David Garrick*, vol. III, p. 1021.

13. British Library, Add. MS 25383.

14. Ibid.

15. An excellent exception is Sybil Rosenfeld, *Strolling Players and Drama in the Provinces, 1660–1765*, Cambridge: Cambridge University Press, 1939.

16. British Library, Add. MS 25383.

17. James Boaden, *Memoirs of Mrs. Siddons*, 2 vols, London: Henry Colburn, 1827, vol. I, pp. 282–3.

18. Ellen Donkin, *Getting into the Act: Women Playwrights in London, 1776–1829*, London: Routledge, 1995, p. 101.

19. On these performances, see Thomas Campbell, *Life of Mrs. Siddons*, London: Effingham Wilson, 1834, pp. 77–9.

20. See Jacky Bratton, *New Readings in Theatre History*, Cambridge: Cambridge University Press, 2003, p. 196.

21. Jane Moody, 'Illusions of Authorship', in *Women and Playwriting in Nineteenth-Century Britain*, eds. Tracy C. Davis and Ellen Donkin, Cambridge: Cambridge University Press, 1999, pp. 99–124.

22. Campbell, *Life of Mrs. Siddons*, pp. 45–6.

23. William Meyler, epilogue for the Bath Theatre, *Felix Farley's Bristol Journal*, 17 December 1785.

24. Prologue to Frederic Reynolds's tragedy, *Werther* (Bath, 1785), spoken by Mrs Bernard.

25. Henry E. Huntington Library, Larpent MS 1740.

26. Tate Wilkinson, *Memoirs of His Own Life*, 4 vols., York: printed for the author, 1790, vol. III, p. 143.

27. For the adaptation of stock plays in America, see Jeffrey Richards's fine study, *Drama, Theatre, and Identity in the American New Republic*, Cambridge: Cambridge University Press, 2005.

28. James Winston, *The Theatric Tourist*, London: T. Woodfall, 1805, p. 1.

29. John O'Keeffe, *Wild Oats; or, The Strolling Gentlemen*, Dublin: [no publisher given], 1791, Act V, p. 76.

30. Wilkinson, *Wandering Patentee*, vol. II, p. 233.

31. Alfred Bunn, *The Stage: Both Before and Behind the Curtain*, 3 vols., London: Richard Bentley, 1840, vol. I, p. 27; vol. II, p. 134.

32. See, for example, the theatrical 'intelligence' about the Philadelphia stage, reported in *Bonner & Middleton's Bristol Journal*, 14 June 1800.

33. Prologue for the Manchester Theatre printed in the *Manchester Mercury*, 16 December 1766.
34. Playbill for the Manchester Theatre, 1 January 1777.
35. On Foote's show, see Jane Moody, 'Stolen Identities: Character, Mimicry and the Invention of Samuel Foote', in *Theatre and Celebrity in Britain, 1660–2000*, eds. Mary Luckhurst and Jane Moody, Basingstoke: Palgrave Macmillan, 2005, pp. 65–89, 83–4.
36. Wilkinson, *Memoirs*, vol. IV, pp. 17–18.
37. Cited by R. J. Broadbent, *Annals of the Liverpool Stage*, New York: Benjamin Blom, 1969, p. 72.
38. Duncombe's edition of 1821 is conveniently reprinted in Richard L. Klepac, *Mr Mathews at Home*, London: Society for Theatre Research, 1979.
39. Klepac, *Mathews*, p. 106.
40. See further, Shane White, *Stories of Freedom in Black New York*, Cambridge, MA: Harvard University Press, 2002, pp. 109–15.
41. *National Advocate*, 8 May 1824, cited in White, *Stories of Freedom*, p. 133.

3

CHRISTOPHER BAUGH

Scenography and technology

Probably the most significant difference between a play written and produced in the mid eighteenth century and one written and produced a hundred years later would be the reliance upon pictorial scenography in the latter. In 1740, with some significant exceptions, the space of the production would display the formal qualities of a scenically neutral theatrical place. This was a place of performance in which scenery served as a decorative background to dramatic action. By 1840 the physical presence of scenic techniques and effects would underpin almost all aspects of production as major elements within dramaturgy and the theatrical experience.

By 1840 the neutral place of performance had been replaced by detailed scenic representations of other worlds involving sophisticated theatrical processes and techniques. This new place of performance was situated within its own discrete architectural space, one that was separated from the audience by a decorated proscenium frame through which the audience looked. Throughout this process of change, important physical and psychological distinctions were established between audience and stage. Fundamentally, however, it would be true to say that spectators in 1740 might have considered it a heresy to connive at losing their sense of identity in the theatre. For that audience, the act of becoming engaged in performance involved balancing a social sense of self alongside admiration of the performer's skill in taking them over the threshold of belief into the world of the play. By 1840 every possible aspect of architecture, scenography and its associated technologies was being used in order to transport the spectator's imagination into the 'other worlds' which the theatre sought to (re)create.

The relationship between the new technologies of the Industrial Revolution, and their integration into theatrical practice was complex and closely reflected the spectators' changing assumptions about theatre. Contrary to some traditional responses, new technologies of spectacle and show need not be understood as invaders and corrupters of dramatic literature, but as a part of the continuum of change whereby the theatrical experience both responded to, and reflected its audiences' concerns and interests. Sheridan's *The School for Scandal* may well be considered as better dramatic literature than his spectacular *Pizarro*, but is it any better as theatre?

Some technical developments proved to be especially significant in enabling the development of theatrical tastes. The chemistry developed in the distillation and processing of coal and other mining industries between 1780–1830 meant that the palette of colour pigments used by scenic artists such as Clarkson Stanfield (1793–1867) or David Roberts (1796–1864) was radically different from that available to Philippe Jacques de Loutherbourg (1740–1812) in the early 1770s. The invention of the Argand lamp and its tubular wick and its later exploitation by the gas lamp enabled the scenic artist and theatre manager to create harmonious stage pictures which integrated all aspects of theatre into a unified pictorial effect. These two technologies may therefore serve to illustrate the radical nature of the reform that scenography underwent during the period.

Representation and *vraisemblance*

New technology rarely initiates significant change but rather enables and expresses a change of taste that may well be already underway. The gradual transformation of scenography centres upon issues of representation and *vraisemblance* which became significant early in the period with resulting effects upon the architecture and scenic arrangement of the stage. For the greater part of the eighteenth century, the playhouse was a building in three parts: a part for the audience, a part for the actors and a part for the scenery. Importantly, the audience and the actors shared the same architectural volume: the space for the actors being a large forestage platform that thrust into the audience space and which was, effectively, surrounded on three sides by spectators. This neutral place, 'owned' by the actors, yet scenically undefined, was placed close to the focal centre of the audience, illuminated by the same light, and sharing the same condition of reality as that of the audience. Yet by consent and convention, this forestage was a threshold, which through the act of performance, could be transgressed and changed into whatever the actor required. As part of the ritualised social event of attending the theatre, the forestage was 'a real place but one that exists outside the boundaries of everyday society or behavior'.[1] The forestage enabled the audience to enjoy the exciting tension that might exist between the close physical presence of great artists such as Susanna Cibber or David Garrick, and belief and absorption in the characters, which the actors created. Furthermore, the forestage had the potential to represent any location that a play might require, being sanctioned by both conventions of representation and of witness. It required very little beyond the action of performance to cross the threshold between a formal, architectural place of performance and a dramatically potent space of performance.

The scenic part of this tripartite arrangement lay to the rear of this platform and, until the early nineteenth century, was a rather dimly lit space that housed the painted side shutters, and the rear shutters which closed the scene. It was considered as a space whose business was to display stock scenes of utility that served as backgrounds to the dramatic action that occurred before them. Money spent on scenery was considered as capital expenditure (as opposed to the consumable expenditure of today) and such expense might be advertised before the season began or after refurbishment of the theatre. The scenic space employed an elegant technology that supported two-dimensional painted surfaces in grooves placed upon the stage, and suspended from the ceiling above. Aristotle's seeming sanction of spectacle (*opsis*) in tragedy meant that, on occasion, extra effort might be expended upon scenes of splendour when technologies of the court masque such as winches, counterweights and pulleys might be employed for special effect such as the appearance of deities and princes descending from the heavens surrounded by glory and clouds.[2] Two quotations from the 1750s characterise the extent and tell us something of the prevailing nature of scenic representation. The first considers the requirements of the stage in Ireland:

> The Stage should be furnished with a competent Number of painted Scenes sufficient to answer the Purposes of all the Plays in the Stock, in which there is no great Variety, being easily reduced to the following Classes. 1st, Temples. 2ndly, Tombs. 3rdly, City Walls and Gates. 4thly, Outsides of Palaces. 5thly, Insides of Palaces. 6thly, Streets. 7thly, Chambers. 8thly, Prisons. 9thly, Gardens. And 10thly, Rural Prospects of Groves, Forests, Desarts, &c. All these should be done by a Master, if such can be procured; otherwise, they should be as simple and unaffected as possible, to avoid offending a judicious Eye.[3]

The second, published in London, would appear to confirm that this approach was not a provincial dilution of metropolitan scenic practice:

> I am not extravagant enough to propose that a *new* Set of Scenes should be produced at every *new Tragedy*. I mean only that there should never be such a *Scarcity* of Scenes in the *Theatre*, but, that, whether the Seat of Action be *Greek, Roman, Asiatic, African, Italian, Spanish*, &c., There may be one *Set*, at least, adapted to *each* country; and that we, the Spectators, may not be put upon to believe ourselves abroad, when we have no *local Imagery* before us, but that of our *own Country*.[4]

In 1759 Sir William Young requested the loan of scenery from Drury Lane for his private theatricals. Garrick's reply indicates the continued use of stock scenery in this period:

> The backscenes of our stage are more than 23 feet wide and 16 feet 6 inches high, and our wings are in proportion, consequently unfit for your place – but indeed we have no useless scenes, what we have are in constant wear, and take their turns as the different plays and entertainments are exhibited.[5]

During the period, however, this rhetorical mode of representation was being challenged. A decided lack of theatrical propriety worried David Garrick as he visited the Comédie Française during his first trip to France in 1751:

> The Appearance of ye house was not as I expected from ye report of others, ye glass branches gave it a rich look, but ye candles instead of lamps at ye front of ye stage are very mean & ye building on ye stage destroys all *vraysemblance* (as ye french call it) & with all their perfection, occasions ten thousand absurdities.[6]

Garrick was concerned about the 'building' of audience seating upon the sides of the forestage – a practice carried out in the English theatre especially on the busy nights of actors' benefit performances. However this relationship between actors and audience began to be seen as damaging to the idea of theatrical representation. In 1762, after a long struggle, Garrick banished the practice of seating spectators upon the Drury Lane stage.

Garrick's bourgeois desire to make the stage a place of elegance led to a considerable increase in expenditure and a concomitant change in production values. As manager of Drury Lane, Garrick's 'tasteful' eye would scan the stage and try to offer his audience a well-tailored and properly 'dressed' theatre experience. In 1759, he spent a considerable sum of money on staging *Antony and Cleopatra* with entirely new scenes, costumes and decorations and, by the early 1760s, Drury Lane had become noted for 'the quantity of different decorations, machinery and dresses'.[7] Towards the end of his career, Garrick concluded: 'I never make any Objection to ye Expence of decorating a play, if I imagine that ye Performance will be of Service to the Author, & the Theatre.'[8] The language of criticism reflected this when the *Theatrical Review* of 4 December 1771 wrote:

> The truth and perfection of Theatrical Representations, in a great measure, depends on proper Decorations; otherwise all that the Player can inculcate will prove ineffectual. In this particular ... Mr. Garrick has generally discovered great judgement; and, we recollect few instances of his erring with respect to this point ... Scenery and Decorations are very important auxiliaries, to the

keeping up the illusion, and carrying on an appearance of reality in Theatrical Representations.[9]

This shifting sensibility with its growing concern for 'an appearance of reality' must have influenced Garrick's decision in 1772 to employ Philippe Jacques de Loutherbourg at Drury Lane. It is important to note that Loutherbourg worked exclusively on spectacles, such as the masque *Alfred* (DL, 1773); on pantomimes, such as Garrick's *A Christmas Tale* (DL, 1773); and on topical and topographical scenes in 'Entertainments' such as *The Waterman* (DL, 1776), which included a 'Grand Representation' of a recent regatta on the River Thames.[10] The playbill for Sheridan's *The Camp* (DL, 1778), for example, promises that the show will conclude 'with a perspective Representation of the Grand Camp at Cox-Heath from a view taken by De Loutherbourg'. However, in spite of Garrick's willingness to spend money on scenes and costumes, the stock scenic system obtained for the majority of plays in the repertoire. But inevitably, the popularity of the scenic artist's work contributed to significant changes in attitudes to representation and its scenic strategies, and one that would fully reflect the period's growing interest in travel and tourism.[11]

A significant feature of this change concerned the degree of harmonisation of all theatrical elements, or at least the degree to which they were subjected to artistic control. Loutherbourg insisted upon an unprecedented degree of scenographic authority as shown in his 'pre-employment' letter to Garrick in 1772:

> I must make a small model of the settings and everything which is required, to scale, painted and detailed so as to put the working painters and machinists and others on the right track by being able to faithfully copy my models, and, if I deem it necessary to retouch something in the final display, to enhance the effect, then I must do so. I shall draw in colour the costumes for the actors and the dancers. I must discuss my work with the composer and the ballet-master.[12]

This unity would have been technically hard to achieve because of the dimly lit stage space, and conventionally improbable within contemporary conceptions of good acting. Its effect was to pull the actors away from the audience into the scenic world of the stage. If we imaginatively transpose a full-scale version of Loutherbourg's scenic models onto an eighteenth-century playhouse, two things become apparent. Firstly, we cannot imagine such scenes as merely providing an upstage background to dramatic action taking place on the forestage. Secondly, the setting suggests that the performers must belong within and become part of the created scenic world. The implications are significant: costume can no longer be fully contemporary or have the charade-like tokenism of historical period. The actor James Quin had worn contemporary clothes of the 1730s including a heavy wig along with a Roman breastplate to indicate his role within *Cymbeline*. Garrick performed *Macbeth* throughout his career in a contemporary scarlet military jacket and wig. As the scenographic unity implied by Loutherbourg becomes accepted, such costumes begin to look increasingly absurd. The large forestage becomes almost a redundant area except for aria-like direct address to the audience and the performer becomes a scenographic ingredient. All these developments had major effects upon acting styles and created new challenges and problems.

In January 1779, Loutherbourg presented *The Wonders of Derbyshire* at Drury Lane. The centrepiece of this pantomime depicted Harlequin and Columbine being chased by Pantalone through the tourist 'wonders' of Derbyshire. The *London Packet*, 8–11 January 1779, describes the succession of beautiful scenes which transfixed the audience: 'few attempts were made to move the muscles of the audience, or to interrupt the admiration excited by the exhibition'. However the *St James Chronicle* of 7–9 January comments, 'The subject of the pantomime was judiciously chosen for the display of Mr. Loutherbourg's abilities; but he should have been accompanied into Derbyshire by a Man of some dramatic Genius, or at least of Talents for the Invention of a Pantomime.' Audiences for such spectacular productions, it is implied, should become quiet, absorbed individuals looking with wonder into the 'window-on-the-world' picture frame: the illuminated auditorium becomes something of an embarrassment to these attempts at verisimilitude.

Henry Woodward's 1780 pantomime, *Harlequin Fortunatus*, had not been acted for some thirteen years, and the playbill announces the introduction of a new topical denouement featuring 'a Representation of the Storming [of] Fort Omoa in the Bay of Honduras' (it was captured by the British from the Spaniards on 26 October 1779). The *Whitehall Evening Post* of 11–13 January 1780 remarked: 'It is said that the apparatus for this display, the scenery, and the paintings, have been finished for some time, and lying ready cut and dry waiting the first achievement that should arise, and wanting only the finishing stroke from some peculiar incident to prepare them for exhibition.' Topical scenes of military action would soon become a significant feature of theatrical culture and the explosions, huge stage armies, patriotic songs and equestrian skills at Astley's Amphitheatre served to present the most important battles of the British Empire from Waterloo to the Crimean War.[13]

It is clear that Loutherbourg's scenographic ambition conflicted directly with the conventional potency of the traditional performer on a liminal forestage, flanked by proscenium doors. Nevertheless, within fifty years the forestage and the proscenium doors had gone and the proscenium arch stage became the focus and talisman of theatre architecture. It may be significant that shortly after Loutherbourg began work at Drury Lane, Garrick commissioned the Adam brothers to undertake a thorough refit of the hundred-year-old building. The architects' engraving presents a light, rather airy, decorated auditorium which glittered with coloured glass on the pilasters. Less than a decade later however, the house team of scenic artists, Thomas Greenwood and William Capon, refashioned the building, producing a more sombre, darker toned auditorium which focused increasing attention on the pictorial proscenium stage.

Loutherbourg left Drury Lane during the winter of 1780–1781 but his theatrical interests continued. In Lisle Street, just off Leicester Square, he set up a miniature theatre called the *Eidophusikon*. It is tempting to see this as Loutherbourg's opportunity to create on a miniature stage (8 feet by 6 feet) visual effects which could not be achieved at Drury Lane. The *Morning Herald* of 12 March 1782 advertises the second programme of scenes of the *Eidophusikon*:

4. Edward Francis Burney, *The Eidophusikon of Philippe-Jacques de Loutherbourg*, c. 1782.

ACT THE FIRST
Scene 1. The SUN RISING in the Fog, Italian Sea Port.
Scene 2. The CATARACT of NIAGARA, in North America.
Scene 3. (by particular desire) the Favourite Scene (exhibited 60 Nights last Season) of the STORM and SHIPWRECK.

ACT THE SECOND
1st. The SETTING of the SUN after a RAINY DAY, with a View of the Castle, Town, and Cliffs of Dover.
2nd. The RISING of the MOON, with a WATER-SPOUT, exhibiting the effects of Three different Lights, with a View of a Rock Shore on the Coast of Japan.

THE CONCLUSIVE SCENE
SATAN arraying his TROOPS on the BANKS of the FIERY LAKE, with the Raising of the PALACE of PANDEMONIUM, from Milton.

The *Eidophusikon*'s effect was significant and was remembered by scenic artists and painters for several decades after its presentations during the 1780s. It served as a stimulus to scenic invention and almost as a sample book of scenographic tropes, such as adverse meteorology, avalanches, collapsing mountain bridges, volcanic eruptions, explosions in colonial outposts, prisons, and nostalgic views of pre-industrial landscapes. Scenes such as these were advertised in theatres throughout the country for the next fifty years.

In making a history of eighteenth-century scenography, it is tempting to concoct a complex recipe of cultural ingredients: to place the spectacular talents of Loutherbourg alongside the Theatre Representations Act (1788), which created a huge increase in provincial theatre and theatre building; the significant increase in the proletarian urban audience; the popular taste for lurid gothic dramas, which located their narratives in ancient castles and required storms and tempests to accompany them, and the considerable increase in the size of Drury Lane and Covent Garden when they were both rebuilt during the 1790s. Yet such a trajectory does not account for the wider spread of interest in the visual and the topographical among all social classes. Artists such as Gainsborough and Reynolds applauded the *Eidophusikon* and thought of it as a major contribution to art. The military campaigns of the 1790s found expression in huge canvases and theatrical displays, and the impact of the French Revolution needed a dramaturgy and a theatrical form to express and respond to its social and cultural effects. The theatre's pictorialism and its ability to control the world by organising it into structured and repeatable views were deeply significant for the world's first industrial society.

The concern for Britain's past and especially for its medieval and Tudor heritage found expression in antiquarian studies of Shakespeare's plays and a desire to stage them with a degree of historical authenticity. William Capon (1757–1827) designed scenes of Gothic streets, chambers and Tudor halls for J. P. Kemble at Drury Lane and then at Covent Garden Theatre. His meticulous approach to scenography earned him the nickname 'pompous Billy' but frequently confirmed the new potential of scenery as the theatre's leading performer and protagonist. He expanded scenic technology by developing built-up three-dimensional scenic units that were used alongside the traditional wing shutters and back-cloths. However, the fifteen new scenes that were prepared for Kemble's *Macbeth* (1794) required the services of a scene-drop to hide the lengthy scene-changes, which a testy critic referred to as the 'perpetual curtain'.[14] Yet the *Gentleman's Magazine* remarked of Joanna Baillie's *De Monfort* (DL, 1800) that 'The artist, at great pains and labour, followed the style of building of the 15th century ... whereby, the spectator, for a short space, might indulge his imagination to believe he was in some religious pile, forgetting both his station in a playhouse, or how allowable such an appearance was on theatre boards.'[15]

New technologies

As the focus of theatrical attention moved beyond the proscenium arch and scenic representation became more precisely descriptive and atmospheric, new and more effective methods of lighting the stage became essential. Oil lamps had little significant advantage over candles as a means of illumination, although their oil supply might give greater longevity and the centre of the light could be more easily intensified by the careful placing of a polished reflector. Nevertheless the light source still consisted of a burning narrow ribbon of plaited fabric which was impregnated with oil. The light's intensity or power depended upon the size of the wick that was ignited. Garrick imported French oil burners which deployed multiple wicks, but the more wicks used, the more disparate and diffuse the light's focus became. However, these burners were evidently capable of producing sufficient light as foot or wing lights to enable the removal of the overhead candelabra traditionally suspended over the forestage. Popular genre paintings by artists such as Zoffany, Wilson, Roberts and Loutherbourg clearly indicate the developing taste for strong, angled light pouring into the scene from the sides of the composition.

This predilection for strong light and shadow was greatly helped by a technical development to the oil lamp that had an enormous impact upon scenography. Aimé Argand (1755–1803) was a Swiss chemist who developed (c.1780) the principle of using a hollow circular wick surrounded by a glass chimney. This proved to be a revolutionary breakthrough since it increased by just over three times the amount of light which could be produced. A glass chimney placed over the wick created an updraft that intensified the light by sucking oxygen through the flame making it possible to suggest the worlds of strong shadowy light which became such a feature of the period's dramaturgy. Arranged on timber battens, such lights could be quickly hooked onto the back of sliding wing-flats or grouped to form footlights. It is probable that Loutherbourg used Argand lamps to achieve his startling effects of meteorology in the *Eidophusikon* in the mid 1780s.

Argand lamp technology provided sufficient illumination to introduce the possibility of projecting special effects. Etienne Gaspard Robertson (1763–1837) invented a moving version of a magic lantern that he called a phantascope. During the last years of the eighteenth century he created an entertainment called the *Phantasmagoria* in the basement of a deserted cloister in Paris that used the moving lantern to project horrifying and alarming images through smoke onto a translucent screen. The spectators saw frightening, fearsome images such as skeletons, demons, ghosts and other macabre figures appear before their eyes. As the lantern moved, the figures would grow larger, giving the impression that they were rushing towards the audience, or they might shrink and disappear into a point of light, leaving the audience in darkness.

A similar lantern was used to create the storm scene when Robert William Elliston staged *King Lear* at Drury Lane Theatre with Edmund Kean. The playbill for 27 April 1820 advertised 'In Act III. A Land Storm. After the manner of *Loutherburg's* [sic] *Eidophusikon*.' James Winston, the stage-manager, noted in his diary that the storm scene had been lit 'by a new process from the top of the stage'.[16] The actor Joseph Cowell recorded that '[o]verhead were revolving prismatic coloured transparencies, to emit a continuously changing supernatural tint, and add to the unearthly character of the scene [so that] King Lear would one instant appear a beautiful pea-green, and the next sky-blue, and, in the event of a momentary cessation of the rotary motion of the magic lantern, his head would be purple and his legs Dutch-pink.' Cowell concludes by saying that during the first performance the stage carpenters competed to see who could make the most 'storm-like' noise. The thin ropes that made the trees move were distinctly visible, and Kean begged Winston to 'slack it off a bit' for the second performance.[17]

The Argand wick transferred its principal feature into the technology of gaslight, introduced into metropolitan theatres sporadically from 1816, but more universally during the 1820s. However, the overall effect of gas should not be overstated since, in practice, the source of light remained a single burning flame or a small circle of burning gas jets. What gas *could* provide, nevertheless, was a plurality of sources (and the concomitant increase in intensity) as well as the important development of the 'gas table' of levers and taps at the side of the stage which enabled lights to be dimmed and controlled.

The heat-generating quality of gas created a form of theatre lighting of great importance. Originally known as the Drummond light, it was named after Captain Thomas Drummond (1797–1840) of the Royal Engineers who in 1824 was charged with mapping the west coast of Scotland and needed to produce a light bright enough to be used in trigonometric calculations. He found that using a blowpipe in which oxygen and hydrogen were mixed at the point of ignition could produce a flame of considerable heat and intensity. This in turn could be played upon a stick of lime that would glow white-hot. The limelight, under the beguiling name of the 'Phoshelioulamproteron', was introduced into the theatre by Frederick Gye at the Rotunda in Vauxhall Gardens in June 1837 for an entertainment called *L'Atelier de Canova*. In November 1837 the Royal Surrey Theatre playbill for *The Sculptor's Workshop* announces that 'The Stage will be lit by a new light ... equalling the power of 264 Argand lamps', and by the end of November, William Charles Macready used the light at Drury Lane Theatre in Michael Balfe's opera *Joan of Arc*.[18] The limelight was traditionally used as a beam of light from high up on the side of the stage or later from the rear of the auditorium. Incandescent lime produces a wide spectrum, almost identical to that of sunlight, so highlighting the new scenic pigments. Playwrights, performers and critics remembered this prototype spotlight well into the twentieth century. According to Percy Fitzgerald, limelight 'really threw open the realms of glittering fairyland to the scenic artist',[19] and Edward Gordon Craig, remembering the light piercing the darkness, warmly acknowledged 'my debts to the limelight men of the Lyceum and to Rembrandt'.[20]

Of the new technologies that became available as a result of industrial experiment and innovation, it was the chemistry of coal mining and their applied technologies, which had a significant impact upon theatre. The quantities of pigment required by the scenic artist prior to this period meant that the available colours had been limited to the cheaply produced earth colours for the yellows and browns, mineral oxides for reds, greens and blues with the addition of carbon (soot), black and chalk whiting to darken or to lighten. The more saturated and intensely vivid colours of small-scale chemistry were simply too expensive. But new industrial processes unleashed a body of mineral chemistry that produced a radical change in the scenic palette. Colours such as chromium dioxide (a powerful green) and the newly synthesised ultramarine and Prussian blues became available in the quantities that scenic artists required and at prices that theatre managers could afford. By the 1820s, chromium yielded an important range of bright yellows, oranges and clean reds that made the colours of the previous age appear dusty and dim.[21] The more common use of zinc white in place of chalk whiting enabled pigments to be tinted more cleanly and, where necessary, to suggest transparency. The effect was noted by *The Times* (27 December 1828) in its review of Clarkson Stanfield's topical diorama 'Spithead to Gibraltar' for the Drury Lane pantomime *Queen Bee* (DL, 1828):

> When our memory glances back a few years and we compare in 'the mind's eye', the dingy, filthy scenery which was exhibited there – trees, like inverted mops, of a brick-dust hue – buildings generally at war with perspective – water as opaque as the surrounding rocks, and clouds not a bit more transparent – when we compare these things with what we now see, the alteration strikes us as nearly miraculous.

During the 1850s, costumes were also to benefit from the sharp, acid yellows and greens and vivid lilacs and purples which became available with the invention (again as by-products of coal mining chemistry) of aniline dyes.

The pantomime diorama provided an opportunity to use the stage and its new technologies to the full. Their popularity during the 1820s and 1830s reflects the contemporary fascination for spectacular views, visual trickery and optical illusions. Dioramas also represent an extension of the topical and topographical interests that were exploited in the *Eidophusikon*. Clarkson Stanfield and David Roberts vied with each other at Drury Lane and Covent Garden Theatre respectively to stretch the credulity of their audiences.[22] Stanfield used the term 'diorama' at Drury Lane, whilst Roberts used the term 'panorama' at Covent Garden, but they were essentially the same thing. Like a film running across the back of a camera, the diorama/panorama backcloth rolled from one vertical roller at the side of the stage to another on the opposite side. Sections of the canvas cloth were cut out and replaced by sized calico. The images were painted on the canvas in opaque scenic distemper whilst the calico sections were painted with newer transparent pigments, bound into spirit-based paint to provide the true dioramic effects. With this technique, spectacular transitions became the order of the day.

In the pantomime *Harlequin and Little Thumb* (DL, 1831), Harlequin darted into the King's Theatre in the Haymarket to avoid capture by Pantaloon. Within a scenic representation of the Haymarket Theatre, the curtain rose to present 'Mr Stanfield's Grand Diorama of Venice'. The scene presented a journey around the sights of Venice and its lagoon interspersed with special dioramic effects. Cross fading of light from the front to the rear of the backcloth could bring about a thunderstorm at the entrance to the Grand Canal, a tranquil sunset over the island of San Giorgio, starlight over the lagoon, or the moon rising over the Bridge of Sighs. Cut out ground-rows rose and fell to create greater depth, whilst actors and singers were pulled across the stage on wheeled gondolas. This diorama offered a scenic travelogue, a people's tour of the exotic, and Stanfield's detailed sketches and paintings, made on location in Venice, served to provide authority for the stage image. Inevitably, this scenographic capability now began to be used in other productions including Stanfield's panoramic view of Agincourt and the 'vasty fields of France' for Macready's *Henry V* (CG, 1839).[23]

These technological developments enabled the theatre fully to engage with the explosion of visual interests taking place in society. The fascination with the creation of an historical past was mirrored in the archaeological scenes of Capon and the Grieve family of scene-painters, and of course this approach facilitated the historicising of Shakespeare's theatre in the productions of William Charles Macready and Charles Kean. Dioramas and panoramas allowed the stage to offer visions of other worlds and to support Britain's colonial presence: the brilliant colours and 'Dutch' artificial foils and metals provided the glitter and spectacle of the pantomime stage, whilst pictorial landscapes in melodramas such as Thomas Morton's *Speed the Plough* (CG, 1798) became nostalgic reminders to an urban proletariat of a disappearing agrarian past. In this way, the theatre was able to play a fundamental role in both realising the world and responding to the awe-inspiring challenges of the new technological age.

NOTES

1 Arnold Aronson, *Looking into the Abyss: Essays on Scenography*, Ann Arbor, MI: University of Michigan Press, 2005, p. 102.
2 'Every Tragedy, therefore, must have six parts, which parts determine its quality – namely, Plot, Character, Diction, Thought, Spectacle, Song.' Francis Fergusson, *Aristotle's Poetics*, New York: Hill and Wang, 1961, p. 62.
3 Anon, *The Case of the Stage in Ireland; containing the reasons for and against a bill for limiting the number of theatres in the city of Dublin*, Dublin: H. Saunders, 1758, pp. 36–7.
4 Roger Pickering, *Reflections upon Theatrical Expression in Tragedy*, London: W. Johnston, 1755, p. 76.
5 Quoted in *The London Stage 1660–1800, part IV (1747–1776)*, ed. George Winchester Stone, 2 vols., Carbondale, IL: Southern Illinois University Press, 1962, vol. I, p. cxvii.
6 Diary entry, 24 May 1751, from *The Diary of David Garrick, being a record of his memorable trip to Paris in 1751*, ed. Ryllis C. Alexander, reprinted New York: Benjamin, 1928; Blom, 1971, p. 5.
7 J. A. Kelly, *German Visitors to English Theatres in the Eighteenth Century*, Princeton, NJ: Princeton University Press, 1936, p. 30.
8 David M. Little and George M. Kahrl, (eds.), *The Letters of David Garrick*, 3 vols., London: Oxford University Press, 1963, Letter 827, 5 April 1774.

9 *Theatrical Review*, 4 December 1771, I, pp. 253–4.

10 See further, Christopher Baugh, *Garrick and Loutherbourg*, Cambridge: Chadwyck-Healey, 1990, pp. 97–104.

11 See Christopher Baugh, 'Philippe James de Loutherbourg and the early pictorial Theatre: Some Aspects of its Social Context', in *Themes in Drama*, 14 vols., *The Theatrical Space*, ed. James Redmond, Cambridge: Cambridge University Press, 1987, vol. IX, pp. 99–128.

12 Letter from Loutherbourg to Garrick, reproduced in Baugh, *Garrick and Loutherbourg*, p. 123.

13 For a perceptive account see Jacky Bratton, 'Theatre of War: the Crimea on the London Stage', in *Performance and Politics in Popular Drama: Aspects of Popular Entertainment in Theatre, Film, and Television, 1800–1976*, eds. David Bradby, Louis James and Bernard Sharratt, Cambridge: Cambridge University Press, 1980, pp. 119–37.

14 *The Oracle, and Public Advertiser*, 22 April 1794. For a detailed analysis, see Joseph W. Donohue, Jr, 'Kemble's Production of *Macbeth* (1794)', *Theatre Notebook* 21 (1967), pp. 63–74.

15 *Gentleman's Magazine*, May 1801, p. 409.

16 James Winston, *Drury Lane Journal: Selections from James Winston's Diaries 1819–1827*, eds. Alfred L. Nelson and Gilbert B. Cross, London: Society for Theatre Research, 1974, p. 8.

17 Joseph Cowell, *Thirty Years Passed Among the Players of England and America*, New York: Harper & Bros., 1844, p. 47.

18 See M. Lindsay Lambert, 'New Light on Limelight', *Theatre Notebook* 47:3 (1993), pp. 157–63.

19 Percy Fitzgerald, *The World Behind the Scenes*, London: Chatto and Windus, 1881, p. 41.

20 Edward Gordon Craig, *Towards a New Theatre*, London: J. M. Dent and Sons, 1913, p. xi.

21 See Robert L. Feller, (ed.), *Artists' Pigments: a Handbook of their History and Characteristics*, Cambridge: Cambridge University Press, 1986.

22 On Clarkson Stanfield's career and his relationship with the diorama, see P. T. van der Merwe, *The Spectacular Career of Clarkson Stanfield 1793–1867*, Newcastle: Tyne and Wear County Council Museums, 1979.

23 Ralph Hyde, *Panoramania! The Art and Entertainment of the 'All-Embracing' View*, London: Trefoil in Association with the Barbican Art Gallery, 1988, usefully illustrates the way in which the theatre dioramas reflected the nineteenth-century fascination for spectacular views, visual trickery and the persistence of optical illusions which predate the cinema.

4

JIM DAVIS

Spectatorship

The nature of theatrical spectatorship during the eighteenth and early nineteenth centuries was determined by a number of factors. After the Restoration, the democratisation of the theatre accelerated, the realms of box, pit and gallery accommodating and rendering visible different sectors of the community according to class and income. In general the social range of spectators attracted to the eighteenth-century patent theatres was very wide, while in the early nineteenth century the distribution of audiences became rather more variegated. The size of theatres also increased in this period: by the 1790s, both Drury Lane and Covent Garden Theatre could seat in excess of 3,000 spectators.

Audiences comprised a cross section of society: the more aristocratic, fashionable and affluent patrons in the boxes; intellectuals, less affluent gentlemen and professionals in the pit; tradesmen and their wives in the middle gallery and servants, footmen and sailors among the inhabitants of the upper gallery. At the patent theatres, royal command performances, attended by the reigning monarch and members of the royal family, regularly took place. As John O'Brien has observed, audiences went to the theatre not only to a play but with the expectation of seeing their collective gathering as 'an image of the nation ... an ideal "mimic state" that resembled the political state not only in its frequent dramaturgical focus on dynastic affairs but in its material form.'[1]

Once we consider the constitution of audiences in the minor theatres which flourished in the expanding suburbs of London and the newer industrial cities from the late eighteenth century onwards, patterns of spectator attendance and composition become more complicated. Playhouses such as the Surrey and Coburg near the south bank of the Thames, for example, attracted audiences from the neighbourhood and often presented plays with local associations, but improvements in urban communications and the willingness of many spectators to walk long distances make it impossible to define the audience of such theatres precisely.[2]

In surviving descriptions, spectators are regularly depicted in comic mode (although not always intentionally) and in ways suggesting that those with more cultivated tastes may not share ways of seeing with less sophisticated spectators. Garrick, who abolished the custom of allowing spectators on the stage in 1760, gives the audience's behaviour comic treatment in *Lethe* (DL, 1740), when the character of the Fine Gentleman says:

> I stand upon the stage, talk loud, and stare about, which confounds the actors, and disturbs the audience. Upon which the galleries, who hate the appearance of one of us, begin to hiss and cry 'Off, off!' while I undaunted stamp my foot, so, loll with my shoulder thus, take snuff with my right hand and smile scornfully, thus. This exasperates the savages, and they attack us with vollies of sucked oranges and half-eaten pippins.[3]

Descriptions of English spectators by European travellers reveal further reasons for the comical and even satirical treatment of spectators. In 1791, Friedrich Wilhelm von Schutz complained about being robbed of curiosity about the audience after having been struck by a heap of orange peel from the gallery at Drury Lane.[4] And in 1826 Ludwig H. von Pückler-Muskau was similarly unimpressed by the coarseness and brutality of English audiences:

> English freedom here degenerates into the rudest license, and it is not uncommon, in the midst of the most affecting part of the tragedy or the most charming 'cadenza' of a singer, to hear some coarse expressions shouted from the galleries.[5]

In his account of a visit to the Coburg, William Hazlitt acknowledges his own sense of repulsion:

> The play was indifferent, but that was nothing. The acting was bad, but that was nothing. The audience were low, but that was nothing. It was the heartless indifference and hearty contempt shown by the performers for their parts, and by the audience for the players and the play, that disgusted us with all of them.[6]

Despite his intuitive sympathies, Hazlitt finds 'the crucial test of what cultural democracy might entail' too extreme for his own cultivated tastes.[7] Images of audiences, both verbal and visual, disclose powerful assumptions of social and cultural difference in those who depict them.

The freedom of spectators to express dissension, even to riot, when displeased was a recurrent aspect of theatregoing in this period. In 1736 Covent Garden Theatre witnessed violent reactions to an attempt to raise prices, while in 1737 footmen went on the rampage when the privilege of free seats in the gallery was withdrawn (see the essay by Kristina Straub in this volume). In 1755 anti-French sentiment led to rioting during performances of the ballet, *The Chinese Festival*, at Drury Lane. In 1763 Thaddeus Fitzpatrick organised riots at both theatres in protest at the abolition of half-price admissions for late arrivals. The OP (Old Price) Riots, which lasted for sixty-seven nights in 1809, were the consequence of new policies imposed under John Philip Kemble's management. The rioters protested about the raised price of seats in the pits, the removal of inexpensive seats to accommodate more boxes and the employment of the Italian singer, Madame Catalani, at huge expense.

Despite the examples of rowdiness recounted by foreign travellers and the occasional bouts of riotous behaviour, spectators were attentive. In particular, the discourse of sensibility powerfully shaped their responses to performance. Both men and women reacted with tears to the intense tragic performances of Sarah Siddons and some of her female supporters even succumbed to hysteria and fainting fits. As Shearer West points out, 'contemporary accounts give us a picture not only of audiences suffering to the point of illness but taking a masochistic pleasure in that suffering'.[8] We should not bring contemporary expectations about the audience's quiet passivity to an exploration of eighteenth-century spectatorship when the auditorium was fully lit throughout the performance and theatre constituted the largest secular indoor space where people could meet together. Jane Moody draws attention to a statement in the *Examiner* which represents the concept of theatre as the ideal public sphere:

> [Theatres] assemble people smilingly and in contact, not cut off from each other by hard pews and harder abstractions ... They make people think how they shall best enjoy life and hope with each other, not how they shall be best off individually and hereafter. They win, not frighten; are universal, not exclusive.[9]

In a variety of ways, we need to challenge Allardyce Nicoll's view that 'spectators in the larger theatres during the first decades of the century were often licentious and debased, while those in the minor houses were vulgar, unruly and physically obnoxious'.[10] Indeed, recent studies in Romantic sociability have suggested that the 'attainment of sociability' was 'one of the chief advantages of theatre'. Critics such as Hazlitt, Leigh Hunt and Lamb valued theatre for its 'capacity to unite people, humanize them, reconcile their conflicting interests and give them something to talk about'. 'Whoever sees a play', wrote Hazlitt, 'ought to be better and more sociable for it; for he has ... some ideas and feelings in common with his neighbours.'[11]

When spectators looked at the stage, what did they actually see? How were they encouraged to perceive the actors and the spectacle presented to them? What informed and constituted their particular ways of seeing? In a period which saw the growth of theatrical memoirs and the evolution of dramatic criticism, what happened on stage and in the auditorium began to be depicted much more frequently through graphic art.[12] This essay therefore sets out to consider how visual images may have shaped the nature of spectatorship.

Throughout the eighteenth century the print trade grew and flourished, a development apparent in the rapid increase in the number of graphic images – satirical prints, engravings, lithographs, mezzotints – in circulation. In effect vision began to be mediated by new technologies of viewing which shaped the individual's perceptions of the surrounding world. This development has important implications for any discussion of spectacle and spectatorship. Foucault for instance has argued that, while the eighteenth century emphasised spectacle as a means of coercion and control, the nineteenth century adopted surveillance (best exemplified through Bentham's panopticon) to establish order and discipline.[13] Theatre historians have drawn on this argument to explain transactions between the stage and spectator, especially in the nineteenth century. However, this is arguably too schematic an approach to the complex interactions between spectator and spectacle, actor, artist and audience addressed in this chapter.

Portraits of actors, depictions of scenes from plays, engravings and satirical prints may all have influenced spectators' interpretations. The period's art was shaped by its close associations with the theatre: Joshua Reynolds almost performed the process of portraiture as he painted in front of admirers; David Wilkie planned the configuration of his genre paintings as if creating a picture for the stage. From the age of Hogarth and Reynolds to that of Cruikshank and Wilkie the theatre and the theatrical provided visual culture with one of its most important and pervasive subjects. Material objects such as porcelain figures, toby jugs and snuff boxes also contributed to this enhanced visual awareness and highlighted the fame of popular performers.

Performers contributed to the increasing prestige and cultural significance of painting during this period.[14] In a groundbreaking study, Shearer West has shown how the image of the actor was virtually created and defined by eighteenth-century portrait painters. And portraiture of actors aimed not only to create a likeness (of sorts), but also to function as interpretation. As West points out, the images obtained from contemporary prints, paintings and pamphlets were 'not an unmediated reflection of the truth but a construction based on critical canons and aesthetic prejudices'. West emphasises the way in which acting theory 'appropriated the critical formulae and critical methods of art theory' pointing out that 'the actor became an image, responded to, interpreted and analysed like a work of art'.[15] This dynamic interplay between the theatre and visual culture had an important part to play in the formation of the educated spectator's perception. But spectatorship could encompass not only decorum and propriety but also voyeurism and desire. As West points out, the celebrity of eighteenth-century actresses led to 'a kind of scrutiny of the body which could displace or confuse lustful voyeurism with cultivated admiration'.[16]

David Garrick was quick to appreciate the value of portraiture both for the enhancement of social status of the actor and for publicity. At Royal Academy exhibitions, artists and actors vied for status, aided and abetted by critics who often 'shared an overlapping vocabulary, as a reflection of the basic assumption that the two disciplines involved visual display for public consumption'.[17] Paintings, drawings and prints can therefore constitute valuable documents through which to interpret spectatorship. This is not to ignore the theoretical discourse around the 'spectator' instituted by Joseph Addison and Richard Steele in which anxieties around the materiality of stage representation and spectator response are played out.[18] Nor is it to dismiss the importance of critical accounts of spectatorship which, as in the work of James Boaden, Charles Lamb, Leigh Hunt and William Hazlitt, drew on contemporary discourses about the graphic arts. Nonetheless, visual images shaped ways of seeing among potential spectators and influenced the nature of their interaction with performance in a variety of ways.

Though his first satirical print, *The Bad Taste of the Town* (1724), pilloried contemporary theatrical spectacle, Hogarth was to make a major contribution to the visual representation of the eighteenth-century theatre. His paintings of *The Beggar's Opera* (1728–9), in which he arguably fuses academic painting and social satire, are the first paintings to show a scene from an actual performance in an English theatre.[19] His portrait of Garrick as Richard III linked portraiture of actors in role with the genre of history painting, cleverly fusing in an ambiguous way the actor, the stage character and the idealised historical figure. Jenny Uglow considers this portrait a turning point in British art because of its emphasis on '*response* to action, not action itself – the face as mirror of the mind within, worked on by the scene without'.[20] Hogarth's *Strolling Actresses Dressing in a Barn* (1738) used players to create an allegorical and satirical comment on the government and theatre of the day, singling out for particular attention the 1737 Licensing Act and its restrictions on strolling players. The gulf between everyday reality and theatrical illusion is treated mock-heroically and Hogarth draws attention to the voyeuristic spectacle of the half-dressed actresses (including one, appropriately enough, playing the goddess Diana) through the inclusion of a figure staring at them from a hole in the barn roof in the top right-hand corner of the painting. The idea of the spectator as voyeur is implicitly signalled in this work. Moreover Hogarth evidently

5. William Hogarth, *The Laughing Audience* (1733).

conceived his public as theatrical spectators, declaring that 'My picture was my stage and men and women my actors.'[21]

The Laughing Audience (1733) may have set the tone for visual depictions of eighteenth-century spectators.[22] Hogarth contrasts the attentive audience members in the pit with the bored gentlemen in the boxes who seem more interested in flirting with orange girls and their neighbours; interestingly, the gallery spectators do not appear in the image. Originally designed as a subscription ticket for a set of prints of *The Rake's Progress*, *The Laughing Audience* hovers on the edge of caricature and anticipates the grotesque depiction of theatrical spectators common in the work of Thomas Rowlandson, Robert Dighton, Isaac and George Cruikshank, Theodore

Lane and others. Although there are stylistic differences, Rowlandson also depicted audiences comically and satirically in works such as *Side Boxes at the Italian Opera* (1785), *Covent Garden Boxes* (1786), *John Bull at the Italian Opera* (1805), *The Boxes* (1809) and *Pidgeon Hole: A Covent Garden Contrivance to Coop up the Gods* (1809). Indeed, in keeping with the overall notion that Rowlandson's characters are invariably spectators – 'people looking at things' – we find that the inhabitants of the side-boxes at the Italian Opera are torn between the spectacle of the performance and the often lascivious spectacle of each other.[23] The spectator has become the spectacle. George Cruikshank's *Pit, Boxes and Gallery* (1836) also maintains this tradition of comic representation with its depiction of a number of languid, uninterested and sexually voracious spectators in the boxes. By contrast, Cruikshank's depiction of the pit and gallery at the Surrey Theatre reveals a socially diverse audience; some absorbed in the performance, others evidently distracted, inattentive and, in the gallery, quite restless.

Satirical prints enjoyed wide currency and had such an impact on forming public opinion that the print shops themselves became an important cultural institution.[24] Members of the public unable to afford prints could nevertheless observe them in the print shop windows, as depicted in Gillray's famous image, *Very Slippy-Weather* (1808). As Diana Donald points out, these window scenes 'shift the focus of attention from comic spectacle to spectators; the latter become a comic spectacle celebrating the intimate relationship between satire and social reality, between performance and audience reaction'.[25] The spectacle of the spectator, then, is to be found in spheres other than the immediately theatrical.

Performers also became the subject of satirical prints. Marcia Pointon suggests that the art of caricature, 'offering alternative subversive personae for celebrities, both contributed to and profited from the proliferation of portraits and the destabilising of identity that accompanied that proliferation'.[26] Caricature helped both to establish and to undermine the actor's public image or persona and could also be read as a critical commentary in its own right. In effect it countered the impact of more formal modes of representation. By the end of the eighteenth century, self-fashioning through portraiture arguably had a strong influence on the way in which spectators viewed actors: there is something regal or even god-like about the images in circulation of Siddons and Kemble. At a time when the royal family were regularly pilloried in satirical prints, portrait painters elevated tragic actors to the status of monarchy. But within this very elevation lay the possibility of a fall from grace. Thus Siddons's emotional powers are pilloried by Annabel Scratch's *How to harrow up the Soul – Oh-h-h!* (1790) or

Thomas Rowlandson's *Mrs. Siddons, Old Kemble and Henderson, Rehearsing in the Green Room* (1789), while the economic dependency of Kemble and Siddons on the munificence and support of their betters is indicated in James Gillray's *Theatrical Mendicants, Relieved* (1809). Among the next generation of actors, Edmund Kean is brought firmly down to earth and reminded of his lowly social origins in such caricatures as Cruikshank's *Keen-ish Sport in Cox's Court!! Or Symptoms of Crim. Con in Drury Lane* (1824), satirising Kean's adulterous affair with an Alderman's wife. Visual culture thus offered spectators a range of conflicting images ranging from idealised portraits to grotesque and scurrilous caricature.

The dethronement or twilight of the gods was most evident in the Old Price riots of 1809 during which caricature made an important contribution to public perceptions of the dispute.[27] During the riots, satirical prints depicted Kemble as King John in confrontation with John Bull: in one image the Covent Garden manager is ignominiously tossed in a blanket by seven prostitutes on the stage in front of OP protestors. Prints tend to treat the rioters quite sympathetically, while those employed by the management to quell the disturbances are much more brutalised in appearance.[28] These images present the spectator as performer, enacting a bloodless revolt in which the actor, as surrogate monarch, is forced into acquiescence with the will of the crowd.

The visual representation of comic performance owed much to the theories of Hogarth. One of the greatest compliments made by critics of the period was to compare the comic brilliance of actors such as John Liston, Joseph Munden and Charles Mathews to that of Hogarth.[29] Interestingly, both Hazlitt and Lamb, who wrote so vividly about comic performance, produced important essays on Hogarth which helped to re-establish his reputation. Lamb considered that, 'in the grand grotesque of farce, Munden stands out as single and unaccompanied as Hogarth', while Hazlitt claimed, 'I have never seen anything in the expression of comic humour equal to Hogarth's paintings but Liston's face.'[30] Artists such as Clint and Harlow exhibited paintings of Liston and Mathews at the Royal Academy. Clint's restrained painting of Liston in character as Paul Pry, first exhibited in 1827, is a far cry from many of the more exaggerated or even grotesque prints of this popular character in circulation. Notably, many surviving portraits of Munden and Liston carefully remove traces of the comic actor from the image.[31] By contrast, caricaturists liked to draw on the conventions of low comedy to mock forms of off-stage excess: Gillray and the Cruikshanks in particular present the entire world as a low comedy performance. In many of the surviving prints, both the Prince of Wales (the future George IV) and the Duke of Clarence (the future William IV) look like low comic actors. In *A New Bravura* (1802), the

Prince is depicted as the low comedy character Lingo from *An Agreeable Surprise* singing the popular song, 'How happy could I be with either', an allusion to his complicated romantic entanglements. In Gillray's *La Promenade en Famille – a Sketch from Life* (1797) the Duke of Clarence is shown on a family outing with his mistress (the actress Dorothy Jordan) and their children, looking more like a low comedian than a prince of the realm. Such prints use theatrical allusions and quotations to produce analogies between theatrical and extra-theatrical worlds.

Print-making techniques only served to deepen the relationship between theatre and caricature. The constraints under which caricaturists worked in disposing of their characters across the plate compelled a theatrical approach to design which served to highlight the dramatic engagement among the figures. Like the manager of a theatre, the caricaturist usually placed the principal focus of attention at the front of the image, arranging the other figures in radiating lines or an arc. As Robert L. Patten points out, caricature enabled spectators to explore a more diverse world: 'the casual, private, momentary: the vitiated slouch of a debauchee, the effusive energy of roisterers, the indignity of flight. Whereas the classical manner sought a kind of fixity of image, an ideal immobilized, caricaturists put mankind into motion.'[32]

By the eighteenth century, the theatre had become 'the true habitat of man's second nature, his protean capacity not only to personate others, but in Hobbes's terms, to represent (and misrepresent) himself'.[33] Such perceptions were mediated to the public by a number of artists including Hogarth and Johann Zoffany. Garrick, for example, commissioned Zoffany to paint a conversation piece (a picture depicting some form of social gathering in a seemingly everyday situation), representing the actor and family members at his new estate at Hampton. The success of this painting led to a commission to paint a conversation piece based on Garrick's own play, *The Farmer's Return*. These immensely popular pieces, based on scenes from specific plays which Zoffany witnessed and sketched in the theatre, began to offer a visual commentary on theatrical performances. One critical account of *A Scene from the Farmer's Return* (1762) described it as

> a most accurate Representation on Canvas of that Scene, as performed at Drury Lane. The Painter absolutely transports us, in Imagination, back again to the Theatre. We see our favourite *Garrick* in the Act of saying, *for yes, she knocked once – and for no, she knocked* twice. And we see the Wife and Children, [as] we saw them on the Stage, in Terror and Amazement: Such strong Likenesses has the Painter exhibited of the several Performers that played the Characters.[34]

In fact it seems unlikely that these images accurately recorded what spectators saw on stage, especially as regards setting.[35] Nonetheless,

Zoffany clearly captured the spirit and visual memory of the production. The theatrical public would have seen these paintings at exhibitions and some would have bought engravings of them for themselves. By applying the conventions of the conversation piece to the representation of theatrical scenes, Zoffany underlined the genre's innate theatricality and revealed its potential as a vehicle for theatrical representation. His lead was followed by a number of artists including Samuel De Wilde, George Clint and George Harlow. All three exhibited theatrical paintings and portraits at the Royal Academy; De Wilde also specialised in theatrical portraits for the ever-burgeoning print market.

Through the ideas of Hogarth and Reynolds, we can discover important insights into the graphic representation of the actor. Joshua Reynolds had a powerful impact on theatrical spectatorship, both as a painter of theatrical portraits and through the influence of his *Discourses*. In turn, his theories shaped the way in which Sarah Siddons and John Philip Kemble presented themselves to the public. Just as the painter strived to achieve the ideal, especially through the depiction of historical subjects, so Reynolds saw the tragic actor attempting to achieve its theatrical equivalent. James Boaden draws on the language of Reynolds to describe the achievements of Siddons and Kemble. Leigh Hunt, Lamb and Hazlitt were also indebted to his arguments. Like Thomas Lawrence's portrait of Kemble as Coriolanus (1798) Reynolds's portrait of *Mrs. Siddons as the Tragic Muse* (1784) suggests an elevation of character which transcends the mimetic and representational nature of the actor's art.

Reynolds was one of a number of portrait painters who capitalised on the fashion for painting actors. He was fascinated by the points of commonality between painting and the stage and realised that the art of the actor, like that of the painter, might sometimes need to transcend or deviate from nature. Such deviations, he argued, 'arise from the necessity ... that every thing should be raised and enlarged beyond its natural state; that the full effect may come home to the spectator, which otherwise would be lost in the comparatively extensive space of the theatre'.[36] Here as elsewhere, Reynolds's argument highlights the importance of considering the effects of performance on the spectator. Indeed, John Barrell has argued that through the *Discourses*, Reynolds attempted to create a cultural public.[37]

A variety of treatises written in this period drew attention to the nature of the communication which takes place between the actor and the audience. The English publication of Charles Le Brun's *Conférence sur l'expression* in 1701 influenced theories of acting and painting, particularly in relation to ideas about muscular motion and the expression of the passions, and in time influenced spectator reception. In works from Aaron Hill's *The Art of Acting*

(1746) to Henry Siddons's *Practical Illustrations of Rhetorical Gesture and Action* (1807), actors and spectators were encouraged to recognise the representation of the passions as a codified semiotic system. (This is not to suggest of course that such codes were rigidly or systematically followed in performance.) Hogarth strongly advocated the importance of muscular movement as a means of making meaning clear and visible. *The Analysis of Beauty* (1752) concludes with a discussion of stage action which argues that careful observation and imitation from nature are essential components of the actor's (as well as the artist's) physical representation of movement.[38] Later in the century, Lavater's emphasis on the uniqueness of character and individuality in his *Essays on Physiognomy* (1789–98) made possible new ways of perceiving theatrical characters. Charles Mathews, who possessed a copy of Lavater's work, certainly demonstrated his notion of 'infinite variety'. The wide range of characters he devised and performed for his one-man shows in the early nineteenth century encouraged spectators to observe individuals rather than stereotypes.[39]

In a variety of ways, then, the visual arts played a significant role in the shaping of theatrical perception. While this was a process of intersection and mediation rather than of specifically attributable causal relationships, it is nevertheless an essential aspect of our understanding of theatrical spectatorship. Audiences realised that they too were part of the representation taking place within the theatrical space they inhabited. And it was because of this that spectatorship was invested with a freedom and elasticity that makes it one of the most complex and challenging dimensions of theatre in this period.

NOTES

1. John O'Brien, *Harlequin Britain: Pantomime and Entertainment, 1690–1760*, Baltimore, MD: Johns Hopkins University Press, 2004, pp. 68–9. Standard works on eighteenth-century audiences include Leo Hughes, *The Drama's Patrons: a Study of the Eighteenth-Century London Audience*, Austin, TX: University of Texas Press, 1971; James Lynch, *Box, Pit and Gallery: Stage and Society in Johnson's London*, Berkeley, CA: University of California Press, 1953; reprinted New York: Russell & Russell, 1971; Harry William Pedicord, *The Theatrical Public in the Time of Garrick*, New York: King's Crown Press, 1954.
2. See further Jane Moody, *Illegitimate Theatre in London, 1770–1840*, Cambridge: Cambridge University Press, 2000, pp. 164–77 and Jim Davis and Victor Emeljanow, *Reflecting the Audience: London Theatregoing, 1840–1880*, Iowa City, IA: University of Iowa Press, 2001.
3. *The Plays of David Garrick*, eds. Harry William Pedicord and Frederick Louis Bergmann, 7 vols., Carbondale, IL: Southern Illinois University Press, 1980–82, vol. I, p. 12.
4. Quoted in John Alexander Kelly, *German Visitors to English Theatres in the Eighteenth Century*, Princeton, NJ: Princeton University Press, 1936, pp. 150–1.

5. Ludwig H. von Pückler-Muskau, *A Tour in England, Ireland and France*, quoted in *Romantic and Revolutionary Theatre, 1789–1860*, ed. Donald Roy, Cambridge: Cambridge University Press, 2003, p. 148.

6. 'Minor Theatres-Strolling Players', *London Magazine* III (March 1820), reprinted in William Archer and Robert Lowe, *Hazlitt on Theatre*, New York: Hill and Wang, 1957, p. 162. See also John Barrell, *The Political Theory of Painting from Reynolds to Hazlitt: 'The Body of the Public'*, New Haven, CT: Yale University Press, 1986, pp. 336–7.

7. Moody, *Illegitimate Theatre*, p. 177.

8. 'The Public and Private Roles of Sarah Siddons', in *A Passion for Performance: Sarah Siddons and her Portraitists*, ed. Robyn Asleson, Los Angeles, CA: Paul Getty Museum, 1999, pp. 1–39, 18.

9. Moody, *Illegitimate Theatre*, p. 174.

10. Allardyce Nicoll, *Early Nineteenth Century English Drama 1800–1850*, second edn., Cambridge: Cambridge University Press, 1970, p. 8.

11. W. Hazlitt, 'Our National Theatres' (first published in the *Atlas*, 1829), in *Selected Writings*, ed. Jon Cook, Oxford: Oxford University Press 1991, p. 157, cited by Julie A. Carlson, 'Hazlitt and the Sociability of Theatre', in *Romantic Sociability: Social Networks and Literary Culture in Britain, 1770–1840*, eds. Gillian Russell and Clara Tuite, Cambridge: Cambridge University Press, 2002, pp. 145–65, 146.

12. See Charles Harold Gray, *Theatrical Criticism in London to 1795*, New York: Columbia University Press, 1931; reprinted New York: Benjamin Blom, 1964.

13. See Michel Foucault, *Discipline and Punish: The Birth of the Prison*, trans. Alan Sheridan, New York: Vintage-Random House, 1979.

14. Julie Stone Peters, *Theatre of the Book, 1480–1880: Print, Text, and Performance in Europe*, Oxford: Oxford University Press, 2000, p. 265.

15. Shearer West, *The Image of the Actor: Verbal and Visual Representation in the Age of Garrick and Kemble*, New York, St. Martin's, 1991, pp. 2, 89.

16. Shearer West, 'Body Connoisseurship', in *Notorious Muse: the Actress in British Art and Culture 1776–1812*, ed. Robyn Asleson, New Haven, CT: Yale University Press, 2003, pp. 151–70, 161.

17. Gill Perry, 'The Spectacle of the Muse: Exhibiting the Actress at the Royal Academy', in *Art on the Line: The Royal Academy Exhibitions at Somerset House 1780–1836*, ed. David H. Solkin, New Haven, CT: Yale University Press, 2001, pp. 111–25, 112.

18. See O'Brien, *Harlequin Britain*, pp. 72–85 for a useful discussion of this issue.

19. See Mark Hallett, *Hogarth*, London: Phaidon Press, 2000, p. 48.

20. Jenny Uglow, *Hogarth: A Life and a World*, London: Faber and Faber, 1997, pp. 398–400.

21. Quoted in Uglow, *Hogarth*, p. 537.

22. Hallett, *Hogarth*, p. 324 suggests that 'Hogarth's works have continued to function as seminal pictorial blueprints for graphic satire ever since they were first produced.'

23. Ronald Paulson, *Rowlandson: A New Interpretation*, New York: Oxford University Press, 1982, p. 80.

24. Marc Baer, *Theatre and Disorder in Late Georgian London*, Oxford: Clarendon Press, 1992, p. 256.

25. Diana Donald, *The Art of Caricature: Satirical Prints in the Reign of George III*, New Haven, CT: Paul Mellon Centre for Studies in British Art, Yale University Press, 1996, p. 7.

26. Marcia Pointon, 'Portrait! Portrait!! Portrait!!!', in *Art on the Line: The Royal Academy Exhibitions at Somerset House 1780–1836*, ed. David H. Solkin, New Haven and London: Yale University Press, 2001, pp. 93–10, 107.

27. See Baer, *Theatre and Disorder*, pp. 255–62.

28. See the various satirical prints produced by Isaac Cruikshank including *King John and John Bull* (1809); *King's Place and Chandos Street in an Uproar or a Sentimental Opposition: Two of a Trade Can Never Agree* and *Killing No Murder as Performed at the Grand National Theatre* (1809).

29. West, *The Image of the Actor*, pp. 132–3.

30. Charles Lamb, 'On the Acting of Munden', in *The Complete Works in Prose and Verse of Charles Lamb*, ed. R. H. Shepherd, London: Chatto and Windus, 1978, p. 375; William Hazlitt, 'On the Works of Hogarth – On the Grand and Familiar Styles of Painting', in *Lectures on the Comic Writers*, reprinted in *The Complete Works of William Hazlitt*, ed. P. P. Howe, 21 vols., London: J. M. Dent, 1930–4, vol. VI, p. 140.

31. See Jim Davis, 'Self-Portraiture On and Off the Stage: the Low Comedian as Iconographer', *Theatre Survey* 43:2 (November 2002), pp. 177–200.

32. Robert L. Patten, *Cruikshank's Life, Times and Art*, 2 vols, Cambridge: Lutterworth Press, 1992–6, vol. I, p. 52.

33. Jean-Christophe Agnew, *Worlds Apart: The Market and the Theater in Anglo-American Thought, 1550–1750*, Cambridge: Cambridge University Press, 1986, p. 102.

34. *St. James Chronicle*, 29 May – 1 June 1764, quoted in David H. Solkin, *Painting for Money: the Visual Arts and the Public Sphere in Eighteenth-Century England*, New Haven, CT: Yale University Press, 1993, p. 257.

35. See West, *The Image of the Actor*, p. 32.

36. Quoted in James Boaden, *Memoirs of the Life of John Philip Kemble*, 2 vols., London: Longman, 1825, vol. I, p. 178.

37. Barrell, *Political Theory of Painting*, p. 88.

38. *The Analysis of Beauty*, ed. Ronald Paulson, New Haven, CT: Yale University Press, 1997, pp. 112–13.

39. See West, *The Image of the Actor*, pp. 137–42 and Jane Goodall, *Performance and Evolution in the Age of Darwin: Out of the Natural Order*, London: Routledge, 2002, pp. 115–24.

PART II

Genres

5

LISA A. FREEMAN

The social life of eighteenth-century comedy

Toward the end of his 'Thoughts on Comedy,' Horace Walpole opines, 'a good comedy, by the passions being exhausted, is at present the most difficult of all compositions, if it represents either nature or fictitious nature; I mean mankind in its present state of civilized society.'[1] Writing during the last quarter of the eighteenth century, Walpole traces developments in English comedy across two centuries, beginning with the 'old comedies' of Jonson, Beaumont and Fletcher, and ending with a meditation on the particular hazards of writing comedy in his own time. Comedy had indeed changed over the course of the eighteenth century, as playwrights left behind the acerbic wit and libertine cynicism of the Restoration stage and, in response to the changing composition of their expanding audience, increasingly adopted what was heralded as a more 'refined,' 'polished,' or 'genteel' tone in their dramatic works.[2] Accordingly, where critical debate during the Restoration and early eighteenth century focused on the divide between humours comedy and comedies of wit, the second half of the eighteenth century featured fierce battles over the relative merits of laughing comedy – which subsumed comedies of wit and humours – as opposed to sentimental comedy, a new dramatic genre that appealed to the middling classes and that highlighted sentiment, exemplary displays of virtue, and ultimately the more emotive forms of sensibility.[3]

For maximum rhetorical effect, advocates on both sides of the debate represented their cause in much exaggerated and often hyperbolic terms. While defenders of laughing comedies, such as Oliver Goldsmith, portrayed sentimental comedy as a 'species of Bastard Tragedy' that had usurped the place of 'True Comedy', and painted themselves as patriotic crusaders on behalf of a uniquely English comic tradition, those who took up the cause of sentimental comedy cast themselves as no less noble and no less besieged.[4] Mounting a heroic defence of sentimental comedy in the preface to *Duplicity* (CG, 1781), Thomas Holcroft declared, for instance, 'the intention of this comedy is of a far nobler nature than the mere incitement of risibility'.[5] In reality, however, as Robert D. Hume has demonstrated, the laughing stage was never so overrun by sentimental comedies as Goldsmith would have us believe, nor were sentimental comedies without their share of successes and due influence as Holcroft might have us think.[6] Moreover, despite years of critical claims to the contrary, most plays from the period fall neatly into neither category of comedy, presenting instead generic amalgams where wit is softened with sentiment and sentiment is displayed humorously.[7] Rather than take up arms on one side or another, then, it might be more useful to consider the arguments as just two extremes in what was otherwise a much more subtle debate over the functions of comedy.

Unlike tragedy which was called upon in the eighteenth century to produce an ideal vision of national posterity, comedy, in keeping with its traditional function as the dramatic genre most concerned with representing and scrutinising contemporary social conditions, was expected to act like 'a dramatic camera': a mimetic representation, as Walpole put it, of 'mankind in its present state of civilized society'.[8] Following this mandate, comedy thus cast its eyes not on the vices of the aristocratic classes, which dominated the Restoration stage, but rather upon the manners, follies, and concerns of the middling classes whose influence and power were in the ascendancy in late eighteenth-century England.

Powered by the explosive growth of wealth and commerce, those of the middling ranks in this period sought to style themselves as a class worthy of emulation even as they, in turn, emulated their social betters. As the historian Neil McKendrick asserts, 'The avowed intention was to proclaim one's ability constantly to improve on the old and the inherited'.[9] As the middling classes pressed forward to gain social legitimacy and recognition, moreover, the very definition of what it meant to be 'gentle', or in more particular terms, what it meant to be a 'gentleman', underwent considerable change, moving away from a reliance on birth and inheritance to a new emphasis on merit and the acquisition of manners.

Describing the impact of these new social conditions on the writing of comedy, Walpole maintained, 'good-breeding, which seems the current coin of humanity, is no more than bank bills real treasure: but it increases the national fund of politeness, and is taken as current money ... The comic writer's art [thus] consists in seizing and distinguishing these shades, which have rendered man a fictitious animal, without destroying his original composition.'[10] In short, as the influence and aspirations of the commercial classes grew, politeness became the new currency not only in the social economy at large but also in the intrigues particular to comedy.[11] Articulated under the headings of good breeding, good nature, good manners and good conversation, politeness constituted a form of capital, no matter how artificial or cultivated, which could drive plots and with which characters could be invested. Whether they dramatised this new turn in the sincere and exemplary mode of sentiment or in the ironic and satirical mode of laughter, then, comedies in the late eighteenth century fulfilled the Horatian mandate to instruct at least as much as they pleased by working to elucidate 'a way for persons of the middling classes to acquire the outward forms and status of aristocratic refinement even as they adapted those forms to, and directed them toward, the pursuit of material advancement in a commercial society'.[12]

In the readings below, I will explore the ways in which this mandate to represent the conditions and concerns of social life in eighteenth-century England was compounded and made all the more particular and acute by the comic imperative of ensuring marital exchange. Through discussions of four of the most popular comedies from the period – Richard Brinsley Sheridan's *The School for Scandal* (DL, 1777), George Colman the Elder's *The English Merchant* (DL, 1767), Oliver Goldsmith's *She Stoops to Conquer* (CG, 1773), and Elizabeth Inchbald's *Every One Has His Fault* (CG, 1793) – I will demonstrate, first, how playwrights treated marriage as a social institution embedded in and regulated by the economic and class interests of the period, and, secondly, how the plots of those comedies administered a process of character valuation that would exemplify and ensure an apposite exchange of credit, property and status.

Character as value

Opening on 8 May 1777, at the end of Richard Brinsley Sheridan's first season as manager of Drury Lane, *The School for Scandal* solidified his already surging reputation as the premier comic playwright of his age.[13] With a prologue by David Garrick, the revered actor, playwright and former manager of Drury Lane, and a cast that featured the great comic actress Frances Abington in the role of Lady Teazle, Thomas King as Sir Peter Teazle, John Palmer as Joseph Surface and William 'Gentleman' Smith as Charles Surface, the comedy enjoyed a successful run of twenty performances in its first season, with regular revivals in repertory all the way up to the present day. A witty comedy of manners, the play takes as its satiric objects scandal-mongering and the hypocrisy of sentiment and features two major plots. In the first, Sir Oliver Surface returns from the East Indies to assess the character and determine the worthiness of his two nephews, Joseph and Charles Surface. In the second, a former lifelong bachelor Sir Peter Teazle wrangles with his very young wife, Lady Teazle, a country girl, who has become caught up in the fashions of London and has come under the

6. Thomas King and others in Sheridan's *The School for Scandal* by James Roberts, exhibited at the Royal Academy, 1779.

influence of a ruthless circle of scandal-mongers, the titular 'School for Scandal', expertly presided over by Lady Sneerwell. The marital prize in this comedy is Maria, a ward of Sir Peter, over whose affections Joseph and Charles Surface vie. While I shall focus most of my attention on the first plot, both plots invariably reflect and are governed by the concept of character, the base currency of, and an essential source of credit and value in, the social economy of eighteenth-century polite culture.

Before the eighteenth century, the term 'character' designated no more than a letter or a symbol, especially one that could be stamped or impressed on precious metals to signify their worth.[14] Drawing on this original meaning, the term was eventually adapted to stipulate the quality, value, or 'stamp' of an individual. A person of 'good character' came to stand, per the discourse of politeness, for an individual with a reputation for moral integrity and good manners. Thus displacing high rank as the main source of good credit, 'character' became the new form of currency not only in financial markets but also in the social economy. Unfortunately, there were a few problems associated with this new form of currency. In particular, character was vulnerable to specious attacks and reputations, like coins and bills, could be manufactured or counterfeited. Like many comedies of the day, then, such as Hugh Kelly's sentimental *False Delicacy* (DL, 1768) or Hannah Cowley's intrigue *A Bold Stroke for a Husband* (CG, 1783), *The School for Scandal* is a comedy of detection in which the 'true' value of character that lurks, here quite literally, beneath false 'Surfaces,' must be determined before an exchange can take place.

In the opening acts of the comedy, Sheridan vividly dramatises the vicissitudes of a social economy based on an unstable form of currency that could be as wildly inflated as it could be suddenly debased. When the 'school', which features such aptly-named members as Mrs Candour, Snake, and Sir Benjamin Backbite, is in session, 'no character escapes', as they spend all of their time taking up the talk of the town and skewering reputations (Act I, scene i). As Mrs Candour is so good to explain, the stakes involved in such exchanges were very high in a culture where, 'very trifling circumstances often [gave] rise to the most injurious Tales' and 'a Tale of Scandal [was] . . . fatal to the Credit of a prudent Lady' – points all too aptly illustrated by the recounted misfortunes of one Miss Letitia Piper, a young woman who lost 'her Lover and her Character' in one day, when a comment that her sheep had had twins was rapidly transmuted into a report 'believ'd by the whole Town', that the unmarried Miss Piper had herself 'been brought to Bed of a fine Boy and a Girl' (Act I, scene i). Thus rendering 'a character dead at every word', the 'school' blithely wields the instruments of what was tantamount to a form of social death from which it would be all but impossible to recover (Act II, scene ii).

In this kind of social economy, scandal could inflict severe damage not only on reputation but also upon the credit and material benefits that reputation yields. Character, in this sense, can be understood not only as a form of currency but also as a form of property, subject to property crimes such as theft, forgery and fraud. Indeed, nothing was so hazardous to the economy of character, and so pernicious in the social sphere it regulated, as the art of dissembling, a crime that Sheridan associates in this comedy with the hypocritical posturings of a 'man of sentiment'. Thus we can virtually predict the outcome of this comedy when, in the very first scene we discover that Joseph Surface is not the 'amiable Character' who passes with all his acquaintance, 'for a youthful miracle of prudence, good sense, and benevolence', but in fact 'artful selfish and malicious – in short, a Sentimental Knave' (Act I, scene i). Though Charles, in direct contrast to his brother, has a reputation for being 'dissipated and extravagant', a 'Bankrupt in Fortune and Reputation', these traits turn out to be the unavoidable results of his generosity, his general good nature and most importantly his 'benevolent heart', all fundamental characteristics of a truly sentimental hero (Act I, scene i; Act I scene ii). If he is profligate and has used up all of his 'credit', it is only because he is generous to a fault, a defect treated in the play as the fitful quality of extravagant youth rather than as a permanent or indelible mark of character.

Immune to the fashions and talk of the town, then, Sir Oliver is disposed to distrust both Joseph's reputation as a man of sentiment and Charles's reputation as a profligate. Instead, he seeks empirical proof and proposes 'to make a trial of their Hearts' in order to discover their true character (Act II, scene iii). What follows is a delightful series of theatrical scenes, including a parody of an auction scene in which Charles Surface demonstrates his 'plain Dealing in Business' (Act III, scene iii), when he puts his entire family tree under the hammer and sells off all the family portraits save Sir Oliver's (Act IV, scene i); a scene in which Joseph Surface refuses to help a distant relative named Stanley, as impersonated by Sir Oliver, and maligns Sir Oliver's character when he claims that his uncle has sent him 'a mere – nothing', when he has actually transmitted £12,000 both to Joseph and to his brother (Act V, scene i) and, though it is arguably immaterial to the resolution of the plot, the famous screen scene, in which Joseph's plan to seduce Lady Teazle is exposed and becomes the talk of the town (Act IV, scene iii). Found '[d]estitute of Truth – Charity – and Gratitude', Joseph Surface's certainty that he could bank on his brother's 'imprudence and bad character' proves improvident (Act V, scene iii; Act IV, scene iii). For in an economy that requires 'plain dealing in Business' to run efficiently, calculated hypocrisy is judged a greater threat to the public good than guileless 'imprudence'. Charles is thus rewarded with Sir Oliver's fortune for his sentimental extravagance of heart, that is, for his good character, even as he secures not just Maria's hand but her fortune as well.

Comedic plots in which a trial of character occurs and in which sons or surrogate sons are rewarded for their good nature with great property proved quite popular in the eighteenth century. In the sentimental variation on these plots, revelations of paternity often reinforced both the adjudication of the value of, and the transfer of property to, these sons. In one of the most successful comedies of the period, Richard Cumberland's *The West Indian* (DL, 1771), for instance, Belcour, a supposed foundling who has arrived in London from the West Indies after having inherited his adoptive (and actual) grandfather's estate, is put to just such a test by his clandestine father Stockwell, a once poor clerk who has risen to become a wealthy London merchant and a member of Parliament. Once Stockwell has been able to 'make some experiment of [his] son's disposition', and discover beneath a 'veil of some irregularities, a heart beaming with benevolence, an animated nature, fallible indeed, but not incorrigible', he publicly reveals himself and offers his blessing for Belcour's marriage to Louisa Dudley.[15]

Significantly, aside from the trials of good nature that *The School for Scandal* and *The West Indian* have in common, each comedy also features a wealthy merchant who is represented both as 'a fine, sanctified fair-dealing man of conscience', and as a benevolent authority figure, whose discerning good judgment can see through the fluctuating value of reputation to detect the hard currency of 'real character' and thus ensure the appropriate distribution of patrilineal property (*West Indian*, Act V, scene viii, lines 5–6; Act I, scene i, l. 104). Appearing in any number of eighteenth-century comedies, both in the laughing and the sentimental variety, these figures mirrored the rising prestige of the commercial branches of society, even as the plots over which they presided with benevolence and wisdom provided the ideological justification for their assimilation into the ruling classes. Simply put, just as good character was construed as the condition for being a character of property, so too did the unimpeachable character of the good merchant in eighteenth-century comedies provide a vivid justification for the massive fortunes generated through trade in the East and West Indies.

The value of comedic daughters

If the transfer of property in these comedies was secured both by the benevolent industry of the father and by the discovery of good nature, or 'conscious worth', in the son, comic plots in which the lost child in question was a daughter rather than a son looked instead to 'conscious innocence' or 'virtue' as the necessary measure of character. In these plays, moreover, the comic resolution required not merely the transfer of property to the son but rather the transfer of the daughter *as* property to a husband. Taking up what has come to be known as the *incognita* plot, first exemplified in its sentimental variation by Richard Steele's *The Conscious Lovers* (DL, 1722) and later repeated in such popular comedies as Edward Moore's *The Foundling* (DL, 1748) and Frances Sheridan's *The Discovery* (DL, 1763), George Colman the Elder's *The English Merchant* (DL, 1767) illustrates the particular perils faced by a woman of unknown provenance who has neither a father nor a husband to defend her character or to own her as his property.[16] The good character of a marriageable young woman in such a position in the eighteenth century was particularly vulnerable to the rapacious proclivities of scandal, for without a family name to fall back on, her only asset and defence in the marriage market was her reputation for virtue, a property, which as we have seen, could all too easily be tainted and debased. In a culture, where, as one character in David Garrick's and George Colman's comedy *The*

Clandestine Marriage (DL, 1766) put it, the marriage of a daughter was often thought of as 'no more than transferring so much stock', the *incognita* plot required that the daughter prove the value of her virtue and be owned by a father before she could be duly transferred, by lawful title and deed, as property to a husband.[17]

In *The English Merchant*, which featured Frances Abington and Thomas King in Colman's last play at Drury Lane before his move to manage Covent Garden, Sir William Douglas, a Scottish Jacobite who was forced to flee the country in 1745, returns to England after twenty years in search of his daughter Amelia. Stripped of his title and estates and still under threat of prosecution, Sir William reveals that he has engaged in this daring home-coming because, 'Her sex demands protection; and she is now of an age, in which she is more exposed to misfortunes than even in helpless infancy' (Act I, p. 11). Distracted by thoughts that his daughter's virtue, and hence her character, might be compromised, he takes up lodgings at Mrs Goodman's, where unbeknownst to him, Amelia has been living in an impoverished condition, beset by the 'ungenerous conduct' and 'dishonourable proposals' of Lord Falbridge, who is ignorant of her 'illustrious extraction' and all too willing to take advantage of her unguarded position, and taunted by a scandalmonger named Spatter, an agent of Lady Alton, who seeks revenge against Amelia for having usurped her place in Lord Falbridge's affections (Act I, p. 14; Act IV, p. 52).

As the comedy makes pointedly clear, Amelia's lack of a 'history', which is to say known genealogical origins, represents a liability upon which Spatter can capitalise by generating and putting into circulation a story to suit his own interests (Act I, p. 2). Indeed, when Amelia attempts to defend her virtue, she is easily put in her place, as the comically histrionic Lady Alton interjects, 'If you are a woman of virtue, what is the meaning of all this mystery? Who are you? What are you? Who will vouch for your character?' (Act II, p. 20). In short, with no one to vouch for her character, that is, with no one to tell the tale of her identity and pronounce both 'who' and 'what' she is, Amelia lacks both credit and credibility. Further, since she apparently belongs to no one, Spatter is free to make her into his own property in any tale he chooses, so long as he can provide that tale with probable weight. Relying on the strong suspicions of Jacobite conspirators that still circulated in late eighteenth-century England, then, Spatter is able to lodge what was termed 'an information' with the authorities that results in Amelia's arrest. Ironically, of course, Spatter has no idea how close he has come to hitting the mark, until he intercepts a letter from Lord Falbridge, which reveals Amelia's identity. But this revelation only confirms the supposition that drives both the sentimental and laughing plots of *The English Merchant* and *The School for Scandal* respectively which is that scandal is an effective weapon precisely because character is at once the essential coin of the realm and the greatest subject of speculation.[18]

Under these circumstances, the comedy informs us, only someone who has firmly established his credit, that is, someone, 'of very large property, and known character', can provide the necessary security not only to post bail for Amelia but also to procure her father's pardon (Act III, p. 40). Not surprisingly, then, the English merchant Freeport intervenes in just such a fashion, acting in a typically benevolent capacity to bring about this part of the comic resolution. When we learn, moreover, that Freeport's mercantile ties have succeeded where Lord Falbridge's aristocratic interests have failed, the extent to which the trading classes have assumed prerogatives and privileges that were formerly reserved for the upper classes is made clear. Under Freeport's direction, Amelia's status as property is finally settled, when, in response to Sir William's desire to 'make some acknowledgement of [Freeport's] extraordinary generosity', the good merchant declines Amelia's hand for himself and begs the favour of joining her with Lord Falbridge (Act V, p. 67). In this manner, Amelia's good character, signified not only by her revealed value as the daughter of a nobleman but also by her earned value from insisting on owing her subsistence to her 'industry and virtue' (Act I, p. 12), becomes the token or property exchanged in a binding transaction among men that both discharges and cements their mutual obligations.

Marriage values

Notably, the same set of preoccupations drives the plot of Goldsmith's last play, the still widely-produced comedy *She Stoops to Conquer* (CG, 1773) as it works to fulfil its generic mandate and, by virtue of marital exchange, 'make [a] personal friendship hereditary'.[19] In a comedy which Garrick rejected only to watch it succeed at Covent Garden Theatre under Colman's new management with the great comic ensemble of John Quick, Edward 'Ned' Shuter and Charles Lee Lewes, we find Young Marlow, the son of Sir Charles Marlow, who has been sent to the country to meet Kate Hardcastle, a daughter of his father's old friend, and to decide whether she might satisfy his tastes in a wife. This project is hampered, however, by an odd quirk of Marlow's character – when he finds himself 'in the company of women of reputation', he loses all confidence and becomes a stammering 'idiot ... a trembler' (Act II, scene i). In contrast, when he is among 'creatures of another stamp', which is to say, women considered available for purchase such as serving girls, milliners' apprentices and prostitutes, he becomes positively 'obstropalous', a 'loud confident creature', a regular 'Rattle' at 'the Ladies Club'. Marlow's extreme modesty and his boorish-ness both arise from the fact that he has spent most of his life 'in seclusion from that lovely part of the creation that chiefly teach men confidence' (Act II, scene i). Isolated from women, in other words, he has not had the chance to acquire what was considered a requisite skill in eighteenth-century social life, the ability to display good character and good manners when engaging in polite conversation. Thus playing on the two extant meanings of 'con-versation' – as either spoken or sexual intercourse – Marlow laments that he is doomed to 'converse with the only part of [the sex] I despise' (Act II, scene i). For Marlow to be found worthy of Kate Hardcastle, he must learn not only how to employ the proper modes for addressing a woman of virtue but also how properly to determine a woman's value.

Following the widely-held notion that discourse with women was the best instrument for bringing about the improvement of male conversation, Marlow's education begins when, in a plot contrivance that provides for any number of comic misunderstandings, the mischievous Tony Lumpkin leads him and his fellow traveller Hastings to believe that they have arrived at an inn along the road rather than at Hardcastle's home. There Marlow first stammers and fails even to look at Kate in her fashionable town attire and then impudently mistakes her for a barmaid when she appears later in simple dress. Under her surreptitious tutelage, however, he soon learns to appreciate 'refin'd simplicity', 'courageous innocence', and 'conscious virtue'; to value a woman whose only fortune is her character; and to desist from his habitual indulgence in 'uninteresting conversation'. But the comedy only allows him to go so far. Just as Marlow is mocked for his severe modesty, so too is he satirised when, in the midst of a romantic frenzy, he offers to eschew his filial obligations and forego a marriage of equal 'birth, fortune, and education'. Both modes of expression are cast as sentimental follies – the one because of its false delicacy, the other because of its economic naïveté. Only when merit is joined with 'equal affluence' (Act V, scene ii), can the 'bargain' be struck (Act V, scene iii), as it is when Hardcastle joins Marlow's hand with Kate's to close the comedy.

The new value of sensibility

Whether in laughing or in sentimental comedies, or in an amalgam of the two, then, the protagonists in late eighteenth-century comedy, in contrast to the capricious protagonists of Restoration comedies, were constrained by a broader awareness of the social and economic concerns that regulated both the marriage market and the assignments of value to character that generated its currency. As the turn of the century approached, however, a new ethos began to influence writers of comedy, an ethos that was shaped less by the social mandates of rational or polite sentiment and more by the effusive, and sometimes revolutionary, affective ties of sensibility. Comedy up to this point had been flexible enough to adapt its plots to the new economic and social realities of late eighteenth-century England, both reflecting and accommodating the demands for credit, property and status. Yet there was at least some feeling in the 1780s and 1790s not only that the conventions of polite society had hardened into the empty forms prognosticated by comic satirists but that those polite forms were insufficiently disposed to support complex representations of human emotion. Hence, while some of the best playwrights of the period, such as Hannah Cowley in plays like *The Belle's Stratagem* (CG, 1780) or *The School for Greybeards* (DL, 1786), continued to write excellent comedies of manners and intrigue, others, such as her equally successful counterpart Elizabeth Inchbald, began to experiment with comedies marked by a sustained interest in affective relations among characters. In trying to close this gap, moreover, comic dramatists not only developed an ironic and critical posture towards the conventions and material interests of comedy but also incorporated a strain of sensibility that verged on the melodramatic.

Both of these tendencies are particularly evident in Inchbald's *Every One Has His Fault* (CG, 1793).[20] Performed for the first time on 29 January 1793, the comedy was immediately assailed in the *True Briton* for its subversive tendencies, a charge which did nothing to prevent the play from enjoying an unusually successful run of thirty-two performances in its first season. Drawing on the long-standing patriotic tradition associated with a defence of English comedy, the pro-government journal took exception not only to one character's frequent allusions to the 'dearness of provisions in the Metropolis', but also to Inchbald's 'unaccountabl[e] blending' of the 'ludicrous' with the 'pathetic'.[21] Given our focus here on comedy's generic conventions, it is worth considering, then, not just how, as Jane Moody has shown us, the *True Briton* deployed, 'an ostensibly *aesthetic* framework for the reviewer's political critique', but also how Inchbald's play proffered an actual threat to the political order by representing the forms that regulated polite culture, including comedy itself, not only as insufficient but, worse, as morally bankrupt.[22]

Significantly, almost all the plots in the comedy treat marriages that have already been formed, implicitly suggesting the inadequacy of comic plotting that stops at this crucial threshold.[23] In the opening scene, we are introduced to Solus, an old bachelor who is suddenly determined to marry, as well as to Mr Placid, who, bedevilled by an always contrary wife, seeks, if not a divorce, at least a legal separation. In the third scene, we encounter Captain and Lady Eleanor Irwin, who, after marrying against her father's wishes and failing at an attempt to make an independent life in America, find themselves back in London 'without friends – without money – and without credit', seeking the child they had been forced to leave behind (Act I, scene iii, lines 99–100). Finally, in the first scene of the second act, we encounter Sir Robert Ramble, who finds himself abjectly insisting on a second marriage to Miss Wooburn from whom he had previously obtained a Scotch divorce.

Set in this manner, Inchbald's ironic critique of the limits and inadequacies of comedy is hard to miss. While Sir Robert's abjection and the Placids's bickering might provide us with some comic relief, Solus's farcical vacillations over whether to marry or not and Mr Harmony's deceptive interventions to bring about reconciliations among all the parties involved only signal the arbitrariness of comic conventions. This sense not just of arbitrariness but also of emptiness is compounded even further by Inchbald's almost relentless anatomisation both of the fiscal circumstances undergirding each marriage and of the extent to which women are regarded as property in those marriages. Indeed, the failure of these social forms to accommodate any notion of female identity that is not linked to property is betrayed when Lord Norland, Lady Eleanor Irwin's father, expresses his exasperation at Miss Wooburn's liminal social status: 'What are you now? Neither a widow, a maid, nor a wife. If I could fix a term to your present state, I should not be thus anxious to place you in another' (Act III, scene i, lines 364–7). What Inchbald resists in this comedy, then, is the 'fix[ing]' of 'states' or forms of marriage under terms of interest that are devoid of affective content. Moreover, where character, credit and status served in earlier comedies as the currency that facilitates happy and fortunate endings, in Inchbald's play those material categories are indicted as morally bankrupt; for they provide only the polite forms for the unfeeling and ungenerous shows of civility to which the impoverished Irwins are repeatedly treated by friends and family alike. The comic resolution comes only, then, when Harmony, who from infancy has felt the 'most unbounded affection for all [his] fellow creatures' and 'lament[s] that human beings should be such strangers to one another' (Act I, scene ii, lines 14–15, 124–6), provides the catalyst not merely for polite displays of sentiment but for repeated effusions of sensibility. The most extravagant of these emotional spectacles occurs when the Irwins (played for poignant effect in the original production by the husband and wife acting team, Alexander and Elizabeth Pope), are reconciled to Lord Norland, after he has been jolted from misery to joy on the unmasking of Harmony's deliberately false report of Captain Irwin's suicide (Act V, scene iii). As the rediscovered son, the parents and the grandfather, all fall to their knees in a series of melodramatic embraces, sensibility supersedes polite sentiment as the driving force of the comedy. A new set of social interests had indeed become the order of the day on the comic stage.

NOTES

1. Horace Walpole, 'Thoughts on Comedy', in *The Works of Horatio Walpole, Earl of Orford*, 5 vols., London: Pickering & Chatto 1798, vol. II, p. 320.
2. For information about eighteenth-century audiences, see Harry William Pedicord, 'The Changing Audience', in *The London Theatre World, 1660–1800*, ed. Robert D. Hume, Carbondale, IL: Southern Illinois University Press, 1980, pp. 236–52.
3. For a discussion of Restoration and early eighteenth-century comedy, see Brian Corman, 'Comedy', in *The Cambridge Companion to English Restoration Theatre*, ed. Deborah Payne Fisk, Cambridge: Cambridge University Press, 2000, pp. 52–69.
4. See Oliver Goldsmith, 'An Essay on the Theatre; or, A Comparison between Laughing and Sentimental Comedy', in *The Collected Works of Oliver Goldsmith*, ed. Arthur Friedman, 5 vols., Oxford: Clarendon Press, 1966, vol. III, p. 212.
5. Thomas Holcroft, *Duplicity*, London: G. Robinson, 1781, p. vi.
6. See Robert D. Hume, 'Goldsmith and Sheridan and the Supposed Revolution in "Laughing" Against "Sentimental" Comedy', in *Studies in Change and Revolution: Aspects of English Intellectual History 1640–1800*, ed. Paul J. Korshin, Menston: Scolar Press, 1972, pp. 237–76.
7. See Shirley Strum Kenny, 'Humane Comedy', *Modern Philology* 75 (1977), pp. 29–43.
8. B. Walwyn, *An Essay on Comedy*, London: M. Hookham, 1782, p. 2; Walpole, *Works*, vol. II, p. 320.
9. Neil McKendrick, introduction to *The Birth of a Consumer Society: the Commercialization of Eighteenth-Century England*, eds. Neil McKendrick, John Brewer and J. H. Plumb, Bloomington, IN: Indiana University Press, 1982, p. 2.
10. Walpole, *Works*, vol. II, pp. 317–18.
11. On the discourse of politeness, see Lawrence E. Klein's *Shaftesbury and the Culture of Politeness: Moral Discourse and Cultural Politics in Early Eighteenth-Century England*, Cambridge: Cambridge University Press, 1994.
12. Lisa A. Freeman, *Character's Theater: Genre and Identity on the Eighteenth-Century English Stage*, Philadelphia, PA: University of Pennsylvania Press, 2002, p. 203.
13. All citations will be taken from Richard Brinsley Sheridan, *The School for Scandal* (1777), in *The Dramatic Works of Richard Brinsley Sheridan*, ed. Cecil Price, 2 vols., Oxford: Clarendon Press, 1973, vol. I.
14. On the concept of character in the eighteenth century, see Deidre Lynch, *The Economy of Character: Novels, Market Culture, and the Business of Inner Meaning*, Chicago, IL: University of Chicago Press, 1998; Patrick Coleman, 'Character in an Eighteenth-Century Context', *Eighteenth Century: Theory*

and Interpretation 24 (1983), pp. 51–63 and James Thompson, *Models of Value: Eighteenth-Century Political Economy and the Novel*, Durham, NC: Duke University Press, 1996.

15. Richard Cumberland, *The West Indian* (1771), in *British Dramatists from Dryden to Sheridan*, ed. George H. Nettleton and Arthur E. Case, revised by George Winchester Stone, Jr, Carbondale and Edwardsville, IL: Southern Illinois University Press, 1969, Act I, scene i, lines 100–1, Act V, scene viii, lines 128–30. For a more extensive account of Cumberland's *The West Indian*, see Freeman, *Character's Theater*, pp. 228–33.

16. George Colman, *The English Merchant*, London: T. Becket, 1767.

17. David Garrick and George Colman, *The Clandestine Marriage*, in *The Plays of David Garrick*, eds. Harry William Pedicord and Frederick Louis Bergmann, 7 vols., Carbondale and Edwardsville, IL: Southern Illinois University Press, 1980–2, vol. I, Act III, scene i, l. 234. For a valuable discussion of the *incognita* plot, see Thompson's *Models of Value*, pp. 18–22.

18. On Sheridan's use of Colman's Spatter as a model for the scandal-mongering Snake, see Mark S. Auburn, *Sheridan's Comedies: Their Contexts and Achievements*, Lincoln, NE: University of Nebraska Press, 1977, pp. 112, 139.

19. Oliver Goldsmith, *She Stoops to Conquer*, ed. James Ogden, London: A. & C. Black, second edn. 2001, Act V, scene i.

20. All citations will be taken from Elizabeth Inchbald, *Every One Has His Fault* (1793), in *The Broadview Anthology of Romantic Drama*, eds. Jeffrey N. Cox and Michael Gamer, Peterborough: Broadview Press, 2003.

21. See the extract of this review reprinted in *The Broadview Anthology of Romantic Drama*, p. 319.

22. Jane Moody, *Illegitimate Theatre in London, 1770–1840*, Cambridge: Cambridge University Press, 2000, p. 49.

23. For a more extensive reading of Inchbald's *Every One Has His Fault* which takes up many of the same issues, see Misty Anderson's *Female Playwrights and Eighteenth-Century Comedy: Negotiating Marriage on the London Stage*, New York and Basingstoke: Palgrave, 2002, pp. 171–99.

6

SUSAN STAVES

Tragedy

The English relation to tragedy during the long eighteenth century was paradoxical. On the one hand, literary people continued to venerate tragedy as a high art form which required poetical gifts and profound thought and which had a special capacity to affect audiences and readers deeply. About one hundred new tragedies premiered in London during the second half of the eighteenth century and still more tragedies were published than performed.[1] Tragedy was an important subject in the period's literary scholarship, theory and criticism. With particular intensity, theorists and critics debated the relative merits of the neoclassical tragedies of Racine and Corneille versus those of indigenous Elizabethan tragedians, especially Shakespeare. The pioneering work of editors and critics such as Lewis Theobald and Samuel Johnson also contributed to a revival of Shakespeare's tragedies in performance. The reputations of famous actors were significantly based on their successes in tragic roles from Shakespeare and from Restoration tragedies by Thomas Otway and Nicholas Rowe. Contemporaries were absorbed in acting and in the psychology and physiology of the passions. By mid-century, a growing print record included magazine drama reviews, engravings of scenes and pamphlet controversies over the relative merits of different actors. These left us with unusually detailed descriptions such as this one about Garrick's performance as Lear cursing Goneril:

> You fall precipitately upon your Knees, extend your arms – clench your Hand – set your Teeth – and with a savage Distraction in your Look – trembling in your Limbs – and your Eyes pointed to Heaven ... begin ... with a *broken, inward, eager* Utterance; from thence rising every Line in Loudness and Rapidity of Voice.[2]

On the other hand, box-office receipts suggest that audiences preferred new comedy to new tragedy. As his extensive correspondence reveals, Garrick felt persecuted by the many earnest writers who kept submitting new tragedies to him in the hope of seeing them performed. When Sheridan became manager of Drury Lane, he wrote to his father-in-law remarking, 'I would much rather you would save me the disagreeableness of giving my opinion to a fresh tragic bard, being already in disgrace with about nine of that irascible fraternity.'[3] Ambitious men, and sometimes women, found their tragedies rejected by managers, or witnessed the often ignominious failure of their play on stage. For example, Tobias Smollett came from Scotland to London with *The Regicide, or, James the First of Scotland* and tried unsuccessfully for ten years to have it produced. Smollett's satiric talents appear in his outraged preface to the published *Regicide* (1749) and in his novel *Roderick Random* (1748), a comic, if bitter, narrative about the sufferings of Melopoyn, a talented poet named after the muse of tragedy, at the hands of supposedly deceitful theatre managers and an actor named Marmozet (Garrick). Even Johnson experienced unhappy moments with *Irene* (DL, 1749), his tragedy of a Christian captive presented to a Turkish Sultan as a mistress. Of *Irene*, Johnson's fine modern biographer Walter Jackson Bate candidly observed, 'There is probably no lengthy work ... by any writer of Johnson's standing that has aroused less curiosity ... or provided less enjoyment than *Irene*.'[4]

In some ways, critics' belief that there was a gulf fixed between serious tragedy and popular theatrical representation intensified at the beginning of the nineteenth century. Thus, Charles Lamb, a constant theatregoer and important drama critic, wrote a calculatedly perverse essay, 'On the Tragedies of Shakespeare, considered with reference to their fitness for stage representation' (1811). Lamb argued that stage representation 'sullied' Shakespeare's great tragedies by bringing down 'a fine vision to the standard of flesh and blood' and even claimed that *Lear* 'cannot be acted'.[5] Of the two significant Romantic tragedies we shall consider, Shelley's *The Cenci* (1819) was unperformable in the contemporary theatre and Byron's *Marino Faliero* (DL, 1821) was performed despite his securing an injunction against performance and was unsuccessful.[6]

Admittedly, good tragedy is rare in many cultures in many periods. In eighteenth-century England the capital investment required to produce a London play and the prospects of financial reward made play writing more competitive than the publication of novels or poems. Nevertheless, this combination of cultural fascination and literary failure – with a few exceptions, which we will consider – is a significant phenomenon.

Why should the eighteenth century's relation to tragedy have combined such fascination and such failure? One important reason was that the lingering appeal of the epistemologies and forms of Greek, Roman, Elizabethan and neoclassical French tragedy butted up against forms of knowledge more

characteristic of the Enlightenment. Older tragedy presents a world of epis-
temological and ethical mystery in which moral effort does not ensure moral
success. Answers to the questions of why protagonists suffer as they do or
how the tragedy we witness could have been averted are not conveniently
provided in Sophocles, Shakespeare or Racine. But Enlightenment thinkers
characteristically turned away from such mysteries and towards an analyti-
cal understanding of social and political structures and institutions. They
were meliorists committed to the improvement of people and their world.
That is why the characteristic form of Enlightenment drama is comedy, and
of serious drama, not tragedy, but romance.

Romances called tragedies

If we examine serious plays of the period classified as tragedies, we discover
that many of them are in fact romances, that is, works concerned to exhibit
ideal virtue. Although the protagonists suffer trials and may face the threat of
death, in the end their deaths are averted and their virtues vindicated. It is not
an accident that the period became infamous for its resistance to tragic
denouements, most memorably for refusing to allow Cordelia to die in
King Lear. Many eighteenth-century Roman plays are descended from
Nathaniel Lee's *Lucius Junius Brutus* (1680), John Dennis's *Liberty
Asserted* (1704) and Joseph Addison's *Cato* (1713). Although not necessarily
set in Rome, these dramas present exemplary heroes who embody civic virtue
and celebrate republican love of liberty and sacrifice of private desire for the
public good. (Occasionally, as in *Cato*, the protagonists may die, but they do
so in order not to compromise their exemplary virtue. Secondary characters,
especially women, may also perish.) Many an English patriot was fond of
stirring lines like these from *Cato*:

> . . . What Pity is it,
> That we can die but once to serve our Country![7]

Audiences enjoyed high-minded, polished, political rhetoric and declamatory styles in the theatre and in parliament. Here the theatre played a role in
cultivating national patriotic spirit. These Roman plays replaced older paradigms of unquestioning fealty to an hereditary monarch with a newer, more
democratic paradigm of civic virtue which asserted, like John Locke's *Two
Treatises of Government* (1690), the people's right to a government which
promoted the people's welfare.

A good example of contemporary romance calling itself tragedy is *The
Grecian Daughter* (DL, 1772), a successful stock play by Arthur Murphy
who was a prolific playwright and drama critic. The play is set in ancient

7. *David Garrick in the Character of the Roman Father.* Drawing (1750) showing (left to right) Mrs Ward as Valeria, Mrs Pritchard as Horatia, Spranger Barry as Plobius and David Garrick as Horatius.

Syracuse where a tyrant has deposed the rightful king. The king's daughter, Euphrasia, saves her father, who is starving to death in prison, by suckling him at her breast and finally stabs the tyrant. Evil-doers are to learn that:

> . . . virtue can keep pace
> With your worst efforts, and can try new modes
> To bid men grow enamour'd of her charms.[8]

Another example, closer to tragedy but still romance, is *The Roman Father* (DL, 1750) by William Whitehead, who became Poet Laureate in 1757. Based on a narrative from the Roman historian Livy and on Corneille's *Horace*, this drama explores a key dilemma that animated many serious eighteenth-century plays: how should an individual weigh his relative duties to country and to family? Together with his two brothers, the young Roman Publius Horatius defeats three Alban enemy champions. Publius rejects his sister Horatia's plea not to fight the Alban Caius Curiatus to whom she is engaged, explaining that 'private Duties' and 'Partial Ties' are 'subordinate' to public duty because our enjoyment of them depends upon 'public Safety'.[9] Their aged father is ashamed of his daughter's weakness and rejoices in his son's bravery, proclaiming:

> ... if from their glorious Deaths
> *Rome*'s Freedom spring, I shall be nobly paid
> For every sharpest Pang the Parent feels.
>
> (Act II, scene i, p. 17)

Yet when Publius returns victorious, Horatia greets him as a 'Barbarian' and cries out:

> Curse on my Country's Love, the Trick ye teach us
> To make us Slaves beneath the Mask of Virtue,
> . . .
> I scorn the impious Passion.
>
> (Act IV, scene ii, p. 60)

At first Publius maintains the calm rationality the play defines as Roman. But Horatia has determined to make him the agent of her suicide and persists until she arouses him to stab her with the sword still wet with Curiatus's blood. There is ambiguity about whether the distinction between rational patriotism and barbaric rage can be maintained as Publius has claimed. A Roman crowd demands Publius be condemned as a murderer, but his father and the wise King defend him. As she dies, Horatia declares that her words have been a feint to ensure her destruction: she seems finally to have controlled her passions and sought a virtuous Roman's death. In the end, we are told that love of country is the hero's 'first, best Passion' (Act V, scene ii, p. 83).

Prose tragedy

The experiment of writing tragedy in prose was the period's most radical break with dramatic convention. The early eighteenth century was a period of generic self-consciousness and experimentation. In 1731, George Lillo had dared to seem ridiculous when he offered Drury Lane his profoundly original *The London Merchant*, a prose tragedy which had not a great ruler but an ordinary merchant's young apprentice for its hero. Although *The London Merchant* would have a major influence on French and German dramatic theory and practice, including that of Denis Diderot and Gotthold Lessing, Lillo's radical experiment had few imitators in England. Ultimately, though, Lillo's drama laid the foundation for the prose tragedy of Ibsen.

Lillo's most significant English follower in the eighteenth century was Edward Moore, whose successful prose tragedy, *The Gamester* (DL, 1753) also became a stock play and a significant influence on Continental drama. The central characters in *The Gamester* are Beverley, a gentleman addicted to gambling, his virtuous wife, and Stukely, an inventive villain who profits from pretending to be Beverley's friend and gambling companion while

8. *The Last Scene in the Tragedy of the Gamester* by Mather Brown, exhibited at the Royal Academy, 1787.

covertly cheating and betraying him. Like *The London Merchant*, *The Gamester* is a domestic tragedy of private life. Unlike its predecessor, however, *The Gamester* takes place in modern London and includes many scenes in the shabby lodgings to which the husband's gambling has reduced his family. The naturalism of the setting and acting particularly affected spectators. Murphy, for instance, commented that Hannah Pritchard as Mrs Beverley 'did not appear to be conscious of an audience before her: She seemed to be a gentlewoman in domestic life, walking about in her own parlour, in the deepest distress, and overwhelmed with misery.'[10] A reviewer in the *Gentleman's Magazine* found the play's language 'perfectly colloquial': Moore did better than Lillo in crafting a prose which had sufficient elevation for tragedy while avoiding the hazards of high style as spoken by contemporary characters.[11]

In social rank, Beverley is a gentleman, yet he is driven by a desire for something far beneath the dignity of older tragic heroes: money. Lillo and Moore addresssed a crucial issue in the new capitalist economy: that personal identity increasingly depended not on birth into a particular social rank but on the possession of money. At the beginning of the play,

Beverley had been a kind and generous member of the upper classes. But having failed to inherit sufficient money to maintain that status, he turned to gambling in the hope of supplying the deficiency. In earlier plots, a man like Beverley would come providentially into money. But in *The Gamester* Beverley reduces himself to debtors' prison, sells the reversion (or future interest) he has in an old uncle's estate and thus his son's inheritance (the market estimated prices for such things, depending on probabilistic calculations using the possessor's age and state of health) and finally can think of nothing to do but drink poison.

Critics have complained that Beverley is too passive and therefore unworthy of his heroic position. Yet a serious issue in this tragedy is his active loyalty to Stukely, the man he thinks his friend. At a cultural moment when traditional male homosocial bonds were being challenged by a new emphasis on the nuclear family of husband, wife and children, Beverley ruins his family in part because he feels obligated to recompense Stukely, who has lent him money and now professes to be on the brink of debtors' prison. 'There's the double Weight that sinks me,' Beverley laments, 'I have undone my Friend too; one, who to save a drowning Wretch, reach'd out his Hand, and perish'd with him.'[12] Beverley asks his wife for her jewels and sells them. Despite his own desperation, we see him repeatedly offering the proceeds to Stukely. In a night scene (Act IV), Beverley, having refused to go home, prostrates himself on the stones of the street. An old servant urges him to 'rouse your Manhood', but Beverley's old-fashioned style of manhood seems to be helpless in the face of Stukely's proto-capitalism. Stukely ignores the challenge to a duel from the fiancé of Beverley's sister, talks of suing instead, and puts Beverley in prison by taking out an action for debt against him. Beverley's version of masculinity has not yet acknowledged the importance of the nuclear family, an ideal his sister Charlotte invokes when she rebukes Mrs Beverley for giving her husband jewels which would have enabled her to support herself and her son. Despite moments of unfortunate sentimentality, *The Gamester* is a significant work which moved audiences by addressing contemporary conundrums over competing moral values. Like many tragedies, it offers an elegy for ideals no longer viable.

Political tragedy

The Licensing Act of 1737 was motivated in part by the government's fear that theatre might be an instrument of political subversion. Shortly after the passage of the Act, the Lord Chamberlain denied permission for the performance of two tragedies with political implications, Henry Brooke's *Gustavus Vasa* (1739) and James Thomson's *Edward and Eleonora* (1739). The Lord

Chamberlain was not required to explain his decisions, but both Brooke and Thomson were associated with the opposition to the Prime Minister, Sir Robert Walpole, and their rhetoric about a nation's people suffering because of a ruler's evil counsellors was presumably among their plays' objectionable features. Although literary historians have often blamed the subsequent weakness of eighteenth-century tragedy on the Licensing Act, it was possible for dramatists to succeed in writing challenging plays despite such censorship. In practice, however, eighteenth-century dramatists usually wrote political plays that supported conventional political opinions.

Dramatists did, however, invent protagonists with complex characters and authentically tragic clashes of values. The Scottish writer James Thomson (better known as the poet of *The Seasons* and 'Rule Britannia') did so in his blank verse tragedy, *Tancred and Sigismunda*, performed at Drury Lane in 1745, the year of the last serious Jacobite uprising in favour of the deposed Stuart claimants to the British throne. Thomson's play is set in medieval Sicily against a background of civil war. A good ruler dies leaving a will that seeks to avert civil strife by settling the crown on the young heir of one faction, requiring him to marry Constantia, the only survivor of the line of the dead tyrant supported by the opposition. An old, public-spirited statesman, Siffridi, has invented this plan. He is sincerely committed to public virtue and to the ideal of the patriot king developed by Thomson's contemporary, Henry St. John, Viscount Bolingbroke: a ruler who serves his people, protects their rights and scrupulously adheres to the law. Moreover, Siffridi has adopted the orphaned Tancred and brought him up with these ideals of civic virtue. In the first act, Siffridi reveals to Tancred that he is the heir of Roger the First and the person chosen by the King's will to succeed to the throne.

Tragedy in *Tancred and Sigismunda* arises both from a familiar conflict between duty and love and from a more original questioning of the limits of civic virtue to which Thomson and his fellow Whigs had allegiance. Without Siffridi's having realised it, young Tancred has fallen in love with Sigismunda, Siffridi's daughter, and proposed to her. Siffridi tells Tancred that Sigismunda cannot be his Queen, that he has an obligation to avert civil war in his country by marrying Constantia. Shocked by these sudden revelations, Tancred resists Siffridi's advice and, perhaps more interestingly, he questions the moral logic of elevating public virtue over private virtue:

> They whom just Heaven has to a Throne exalted,
> To guard the Rights and Liberties of others,
> What Duty binds them to betray their own?[13]

Convinced that he is acting in the public interest, Siffridi offers the Sicilian assembly a falsified document purporting to show that Tancred has assented to the will. Tancred, Sigismunda and Constantia are all present in the assembly. Stunned by the dizzying sequence of events and unused to public life, Tancred remains silent and instead of challenging the authenticity of the document goes off with Constantia. Because Thomson elects not to dramatise this scene but to allow different characters to give their own versions of it one after the other, this episode comes to resemble a traumatic event which is repeated in memory as the mind tries out different narrative versions, none of which can offer an escape from grief. Having seen Tancred betray his love, Sigismunda allows herself to be persuaded that it is her duty to marry Earl Osmond, Constantia's adviser and a leader of the opposition. When he is told of Sigismunda's marriage, Tancred begs her to flee with him. She refuses, but Osmond – surprising the two in a night assignation – concludes that Tancred is displaying the character of a tyrant in appropriating a wife of a subject. In the ensuing duel, Tancred kills Osmond, but not before Osmond kills Sigismunda. As Siffridi acknowledges, neither he nor Tancred has succeeded in demonstrating the ideals of civic virtue which they articulated.

Plays depicting the triumph of a champion of republican liberty are succeeded in the early nineteenth century by Romantic tragedies which show the state as nightmarishly oppressive, crushing private virtue. Byron's *The Two Foscari* offers an intriguing coda to earlier Roman plays. It is set in Renaissance Venice, site of an early European republic with a crucial position in English political theory. Byron depicts an imperial Venice ruled by an aged Doge, Francis Foscari, and a council more powerful than the Doge. Foscari is willing to imitate the republican virtues of Lucius Junius Brutus by allowing the law to take its course against his son, Jacopo Foscari, who has committed acts prosecutable as treason against Venice. Jacopo has risked death by plotting to return from his enforced exile to the city he loves. In him patriotism has become not willingness to sacrifice self to serve country but cathection to a geographic place. This Venetian state, however, combines its republican constitution and public pageantry with regular recourse to torture and secrecy. One senator comments:

> . . . men know as little
> Of the state's real acts as of the grave's
> Unfathom'd mysteries.[14]

In a plot line reminiscent of Jacobean tragedy, Loredano is convinced that the Doge has had his father and his brother poisoned and seeks vengeance. The Doge denies this accusation, insisting plausibly that he has sacrificed his own son for the welfare of the state. Yet in this state the individual virtue celebrated in Restoration heroic drama and the eighteenth-century Roman play is no longer possible. Secrecy and repression, which Byron saw as also characteristic of the reactionary English state, poison all human relationships.

Like many serious plays of the period, *The Two Foscari* explores not only the question of how far an individual's duty to the state might extend, but also the significance of gender in such a question. Some women writers had explicitly rejected the common idea that while men's highest duty might be to the state, women's highest duty should be to her family. Thus, Catharine Trotter in *The Revolution of Sweden* (HM, 1706), another play about Gustavus Vasa, has her heroine foil her husband's treasonous plot by reporting it to Vasa, helping to liberate Sweden.

In *The Two Foscari* Byron pits Frances Foscari's words about obligation to public duty and law against a scathing critique of the state by Jacopo's wife, Marina. Bitter about the Doge's unwillingness to try to save his son, Marina argues that deference to the state is merely the effect of state terror on individuals less brave and independent than she. Keep your 'maxims' of 'deference', she tells the Doge, for 'dumb citizens' to whom 'your midnight carryings off and drownings' and 'unknown dooms, and sudden executions' have made you seem the 'beings of another and worse world!'

Whereas Horatia in *The Roman Father* retracts her accusations that men's devotion to the country violates primary natural duties, Marina continues to insist that men have made a false god of the state. She denies that her children belong to the Venetian republic and pleads that as 'a woman' her husband and her children '... were / Country and home' (Act V, scene i, p. 198). Nevertheless, Marina adopts rhetoric typical of the eighteenth-century Roman play:

> The country is the traitress, which thrusts forth
> Her best and bravest from her. Tyranny
> Is far the worst of treasons ...
>
> (Act II, scene i, p. 161)

Given the play's emphasis on the Machiavellian manipulation of public justice and the depiction of Jacopo's sufferings in the dungeon (including his shrieks under the torture which eventually kills him), an audience is likely to sympathise with Marina's point of view. The Council deposes Foscari, who sees the state inhabited not by a democratic 'people' but by a cowed 'populace' (Act V, scene i, p. 205). After Loredano poisons Foscari, the Council decides to bury him with public honours as Marina proclaims their hypocrisy (Act V, scene i, p. 209).

Byron was vividly aware that *The Two Foscari* contrasted sharply with the majority of contemporary political plays. As Gillian Russell has shown, British theatre in this period helped to construct a new kind of patriotism designed to counter first the radicalism of the French Revolution and then France's direct military threat in the Napoleonic Wars.[15] Much of this theatre was sheer pageantry, but the older Roman play sometimes became the new patriotic tragedy. Such plays were more concerned with articulating patriotic sentiments and providing inspiring spectacles of military victory than with the profound problems Byron explored of an individual's impotence before larger historical forces.

Domestic tragedy

Traditionally, the high literary status of tragedy was linked to the social status of its protagonists and to the belief that the actions of kings and statesmen had consequences which reverberated through the social world. The actions of more ordinary people seemed the proper subject of comedy. In the eighteenth century, however, writers such as Lillo and Moore challenged generic forms and the assumptions behind them. Inspired in part by their example, the French theorist and playwright Denis Diderot developed the idea of a modern serious *drame*, neither comic nor tragic, yet nevertheless representing sublime feeling and moral inspiration. Like other contemporary theorists, Diderot argued that the uncomplicated representation of the misfortunes of ordinary private people would move audiences more than 'the fictitious death of a tyrant, or the sacrifice of a child on the altars of the gods of Athens or Rome'.[16] In an age of sensibility, many also shared Diderot's love of affecting stage tableaux and sentimental maxims. Bourgeois drama in this period represented suffering and aimed to evoke pathos, but tended to avoid tragic conclusions. Indeed, the adaptation of *The Gamester* most frequently staged on the continent, by the Frenchman Bernard-Joseph Saurin, allowed Beverley to live.

Only rarely are domestic plays of this period tragic rather than pathetic and sentimental. The starkest and most powerful domestic tragedy is probably Lillo's *The Fatal Curiosity* (HM, 1736), a verse play which could reduce an audience to stunned silence rather than the more usual tears. Lillo's social position as an artisan rather than a gentleman seems to have freed him to observe how profoundly the presence or absence of money and its concomitant social respect could affect character. His Calvinism may have insulated him from the more usual optimism of the Enlightenment.

Based on a news report rather than on mythology or history, *The Fatal Curiosity* represents a formerly genteel but now impoverished and aged husband and wife, bitter about their fall from prosperity and independence. Their only son has gone to the Indies and is presumed dead. Old Wilmot, formerly generous and sagacious, is now despairing; he sells his copy of

Seneca's philosophy to buy bread and refrains from suicide only because he loves his wife. Faced with the 'insolent contempt' of people who used to respect her, Agnes becomes angry and fiercely proud rather than humble.[17] 'Nature only favors youth', Old Wilmot says,

> ... No second hope shall spring
> From my dead loins, and *Agnes'* sterile womb,
> To dry our tears, and dissipate despair.
>
> (Act II, scene iii, p. 321)

One day they entertain a shipwrecked stranger and notice that he carries jewels. The stranger praises the good fortune of his survival and celebrates the grace and mercy which appear when least expected. Old Wilmot retorts that fortune is more capricious than comforting and asks how many others died in the shipwreck. After the stranger goes to bed, Agnes's curiosity leads her to open his casket, where she discovers jewels that could end their poverty:

> ... the cold neglect of friends;
> The galling scorn, or more provoking pity
> Of an insulting world –
>
> (Act III, scene i, p. 323)

The Wilmots determine to stab the stranger in his sleep and keep the jewels. As Wilmot carries out the deed, the young man awakes and cries out, 'father!' (Act III, scene i, p. 328).

Young Wilmot's death is the result of his decision to withhold his identity from his parents. As a man of sensibility and curiosity, he had hoped to 'refine' the happiness of their reunion by staging a scene of gradual recognition in which his friends could witness the 'floods of transport' his self-revelation would release (Act II, scene ii, pp. 318–19). Immediately discovered as a murderer, Old Wilmot pronounces his own elegy:

> Curses and deprecations are in vain:
> The sun will shine, and all things have their course.
> When we, the curse and burthen of the earth,
> Shall be absorb'd, and mingled with its dust.
>
> (Act III, scene i, p. 329)

The Fatal Curiosity and *The Gamester* were among the very few plays that William Hazlitt, writing in 1820, exempted from his complaint that eighteenth-century tragedy had 'degenerated ... into the most frigid, insipid, and insignificant of all things'. After the French Revolution, though, the new German drama of Friedrich Schiller and August von Kotzebue startled audiences 'by overturning all the established maxims of society'.[18] Kotzebue's

Menschenhass und Reue (1789) adapted as *The Stranger* (1798) for instance, shocked by showing a husband being reconciled with his adulterous wife. These German plays were not necessarily tragedies, but their challenges to contemporary morality aligned them with contemporary protests against established convention and established power.

Shelley's *Cenci* is a tragedy sympathetic to revolution, one that focuses on the domestic but also points to ways in which the domestic world is constructed by the political. Shelley's two principal characters are Francesco Cenci, a powerful Renaissance Count, and his daughter, Beatrice. Cenci is a moral monster whose crimes include avarice, blasphemy, theft and murder. Like the protagonists of Restoration villain tragedy, including Nathaniel Lee's *Caesar Borgia* (1679) and Gothic tragedies, Cenci revels in his hyperbolic capacity to multiply evils. Although the ultimate wellsprings of his conduct remain mysterious, Shelley highlights his psychology, suggesting that his libertine sexual indulgence has now given way to a sadistic 'joy' in inflicting pain and terror on others. Cenci's crimes proceed virtually unchecked because, in a state still more unjust than Byron's Venice, the avaricious Pope and the Church hierarchy in Rome prefer profiting from his fines and bribes to punishing him. Moreover, the Pope considers it

> . . . of most dangerous example
> In aught to weaken the paternal power,
> Being, as 'twere, the shadow of his own.[19]

In *The Cenci*, however, the state has become the context for a tragedy primarily domestic. Huddled together in the confines of Cenci's Sadean abode, we find a virtuous, loving, sentimental family. His wife Lucretia has devoted herself to her stepchildren, Beatrice and the younger Bernardo, who love her in return. While they have tried to reform the homicidal Cenci, he has

> . . . given us all
> Ditch-water, and the fever-stricken flesh
> Of buffaloes, and bade us eat or starve,
> And we have eaten . . .
>
> (Act II, scene i, p. 762)

All her prayers and expostulations having proved inefficacious, Beatrice takes the opportunity of a rare party in the palace to petition the authorities. At the banquet, Cenci announces the news – to him happy news – that his two older sons have been killed in Spain. The notables murmur displeasure, but are too intimidated by Cenci to heed Beatrice's appeal.

A major trope of eighteenth-century political drama was the rape of Lucretia by the tyrant Tarquin; Lucretia heroically kills herself, but Lucius

Junius Brutus leads an insurrection which drives out the tyrant. Drama consistently used the rape of a woman by a ruler as a figure for the state's unjust taking of private property, a common political grievance. In *The Cenci*, however, Cenci rapes his own daughter. He sends the guests home, declaring that he declines to make them 'spectators of our dull domestic quarrels' and rages at Beatrice, threatening, 'I know a charm shall make thee meek and tame ...' (Act I, scene iii, p. 758). In Act III, Beatrice staggers onto the stage, dishevelled and speaking wildly:

> The beautiful blue heaven is flecked with blood!
> The sunshine on the floor is black!
>
> (Act III, scene i, p. 777)

Beatrice considers suicide but rejects that possibility as betraying her faith in God. The Machiavellian priest Orsino, who wants to possess Beatrice's body and her fortune, insinuates that she has a duty to kill her father lest he continue to have intercourse with her and she become

> Utterly lost; subdued even to the hue
> Of that which thou permitest
>
> (Act III, scene i, p. 786)

Like Satan and Richardson's Lovelace after the rape of Clarissa, Cenci aspires to subdue 'her stubborn will' so that 'by its own consent' it 'shall stoop as low/ As that which drags it down' (Act IV, scene i, p. 803). Assisted by Lucretia, Beatrice hires murderers who strangle Cenci. Realising that the name of 'father' has become entirely disjunct from what are supposed to be the moral attributes of fatherhood, sheltering instead 'impious hate' (Act I, scene iii, p. 755) Beatrice declares:

> I am more innocent of parricide
> Than is a child born fatherless ...
>
> (Act IV, scene iv, p. 828)

Her stepmother and a brother involved in the plot confess under torture; Beatrice alone is bold enough to defy the judges. Rejecting didacticism, Shelley insisted that his tragic heroine was neither right nor wrong to kill her father. Critics debate whether she was in an existential sense justified or whether the tragedy is that her father has unleashed in her the dark passions he indulged.

In his imagination, Shelley had cast Edmund Kean and Eliza O'Neill, then leading tragic actors of the day, as Cenci and Beatrice. But Shelley was not close enough to the London patent houses to realise how unacceptable his tragedy would be to them. Shelley, Byron and Lamb all disliked the contemporary theatre's emphasis on visual spectacle and music as opposed to words and hoped for a theatre in which the poet's words were primary. Byron did create a political tragedy reflecting the late Enlightenment's understanding of human character as significantly constructed by the political world, yet the question remains whether political truths can best be represented in stage tragedy or the longer, non-fiction prose works more characteristic of Enlightenment literary success – like Adam Smith's *The Wealth of Nations* or Gibbon's *The Decline and Fall of the Roman Empire*. Though fascinated by tragedy, many writers of the long eighteenth century failed to write tragedies that satisfied either their contemporaries or posterity. Yet artists thrive on doing what commentators deem impossible and there is no reason why we cannot join Romantic writers in hoping for a revival of poetic political tragedy. Certainly the twenty-first century offers suitable subject matter.

NOTES

1. Robertson Davies, 'Playwrights and Plays', in *The Revels History of Drama in English*, eds. Michael R. Booth et al., 6 vols., London: Methuen, 1975, vol. VI, p. 153.
2. Samuel Foote, *An Examen of the New Comedy*, quoted in Kalman A. Burnim, *David Garrick, Director*, Pittsburgh, PA: University of Pittsburgh Press, 1961, p. 144.
3. *The Letters of Richard Brinsley Sheridan*, ed. Cecil Price, 3 vols., Oxford: Clarendon Press, 1966, vol. I, p. 103.
4. Walter Jackson Bate, *Samuel Johnson*, New York: Harcourt, Brace, Jovanovich, 1977, p. 157.
5. *The Works of Charles and Mary Lamb*, ed. E. V. Lucas, 7 vols., London: Methuen, 1903, vol. I, p. 98, p. 107.
6. Alan Richardson, 'Byron and the Theatre', in *The Cambridge Companion to Byron*, ed. Drummond Bone, Cambridge: Cambridge University Press, 2004, p. 141.
7. Joseph Addison, *Cato: A Tragedy*, The Hague: J. Tonson, 1713, Act VI, scene i, p. 61.
8. Arthur Murphy, *The Grecian Daughter: A Tragedy*, London: W. Griffin, 1772, Act II, p. 23.
9. William Whitehead, *The Roman Father. A Tragedy*, London: R. Dodsley, 1750, Act II, scene i, pp. 23–24. Subsequent references are cited within the text. An anonymous pamphlet, *A Comparison between the Horace of Corneille and the Roman Father, of Mr. Whitehead*, London: [no publisher given], 1750, is an interesting example of how detailed and sophisticated some contemporary drama criticism had become.
10. Arthur Murphy, *The Life of David Garrick*, 1801; reprinted New York: Benjamin Bloom, 1969, p. 235.
11. *Gentleman's Magazine*, February 1753, p. 61.
12. Edward Moore, 'The Gamester', in *Eighteenth-Century Tragedy*, ed. Michael R. Booth, London: Oxford University Press, 1965, Act II, p. 178.

13. *The Plays of James Thomson, 1700–1748*, ed. John C. Greene, 2 vols., New York: Garland, 1987, vol. II, Act I, scene vi, p. 413.

14. George Gordon, *Lord Byron, The Complete Poetical Works*, eds. Jerome J. McGann and Barry Weller, 7 vols., Oxford: Clarendon Press, 1980–93, vol. VI, Act I, scene i, p. 138.

15. Gillian Russell, *The Theatres of War: Performance, Politics and Society, 1793–1815*, Oxford: Clarendon Press, 1995.

16. 'Conversations on *The Natural Son*' (1757), in Denis Diderot, *Selected Writings on Art and Literature*, trans. Geoffrey Bremner, London: Penguin, 1994, p. 57.

17. *The Dramatic Works of George Lillo*, ed. James L. Steffenson, Oxford: Clarendon Press, 1993, Act I, scene ii, p. 304.

18. *The Complete Works of William Hazlitt*, ed. P. P. Howe, 21 vols., London: J. M. Dent, 1930–34, vol. VI, pp. 359, 360.

19. *The Poems of Shelley*, eds. Kelvin Everest and Geoffrey Matthews, 4 vols., Harlow: Longman, 1989– , vol. II, Act II, scene ii, p. 771.

7

JOHN O'BRIEN

Pantomime

Throughout this period, an evening's programme at the theatre did not end when the curtain fell on the mainpiece play. Most evenings, that play – a revival of Shakespeare's *Hamlet*, say, or a new work such as Richard Sheridan's *The School for Scandal* (DL, 1777) – would be followed by an afterpiece: a one-act comedy such as David Garrick's *Miss in her Teens* (CG, 1747), or, on many occasions, a pantomime. These pantomimes did not much resemble anything we might today associate with the term, however. Rather, they involved a cast of characters drawn from the continental commedia dell'arte – Harlequin, Colombine and Pantaloon, among others – performing their characteristic story: Harlequin pines after Colombine; her guardian or father Pantaloon attempts to block their romance; Harlequin tricks Pantaloon and gains Colombine. This part of the performance, known as the comic or grotesque, would typically be interwoven with a serious story, one drawn from classical mythology, fairytales or popular works of fiction, such as *Robinson Crusoe* or *The Castle of Otranto*. But the true heart of pantomime lay in acrobatics, spectacle, song, dance, travelogue, slapstick and special effects. Pantomime exploited all the material resources that playhouses had to offer in order to create a kind of fantastic world where the usual rules of cause-and-effect did not apply, where spectacular transformations happened as a matter of course. The magic tricks that took place within each performance – as Harlequin transformed his environment the better to pursue Colombine, or the Clown constructed machines or vehicles out of random objects that came to hand – relied upon, and also celebrated, the magic of the theatre itself.

From the moment of its emergence in the 1720s, pantomime had most of the features that would remain a part of the form for the next century and more: the commedia dell'arte characters, for whom the plot becomes the pretext for a variety of set-piece comic scenes, transformations, tricks and chases; music, ranging from operatic-style arias to popular songs; spectacular scenery; magical transformations and special effects. The classical stories which dominated the 'serious' plots in the middle of the eighteenth century were soon supplemented by a wide variety of stories, drawn from various domains of folklore and popular culture: English folklore (*Harlequin Dick Whittington, Harlequin Robin Hood, Harlequin Horner*); bestselling fiction (*Harlequin Robinson Crusoe, Harlequin Gulliver*); current events (*Harlequin Incendiary*, about the 1745 Jacobite rebellion; *Harlequin Omai*, referring to the Tahitian brought to Britain by Captain James Cook in 1774); fairytales (*Harlequin Blue Beard, Harlequin Mother Goose*) and the Arabian Nights (*Harlequin and the Red Dwarf*). Pantomime's various elements were often not unified by any overarching design, nor were they necessarily linked one to the next by any recognisable principle of narrative logic. But this does not seem to have bothered audiences much, as there is ample testimony that theatregoers enjoyed this mixture of spectacle and sensation. As one reviewer in the *Times* put it, pantomime was best considered as 'an enchanting fascination that monopolises the mind to the scene before it'.[1] Many of pantomime's most salient pleasures were visual ones: the motions of the performers, the magic of stage machinery, the beauty and grandeur of the scenery. Pantomimes were never fully wordless – they were filled with song, for example, and sometimes did contain dialogue – but they certainly placed much less emphasis on the spoken word than did the legitimate drama.

This emphasis on spectacle and sensation rather than language poses obvious problems for understanding and researching pantomime. The documentary evidence is scanty: some descriptions from theatregoers have survived, as well as reviews from newspapers and magazines, particularly in the later part of the century. Also extant are a fair number of pantomime libretti although these frequently printed only the songs performed in each entertainment; images of pantomime performers, particularly famous ones like John Rich, the first British Harlequin of note, and Joseph Grimaldi, the nation's most famous Clown; and prints showing examples of pantomime scenery. But even these records are suggestive rather than conclusive, and no printed record can hope to convey the full impact of human bodies in motion, or to capture pantomime's multiple appeals to the eye and ear. What is true of pantomime is also true of any performance, even one for which we have a full record of the spoken text: written and printed records are like musical notation, a pointer to a live, embodied, performance, but not a comprehensive summation. Pantomime relied less on characterisation and plot than on those elements of the theatre which serious drama marginalised, or even suppressed: spectacle, slapstick, the frailties of the human body. In pantomime we see that theatre, an art form that has frequently tried to downplay its materiality – that is, its reliance on scenery, costume and stage effects – can offer some of its purest pleasures when those are brought to the fore.

Pantomime was widely mocked and criticised, and even most of those who recorded their admiration also express some misgivings about endorsing a form so devoted to spectacle and sensation. Its enduring popularity was occasionally a source of embarrassment to critics, as well as to theatre managers, actors and dramatists, who believed that the British theatre was undermined by so seemingly frivolous a form of entertainment. That audiences enjoyed performances filled with slapstick and spectacle rather than edifying speeches was galling. Observers of early pantomime like Alexander Pope, William Hogarth and Henry Fielding took its ascendancy to be a sign of the British theatre's decline, and they satirised pantomime ruthlessly. Pantomime's many critics frequently dismissed it as a meaningless spectacle, as mere sensation that bypassed or, even worse, undercut the kinds of message that the theatre was intended to convey to its audience. In his journal *The Prompter*, for example, Aaron Hill imagines the voice of 'Common Sense' lambasting the theatre for the way in which it has 'foster[ed] and idolise[d] my bitter enemy Pantomime' which has 'introduced her constant attendants – Absurdity, Noise, Nonsense, and Puppet-show.'[2] To critics like Hill who understood the theatre to be primarily a domain of language, pantomime's sensual feast threatened to incapacitate spectators' ability to exercise critical judgment, trumping their reason by flooding their senses with an excess of stimulation.

Even the most sympathetic view of pantomime is duty bound to note that there is an element of truth to these complaints, especially to the extent that we too think of the theatre primarily as a linguistic, literary medium. Pantomime did downplay traditional aspects of drama such as characterisation and plot development: there is only one basic plot in the commedia sections, and the stories chosen for the 'serious' framework were so familiar that they could be told in a kind of visual shorthand. Any attempt to analyse pantomime with the critical tools usually deployed to explicate literary texts is bound to find these performances lacking. But scholars working in film, media, performance studies and mass culture have made it possible to explore forms that fall outside the domain of the literary without apology, and have provided tools to do so. If we consider pantomime not as failed drama but as successful popular entertainment the form opens itself up to a rich variety of meanings.

Far from contradicting the values of eighteenth-century literary culture, pantomime actually fulfils some of them, albeit in an unexpected, even ironic way. For instance, pantomime clearly took part in the period's neoclassicism, that attempt to articulate a culture and potentially an empire as the successor to Rome. The term 'pantomime' was imported into English from Latin, where it denoted a class of dancers in the Roman theatre who were said to be capable of imitating anything just through the movements of their bodies. In the first decades of the eighteenth century, John Weaver, a dancing master, published several essays and pamphlets calling for the revival of the kind of dances once staged by the ancient Roman *pantomimi*. By the 1710s, Weaver was exhibiting examples of dances 'in imitation of the Roman pantomimes' at the London patent houses in the hope of promoting the form. Weaver's demonstrations do not seem to have had great success at the box-office, and there is no indication that anyone else followed suit. This classicising impulse remained, however, for much of the rest of the century in the form of the myths – Perseus and Andromeda, Orpheus and Eurydice, the Rape of Proserpine, among others – that frequently lent their plots to the serious parts of pantomime performances.[3] As John Rich observed in the preface to *The Rape of Proserpine*, his 1727 collaboration with librettist Lewis Theobald, pantomime brought classical stories to a broad audience, including these narratives as part of a 'general Diversion' rather than a performance aimed only at the wealthy, sophisticated and educated.[4]

At the same time, eighteenth-century pantomime also fulfilled the Horatian dictum that aesthetic productions must combine the *dulce* and the *utile*, the pleasing and the useful. These shows typically had a bifurcated structure, one where the comic, harlequinade episodes alternated with the serious, mythological ones, a pattern that had the effect of objectifying *dulce* and *utile* into distinct sections, separating them out as alternating components of the theatrical experience. The evidence suggests that in at least some cases, pantomimes did make efforts to link the two modes. In the Rich/Theobald *Orpheus and Eurydice* (CG, 1740), for example, the serious sections emphasise the point of view of Rhodope (the woman Orpheus has left behind to pursue Eurydice), a thematic point that knits this narrative more closely to the conventional love plot of the comic episodes. In *Perseus and Andromeda* (CG, 1730), another collaboration between Rich and Theobald, the transition between serious and comic sections is marked when, in successive scenes, Harlequin and Perseus are given the magic instruments – a magic slapstick bat in Harlequin's case, a hat and sword for Perseus – which will enable them to accomplish their respective tasks. Pantomimes reified the Horatian *dulce* and *utile* and then placed them in thematic, visual and perhaps musical relationship to each other. By yoking together this seemingly various content, pantomime reproduced within itself the heterogeneous character of the period's theatre in which serious fare was frequently intermingled with singing, dancing, acrobatics and farce. In content and structure, then, pantomime stands as an example of what we can call popular neoclassicism, a mode of performance intended to bring classical stories and motifs to audiences who would not be able to encounter them in other media.

Continuity and innovation: pantomime and the culture industry

Pantomime changed, of course, over time, and while a full account of such changes is well beyond the scope of this essay, simply raising the question encourages us to think about the nature of change within a form that cannot really be assessed in terms of authorial influence or innovation. To talk about the evolution of pantomime in this period requires us to think about the theatre as an institution, whether in relation to commercial factors such as the intense rivalry between the playhouses or the theatre's relationship to changes in the culture at large. For in the case of pantomime, the most conspicuous human agents behind the performance were not, clearly, the authors, and were frequently not the actors, either. A few pantomime performers achieved great renown and popularity, but most were comparatively anonymous, their individuality subsumed into the conventions of the harlequinade and the sensory delights of the spectacle. It was, rather, the theatre managers who bore the brunt of critical attention for programming and orchestrating pantomime entertainments, and the net effect of this attention was to bring the institution of the theatre into the light of day as a capitalist, money-making enterprise. To this extent, pantomime's great popularity with theatre audiences and its prominence in the public discourse *about* the stage may be said to mark the maturity of the British theatre as a nascent branch of what Theodor Adorno and Max Horkheimer would later dub the culture industry. The image of a cynical and manipulative apparatus of entertainment openly duping the public is surely too oppressive to fit our period, which was incapable of mounting anything as organised as Horkheimer and Adorno, writing in the middle of the twentieth century, described. But their model is useful nonetheless, for it highlights features of the period's theatre, and pantomime's place within it, that might otherwise be ignored.

Pantomime, for example, may be said to anticipate the complicated relationship between conventionality and innovation that Horkheimer and Adorno saw to be rampant in twentieth-century American mass culture. It was an extraordinarily conventional form, using not just character types and familiar situations but the same characters acting out virtually the same plot over and over again. What is more, the intense competition between the London theatres led to a great deal of imitation, as successful offerings would quickly be copied by other playhouses; thus both the London patent theatres staged pantomime productions of the Faust story, Perseus and Andromeda, and Orpheus and Eurydice. But the theatre managers also had to assert the novelty of each new production, to maintain a constant stream of innovation. According to Horkheimer and Adorno, such innovation was largely a mirage: '[t]he constant pressure to produce new effects (which must conform to the old pattern) serves merely as another rule to increase the power of the conventions when any single effect threatens to slip through the net.'[5] Their words usefully caution us not to take claims for the novelty of any particular production at face value. And they suggest that innovation needs to be understood as an effect of a larger system than the product of individual authorial inspiration.

Charles Dibdin's pantomime *The Touchstone, or, Harlequin Traveller* (CG, 1779), provides an interesting case of a work which both affirmed and challenged convention, while also pointing the way to features that would become a larger and larger part of pantomimes in the Regency period. In his advertisement to the printed lyrics for *The Touchstone*, Dibdin claimed that this 'Operatical Pantomime' offered 'new and various' ways in which to combine music with action.[6] In a sense, Dibdin's claim marks the degree to which the operatic pretensions of Rich's pantomimes of the 1730s and 40s had been forgotten four decades later as Dibdin's innovations probably marked a return to patterns that had fallen out of use to the point where they only appeared to be fresh and new. More important, however, are the innovations that *The Touchstone* can rightly claim as its own. In Dibdin's pantomime, Harlequin *speaks*. Harlequin's speech was not completely unprecedented, either; Harlequin always spoke in the many eighteenth-century revivals of Aphra Behn's 1687 play, *The Emperor of the Moon*, itself an adaptation of a French commedia dell'arte scenario, and David Garrick had included a speaking Harlequin in *Harlequin's Invasion* (DL, 1759). Here, however, Dibdin explicitly makes speech itself into a theme, as the titular touchstone which Harlequin carries forces his interlocutor to utter the truth. Thus Mezzetin first dissembles, claiming that he has been missing Harlequin, but when touched with the stone, Mezzetin expresses how fully he detests Harlequin, and that he has been seeing Harlequin's old flame Marinette, going on at such length that Harlequin has to wrest the stone from his hands. *The Touchstone*'s truth-telling goes on until Harlequin finally encounters a British sailor, for whom the touchstone is superfluous, as he speaks with complete candour anyway. Harlequin takes this to be 'an instance of national Character', a typical feature of a sailor and the nation for which he serves.[7] Harlequin's testimonial picks up a patriotic, nationalistic theme that would become an ever greater part of pantomime in the decades to come.

Speaking Harlequins like the one in *The Touchstone* never became a regular part of pantomime entertainments and dialogue of any kind remained comparatively rare. What Dibdin's innovation signals, perhaps, is the decline of Harlequin as the central figure in pantomime, as though his usual antics were no longer sufficient and required something more to sustain interest. Harlequin would remain a key figure for pantomime, his name appearing in virtually every title for decades to come, but by the early nineteenth century, his central place in the performance had been taken over by the Clown, especially after the rise to stardom of Joseph Grimaldi, the period's most famous Clown and one of the most popular figures in the history of British theatre. (Grimaldi's Clown spoke, but rarely and with seeming reluctance, eking out a single word, such as 'No' when confronted with someone who seemed to have hurtful designs on him.)[8] But the innovation that *The Touchstone* helped establish is best indicated in its subtitle, *Harlequin Traveller*. In the course of the performance, characters travel from an unidentified desert island (Harlequin is first shown as the survivor of a ship-wreck) to real places like Italy, Paris, Dover and Whitehall, and then to imaginary places like a 'Temple of Fortune', a 'Wood of Oaks', a 'Gloomy Cavern', and, finally, a 'Luminous Grove'. Increasingly, pantomimes would offer spectators the pleasures of a kind of travelogue, whether within Britain (Oxford in *Harlequin and Friar Bacon* [CG, 1818], Brighton in *Harlequin and Fortunio* [CG, 1815], Canterbury in *Harlequin Habeas* [CG, 1802], Glasgow and other Scottish locations in *Goosey, Goosey, Gander* [P, 1832]), or abroad (Constantinople in *Harlequin Munchausen* [CG, 1818], Venice in *Harlequin and Little Thumb* [DL, 1831], Egypt in *Harlequin Colossus* [CG, 1812]), or to imagined palaces: caves, woods and grottoes too numerous to list. *The Touchstone, or Harlequin Traveller* was popular enough to be revived fre-quently over the next decade or two, but we can also think of it as a transi-tional work, one that forecasts some of the key changes between mid-century pantomime and its early nineteenth-century descendant.

A good example of a Regency-period pantomime, one worth examining in some detail, is *Harlequin and the Red Dwarf, or, The Adamant Rock* (CG, 1812).[9] In its opening scenes, the pantomime recounted a story from the Arabian Nights: Prince Cherry, looking for his love Princess Fair Star, the daughter of Emperor Longoheadiano and Empress Rondabellyiana, finds him-self shipwrecked when his boat is drawn to the magnetic adamant rock. (The Emperor and Empress's names point to one of the key features of these char-acters, namely the oversized – long in one case, round in another – papier-mâché heads worn by the characters and their retainers.) The princess is being held prisoner by the Red Dwarf, to whom she has been promised by her parents, a betrothal against which she is rebelling. A Green Bird (who is actually a good fairy transformed by the dwarf) rescues Prince Cherry and leads him to Princess Fair Star whereupon Prince Cherry frees her with his magic bow and arrow. The Green Bird transforms Cherry and Fair Star into Harlequin and Colombine, momentarily transfixing the dwarf like a statue to give them time to escape to England. There, they must find the 'Dancing Water' that will enable them to return to their original forms. Once he is reanimated, the dwarf changes the

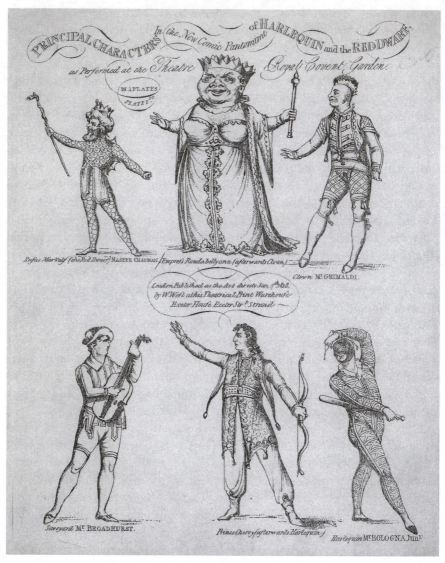

9. *Harlequin and the Red Dwarf* by William West, c. 1812.

Emperor to Pantaloon and the Queen to Pantaloon's servant, the Clown; he sends them to England in pursuit of the transformed lovers.

Sixteen scenes of harlequinade action followed in rapid succession, each set in a different location, and most centred on the escapades of the Clown. As Pantaloon's servant, the Clown had the mission of thwarting Harlequin in his pursuit of Colombine; their cat and mouse game delayed Harlequin's eventual union with Colombine, and created the opportunity for a wide variety of disparate episodes to take place. In *Harlequin and the Red Dwarf*, these included a London street scene where a man with an enormous camera obscura showed images of British frigates, seaside resorts and fashionable London walks; a series of chase scenes where the Clown *almost* caught up with Harlequin, but was always thwarted when Harlequin confused him by changing the scene with a stroke of his magic bat; an extended scene at an auction shop, where the Clown and the auctioneer engage in a duet, and a scene in Epping Forest, where the Clown takes part in a parodic version of the Epping Hunt. In each scene, the pursuit came to a halt as the Clown initiated a number of set-piece episodes, dressing up, for example, in imitation of a Hussar (cavalry officers whose taste for extravagant clothing made them an object of mockery) and feeding a miniature Napoleon to a Russian bear. *Harlequin and the Red Dwarf* concludes with a final scene in a fairy palace: the Clown steals Harlequin's magic bat, but the Green Bird gets enough of the Dancing Water to transform herself back into the Good Fairy and to return the lovers to their original forms, in which they are united at last.

It is just possible that some theatregoers may have lived long enough to have seen both a mid eighteenth-century pantomime and a Regency example such as *Harlequin and the Red Dwarf*, and if so, he or she would have recognised some features of the former that return in the latter: the commedia dell'arte characters, the centrality of a love story, the bifurcated structure, the emphasis on song, spectacle and magical transformations rather than dialogue. But the differences are more obvious. By the early nineteenth century, the 'serious' sections of the pantomime had been gathered to the beginning, where they formed a very loose framework for the comic episodes, which now far outnumbered the serious scenes. The transition from serious to comic modes took place only at the beginning and the end, and was not only marked – by the removal of the big heads, for one thing – but also *motivated*; the shift into the magical world of the harlequinade happened at the moment when events in the 'serious' plot had reached an impasse. And as I have already suggested, the comic scenes were now dominated, not by Harlequin, but by the Clown, a character who had been present in earlier pantomimes, frequently as a servant of Pantaloon, but typically as a secondary figure rather than a focus of attention in his own right.

The Clown's rise to prominence is hard to separate from the charisma of Joseph Grimaldi, the most popular pantomime performer of the period. From the time of his first big success in *Harlequin and Mother Goose* in 1806 until his retirement from performance in 1824 (owing in part to injuries sustained from his falls on stage), Grimaldi achieved a kind of popularity and celebrity on a par with someone like Charlie Chaplin in the early twentieth century. Grimaldi's Clown was a figure of anarchy and criminality, but also of naïveté; he could not be held accountable for his actions because his cruelty to other characters seemed more the effect of carelessness than malice. With the emergence of the Clown as the central character, the dominant mode of magic shifted. Where Harlequin had exploited his capacity to transform objects (a chair into a coach, a coach into a cage), and to shift scenes, the Clown engaged in what David Mayer has usefully termed 'tricks of construction', putting together disparate objects in new ways.[10] The Clown's Hussar costume in *Harlequin and the Red Dwarf*, for example, was constructed from coalscuttles, which became boots, horseshoes, which turned into heels, candlesticks which became spurs, a bear skin which became a coat, a woman's muff that was commandeered to become his hat, and a black tippet, which turned into enormous moustaches. In *Harlequin and Asmodeus* (CG, 1810), Grimaldi's Clown assembled a monster out of vegetables found in the stalls at Covent Garden market. The monster turned on its creator, a pattern that, intriguingly, is replicated in Mary Shelley's *Frankenstein* (1819). The connection becomes less fanciful once we observe that Byron, a member of the storytelling party from which *Frankenstein* was produced, was a friend of Grimaldi's. Because the Clown was not himself a protagonist in the love story, pantomimes which concentrated on his activities became even less plot-oriented than before as the former harlequinade became a framework for a miscellaneous series of set-pieces set in widely disparate and often exotic locations.

What meanings can we derive from a form that so frequently seems to flaunt its embrace of nonsense? How do these performances express the concerns of the culture that loved them? I would argue that the popularity of harlequinade in eighteenth- and early nineteenth-century Britain reflects the period's growing urbanisation. Even early eighteenth-century Britons thought of themselves as living in a modern age, one that was fundamentally unlike the predominantly rural, traditional world of old England. Such a belief had its pleasures, but it also brought with it a sense of nostalgia for what had been lost. In such a context, characters such as Harlequin, Colombine and Pantaloon are best understood as stylised, stereotypical representations of the common folk, inhabiting a timeless, pastoral world. To eighteenth-century Londoners, the experience of returning to these characters and their stock situations offered a reassuring trip into an idealised past, into the kind of merry England for which they felt nostalgia only when they realised that it was passing. After mid-century, pantomime became strongly associated with the Christmas season; new pantomimes, originally produced to no particular schedule, now appeared every year on Boxing Day.

This had the effect of domesticating pantomime, identifying it as one of the shared pleasures of the holiday season and defining it as an annual tradition and national custom.

By the early nineteenth century, pantomime's association with British nationalism had become strong, its long popularity with generations of theatregoers having accomplished the remarkable trick of making Continental commedia dell'arte characters seem always to have been British. The figure of Harlequin became so familiar an emblem of the British stage that an 1829 dramatic journal was entitled, simply, *Harlequin*. For his part, Grimaldi's mockery of the pretensions of the powerful and his parodies of Napoleon made him seem almost the incarnation of John Bull, his plucky determination mirroring the stereotype of the British national subject.[11] It is surely no coincidence that the years of Grimaldi's greatest popularity correspond so closely to the Napoleonic Wars, a particularly intense period of nationalism. And Regency pantomimes also responded to the face of modernity in their own time. However foreign the subject matter of the frame stories might be, the real subject of many early nineteenth-century pantomimes is the city itself. As the pace of urbanisation accelerated, the city's chaos found a fitting analogue in pantomime's rapid-fire changes of scene. As Jane Moody puts it, 'The unexpected metamorphosis of urban goods and shops in pantomime, as hat-boxes turn into watch-houses, and apple-stalls to printer's shops, seems to transform into laughter the experience of endless change and social mobility.'[12] And the expansion in the range of places to which pantomime took its spectators maps the imaginative spread of British culture in our period, its expansion outward to embrace a world and an empire.

Perhaps most of all, pantomime was motivated by a levelling impulse, a desire to undercut pretension by suggesting that high and low share common characteristics. As Mayer has argued, the effect of Harlequin's transformations – turning old women into judges, for example – can be thought of as 'visual similes', tricks that reveal how 'one thing has a hidden likeness to another'.[13] Classical mythology is revealed to have much the same interests as popular comedy; London dandies are easily imitated by a clown. Pantomime can be thought of as a multimedia framework for satire, one that for more than a century enabled pantomime artists and producers to mock targets that changed with the passage of time.

After Grimaldi's retirement, pantomime would undergo another evolution, this time even further in the direction of spectacle. During the Victorian period, the opening, fairytale framework expanded to take up the bulk of the performance and typically ended with a splendid transformation scene. The harlequinade shrank, becoming a short coda to the rest of the piece. It was increasingly understood to be a vestige of the past, an archaic example of the kind of performance that had once pleased the audience's ancestors. By the early twentieth century, the harlequinade had disappeared entirely, and pantomime had become cast largely as a Christmas entertainment for children. But during its heyday, in our period, British pantomime was a vital and frequently exciting form, one that called on the full resources of the theatre to entertain spectators of every age and class. If pantomime scandalised some observers who wanted to think of the playhouse solely as the domain of uplifting language, it also fulfilled the theatre's potential for appealing to the human senses. Pantomime was an essential part of the British theatre.

NOTES

1. 'Pantomimes. Omai', *The Times*, 28 December 1785.
2. A. Hill and W. Popple, *The Prompter: a Theatrical Paper (1734–1736)*, eds. William W. Appleton and Kalmin A. Burnim, New York: Benjamin Blom, 1966, p. 17.
3. For a fuller description of *Perseus and Andromeda*, see my book, *Harlequin Britain: Pantomime and Entertainment, 1690–1760*, Baltimore, MD: Johns Hopkins University Press, 2004, pp. 5–10.
4. John Rich, 'Preface' to Lewis Theobald, *The Rape of Proserpine*, London: T. Wood, 1727, p. iv.
5. Max Horkheimer and Theodor Adorno, 'The Culture Industry: Enlightenment as Mass Deception', in *Dialectic of Enlightenment*, trans. John Cumming, New York: Continuum Books, 1944, p. 128.
6. Charles Dibdin, *The Touchstone, or, Harlequin Traveller* (1779), London: Stainer and Bell, 1990, unpaginated.
7. Dibdin, *The Touchstone*.
8. See Jane Moody, *Illegitimate Theatre in London, 1770–1840*, Cambridge: Cambridge University Press, 2000, p. 216.
9. I base the following description on the account in A. S. Jackson's 'The Production and Staging of the English Pantomime as Illustrated by *Harlequin the Red Dwarf; or, the Adamant Rock*, performed at Covent Garden Theatre December 26, 1812', MA thesis, Ohio State University, 1959, as well as the review published in the *Times* on 28 December 1812.
10. David Mayer III, *Harlequin in His Element: the English Pantomime, 1806–1836*, Cambridge, MA: Harvard University Press, 1969, p. 49.
11. Moody, *Illegitimate Theatre*, p. 213.
12. Moody, *Illegitimate Theatre*, p. 219.
13. Mayer, *Harlequin*, p. 39.

8

JACKY BRATTON

Romantic melodrama

I remember being taken somewhere and there was a large rock with a door in it and a handsome lady was outside fastened with a chain to a stake, by the door or entrance to the cave. Her long black hair, refined and yet withal a pronounced Semitic face, showed to me Aunt Eliza. While spell-bound to see her under such extraordinary circumstances, a huge reptile, hideous in green scales and large fiery eyes, made its appearance over the brow of the rock, flapped its wings and swung its tail. My scream of terror, my shout for Aunt Eliza's assistance, my puny efforts to go to her assistance made, it seems, quite a sensation, and the hero spoiled tragic effect, and caused much laughter. Thus early I made a melodramatic comedian's success.[1]

Thus James Frowde (1831–99), whose mother had been one of the famous Hengler family of pyrotechnists, rope-dancers, tragedians and circus proprietors, recalls his first memory of performance, some time around 1835. As he himself recognises, what he describes is an archetypal melodramatic moment. The play would seem to be one of the many stage versions of the heroic fable of St George and the Dragon, whose 1833–4 enactment on the classic boards of Drury Lane by Andrew Ducrow and his famous horses from Astley's Amphitheatre caused critical disgust. The drama clothed nationalist mythologising in gothic fairytale, spectacular horsemanship and special effects (Ducrow had a flying dragon that lifted him bodily from his saddle during the climactic combat). In little James's primal scene, evil – embodied in the scaly, tale-swinging beast of nightmare – menaces feminine innocence embodied in his handsome aunt. His telling of the story invokes the trope of the naïve theatregoer carried away by the fiction, overlaid with the intertheatrical joke of the boy's family relation to the stage: he not only took the dragon for real, but really knew and wished to protect the human performer. Most significantly, his comment reveals much about the structure of feeling in melodrama. He recalls that the audience laughed good-naturedly at the little boy who did not understand play-acting and undercut the tragic effect; as an adult, Frowde recognises that such comic moments have a place in heroic drama. He precociously took on a professional role which he was to occupy later – that of 'melodramatic comedian'. The thrill of sexualised menace and heroism is interlaced with laughter, mocking or at least end-stopping the emotions just created. This is melodrama, which is arguably the stage manifestation of the Romantic understanding of humanity: a form which dramatises the newly conceptualised subconscious and displays a marked idealism and optimism about human potentiality. All this is clothed in supernatural manifestations, exotic tales, beautiful costume, spectacular effects and scenery, all often doing the work of nascent imperialism and class redefinition. Finally, melodrama distances and complicates its themes and understanding of the world through humour.

Defining the genre

Melodrama as a term has suffered much from pejorative use and, curiously, post-modern efforts to reclaim the form have not so far succeeded. Its ideological position as the perceived opposite of realism,[2] and thus as a handy demotic term for bad drama, is no doubt a large part of its current problem; but it is not the whole story. Abusive definitions begin with the critical crisis in the life of tragedy in the late eighteenth century. As the pioneering French melodramatist Guilbert de Pixérécourt later complained,

> an inexplicable mania impels a throng of critics to denounce this new genre with a kind of fanaticism. These rabid censors, convinced that nature has sanctioned only tragedies and comedies, took any dramatic work that did not bear one of these two names for a literary monster that had to be strangled at birth.[3]

Pixérécourt's work was part of a theatrical renaissance across Europe during which many new theatres were built and new forms evolved to suit eager new audiences. But in most countries critics saw this expansion as a threat and the emerging culture as inferior. It was almost impossible for literary establishments to see the upsurge of theatre amongst the growing urban populations as a good thing. Romantic critics and poets in England were unanimous about both the importance of theatre and also the slough into which dramatic writing had fallen.

Critical interpretations of the Romantic poets' dilemma over tragedy and the poetic drama continue the abjection of melodrama. George Steiner asserts that 'at the origins of the romantic movement lies an explicit attempt to revitalize the major forms of tragedy'. The historicity of modern times, he argues, lies at the heart of this failure: '[t]he new "historical" man ... came to the theatre with a newspaper in his pocket.' He asks rhetorically, 'How was the playwright to ... rival the drama of actual news?' and answers, 'Only by crying even louder havoc, by writing melodrama.'[4] Heilman's influential contrasting of tragedy and melodrama reifies this binary opposition, categorising 'all nontragic conflict that invokes ideas of good and evil' as melodrama. This definition requires us to understand that '*Tragedy* connotes profound experience' because of its preoccupations with inner or spiritual and moral dividedness, while melodrama is 'monopathic', neither invoking internal conflict nor requiring the spectator to feel any complexity of response. Heilmann is seeking to rehabilitate the term melodrama, and to use it as 'a precise instrument', but even in so doing he reasserts literary hierarchies, simply asserting that 'what we call "popular melodrama" has reduced to stereotypes and thus has trivialized the basic structural characteristics of a literary form'.[5]

What is amiss in this redefinition is the assumption that melodrama *is* 'a literary form'. If this is the case, then we need to think of melodrama using Susan Stewart's formulation as a 'crime of writing', or, in John O'Brien's useful phrase, as a 'crime *against* writing'. Stewart coined this term to describe practices which seem to be 'inversions or negations of cultural rules'; O'Brien modifies the concept to explain the cultural threat posed by pantomime's popularity in early eighteenth-century London. The triumph of melodrama a hundred years later extends that threat. In the 1720s, O'Brien argues, pantomime's sensuous, spectacular aesthetic, largely wordless except for the lyrics of the songs, challenged the contemporary demand that the drama should be moral and exemplary, thereby undercutting 'the theater's desire to define itself as a space of language, and therefore as a literary medium on a par with epic poetry'.[6] How much more threatening, then, was melodrama, which took sensuous and spectacular performance to new heights of illusion and invaded the drama's realm of moral and exemplary story-telling.

The roots of Romantic melodrama

Why this genre should have come to dominate the Romantic stage, and how it was related to late eighteenth-century upheavals in European society and revolutionary politics is a question with several answers. In Britain growing urban populations offered the possibility of larger audiences: theatres increased in size, both in their auditoria and, necessarily, in the dimensions of the stage. In turn, this growth led to technical developments in scenery and lighting as well as the use of large casts and orchestras. The forms of theatre which developed under this impetus relied less on the individual actors' interpretation of a writer's work, but rather more on an expanded palette of effects: opera and ballet flourished, and the dominant dramatic form became melodrama, a genre which weaves its meanings from music, mime, comedy and spectacle. In Britain this phenomenon was regarded by critics and reviewers as foreign – the usual stick used to beat theatrical innovation – and was attributed to the invasion of the serious stage by tastes generated in the minor theatres: Astley's St George should not be entertaining the multitudes at Drury Lane. But in fact the patent houses often led the way in the development of an outrageously attractive artform which responded to the challenge of technical and demographic change in a way that made a vital contribution to the discourses of Romanticism.

Peter Brooks's influential view is that melodrama represents a creative expression of French revolutionary culture. But the form also has its roots in the dramatic trends of the eighteenth century in both France and Britain. The analysis initiated by Anne Ubersfeld and taken up by Thomas Elsaesser and Frederick Brown stresses that the genre emerged from the tradition of the French *drame bourgeois* and corroborated its values.[7] This is borne out by Pixérécourt's claim that melodrama was 'patterned on the model of Sedaine's plays' meaning, presumably, *drames* like his *Le Philosophe Sans le Savoir* (1765), a play much admired by Diderot, rather than his opera libretti.[8] In Britain one could point to similar interests in class and sensibility in sentimental comedy, but the distinctively British mixture of low comedy and refined sentiment was already evident. As far back as Steele's *The Conscious Lovers* (DL, 1722) virtue, pious common sense, good feeling and wordless mutual understanding are intercut with vulgar fun in a mixture that might be identified as proto-melodramatic. Lillo's domestic tragedies are also part of the melodramatic matrix, especially *The London Merchant* (DL, 1731), a tale of seduction and murder ending on the gallows. This unrelievedly solemn play came to occupy a special place in eighteenth-century London theatre as the traditional prelude to the Boxing Day panto-mime. That carnival audience, full of potentially dangerous young people, received the traditional sermon on the ghastly fate of the bad apprentice as their pre-pantomime mock-penance and their due, a ritual in which they delighted, though they did not necessarily pay any attention. So the British version of the sentimental drama was, from the first, received with irony as well as enthusiasm; it only remained for melodrama to combine serious theme and comic counterpoint into a single dramatic pattern.

Romantic melodrama's rise to domination over tragedy was a conse-quence of social, demographic and aesthetic shifts occurring across much of Europe. Peter Brooks has argued for the form's conceptual modernity, its theatrical articulation of a secular world order.[9] The plays express and to some extent explore and question an anthropocentric moral order and its changing values, from the eighteenth-century focus on personal sensibility and the nationalism and prescriptive gender roles characteristic of Victorian society to the emphasis on family values and individual heroism in the twentieth century. The result is a genre which acts out conflicts and personifies cultural meanings in iconic roles – hero, heroine, villain. The forces of nature or the supernatural are made manifest in a waterfall, an erupting volcano, a ghost, dragon or providential coincidence. Melodrama renders tangible an inner or abstract action through the entire repertoire of physical performance: music, song and dance combine with elaborate, gestural acting, employing the whole body to express emotion. Complexity, ambiguity and irony are conveyed by dramatic rather than poetic or literary means. The verbal script may be slight, but rapid exchanges between the many sign systems (plot, spectacle, fighting, music, humour) create complex meanings as we shall see in *A Tale of Mystery*. Exploration of 'character' is not integrated and intellectualised but fragmented and acted-out. In melodrama we should not seek 'an interior conflict, the "psychology of melodrama," because melodrama exteriorizes conflict and psychic structure, producing instead what we might call the "melodrama of psychology"'.[10]

Manichean struggle? melodrama and the gothic

The beauty of humble virtue, the hegemonic interpellation of the poor as honest, was centrally important in melodrama, especially as the theatres responded to rising social consciousness in the nineteenth century. In its Romantic first flowering, the epitome of goodness was often made so innocent as to be incapable of verbal expression: a child, a mute character, a wild man, or indeed a dog or a horse. The Rousseauvian appeal to the language of the heart, rejecting the potential deceptiveness of words, was effectively embodied on the melodramatic stage, where all the resources of music, spectacle and pantomime action could spell out the message that here was innocence, threatened but for ever true to itself. The spectacle of such helplessness as power was alluring; but still the other pole of the binary, the theatrical embodiment of evil, was more dramatically important. This is a truism of the stage at all times, but the dramatic interest of evil comes to dominate melodrama: Peter Brooks stresses that '[i]n the clash of virtue and villainy, it is the latter that constitutes the active force' and also dominates the affective structure of the genre. The action reaches towards evil in excess, 'so that we accede to the experience of nightmare'.[11]

It was through the importation of Pixérécourt's plays that the Romantic melodrama first came to the London stage. The first play named as 'a melodrame' was *A Tale of Mystery*, translated by the radical playwright Thomas Holcroft from Pixérécourt's *Cœlina, ou l'enfant du mystère* (Paris,

1800), and staged at Covent Garden in 1802. From it we may derive a catalogue of the features of such dramas. In a picturesque alpine setting, an innocent young woman is threatened by a rapacious aristocrat, Romaldi, who has power over her bourgeois guardian. He is defeated by the self-sacrifice of a mysterious dumb man who is revealed to be his own brother, Francisco, whose tongue was cut out by robbers at Romaldi's order many years before. In the climactic scene Romaldi is revealed and his brother forgives him:

> *Thunder heard, while the scene changes. Music.*
>
> *Scene III. – the wild mountainous country called the Nant of Arpennaz; with pines and massy rocks. A rude wooden bridge on a small height thrown from rock to rock; a rugged mill stream a little in the back ground; the miller's house on the right; a steep ascent by a narrow path to the bridge; a stone or bank to sit on, on the right-hand side. The increasing storm of lightning, thunder, hail, and rain, becomes terrible. Suitable music.*
>
> *Enter* ROMALDI *from the rocks, disguised like a peasant, with terror; pursued as it were by the storm.*[12]

The set itself is a character here, and an archetypally Romantic one: a sublime landscape, a storm embodying the moral force of nature, steep paths, crags and narrow bridges. The villain acts with the scenery and delivers speeches of horror and repentance in dialogue with the sound effects and music. The play is dubbed a 'melodrame' precisely because music does not accompany but actively participates in the scene, shaping the narrative and extending what the characters do and say as well as framing the audience's responses. Here the orchestra has the last word, moving from remorse to pastorale as the good peasant who is to recognise Romaldi enters:

> ROMALDI: *Falls motionless again. Music of painful remorse; then changes to the cheerful pastorale, &c.*

Early French melodramas normally work upon a relatively straightforward if rather illogical dynamic between helpless, but invulnerable, good and dominant, but defeated, evil. In this sense melodrama is an expression of radical optimism about human nature, and is born, as Brooks argues, of a 'thirst for the Sacred', a wish to believe the best is possible.[13] Contemporary English audiences, schooled on Shakespeare's mixed modes rather than in the French stage tradition would not have been likely to respond to such a notion if too solemnly expressed; for them, Holcroft has added to Pixérécourt a layer of humour. The affective qualification of comedy – nothing should be taken seriously for too long – immediately became indispensable to the English version of the genre. Melodrama's comic characters both undercut and protect the heroic view of humanity. Innocence is dumb, as in the case of the saintly Francisco, and it is the comic serving-woman

Fiametta who alone can interpret his gestures and also make sure the audience laughs at her rather than at him. Such a pattern became a way to contain contradictory views of mankind as both supreme and vulnerable and to manage scepticism. The trajectory of the plot thus carries a powerful representation of evil's fascination and a positive construction of virtue's power, while the time and stage space occupied by comedy convey a different and ironised appreciation of human compromise and fallibility.

It is perhaps the theatrical usefulness of the gothic as a semiotic with instantly recognisable signs for the major emotions that has extended its life in British melodrama. The earliest examples predate *A Tale of Mystery*. Monk Lewis's *The Castle Spectre* was a great success at Drury Lane from December 1797 while the travelling theatre of Samuel Richardson was still founding its repertoire upon pieces with such titles as *The Monk and the Murderer*!!! in the 1830s; *The Rocky Horror Picture Show* continues to provoke a self-conscious mixture of screams and laughter today. At patent, minor and unlicensed theatres, pantomimes set either in medieval or exotic locations developed into the gothic melodrama. Grand spectacles like Lewis's *Timour the Tartar* (CG, 1811) a highly successful exotic drama with parades, horseback fighting and burning castles, was revived for years on every stage from the patent houses to the Hengler touring circus during the 1850s; the text includes a very good role for a comic man, played at Hengler's by Frowde. Small new theatres like Jane Scott's Sans Pareil in the Strand were not deterred by lack of space. In 1812, she produced the 'serious pantomime' *Asgard the Demon Hunter*: a melodrama in all but name and an exercise in what we would call high camp, featuring a dancing and singing chorus of inquisitors. This success led to a string of full-blown gothic pieces written by and starring Scott, supported by her company of dancers and comedians.

Many early melodramas displaced their narrative into distant times and places. The stage land of these plays has a recognisable performance language, a set of shorthand emotional cues, and also permits a handy reuse of kit (workable bridges, cut-out crags, scarlet-lined cloaks, ghost projections, pop-up skeletons). Despite the familiarity of these scenes and conventions, however, such plays might be doing urgent cultural work.[14] Jane Scott's only published play, *The Old Oak Chest* (SP, 1816) is a tale of robbers, smugglers and spectres which gained a wide currency in the illegal radical theatres of the 1820s and 30s, as well as a permanent place in the repertoire of the portables, because it could be read as a political allegory about democracy and the claims and responsibilities of the rulers. John Fawcett's *Obi; or, Three Finger'd Jack* (HM, 1800) is a pantomimic melodrama on the subject of racial conflict and the deep-seated fears of the colonising British.[15] The developing genre could be put to political work, despite the Lord Chamberlain's censorship prohibiting overt politics on the stage. Melodrama's laminated structure, contrasting moods and potentially contradictory values allowed for varied responses from audiences at different theatres who would choose, night by night and even moment by moment, what political message they read, and which opinions they supported.

The melodrama of psychology

The extended life of the gothic on stage and screen relates in interesting ways to the status of melodrama as a crime against writing. On stage the gothic frisson can be intensified by the manipulation of what is seen: one might argue, indeed, that the more use melodrama makes of the non-verbal image the more powerful is its bodying-forth of interiority. Eighteenth-century dramatists writing for the patent houses tended to use conventional drama-turgy: their work was trapped for a time in an indeterminate space where the disintegration of genre and conventional critical judgments went against them. The critic John Genest condemned George Colman the Younger's version of *Caleb Williams*, called *The Iron Chest* (DL, 1796) 'one of those jumbles of Tragedy, Comedy, and Opera ... which every friend of the legitimate Drama must reprobate' and wished, '[i]n a literary point of view', that the dramatist had suppressed the play.[16] Similarly, Genest declared that William Dimond's powerful play, *The Foundling of the Forest* (HM, 1809), 'would have been a very good piece, if it had not been degraded from a place in the legitimate drama by the introduction of 6 or 7 songs'.[17] He is right that the songs, and the comic-servant plot in which they occur, could be omitted without undermining the effect of the main plot: Dimond has not achieved the full blending of tones which gives melodrama its complexity. But the interest of this play lies in its pre-Freudian realisation of a family drama: the Count De Valmont's wife and heir, lost many years before to the murderous rapacity of his cousin Longueville, are found not to have been killed, but rather concealed from him and from themselves in madness and namelessness. The climax of the piece is the reuniting of the family: Florian, the foundling child, recognises his mother by the impulse of blood and she him by the scar upon his hand sustained in their near-fatal parting. Both are restored to De Valmont, who has brought Florian up out of charity while still grieving for his own lost wife and son. Dimond's attempts to fashion a realistic character for the bereaved father, and to make him express in words the strain of loneliness upon his essential benevolence, only weaken the exposition and progress of the drama through the mute signs of feeling. The play lived on in the theatre by virtue, chiefly, of the powerfully silent figure of Eugenia, the mad mother lost in the forest, though its many lines of verbose and superfluous dialogue were probably abandoned when it was played beyond the Haymarket.

Paradoxically, then, one might say that the aspiration of some dramatists to create literature militated against their success as melodramatists or that melodrama gives limited importance to the word. A clear demonstration of this is the 1804 text of the chapbook tale *Valentine and Orson*. This story had been a carnival play in several European countries during the early modern period, and a performance can be seen in a corner of Breughel's *Battle of Carnival and Lent*, painted in 1566; a lost play on the subject is also mentioned in Philip Henslowe's diary. The play, arranged by the manager Mark Lonsdale, was a hit at Sadler's Wells – a theatre without a licence for the spoken drama – in June 1794. Orson, the 'wild man' raised in the forest by a bear, was the creation of the virtuoso mime and clown, Jean Baptiste Dubois. When the play was staged at Covent Garden by Thomas Dibdin in 1804, he was able to use Dubois as Orson and Charles Farley, who had played Francisco, the dumb hero of *A Tale of Mystery*, as Valentine. At Covent Garden, of course, Dibdin did not need to confine himself to pantomime. George Daniel's preface to the printed text of Dibdin's play calls it 'a catalogue *raisonnée* of the various characters of mankind – a textbook for observations, on men and manners – a phantasmagoria of the real and the unreal, the natural and the supernatural'.[18] With the benefit of hindsight and the insights of Lacan, we might agree that Dibdin's *Valentine and Orson* offers a spectacular realisation of the period's psychological discoveries and the reframing of the relationship between the individual and society. But it does so by the deployment of far more than words. Indeed the verbal skeleton with which we are left is a very inadequate guide to the stage effect of the play's climactic moments.

The encounter between Valentine, the perfect chivalric hero, and Orson, his natural brother, is the climax of the first act. It is prefaced by demi-choruses of peasants and pilgrims, singing a glee and exchanging rhymes, before the wild man enters, in a state of nature, carrying a dead animal as food to entertain his foster-mother, the bear. Orson is playful as well as fearsome and the comic temper continues through the rest of the build-up. Valentine enters with his servant Hugo (played in this version by the droll comedian William Blanchard) who is scared of the forest. Having been left alone, Hugo is chased across the stage by Orson and escapes, leaving his mauled cloak for Valentine to find. The play highlights the physical strength of the wild man as well as his generosity to his ursine foster mother:

> *Re-Enter* **Valentine**, R. – *he cannot find the wild man* – *sees* **Hugo's** *cloak, laments his supposed death, and mounts the tree to look out for his enemy.*

Re-Enter **Orson**, *expressing disappointment at not having overtaken* **Hugo** – *he approaches the tree* – **Valentine** *plucks a branch, and throws it at him* – **Orson** *looks up with astonishment, chatters uncouthly to* **Valentine**, *throws the branch back to him, and beckons him to come down* – **Valentine** *hesitates* – **Orson**, *enraged, immediately ascends the tree* – *and while he is climbing up on one side*, **Valentine** *gets down on the other, and in turn beckons his opponent* – **Orson** *makes but one jump from the tree to the ground* – *runs to* **Valentine**, *who opposes his polished shield* – **Orson**, *seeing his own figure reflected in it, suddenly starts back* – **Valentine**, *with his sword drawn, keeps* **Orson** *at bay, and leads him round the stage, still wondering at the spectacle he beholds reflected* – **Orson** *at length struggles for the shield, takes it from* **Valentine**, *and throws it away* – **Valentine** *has another shield at his back, which he immediately uses, slightly wounds* **Orson**, *at which he, enraged, looks round for a weapon, pulls up a young tree by the roots, and uses it as a club.*

'A Fierce Combat' ensues before the bear re-enters. Valentine threatens her, and in his anxiety to defend his mother Orson allows himself to be taken prisoner. He accepts fruit and wine from Valentine and offers them to his mother, who then falls down and dies upon the stage. Orson grieves, and Valentine caresses him:

Orson *seeing* **Valentine's** *attention to himself and the Bear, seems pleased and overcome by it* – *presents* **Valentine** *with one end of the cord, and holding the other, suffers himself to be led off, looking back from time to time, at the dead Bear, and making an uncouth and mournful kind of lamentation.*

(*Valentine and Orson*, pp. 17–19)

The mastery of nature is performed here in a complex patterning that allows multiple responses and readings without predetermined closure. The audience is presented with competing images of man as wild and civilised, displaying strength against agility. The wild man Orson is confronted not with his opposite but with himself, seen in a mirror. He is enraged, but enters willy-nilly into self-consciousness, and immediately begins to move away from unity with his mother –whom he discovers to be less than human and who inevitably dies – to surrender himself to the law of the father. In the next act he will be led into the city and rapidly immersed in the rules of society. Very little of this is put into dialogue even in the printed version, and presumably almost nothing was spoken at Sadler's Wells, but the play's presentation of contemporary issues becomes clear if we can somehow read through the bareness of the text to the stage action. Watching the interplay between the brothers, and between them and the bear, the audience would feel the paradoxes which inform Romantic thought: the generosity of nature and the superiority of civilisation; the pity and the inevitability of civilisation emerging from the woods.

Home, sweet home

Early melodrama challenged the claims of poetic tragedy to stage supremacy, and brought down upon its writers the condemnation of the literary establishment. This preoccupation with social order and class interaction also led melodramatists onto ground previously considered the territory of modern comedy: settings and characters drawn from everyday life. Thomas Postlewait has made it clear that 'melodrama is not an early stage of modern realistic drama'; rather it shares many of the topics and concerns of realism, but frames them differently.[19] Steiner's 'historicised' nineteenth-century spectator – the man with the newspaper in his pocket and, one might add, the woman waiting for the return of her husband or sons from naval, military and imperial service – was attracted to the theatre by spectacular dramatisations of international current events, like the battles staged in the water tank at Sadler's Wells and in the circus ring at Astley's. These plays dramatised the experiences of gallant Jack tars or outnumbered British officers. Before long, as anxieties overseas subsided, such figures came to be deployed in staging excitements nearer home which involved social rather than military upheaval and threat. Jerrold's *Black-Ey'd Susan* (S, 1829) is probably the obvious transitional instance. William, a working-class hero out of a broadside song, is saved from being hanged for having struck a superior officer who was assaulting Susan, his wife, when it is revealed that, at the time of the incident, he was already discharged from the naval service, and therefore free to act as a husband rather than as a serving sailor. The switch here is from gothic representations of revolution to the exploration and usually the endorsement of the current social order, despite its manifest injustices, in the domestic sphere. These dramas of contemporary life deserted the purely comedic frame for a melodramatic interlarding of comic characters and commentary with high-minded social prescription and interpellation. Melodramatists of the second generation, like William Moncrieff, Douglas Jerrold and Edward Fitzball, were advised to scour the newspapers to find their stories, and they plotted plays round issues like the press gang and the new police or sensations such as a murder, a crash or a strike. In this melodramas resembled and drew upon contemporary visual culture: Jerrold's *The Rent Day*, for example, staged at Drury Lane in January 1832, at the height of the democratic excitement over parliamentary reform, comments from his own radical position upon the class tensions, oppressions and aspirations which filled the newspapers. The play employs the newly developed technique of 'realising' a picture upon the stage. In this case a drama about rural poverty is constructed around two genre paintings by David Wilkie: *The Rent Day* (1807), presented as the curtain rose, and *Distraining for Rent* (1815) with which the first act ends.[20]

Melodramatists also drew upon the latest novels, making spectacles of nationhood from Walter Scott and forging a domestic typology from such writers as Amelia Opie and, later, Charles Dickens. Sometimes the two could be intercut: George Soane in *The Falls of Clyde* (DL, 1817) uses a setting from Scott together with a plot taken from Opie. In this play, a farmer's daughter, played by the famous soubrette Fanny Kelly, is seduced by a young laird. Her brother challenges and almost kills him, but he is rescued by gypsies – led by T. P. Cooke, the leading exponent of the heroic stage tar – and carried off to a picturesque cavern behind the Falls. The laird recovers, escapes, rescues the brother from the gallows and in the end marries Ellen. Moncrieff wrote a play in which Junius Brutus Booth, fresh from playing Nahum Tate's adaptation of *King Lear* at Covent Garden, could appear at the Coburg in a similar role, and so transformed Opie's *Father and Daughter* into *The Lear of Private Life*. The heroine, seduced and cast off, wanders through the snow with her baby in her arms; in the last act her song about repentance and weeping restores her father to health after five years of madness. Bishop's song, 'Home, Sweet Home', has a similar power in John Howard Payne and James Robinson Planché's *Clari, The Maid Of Milan* (CG, 1823) when the maid of the title, having preserved her innocence in the house of her ducal would-be seducer, is prompted by hearing the song to flee back to her humble parents' home.[21] Such songs and motifs came to embody the moral world of dramatic art in the first half of the nineteenth century. These plays were also widely parodied and burlesqued, often for the enjoyment of the same audiences who wept over them in all seriousness; both modes were aspects of the melodramatisation of modern life. Such melodramas are not simply 'realistic', nor are they meant to be; they are as complex in their signification as the new world they framed and reflected, captured and distorted.

NOTES

1. Jacky Bratton and Ann Featherstone, *The Victorian Clown*, Cambridge: Cambridge University Press, 2006, p. 41. The performer is Eliza Ann Hengler, daughter of Henry Michael Hengler and wife of William Powell, equestrian and circus proprietor. She was primarily a rope-dancer.
2. See Thomas Postlewait, 'From Melodrama to Realism: the Suspect History of American Drama', in *Melodrama: The Cultural Emergence of a Genre*, eds. Michael Hays and Anastasia Nikolopoulou, New York: St Martin's Press, 1996, pp. 39–60.
3. Guilbert de Pixérécourt, 'Melodrama', in *Le Livre des cent-et-un, Vol. 6*, Bruxelles: Louis Hauman, 1832; reprinted in *Four Melodramas*, ed. and trans. by Daniel Gerould and Marvin Carlson, New York: Martin E. Segal Theater Centre Publications, 2002, pp. 311–14, 313.

4. George Steiner, *The Death of Tragedy*, New York: Knopf, 1961, pp. 108, 117.
5. Robert B. Heilman, *Tragedy and Melodrama: Versions of Experience*, Seattle, WA and London: University of Washington Press, 1968, pp. 74–7, 84–6, 75–6.
6. See Susan Stewart, *Crimes of Writing: Problems in the Containment of Representation*, Durham, NC and London: Duke University Press, 1994, p. 3 and John O'Brien, *Harlequin Britain: Pantomime and Entertainment, 1690–1760*, Baltimore, MD: Johns Hopkins University Press, 2004, p. xviii. For a twenty-first century discussion of this protracted dispute, see Jane Moody, *Illegitimate Theatre in London, 1770–1840*, Cambridge: Cambridge University Press, 2000.
7. See further Anne Ubersfeld, *Reading Theatre*, trans. by Frank Collins, Toronto: University of Toronto Press, 1999; Thomas Elsaesser, 'Tales of Sound and Fury: Observations on the Family Melodrama', in *Home Is Where the Heart Is: Studies in Melodrama and the Woman's Film*, ed. Christine Gledhill, London: British Film Institute, 1987 and Frederick Brown, *Theater and Revolution: the Culture of the French Stage*, New York: Viking Press, 1980.
8. Pixérécourt, 'Melodrama', p. 311.
9. Peter Brooks, *The Melodramatic Imagination: Balzac, Henry James, Melodrama, and the Mode of Excess*, New Haven, CT: Yale University Press, 1976, p. 21.
10. Brooks, *The Melodramatic Imagination*, p. 35.
11. Brooks, *The Melodramatic Imagination*, pp. 34–5.
12. *A Tale of Mystery*, Dolby's British Theatre (London: n.d.) pp. 26–7.
13. Brooks, *The Melodramatic Imagination*, p. 16.
14. See Paula R. Backscheider, *Spectacular Politics: Theatrical Power and Mass Culture in Early Modern England*, Baltimore, MD: Johns Hopkins University Press, 1993, p. 190.
15. See a recent discussion of the play and a copy of its text at http://www.rc.umd.edu/praxis/obi/obi_melodrama_act1.html. On the play's political resonances when presented at the Coburg in December 1819, see Jacky Bratton, *New Readings in Theatre History*, Cambridge: Cambridge University Press 2003, pp. 61–3.
16. John Genest, *Some Account of the English Stage: from the Restoration in 1660 to 1830*, 10 vols., Bath: H. E. Carrington, 1832, vol. VII, pp. 233, 237.
17. Genest, vol. VIII, p. 151.
18. D-G [George Daniel], 'Remarks' to *Valentine and Orson*, London: John Cumberland, 1831, p. 5.
19. Postlewait, 'From Melodrama to Realism', p. 55.
20. See Martin Meisel, *Realizations: Narrative, Pictorial, and Theatrical Arts in Nineteenth-Century England*, Princeton, NJ: Princeton University Press, 1983, pp. 147–50.
21. This line of development was first traced in Maurice Willson Disher, *Blood and Thunder: Mid-Victorian Melodrama and its Origins*, London: Frederick Muller, 1949, pp. 82–5.

PART III

Identities

9

KRISTINA STRAUB

The making of an English audience: the case of the footmen's gallery

The story of London theatre audiences in the eighteenth century has been told by cultural historians Peter Stallybrass and Allon White as the gradual displacement of rowdy, carnivalesque participation by the decorum of high-art consumption. Drawing on Norbert Elias's *History of Manners* and the work of sociologist Pierre Bourdieu, Stallybrass and White narrate emerging demands for the audience to assume the docile role of quiet attentiveness and 'appropriate' reaction to the performance on the stage: 'what is new . . . is the urgent attempt to expel the lower sort altogether from the scene of reception, to homogenise the audience by refining and domesticating its energy, sublimating its diverse physical pleasures into a purely contemplative force, replacing a dispersed, heterodox, noisy participation in the *event* of theatre by silent specular intensity'.[1] Stallybrass and White frame this story about audiences in the grand narrative of the middle class' ubiquitous 'rise' and the emergence of a 'bourgeois public sphere'.[2] Unfortunately, their narrative, however elegant, has limited studies of eighteenth-century spectatorship by obscuring the specific processes by which particular audience members, struggled for and ultimately lost the right to public voices and behaviours not consonant with the 'bourgeois public sphere'.

We need more information about the social identities and relations of eighteenth-century British audiences; more is at stake in this knowledge than a history of dramatic reception. As Lisa A. Freeman concludes, 'the semiotics of placement within the theater provided for an intense experience of the socioeconomic conditions that regulated society at large and made patently clear the kinds of competing interests that had to be negotiated within that culture. Social rank was as significant an element in the experience of the theatrical space as it was in the meaning of the plays performed.'[3] I propose to further this search for knowledge about particular social identities and dynamics by looking at the case of footmen in Drury Lane Theatre as a highly visible portion of the London audience from the time that they were admitted into the upper gallery by Christopher Rich in the late seventeenth century until David Garrick abolished this practice in 1759. Print reactions to the footmen and their depiction in a number of afterpieces during this period constitute a case study in cultural identities and social relations rendered invisible by the grand narrative of an emergent, middle-class decorum. Newspaper commentary on and dramatic representations of footmen's behaviour tell a very different story about public conflict between distinct groups of theatregoers and the powerful roles which ideologies of sexuality and gender played in the negotiations of that conflict.

The footmen's gallery

During the first half of the eighteenth century, the footmen's gallery at Drury Lane was the focus for public opinion on the presence and behaviour of domestic servants in urban places of leisure. From the Restoration, footmen, sent early to the theatre to hold places for their masters, had free access to the upper gallery after the performance of the fourth act. In 1696, that access was extended to the whole performance, and London footmen took full advantage of this free entertainment, making Drury Lane Theatre a place where one could encounter one of the largest, most highly visible and vocal groups of footmen in the city. According to Colley Cibber, Rich opened the gallery to the footmen for the whole play during a period of intense competition between London theatres in order to curry favour with their aristocratic employers: 'This riotous Privilege, so craftily given, and which from Custom, was at last ripen'd into Right, became the most disgraceful Nuisance, that ever depreciated the Theatre. How often have the most polite Audiences, in the most affecting Scenes of the best Plays, been disturb'd and insulted, by the Noise and Clamour of these savage Spectators?'[4] As Cibber suggests, a 'Privilege' granted because of the footmen's association with 'People of Quality', was taken up by men servants as a 'Right', which, over the course of sixty years, was noisily asserted by the footmen and resented by other audience members with physical and verbal aggression on both sides.

In general, the footman's obtrusive presence in public spaces of urban amusement was viewed with considerable ambivalence. On one hand, no one approved of the often rude and insubordinate behaviour of footmen in public; on the other hand, as masculine subjects, footmen were seen as having certain claims to respect within the public realm. A 1743 writer in the *Champion* laments, 'when I see four or five able Fellows swinging behind a gilt Chariot, and reflect, that they have no other Business to do than what, perhaps, might be better undone; that they are ... of so little Use to Society that in the Course of their whole Lives not one of them adds a Shilling to the publick *Stock*, I am grieved to see *Englishmen* in such a Situation.'[5] Footmen, as 'Englishmen', were distinguished from other European servants, as many British writers at the time were not only acutely aware, but curiously proud.

The status of the footman as 'Englishman' is rooted at least partially in the emergent ideal of English justice. The legal protection of servants' rights was seen as a distinguishing feature of English national identity. *The Laws Relating to Masters and Servants*, a frequently reprinted pamphlet, proudly declaims, 'the Commonality are upon the same Footing, as to Liberty and Property, as the Gentry; and Servants of the lowest Class, being under the Protection of the Laws, if mal-treated, have the same Remedy and Redress as their Masters'.[6] While this egalitarianism under the law was more theoretical than actual, a respect for men servants' rights seems to have influenced attitudes towards their public presence. As Leo Hughes notes, the Comédie Française did not tolerate bad behaviour from waiting servants: 'the state intervened, and lackeys were banned ... In England such intervention would have seemed impolitic, not to say tyrannical.'[7] Indeed, the footman's gallery in the London theatres logged a history of troublesome to riotous behaviour, a situation that was apparently tolerated as an unpleasant byproduct of English liberty. A 1728 *Touch-Stone* article comments,

> Our Servants (because not Slaves) are suffer'd to disturb at Will our politest Amusements: At an immense Sum we support these Entertainments, and they are allow'd gratis to put the Negative upon our hearing them: The Bread they eat, the Cloaths they wear are ours: yet, with one in their Belly, and the other on their Back, their Rudeness dare stand betwixt Us and our Pleasures; and the meanest Footman unpunished, fly in the Face of the Whole Court.
>   ... no such Liberties or Insolencies would be tolerated in any Part of the Globe, but Great Britain.[8]

On the one hand, the behaviour of the Drury Lane footmen was an offence to their superiors; on the other, it was a source of pride in an English social system that did not countenance treating servants like 'slaves'.

The footmen's gallery gave a permanent place and, consequently, a voice to footmen's claims to participation in urban leisure activities,[9] claims that can be best understood in the context of general concerns over the public presence and agency of the male servants employed by the aristocracy and landed gentry while resident in London. The presence and voices of footmen were common objects of complaint by conservative polemicists on 'the servant problem'.[10] The ubiquitous presence of footmen in the theatres and other places of public leisure and amusement takes on a more threatening aspect in the larger context of print anxiety over London servants' new economic mobility: the practice of servants 'giving warning' and moving from place to place. Closely linked to this concern about servants 'giving warning' is a considerable amount of worry about how servants in London were spending their free time. London footmen were objects of the most intense expressions of anxiety, in part because the footmen's leisure was, in a sense, part of their job. As J. Jean Hecht notes, aristocratic status was signalled in the opulent spectacle of richly liveried footmen standing around not doing very much: the brawnier the footman and the richer his livery, the more his allegedly labourless existence signified his master's economic and social power.[11] The bodies and voices of footmen taking up space at fashionable London places of amusement suggested to many, however, not only aristocratic 'luxury', but a public presence, even a power, that was subversive of class hierarchy and the public order.

The footmen in the gallery were often written about as nuisances to other audience members, but they were also feared. The *Gentleman's Magazine* reports in 1732 on the obnoxious behaviour of wise-cracking, snuff-taking footmen sent to hold their masters' traditional places in the 'Boxes', but annoyance could turn to trepidation when the footmen assumed 'their' place in the upper gallery: 'After the Play is begun, we have often seen the noblest parts of it interrupted by their *Bear-Garden Quarrels* in the *Upper Gallery*. For these Reasons they ought to be banish'd out of the *Playhouse* for ever. But perhaps this may be dangerous, considering they lately *rioted* an *Assembly* they could not be admitted to, and opposed the *Guards* that were plac'd for the Safety of their Masters.'[12] The image of the footman that emerges from such printed comments separates him from a resentful 'Audience' that upholds, in contrast, a standard of polite behaviour. Drury Lane footmen were a highly visible, collective 'other' to what was considered proper public behaviour, but they were also seen as too powerful a presence to be dismissed, either figuratively or literally. Dramatic representations of footmen contribute to the footman's ambiguous public image in the form of a dualistic, even contradictory sexuality. On the one hand, footmen on the stage incorporate the aggressive sexuality associated with their class in the polemical literature on 'the servant problem'. On the other hand, they embody a naturalised 'English' masculinity transcendent of class difference. That the English stage styled itself and its privileged audience as 'manly' (as opposed to 'effeminate' entertainments such as Italian opera or French dance) is a truism of the period. If the footmen in the gallery could not be beaten back, footmen on stage asked them to join the ranks of a decorously 'manly' British audience.

Representations of footmen on the London stage

This invitation was proffered in a spate of dramatic works performed in the course of a decade marked by considerable publicity about the Drury

Lane riots of 1737 over the footmen's 'right' to the upper gallery. Plays in which servants play a predominant role on the eighteenth-century stage are ubiquitous and highly varied, from the trickster figures of Fielding's *The Intriguing Chambermaid* (DL, 1733) and Garrick's *The Lying Valet* (GF, 1741) to the loyal retainers of the more sentimental melodrama. These dramatic works have received little critical attention, perhaps in part because many of them are afterpieces, part of a night at the theatre obscured by our post-Victorian view of the stage. It may not be coincidental that themes pertaining to servants' social status and agency are taken up by many of these afterpieces. The timing of their performances was likely to bring artisans, tradesmen, apprentices and servants, including footmen, together with their gentle counterparts to form a notably heterogeneous audience. These afterpieces, featuring footmen and other personal men servants such as valets, satirise greedy servants and their duped masters, but they do not follow a specific, political 'line' on 'the servant problem'. Interpreted in the context of the highly visible and audible presence of footmen in the London theatre, these afterpieces can be read as negotiations between the different feelings created in audience members by the footman's ambivalent public status.

Three short theatrical pieces, the anonymous imitation of *The Beggar's Opera* entitled *The Footman* (GF, 1732) and two farces by Henry Fielding, *An Old Man Taught Wisdom; or, The Virgin Unmasked* (DL, 1735) and *Miss Lucy in Town* (DL, 1741), comprise a model for thinking about how gender and sexuality shape the image of domestic men servants into a 'manliness' that blurs class boundaries. Read together, with the controversy over the footmen's gallery in mind, these afterpieces are both responses to the politics of urban spaces shared by servants and their masters, and a means of shaping that politics. The footman's sexuality emerges as crucial to managing the general threat of urban servants' leisure and the more specific concern that men servants might gather together and even assert proprietary control over the public space of London theatres.

All three plays culminate in the fantasy of the footman's escape from service into financial independence. This change in economic status is inextricably coupled with the footman's marriage and his transformation from suspect sexual object/predator into 'English husband', his problematic virility turned into an authoritative masculinity. *The Footman: An Opera*, performed and printed in 1732, is dedicated to 'The Society of Footmen in Great-Britain': 'How many, who now make the most conspicuous Figures with the brightest Equipage, would, without your Aid, make no Figures at all?'[13] *The Footman* is one of many imitative 'operas' performed after John Gay's highly popular *The Beggar's Opera* (1728), whose social satire turns on lower-class characters – in this case servants – playing out the manners and the vices of their 'betters'. The play begins, in imitation of *The Beggar's Opera*, with a dialogue between poet and player which establishes that, not only is the hero a footman, but the characters are 'All Footmen!' (*The Footman*, p. vii). The footman/hero is Charles, whose service includes pimping for his master; Charles, himself a ladies' man, is teetering on the verge of true love for the virtuous Jenny Jessamy. Charles embodies the stereotype of the sexually and financially 'loose' London footman. He tells Jenny, 'I'd marry you, if my Fortune cou'd bear it, But really, I have so many Expences upon my hands, what with fine Clothes, Chair-hire, Taverns, Plays, and the like' (*Footman*, p. 28). Following the formula of *The Beggar's Opera*, servants parody the materialism and libertine sexuality of their masters; in a twist on Gay's contrived happy ending, however, Charles reforms his spending habits in order to marry Jenny: 'I don't question but I shall be capable of supporting you in a tolerable genteel Manner. I'll retrench my Superfluities, and as you affect nothing of Gaudiness, you shall make as decent, tho' not as glaring a Figure, as any Lady about Town' (*Footman*, p. 53).

On stage as in life, marriage for the footman means leaving service, as domestic servants are not, at least in theory, allowed to wed. Hence, it means changing economic and social status, a transition that carried its own social and financial complexities in the second quarter of the eighteenth century. Wrapped deep inside the satiric plot of *The Footman* is the model of life-cycle service (the traditional relationship between servants and masters) in which servants grow out of their master's families and into their own. Life-cycle service was, certainly by 1732, a dying institution and very far from the experience of many London footmen in the gallery. *The Footman*'s ending encodes both the traditional hope of the male domestic servant for this change in social and economic status and its new arbitrariness. In the decadent world of fashionable London, this transition comes about through chance and corruption rather than the 'natural' transition from servant to master. Charles is able to reform and marry Jenny because of a lottery ticket which his master has given him for 'some Considerations': 'So, this comes of pimping! 'tis certainly the most profitable Employment in Life' (*Footman*, p. 72). Ironically, the servant's recuperation into an English husband to a virtuous wife is a by-product of aristocratic decadence, a cynical view of class relations that sets the footman/husband on a par with the sexual and financial excesses of aristocratic masculinity. As in *The Beggar's Opera*, both classes, master and man, offer comments on the decadent materialism of modern society. But as with Gay's mock-heroic character Macheath, this footman/hero carries a masculine charisma that floats free of the play's social satire.

For his rejection of the luxurious life of a London footman, Charles is rewarded with Jenny, a prize equally sought as a mistress by his Lord Gaylove. Charles crows, 'He'd give the World to obtain his Desires: in that Point I shall triumph over him with all his Titles' (*Footman*, p. 61). As in other plays I shall examine, Charles assumes the privileged position of 'an English Husband', the footman's dangerous sexuality transformed into conjugal virility and a mastery over women that transcends class difference. At the same time, Charles assumes this culturally valuable form of manliness by leaving service; in this play, the fading tradition of life-cycle service is evoked to give the problem of men servants' agency a socially acceptable form. But in the context of modern economic relations between serving and master classes, its evocation is an ironic echo of past relations between masters and servants that only serves to throw into relief the gross materialism and corruption of the present.

Two popular afterpieces by Henry Fielding, the musical entertainment, *An Old Man Taught Wisdom*, first performed with the highly popular actress Kitty Clive in the title role, and its sequel, *Miss Lucy in Town*, also starring Clive, and performed throughout the century, offer audiences a manly footman-hero who embodies the worst nightmare of polemicists such as Defoe and Swift on 'the servant problem': the footman who marries his master's daughter.[14] Social mobility and sexual transgression come together in this recurrent form of paranoia. While Defoe imagines murder and mayhem as the result of this sexual encroachment and Swift the moral and physical pollution of aristocratic families, Fielding seems to be presenting the possibility that a cross-class marriage might be successful if the daughter is a handful and the footman a good sort. And so the sexually opportunistic footman is transformed, in Fielding's comic afterpiece, into a manly 'Englishman', a more-than-adequate addition to the English squirearchy.

An Old Man Taught Wisdom presents Thomas, footman to Lord Bounce, as object of desire to the pretty but clueless Miss Lucy, daughter of Goodwill, a benign but bumbling squire. Thomas and Miss Lucy come to the stage stereotyped as ridiculous or dangerous by many satiric and didactic warnings: the lustful daughter of the middling gentry and her paramour, the laced, white-stockinged, and sexually and economically opportunistic footman. Fielding's Thomas echoes the almost feminine appeal of the sexy footman. According to Miss Lucy, Thomas 'looks a thousand times more like a gentleman than either Squire *Foxchase* or Squire *Tankard*, and talks more like one, ay, and smells more like one too. His Head is so prettily drest, done all down upon the Top with Sugar, like a frosted Cake, with three little Curls of each side, that you may see his Ears as plain!' (*An Old Man*, p. 5).

Thomas's attractions for Lucy evoke the idea that the footman can be easily mistaken for his aristocratic master.

The livery servant's finery is an ambiguous signifier of both his master's affluent status and his own, dangerous attractiveness. It both feminises him and makes him the marker of his employer's masculine power. Thomas incorporates both feminine charms and a highly serviceable male strength: 'he always carries a great swinging Stick in his Hand, as big as himself, that he wou'd knock any Dog down with, who was to offer to bite me' (*An Old Man*, p. 5). This portrait draws on a pre-existent discourse on the finery of livery servants as both effeminate and, combined with a strong, healthy body, a marker of the status and authority of his employer. Miss Lucy's attraction to Thomas suggests that he also embodies more than just aristocratic decadence; he also wields a masculine power that is validated by gender relations: the 'natural' ability to protect women.

Thomas's naturalised masculine authority over Lucy at the play's end contrasts strikingly with the play's satiric allusions to sexually opportunistic footmen. Thomas becomes an English husband whose sexual qualifications underwrite, rather than undercut his moral authority. He declares to Goodwill, 'I trust that, by my future conduct, I shall not prove myself totally unworthy of your respect', and the latter replies, 'Thou talkest like a pretty sensible fellow; and I don't know whether my daughter has not made a better choice, than she could have done among her booby relations. I shall suspend my judgment at present, and pass it hereafter, according to your behaviour' (*An Old Man*, p. 21). The footman's equivocal masculine worth is relative, of course, to Miss Lucy's other, obviously worthless suitors (an apothecary, a dancing master and a singing teacher), making another satirical point about the degeneracy of the lower squirearchy. The sequel, *Miss Lucy in Town*, however, makes less equivocal claims for Thomas's status as husband to the desiring Lucy by investing it in an idealised English masculinity.

Miss Lucy in Town begins with the newly married couple on their first trip to London. The action is confined to a bawdy house that the inexperienced Lucy and her husband mistake for respectable lodgings. Thomas is absent for most of the play in a quest for proper 'Londonised' clothes while his landlady attempts to sell Lucy by manipulating her 'natural desires' into 'fashionable' vices. Under the whores' tutelage, Lucy's countrified lust – what she calls her 'plain country wooing' – is supplanted by material greed as Zorobabel, a Jew, and Lord Bawble, a decadent aristocrat, vie for the 'goods'. The country wife is hardly passive baggage, however, and Lucy pursues her own material and sexual goals, manipulating Zorobabel into giving her jewels while pursuing her desire for Lord Bawble who appears to her as a better-dressed version of her footman/husband. The footman's sexual charisma is never displaced by that of more wealthy or aristocratic males. Her husband's body is temporarily supplanted as object of desire not by the bodies of her lovers but by those of the footmen which they promise her: she must choose Zorobabel, she tells Lord Bawble, because he 'promised to keep two tall lusty fellows, for no other business but to carry me up and down in a chair'. Lord Bawble counters, not with his own physical charms, but with the addition of 'two other tall fellows for no other use but to walk before your chair' (*Miss Lucy*, p. 54). Fielding's satire of urban materialism raises the common figure of the 'tall lusty' footman as status symbol and sexual object only to counter it, in the play's ending, with Thomas's husbandly authority.

Lucy's unmastered sexuality can be stabilised only by the male domestic authority invested in her husband. The sexy footman gets the sexually loose but 'gentle' daughter, but this apparent transgression across class lines only makes for a more potent patriarch. Thomas returns in his London finery to discover his wife with Lord Bawble:

THOMAS: I give your lordship joy of this fine girl.
LORD BAWBLE: Stay till I have had her, Tom. Egad she hath cost me a round sum, and I have had nothing but kisses for my money yet.
THOMAS: No, my lord! Then I am afraid your lordship never will have any thing more, for this lady is mine.
LORD BAWBLE: How! What property have you in her?
THOMAS: The property of an English husband, my lord

(*Miss Lucy*, p. 61)

Thomas removes sexuality from the corrupt economy of the London marketplace, in which his wife is, literally, for sale, and plants it firmly in the ground of a naturalised, national identity: 'Fortune, which made me poor, made me a servant; but nature, which made me an Englishman, preserved me from being a slave. I have as good a right to the little I claim, as the proudest peer hath to his great possessions; and whilst I am able, I will defend it' (*Miss Lucy*, p. 61).

There is more going on in Fielding's footman as English husband, however, than playing to a particular portion of the audience. Thomas – and his later, novelistic counterpart, Joseph Andrews – are, I would argue, expressive of the public ambivalence towards footmen as, simultaneously, English citizens with a tolerated public presence and voice, and threatening, even dangerous members of an urban 'mob'. Fielding's sexy footman as 'English husband' offers the potential for a male identity that can be shared across class lines. While the theatre did not sustain the 'property' claims of the London footmen to their own public space after 1759, Fielding's Thomas offered diverse members of the audience a masculine ideal that gestures towards the possibility of a gender-based rather than class-based hegemony. Under the banner of 'Englishmen', the men, at least, in London audiences were offered a model that sidesteps class differences in its concerted rejection of 'unmanly' behaviour – both on and off the stage.

The end of the footman's gallery

This ideological solution to the problem of the London footman's public identity must be understood, however, in relation to the material struggles over place and voice which gave rise to it. Fielding's image of gender relations covers over, rather than resolving, a highly specific, class-based conflict. In 1737, when the struggle between footmen and other audience members erupted into more than the usual shoving and verbal abuse, the contest ended in a draw. On Saturday night, 19 February 1737, Drury Lane audience members snapped. As Leo Hughes reports, 'the pit at Drury Lane led a revolt in which other members of the audience ardently joined', evicting the footmen and forcing from manager Charles Fleetwood the promise to abolish the footman's gallery. The footmen returned, however, on 21 February and forced entrance into the closed gallery. As the *London Magazine* reported, 'This Night a great Disturbance happened at Drury-Lane Play House, occasioned by a Great Number of Footmen, who assembled themselves there in a riotous Manner, with great Out-cries of burning the House and Audience together, unless they were immediately admitted into what they call their Gallery; and in order to strike a Terror, they began to hew down the Door of the Passage which leads to the said Gallery.'[15] Order was temporarily restored, but two weeks later the footmen returned: 'This Night a great Number of Footmen assembled together with Sticks, Staves, and other offensive Weapons, in a tumultuous and riotous Manner, and broke open the Doors of *Drury-Lane* Play-house, for not being let into what they call their *Gallery*, and fought their Way in so desperate a Manner to the Stage Door (which they forced open) that 25 or 26 Persons were wounded in a very dangerous Manner, in the Fray'. This time the footmen would not be appeased and 'several of the Ring-leaders' were taken into custody. These events were reported as all the more disturbing because they took place in the presence of members of the royal family.[16]

This affront to the most sacred and established forms of British authority contrasts sharply with the mildness of the official response which was to sentence three footmen to six months' hard labour, and to post a guard at the gallery door for a few nights following the second riot. The popular press certainly condemned the behaviour of the footmen, but it also gave them a public voice by publishing an open letter to Charles Fleetwood. If Fleetwood admits them into the gallery 'which is our Property', no further action will be taken: 'if not, our Intention is to Combine in a Body in Cognito, and Reduce the play house to the Ground, Valuing no Detection'.[17] The footmen's right to 'their' gallery was duly restored, and they continued to hold their claim for another twenty-two years, creating a public space in which the seed of cross-class masculinity could be planted.

The story of the footman's gallery ends in 1759 when David Garrick turned the footmen's gallery into regular paying seats. Garrick, who 'civilised' the London theatre in many respects, moving acting towards social respectability and demanding (though not always getting) more polite behaviour from his audiences, had apparently had enough from the footmen's gallery. The social climate was ripe for his decision given widespread opposition to 'vails' (the allegedly exorbitant tips expected by domestic servants from visitors to the household).[18] Servants could 'forget' to pour wine, make fires, or empty chamber pots for visitors who did not reward them sufficiently. Scotland had just banned vails at the time of Garrick's decision and one of the events in Edinburgh leading to the ban was a performance of James Townley's satire on corrupt urban servants, *High Life Below Stairs*. Garrick's decision to stage this play at Drury Lane led to the footmen's inevitable protest and the subsequent end to 'their' gallery.

High Life Below Stairs satirises the dangerous ignorance of the gentry to their exploitation by greedy, wasteful and dishonest servants. Lovel, a young planter from the West Indies, is befriended by Freeman, who reproaches him for taking 'Pride in a Number of idle, unnecessary Servants, who are the Plague and Reproach of this Kingdom'.[19] Lovel disguises himself as 'Jemmy', a young country boy sent into the city to be trained as a house servant by his own servants, Philip and Kitty. In this way, he plans to learn whether or not his servants are treating him honestly. Of course they are not and 'Jemmy' is instructed in how to best to cheat his master and seduce the household maids. In the course of the play, greedy, oversexed servants stage surreptitious class warfare against their 'betters'. The footmen in the Drury Lane gallery were not amused, as the playwright John O'Keeffe documents:

> The whole race of the domestic gentry, on the first night of this excellent little piece, were in a ferment of rage at what they conceived would be their ruin; and from the upper gallery, to which they were admitted gratis, came hisses and groans, and even many a handful of halfpence was flung on the stage at Philip and my Lord Duke, and Sir Harry, &c. This tumult went on for a few nights, but ultimately was a good thing for all theatres, as it gave Garrick, then manager, a fair occasion to shut the galleries from the servants, and ever after make it a pay place, which to this day it has continued.[20]

Besides riding the tide of the anti-vails movement in Britain, Garrick may have had more immediate economic motives for facing down the footmen in Drury Lane Theatre: the 'free-list' (authors and others legitimately claiming free admittance to the theatre) was a substantial drain on his revenues. Abolishing the footman's gallery did not keep servants away, but it did make them pay the reduced price of admission, as well as dispersing them throughout the theatre by taking away their 'special place'.

While theatregoers continued to complain about sitting 'cheek by jowl' with footmen until the practice of reserved seats was introduced, the era of the footmen's 'own place' ended. The curtailment of a particular class of working men's claims to public voice and space is as much a part of the story of London audiences as the 'rise of the middle class'. Accompanying this curtailment is the dramatic literature's creation of the footman as 'English husband'. As men with 'property' in their wives, footmen paradoxically enter the construction of a masculine public sphere through the erasure of the space and role which literally set them apart from their masters. The right to be like everyone else in the London theatre audience – or, at least, like every other man – gave footmen a gendered status while stripping them of their traditional claim to 'their' gallery. The widespread ambivalence towards manservants finds resolution in Garrick's paying customer, just another member of a British public whose heterogeneity is subsumed under the banner of authoritative masculinity.

NOTES

1. Peter Stallybrass and Allon White, *The Politics and Poetics of Transgression*, Ithaca, NY: Cornell University Press, 1986, p. 87.
2. Stallybrass and White, *The Politics of Transgression*, p. 88.
3. Lisa A. Freeman, *Character's Theater: Genre and Identity on the Eighteenth-Century English Stage*, Philadelphia, PA: University of Pennsylvania Press, 2002, p. 4.
4. *An Apology for the Life of Colley Cibber*, ed. B. R. S. Fone, Ann Arbor, MI: The University of Michigan Press, 1968, p. 129.
5. Quoted in J. Jean Hecht, *The Domestic Servant Class in Eighteenth-Century England*, London: Routledge and Kegan Paul, 1956, p. 179.
6. *The Laws Relating to Masters and Servants*, London: H. Lintot, 1755, p. iii.
7. Leo Hughes, *The Drama's Patrons: a Study of the Eighteenth-Century London Audience*, Austin, TX: University of Texas Press, 1971, p. 15.
8. Quoted in Hughes, *The Drama's Patrons*, p. 18.
9. Hughes, *The Drama's Patrons*, p. 17, refers to a major scuffle amongst footmen which took place in 1701 at a concert in the theatre at Little Lincoln's Inn Fields.
10. See for example Eliza Haywood, *A Present for a Servant-Maid. Or, the Sure Means of gaining Love and Esteem*, Dublin: George Faulkner, 1743, p. 36.
11. Hecht, *The Domestic Servant Class*, pp. 54–5.

12. *Gentleman's Magazine*, March 1732, p. 661.
13. *The Footman: An Opera; As it is Acted at the New-Theatre, in Goodman's-Fields*, London: Henry Lintot, 1732, pp. iii–iv. Subsequent references are cited within the text.
14. Robert Hume convincingly discredits *The London Stage's* claim that *Miss Lucy in Town* was banned by the Lord Chamberlain. See Robert Hume, *Henry Fielding and the London Theatre 1728–1737*, Oxford: Clarendon Press, 1988, p. 265.
15. *London Magazine*, February 1737, p. 107. Quoted in Hughes, *The Drama's Patrons*, p. 19.
16. *London Magazine*, March 1737, p. 163. Quoted in Hughes, *The Drama's Patrons*, pp. 19–20.
17. *Gentleman's Magazine*, March 1737, n. p.
18. Hecht, *The Domestic Servant Class*, p. 138.
19. [James Townley], *High Life below Stairs*, London: J. Newbery, 1769, Act I, scene i, p. 4.
20. John O'Keeffe, *Recollections of the Life of John O'Keeffe*, 2 vols., London: Henry Colburn, 1826; reissued New York and London: Benjamin Blom, 1969, vol. I, pp. 161–2.

10

MISTY G. ANDERSON

Women playwrights

The story of female playwrights in the later eighteenth century begins with the eclipse of most of the women who preceded them. *The Rover*, Aphra Behn's popular comedy of Spanish intrigue, faded from the repertoire, along with the works of Delarivière Manley, Mary Pix, Catherine Trotter, Penelope Aubin and Eliza Haywood. The exception to this trend was Susanna Centlivre, but frequent revivals of her work and the occasional piece such as Charlotte Charke's *The Art of Management* (York Buildings, 1735) or Kitty Clive's *Bays in Petticoats* (DL, 1750) could not undo the cultural amnesia that was setting in. This eclipse occurred in a period of backlash against the libertine, rough gender play of the Restoration and early eighteenth century. In their place came more sentimental or 'humane' comedies, as well as the next generation of female playwrights including Frances Sheridan, Elizabeth Griffith, Hannah Cowley, Hannah More, Sophia Lee, Elizabeth Inchbald and Joanna Baillie.[1]

The developing sense of bourgeois taste and propriety put the female playwright in a complicated position. Long-standing concerns about sexual impropriety in the theatre and the likelihood of critical censure in the rough-and-tumble world of reviewing made life in the theatre a suspect choice for a 'proper lady'.[2] While many female playwrights successfully negotiated these concerns, women such as Frances Burney found themselves caught between aspirations and expectations. Even with a successful novel, *Evelina*, to her credit, Burney's father Charles was convinced that the production of her comedy, *The Witlings*, would endanger her reputation and that of the family:

> I w^d have you be very Careful, & very perfect – that is, as far so as your own Efforts, & the best advice you can get, can make you. In the Novel Way, there is no danger – & in that, no *Times* can affect you.[3]

Though Charles Burney was overnice about reputation, he was right about one thing: critics in newspapers such as the *Times* could be unforgiving.

A *Times* review of a production of Hannah Cowley's *Which is the Man?* began, 'In this drama there is very little originality, very little wit, and but a small share of humour …'[4] Such were the hard hits that playwrights – by contrast with novelists – could expect.

While audiences were receptive to work by female playwrights, George Colman the Elder's *The Separate Maintenance* (HM, 1779) and Colman the Younger's *The Female Dramatist* (HM, 1782), both of which parodied female playwrights, indicate some hostility among their male counterparts. The sense that it was hard for male playwrights to have 'real' comedies staged because they were being edged out by bad sentimental taste and less talented women was implicit in Goldsmith's condemnation of writers who abandoned true comedy for her 'weeping sister'.[5] Some reviewers, quick to place even a successful play by a female playwright below what they perceived to be the 'living ornaments of theatrical composition' such as Sheridan, Cumberland and Holcroft, only fanned the flames.[6] Statistically, more women's plays on the stage did mean fewer plays by men at the patent houses, but most of the cuts came from the stock repertoire.[7]

Male mentors proved to be another mixed blessing. David Garrick's interest in producing plays by women, including Kitty Clive, Susanna Cibber, Frances Sheridan, Charlotte Lennox, Dorothy Celisia and Hannah Cowley, is well known, but his support seemed to fade when these playwrights proposed a second or third play which might turn the prodigy into the professional. The prologues and epilogues to women's plays, often written by influential male friends, suggest that they remain trespassers long after they have established a place on the London stage; they 'beg', 'bribe', 'dare', and ask their audiences to 'bear' it as they present their plays.[8] By the end of the eighteenth century women could claim close to ten per cent of all plays being produced on the London stages. Interestingly, this figure is close to the statistics for female playwrights on the London and New York stages at the end of the twentieth century.[9]

Women wrote for the theatre in many different forms from tragedies like Mariana Starke's *The Widow of Malabar* (Mrs Crespigny's private theatre, Camberwell and CG, 1791), or Charlotte Smith's comedy *What Is She?* (CG, 1799), to experimental 'closet' dramas (Jane Collier and Sarah Fielding's *The Cry*, 1754, and Baillie's *Plays on the Passions*, 1798–1812). It is notable that the smash hits of the period written by women, including Cowley's *The Belle's Stratagem* (CG, 1780), and Inchbald's *Every One Has His Fault* (CG, 1793), were comedies. Most female playwrights intent on Drury Lane or Covent Garden gravitated to comedy, not least because such plays had box-office appeal and financial rewards could be significant, particularly after Garrick instituted more regular theatrical bookkeeping practices at mid-century. Hannah Cowley earned an estimated £500 for *Which is the Man?* and over £700 for *The Runaway*. Inchbald, who was born into a Suffolk Roman Catholic farming family and widowed early in life, left an estate of over £6,000 at her death. That estate included receipts from her dark comedy *Every One Has His Fault* (£700), her sentimental and sharply political *Such Things Are* (£900), and her farce *The Mogul Tale* (£300). Compared with her popular novel *A Simple Story*, which sold for a respectable £200, we see why aspiring women like Cowley and Inchbald would choose the theatre for financial as well as aesthetic reasons.[10]

But the theatre also attracted these women because of its capacity to pose challenging questions about gender and power in English society. How do middle- and upper-class women secure their futures when marriage law makes it all but impossible for them to hold property or choose a partner without renouncing their affective obligations to their parents? And what means do wives have for holding a marriage together when a husband's wandering attentions or the threat of divorce (rare and difficult in real life) left them with uncertain futures? Comedy's wish-fulfilment structures, its witty trickster heroines and fifth-act reformations, proved an attractive form for posing some of these questions. Moreover, comedy enabled playwrights to mock the powerful, debate cultural assumptions, and challenge gender roles in ways that were pleasurable and unthreatening to the audience. Experimental pieces like Joanna Baillie's tragedy *Count Basil* (not performed, 1798) remind us that plays which circulated in print are also a part of the theatrical story, sometimes showing us what could not be staged. When female playwrights turned to tragedy, for the stage or the page, they tended to stress themes of female entrapment and the collision of public and private plots, themes that show the breakdown of comic hopes for social reconciliation. But the writing of tragedy, as illustrated by Lord Byron's famous quip about Joanna Baillie needing to borrow testicles, carried strongly masculine associations. Beneath the outlines of eighteenth-century theatrical genres (which have been used, Susan Bennett notes, 'to find [women's] writings less accomplished than those of their male counterparts') we can see moments that challenge expectations, leading eventually to hybrid forms like tragicomedy or melodrama, which attempt to name plots in search of different conclusions.[11]

Female playwrights at mid-century

Kitty Clive, Frances Sheridan, Charlotte Lennox and Hannah Cowley brought their plays to the patent theatres in the 1750s, 60s and 70s. Their works often explored shifts in attitudes about marriage as well as the more recalcitrant nodes of gendered power it preserved. The legal debate in England, marked by Lord Hardwicke's Marriage Act of 1753, illustrates these tensions. The Act, which raised the age of marital consent for females from twelve to twenty-one, protected young women and the assets of wealthy families from predatory adventurers, but it also extended the authority of families and allowed them to make ancillary agreements that restricted the transfer of wealth. Though in principle the Act affirmed the right of wives to make contracts, its details made clear that the property rights of fathers and husbands trumped the contract rights of daughters and wives. The marriage plot is, from this perspective, a very serious thing indeed.

Frances Sheridan had explored the legal and cultural dynamics of marriage in her sentimental novel, *The Memoirs of Miss Sydney Biddulph* (1761) before her first comedy, *The Discovery*, appeared in 1763. *The Discovery* was a solid success at Drury Lane and ran for seventeen nights. With David Garrick as Sir Anthony Branville and Thomas Sheridan as Lord Medway in the original cast, the play had star power. But its subsequent revivals (six in London and others at the Dublin theatres), as well as Jane Pope's two-act adaptation, *The Young Couple*, and multiple print editions prove its enduring appeal. In *The Discovery*, ex-rake Lord Medway wants to marry off his children against their inclinations in order to repair his fortunes, until he discovers that the rich widow Mrs Knightly, for whom he intends his son, Colonel Medway, is actually his long-lost daughter. Medway is also trying to seduce young Lady Flutter and tells Sir Harry Flutter to 'shew [himself] a man' in his 'sneering, ironical treatment' of his wife, advice that echoes passages from Jane Collier's 1753 *The Art of Ingeniously Tormenting*.[12] The recently married Flutters are show-stealers. Medway has coached them into fighting, but their funny tiffs show them to be more childish and affectionate than scheming:

> LADY FLUTTER: Then I'll stay to vex you.
>
> SIR HARRY: Then, Ma'am, I must teach you the obedience that is due to the commands of a husband.
>
> LADY FLUTTER: A husband! Oh gracious, defend me from such a husband – A battledore and shittlecock would be fitter for you than a wife, I fancy.
>
> SIR HARRY: And let me tell your pertness, a doll would be properer for you than a husband – there's for you, Miss.
>
> LADY FLUTTER: You'll be a boy all your life, Sir Harry.
>
> SIR HARRY: And you'll be a fool all your life, Lady Snap.
>
> LADY FLUTTER: I shall be the fitter company for you then.
>
> SIR HARRY: Tchou, tchou, tchou [*Jeering her.*]
>
> (Act II, scene i, pp. 54–5)

Lady Medway attempts to ease their quarrels and offer advice on discretion but the shadow of seduction looms large. Her own marital woes raise questions about the durability of comic reconciliation, questions Sheridan can ask because they are secured by the comedy's happy ending. Sheridan's next comedy, *The Dupe* (DL, 1763), did not shine as brightly. The greater loss was Garrick's rejection of *A Journey to Bath*, which Sheridan wrote while in Blois. The play includes a promising collection of characters with linguistic quirks that reflect their personalities. The overreaching Mrs Tryfort who confuses 'progeny' with 'prodigy', and 'contribute' with 'attribute' may have provided the prototype for her son's famous creation of Mrs Malaprop in *The Rivals*. Indeed, Richard Brinsley Sheridan may have transcribed the surviving copy of his mother's original manuscript.[13]

Hannah Cowley, the most successful female playwright after Centlivre, came into her own only after David Garrick's exit from the London stage in 1776. The versatile Cowley wrote comedies, farces, tragedies, an opera and an interlude, but she excelled at adapting the witty Restoration heroine and the Spanish intrigue plot to the more humane environment of late eighteenth-century comedy. Cowley's distinctive blend of feminine propriety and laughing comedy was successful. Her first play, *The Runaway* (DL, 1776), ran nineteen nights in its first season and saw ten subsequent productions before 1800. In this plot, Emily Morley has fallen in love with George Hargrave at a masquerade; she then turns up next door in the country on holiday but refuses to identify herself because she is hiding from her uncle, who is trying to marry her off. In the first production, Sarah Siddons played the heroine, alongside Richard Yates as her beloved George and Elizabeth Young as the vivacious Bella. The plot of mistaken identity, a cascade of misunderstandings, and lively characters all make for good theatre. Cowley's association of Englishness with virtue and stability, compared to the tyranny of the French and the rebellious liberty of America, was a timely one in 1776. Lady Dinah wishes for 'France! for thy Bastile, for thy *Lettres de Cachet*!' (Act III, p. 39) as a way to persecute her rival Emily, while Justice rebukes Emily, declaring, 'she can be no Patriot, our Patriots don't ride in coaches and six' (Act IV, p. 59). The English virtues which George and Emily exemplify include, most crucially, their ability to contract marriage with one another in harmony with a contractual model of civil society. Cowley lets Bella (Emily's friend, who speaks often and boldly) challenge the asymmetry of Anglican marriage vows: '*Love*, one might manage that perhaps – but *honour, obey*, – 'tis strange the Ladies had never interest enough to get this ungallant form mended' (Act V, p. 72). Though she is reprimanded by the good uncle, Drummond, her comic riposte sharpens the connection between rights, contracts, national identity and the good marriage.

In 1779, apart from a brief and frustrating detour into tragedy with *Albina*, Cowley put her energies into a farce entitled *Who's The Dupe?* (DL, 1779) which mocks the older intellectual, Gradus. Gradus looks like 'a Dictionary-maker' and makes a fool of himself while trying to woo younger women. By showing the learned man outwitted by a younger woman, Cowley satirises the cultural authority of men of letters such as Samuel Johnson, David Garrick and Oliver Goldsmith. At the same time that Cowley was demonstrating the popularity of female social satire, Frances Burney was being advised to shelve *The Witlings* and 'to dance the Nancy Dawson with fetters on'.[14] *The Witlings* skewers bluestockings, bad poets and greedy relatives who prize reputation over love in situations that humiliate the offending parties. Defying the conventional popularity for plays set in the drawing room or country house, the play opens in a milliner's shop, with several women sewing and selling their wares. Food spills, people work and customers bustle in and out of shops; as Margaret Doody observes, this is all unusual stagecraft for a comedy of the period.[15] The sense of the material world of work, food and bodies parallels the circulation of gossip, 'miniscripts', criticism, and laughably horrid poetry (such as 'Epitaph on a Fly killed by a Spider') of the 'Sprit' [Esprit] party. The critical gossip is eventually turned against its leader, Lady Smatter, in order to buy her silence and facilitate the marriage of the young lovers Cecilia and Beaufort. The play reveals the aggressive energies behind laughter, energies which provide the bite in Cowley's farce and which also erupt in Burney's fiction. Though none of her four comedies ever made it to the stage, Burney continued to hope: the margins of the manuscript reveal that she was timing the length of scenes in *The Woman Hater* (1801), thinking and preparing like a writer for the stage.[16]

Hannah Cowley's most successful comedy was *The Belle's Stratagem*, a play which Inchbald preferred to its prototype, George Farquhar's *The Beaux' Stratagem*, for its witty yet moral tone. Cowley's female characters are much more resourceful and energetic than the somewhat mousy Emily Morland in Farquhar's play. Letitia, who borrows Kate Hardcastle's trick from *She Stoops to Conquer*, charms her reluctant intended using a Restoration-style intrigue strategy in which she plays two full characters: the ridiculously unsophisticated country girl named 'Letty' to whom Doricourt is betrothed and a sexy, mystery woman. Letitia plays alternately on Doricourt's fears and desires to reveal herself finally as the *incognita* after he has already dutifully married 'Letty'. Her triumph balances energy and sexuality with propriety. While the play's main device resembles Goldsmith's, the difference between Mr Hardcastle ('I'll never control your choice', Act I, scene i) and Mr Hardy ('I foresee Letty will have her own way, and so I shan't give myself the trouble to dispute it', Act I, scene iv) indicates a shift in power dynamics. Kate is a fine actress, but Letitia is a playwright. As Lisa Freeman notes, 'the stratagem belongs to the Belle, as she maintains control of the script and the spectacle produced for the gaze'.[17]

The emphasis on theatrical female agency extends into Cowley's next success, *A Bold Stroke for a Husband* (CG, 1783), in which Victoria must reclaim her husband Carlos from his mistress Laura, and Olivia must disgust the suitors her father provides so she can seduce and marry Julio. Cowley's decision to set her play outside England (see also *The School for Greybeards*, her 1786 rewriting of Aphra Behn's *The Lucky Chance*), owes something to the Marriage Act of 1753. This legislation had the effect of putting an end to the spousals and *contracts de futuro* (written or spoken promises to marry) which had been stock plot devices of earlier comedies. Cowley's international settings underscore the fact that the limits of English marriage law also shape the terms of English romantic comedy.

The dynamics of marriage were not, however, the sole province of comic playwrights. Writers like Hannah More, who wrote plays for the professional stage as well as pedagogical dramas for use in Sunday schools, used tragedy's domain to show how familial relationships fall apart. *Percy* (CG, 1777) questions whether betrothals have ethical if not legal validity, particularly against the backdrop of marriages forced on daughters by manipulative, domineering or greedy fathers. In *Percy*, the jealous husband Douglas is convinced that Percy and Elwina, who were betrothed before Elwina's forced marriage to Douglas, have plotted their reunion. Douglas kills Percy in a duel, then witnesses the suicide of Elwina. As she explains to Percy, she could withstand her father's fury, '... but his tears, / Ah, they undid me! Percy, dost thou know / The cruel tyranny of tenderness?'[18] In Act V, first Douglas and then her father repent for refusing to honour her betrothal and for demanding her obedience in spite of her love for Percy. Raby, who 'kneels to his wronged child', laments, 'Am I a father? Fathers love their children – / I murder mine! ...' (Act V, p. 87). The culprit here is parental tyranny, which has forced the consistently virtuous Elwina into her impossible situation. More's virtuous heroine charts out the dilemmas that will multiply in Inchbald's dark comedies and threaten comedy's optimistic vision of community.

Problem comedies and social critique

Female playwrights explored a range of social problems in eighteenth-century society. Among them was gambling, which was presented as a fashionable diversion-*cum*-addiction, with narratives of suspense and repentance always at hand. *The Times* (DL, 1779), Elizabeth Griffith's substantial adaptation of Goldoni's French comedy, *Le Bourru Bienfaisant,* rewrites the original to focus on the dangers posed by gambling to a young married couple called the Woodleys. By this time, Griffith already had four comedies to her credit as well as a popular epistolary novel, *A Series of Genuine Letters between Henry and Frances* (1757). *The Times* ran for a respectable, but unspectacular, nine nights.[19] The play is worth our attention for its deft stagecraft, its critique of gambling and its condemnation of men who keep women ignorant in the name of protecting them. Lady Mary Woodley is unaware of their troubling financial situation because her husband fears alarming her, and so the fashionable card games and trips to the jeweller continue. Similarly, her sister Louisa is kept in the dark by her uncle Sir William (the 'beneficent bear' of Goldoni's title) who won't tell her whom he has chosen as her husband. The 'protection racket' of husbands and guardians begins to resemble the treachery of the Bromleys, who exploit Woodley and Lady Mary and drag them into further debt. After a well-crafted fifth-act card party, in which the background player's references to 'monsters', 'beasts', 'renounce!' and 'judgment' (all gambling terms) underscore the depravity of the Bromleys, the Woodleys come to terms with their bankruptcy and happily retire to the country. The avuncular but stern Sir William sets things to rights along with the help of Louisa's beloved Colonel Mountford, but the seriousness of Griffith's critique lingers and unsettles. What is at risk here is not the comedy's conventional ending in marriage but rather the survival of marriage in modern life.

Hannah Cowley's *Which is the Man?* (CG, 1782), a more substantial success with twenty-three nights in the first season and four author benefits, also tackles gambling. Lord Sparkle, who has imposed upon the country squire Bobby Pendragon and his sister Sophy (played by the gifted John Quick and Isabella Mattocks in the first run) in order to get their support for his election, gambles for 'corn-fields, fruitful vallies, and rich herds'.[20] The secondary character Clarinda gloats that Lady Squander's jewels and furniture are at Christie's 'at last'. In contrast to this loss of land and community, Beauchamp, the patriotic and serious soldier who loves the vivacious Lady Bell Bloomer, remains steadfast in defence of his nation, female honour and self-sufficiency (he scorns to be 'quartered on a Wife's fortune' while he can lift a sword). *Which is the Man?* is a picture of a nation at risk: French marriage law offers Julia more individual agency than is possible under English law and the French salon signifies to the widowed Lady Bell a culture more respectful of women than her native England. Meanwhile, Lord Sparkle threatens to consume the very countryside by wearing 'fifty acres in a suit, and the produce of a whole farm for a pair of buckles' as he converts agricultural profits into luxury goods (Act III, scene i, p. 25).

Beauchamp is left to protect the fragile community from enemies foreign and domestic, armed with little more than his passion for 'love and duty'.

Inchbald's colonial plays, including *The Mogul Tale, Such Things Are* and *The Wise Man of the East*, as well as her interest in continental playwrights, particularly Kotzebue and Dumaniant, also reflect a troubled nationalism.[21] The abuses of colonial rule, particularly in *Such Things Are* (CG, 1787) undermine the image of an enlightened, rational and just Britain even as they call on the nation to live up to humanitarian principles. Reviews occasionally underscored Inchbald's Jacobin politics, most notably in the *True Briton*'s review of *Every One Has His Fault*, though most of her plays are implicitly rather than overtly political. The restoration of the fallen or abandoned woman is a key theme in Inchbald's Kotzebue translation, *Lovers' Vows* (the textual source for the infamous amateur theatrical in *Mansfield Park* which sends Sir Thomas Bertram into a rage) as well as in Sophia Lee's *The Chapter of Accidents* (HM, 1780). These plays demonstrate how the hope of reconciliation included in comedy's 'happy ending' could make it so amenable to serious matters and so attractive to female playwrights interested in both popular success and social reform.

Inchbald and beyond

Elizabeth Inchbald's London debut in 1780 marks the beginning of the most commercially successful career of any woman dramatist in the late eighteenth century. Her twenty staged plays (nine adaptations and eleven original pieces), ranged across farce, tragedy, comedy and tragicomedy. Inchbald also produced a significant body of criticism primarily in the form of her 125 prefaces commissioned by John Bell for *The British Theatre* (1806–9). She too favoured the five-act comedy as a form that could 'teach ... an audience to think and to feel, as well as to laugh and applaud'.[22] Inchbald helped to define the shape of late eighteenth-century drama and to present the female dramatist as an 'authorial performer'.[23] Her strong sense of dialogue and stage-worthy action, both prominent features of her first original play, *The Mogul Tale* (HM, 1784) had been honed by her experience as an actress. Inchbald used the contemporary craze for hot-air balloons to launch the farce's action which involved a spectacular backdrop and exotic locales. In the play, the English balloonists are blown off course and land in the seraglio of a philosophical sultan, a situation rife with opportunities for escape plots, 'oriental' costumes, and declamations about political justice.

Inchbald's comedies pressed on the generic limits of the form as it verged into tragicomedy. The dominant theme of her oeuvre was the drive toward community and reconciliation. In *I'll Tell You What* (HM, 1785) and *Every*

10. Elizabeth Inchbald as playwright in *I'll Tell You What*.

One Has His Fault (CG, 1793), husbands compel divorces, but this is not funny. *I'll Tell You What* challenges the ribald humour of Restoration comedies like Wycherley's plays, *The Country Wife* and *Love in a Wood*, by showing the consequences of infidelity on a community of friends and family.

In the play, Anthony Euston has returned from the West Indies to find his nephew Sir George Euston divorced and remarried to his first love, the new Lady Euston, while his ex-wife Harriet is married to Major Cypress. The confusion surrounding the phrase 'my wife' creates a sense of verbal play that provides comic ballast for the play's serious themes. Major Cypress, for example, loves to tell the story of being revealed by Sir George Euston during an assignation with Harriet, the event which prompted the divorce. When asked to explain his presence, Cypress replies, 'I protest my being in that closet was entirely owing to "I'll tell you what" – In short to an – an *undescribable something* – There I made a full stop'.[24] Although Cypress retells this story in order to trumpet his victory over the embarrassed husband, his acquaintance Colonel Downright fails to find it funny.

Eventually, the moral bankruptcy of Cypress becomes public when the new Lady Euston arranges to have Sir George discovered in exactly the same situation by Major Cypress. Lady Euston thus avenges her husband's honour and humiliates Major Cypress for attempting to seduce her. This tightly constructed verbal and visual joke asks the characters and the audience to consider the dangers of relationships 'formed on vice'. Like her *Wives as They Were, Maids as They Are* (CG, 1797), Inchbald raises questions about what we can find funny. In *Wives*, for example, Lord Priory tests his 'old-fashioned' wife to the point of endangering her safety, while the modern 'maid', Miss Dorrillon, illustrates the dangers in store for single women made vulnerable by gambling debts. Inchbald calls readers and viewers to question rigid assumptions about female submission to husbands and fathers in favour of a more supple and humane ethics.

Inchbald's work as a critic overlaps with Joanna Baillie's contributions to drama and dramatic theory, particularly her *Plays on the Passions*, each of which explores a particular emotion, among them, love, hatred and greed. Baillie's movement between the 'closet' and the stage reminds us that plays were designed to be read as well as seen, a theme of Inchbald's criticism as well. Baillie had a genuine interest in the theatre of the imagination and recognised 'the closet's dramatic potential'.[25] She explored domestic relationships as a site of tension between public roles and private bonds. *De Monfort* (DL, 1800) was Baillie's play upon the passion of hatred. Inchbald declared Baillie 'a woman of genius' for having written it, though she found Baillie a better theorist than a playwright.[26] This conversation between De Monfort and his sister Jane, after a confrontation with his enemy, Rezenvelt, at a masquerade, shows the kind of exchange characteristic of her work:

> DE MONFORT: ... Oh curse that villain! that detested villain!
> He hath spread mis'ry o'er my fated life:
> He will undo us all.
> JANE: ... hideous passion tears thee from my heart,
> Blasting thy worth. – I cannot strive with this.
> DE MONFORT: (*affectionately*) What shall I do?[27]

De Monfort is, in one sense, an anti-marriage play, turning on a brother's deep-seated hatred for and eventual murder of the man who would court his sister. It closes on a scene at once chaste and incestuous, as De Monfort leads his sister Jane from the stage, literally walking outside the marriage plot: John Philip Kemble and his sister Sarah Siddons performed these roles to great critical acclaim. While Inchbald stretched the marriage plot to its breaking point, Baillie's experimental plays showed that she was willing to break with it altogether. Baillie wanted what she called 'Characteristick Comedy', the discovery of the human heart which happens when characters work through trying situations.[28] At the heart of these rich psychological plays are emotions, delineated in both 'their bold and prominent features' and through 'those minute and delicate traits which ... are the most difficult of all to counterfeit'.[29]

The work of late eighteenth-century female playwrights displays an awareness of the social experiences of women as well as creative responses to their situations. But ultimately, we are more likely to see genre bending than gender bending in their approaches to the position of women. The domestic matters at the heart of comedy provided material for creative compromises as well as direct critiques of social mores and norms. Navigating between social conventions and generic expectations, these playwrights speak to private and public failures of justice through plays which attempt to draw their characters into ethical communities and, when they cannot, to stretch the boundaries of genre in search of other ways to tell the story.

NOTES

1. Shirley Strum Kenny, 'Humane Comedy', *Modern Philology* 75:1 (August 1977), pp. 29–43.
2. Mary Poovey, *The Proper Lady and the Woman Writer: Ideology as Style in the Works of Mary Wollstonecraft, Mary Shelley, and Jane Austen*, Chicago: University of Chicago Press, 1984.
3. Charles Burney to Frances Burney, Egerton MS 3690 4–5, quoted in Margaret Doody, *Frances Burney: The Life in the Works*, New Brunswick, NJ: Rutgers University Press, 1988, p. 96.
4. *Times*, 17 February 1786.
5. Oliver Goldsmith, *An Essay on the Theatre; or, A Comparison between Laughing and Sentimental Comedy* in *The Collected Works of Oliver Goldsmith*, ed. Arthur Friedman, 5 vols., Oxford: Clarendon Press, 1966, vol. III, p. 212.
6. Review of *I'll Tell You What*, *English Review* VIII (November 1786), 378.
7. Ellen Donkin, *Getting into the Act: Women Playwrights in London, 1776–1829*, London: Routledge, 1995, p. 102.
8. The prologue to Hannah More's *Percy* 'begs' the favour of her audience; Hannah Cowley proposes to 'bribe' her audience to listen to the 'not very common' voice of a female dramatist; Harriet Lee 'hopes, what she dares not expect' (indulgence) in her preface to her comedy *The New Peerage* (1787) and Susanna Centlivre asks her audience to 'Be kind, and bear a woman's treat tonight ... and none but woman-haters damn this play' in the prologue to *The Busie Body*.

9. Donkin, *Getting into the Act*, p. 186.

10. Figures for Cowley's profits are drawn from *The London Stage 1660–1800: A Calendar of Plays, Entertainments and Afterpieces*, eds. William Van Lennep et al., Carbondale, IL: Southern Illinois University Press, 1960–68, parts 4 and 5; Inchbald's come from James Boaden's *Memoirs of Mrs. Inchbald*, London: Richard Bentley, 1833.

11. Susan Bennett, 'Genre Trouble: Joanna Baillie, Elizabeth Polack – Tragic Subjects, Melodramatic Subjects', in *Women and Playwriting in Nineteenth-Century Britain*, eds. Tracy C. Davis and Ellen Donkin, Cambridge: Cambridge University Press, 1999, pp. 215–32, 215.

12. Frances Sheridan, *The Plays of Frances Sheridan*, eds. Robert Hogan and Jerry C. Beasley, Newark, DE: University of Delaware Press, 1984, Act I, scene ii, p. 46. Subsequent references are cited within the text.

13. Sheridan, *The Plays of Frances Sheridan*, p. 35.

14. This was Samuel Crisp's advice to Burney about limiting her freedoms for the sake of propriety. See Charlotte Barrett, (ed.), *The Diary and Letters of Madame d'Arblay*, 7 vols., London: Henry Colburn, 1854, vol. I, p. 38.

15. Doody, *Frances Burney*, pp. 77–8.

16. *The Woman Hater*, Berg Manuscript Collection, New York Public Library. All of Burney's plays are now available in *The Complete Plays of Frances Burney*, eds. Stewart J. Cooke, Geoffrey M. Sill and Peter Sabor, 2 vols., Montreal: McGill-Queen's University Press, 1995.

17. Lisa A. Freeman, *Character's Theater: Genre and Identity on the Eighteenth-Century English Stage*, Philadelphia, PA: University of Pennsylvania Press, 2002, p. 183.

18. Hannah More, *Percy*, London: T. Cadell, 1778, Act III, p. 45.

19. Melinda Finberg, (ed.), *Eighteenth-Century Women Dramatists*, New York: Oxford University Press, 2001, p. xxix.

20. Hannah Cowley, *Which is the Man?* London: C. Dilly, 1783, Act I, scene i, p. 4. Subsequent references are cited within the text.

21. Daniel O'Quinn, 'Inchbald's Indies: Domestic and Dramatic Re-Orientations', *European Romantic Review* 9:2 (Spring 1998), pp. 217–30 and Betsy Bolton, *Women, Nationalism, and the Romantic Stage: Theatre and Politics in Britain, 1780–1800*, Cambridge: Cambridge University Press, 2001.

22. Elizabeth Inchbald, 'Remarks on *The Conscious Lovers*'; reprinted in *Remarks for the British Theatre (1806–1809), by Elizabeth Inchbald*, introduction by Cecilia Macheski, Delmar, NY: Scholars' Facsimiles and Reprints, 1990.

23. Thomas C. Crochunis, 'Authorial Performances in the Criticism and Theory of Romantic Women Playwrights', in *Women in British Romantic Theatre: Drama, Performance, and Society, 1790–1840*, ed. Catherine B. Burroughs, Cambridge: Cambridge University Press, 2000, pp. 223–54.

24. Elizabeth Inchbald, *I'll Tell You What*, London: G. G. J. & J. Robinson, 1786, Act I, scene iii, p. 18.

25. Catherine B. Burroughs, *Closet Stages: Joanna Baillie and the Theatre Theory of British Romantic Women Writers*, Philadelphia, PA: University of Pennsylvania Press, 1997, p. 91.

26. Elizabeth Inchbald, 'Remarks on *De Monfort*' reprinted in *Remarks for the British Theatre*.

27. Joanna Baillie, *De Monfort*, in *Five Romantic Plays*, ed. Paul Baines and Edward Burns, Oxford: Oxford University Press, 2000, Act II, scene ii, p. 136.

28. Joanna Baillie, 'Introductory Discourse' to *A Series of Plays: In Which it is Attempted to Delineate the Stronger Passions of the Mind*, London: T. Cadell and W. Davies, 1798, p. 49.

29. Baillie, 'Introductory Discourse', p. 59.

11

LAURA J. ROSENTHAL

Entertaining women: the actress in eighteenth-century theatre and culture

Actresses and sexual reputation

When English women first appeared on the public stage at the Restoration, some critics slighted them, in part by calling them whores. By the eighteenth century, however, women's place in performance had been fully established: while many public spaces, such as the century's famous coffee houses, excluded women, the playhouse simply could not function without them. Contemporary responses, nevertheless, remind us of the continuing volatility of the female body on stage – a result, at least in part, of the actress's indirect challenge to gender expectations.

Of course, all performers in this period became vulnerable to speculations about their personal lives.[1] Yet sexual suspicion occupied an even greater part of the response to actresses: it is difficult to find a biography of an actress that does not devote significant energy to positioning its subject somewhere on (or off) the spectrum of female virtue.[2] Critics have therefore debated whether contemporaries considered actresses as 'prostitutes or ladies', as 'reified objects or emergent professionals'.[3] We need, however, to place this important question in the broader context of changing constructions of gender, the marketplace and the distinctiveness of eighteenth-century theatre culture instead of debating what might be a false opposition. By doing so, we can arrive at a more nuanced reading of the intertwined reputations of these two female professions (acting and prostitution) and thus achieve a better understanding of the actress's cultural position. The emergence in this period of an urban media culture, which offered to paying consumers an unprecedented variety of entertainment, located theatre as one choice in an expanding cultural market which ranged from the virtuous to the lurid.[4] While conforming in some ways to the new bourgeois rhetoric of propriety, the stage also offered an intriguing though sometimes scandalous alternative to traditional hierarchies of rank and emerging ideologies of gender.

Actresses made their first appearance on the English commercial stage at a moment of larger cultural and aesthetic changes in the theatre. Visual pleasure, in the form of elaborate sets and lavish costumes, became central to the Restoration stage. Intricately costumed and coiffed female (and male) bodies attracted the admiring gaze of spectators. Comic types, such as the fop and the fine lady, revealed their foibles through their costumes, and tragic kings and queens often appeared in aristocratic cast-offs. Dances, special effects and new costume elements, such as Colley Cibber's giant fop peruke and David Garrick's 'fright wig', in which hairs stood on end, attracted audiences. Some critics have thus suggested that this period initiated the modern dynamic of looking, in which the bodies on stage became increasingly vulnerable to visual and sexual objectification.[5] The exposure of female bodies to the male gaze tended to associate actresses with prostitution regardless of their behaviour off stage. Certainly we find no shortage of sexually degrading remarks in either the Restoration or the eighteenth century. But to describe actresses as objectified underestimates the agency, power and privilege some of them enjoyed. Female performers travelled in the most elite circles, sometimes rubbing elbows with aristocrats and even royalty. As Felicity Nussbaum points out, '[t]hough early actresses were underpaid and earned significantly less than men ... the most celebrated women players in the eighteenth century could make more from acting than many male thespians, more than men who laboured in other trades, and – most significantly – more money than any other working women up to that point in history.'[6] With their disposable incomes, leading actresses could perform gentility in key ways: they became philanthropists and patrons of the arts; they borrowed and invested; on occasion they even purchased country estates.

The roles available to women on the eighteenth-century as opposed to the Restoration stage offered the opportunity for a different range of gender performances. The bawdiness of Restoration comedies and the theatre's libertine culture had left little doubt about the sexuality of most female performers. In the eighteenth century, however, the cultural landscape changed, placing greater emphasis on bourgeois propriety as the middle class became more powerful. The popular domestic novel, born in this period, insisted that virtue would find its reward and vice its punishment. The stage came under pressure to reform: *The Country Girl* (DL, 1766), David Garrick's cleaned-up version of William Wycherley's sexually explicit *The Country Wife*, took the place of the original until the beginning of the twentieth century. Playwrights created more sentimental and less overtly sexualised roles for women, diminishing (but not erasing) assumptions about the actress's sexual availability.

Nevertheless, eighteenth-century culture continued to associate actresses with prostitutes, but for reasons not confined to, or even necessarily dominated by, prurience and moral scandal. While Restoration theatre remained profoundly associated with the court, the eighteenth-century stage found its home in the broad spectrum of commercial entertainments in London's urban culture which commodified 'vice' and 'virtue' in the same marketplace. For print entertainment, readers could buy newspapers, domestic novels, scandalous diatribes, conduct books, collections of sermons, political pamphlets and, for the first time, pornography.[7] Guides to brothels describing individual prostitutes and their particular features became available. Those searching for live entertainment could witness David Garrick performing Hamlet, a troupe of rope-dancers, a cross-dressed version of *The Beggar's Opera* or, in a more discreet setting, posture girls who struck erotic poses in various states of undress. As a regular consumer of entertainment, James Boswell was particularly thrilled to be admitted as a lover by 'that delicious subject of gallantry, an actress', a great coup from his perspective.[8] Reformers divided these kinds of pleasure by their moral content and critics attempted to distinguish high-quality 'rational' forms from low pandering; the marketplace, however, offered its own distinction between successful and unsuccessful forms that could cut across other kinds of divisions. In this context, elite actresses and elite prostitutes came to share a unique and unprecedented kind of celebrity status.

Joseph Roach has observed that 'the celebrity of eighteenth-century actors and actresses was at least anticipatory and perhaps generative of modern celebrity because their images began to circulate widely in the absence of their persons, a privilege once reserved to duly anointed sovereigns and saints'.[9] Images of elite prostitutes, however, also circulated briskly. While Restoration writers represented prostitutes as uncontrolled and overly indulgent, eighteenth-century writers were just as likely to see them as social performers, trendsetters and even fashion plates.[10] Like actresses, famous prostitutes had their portraits painted by renowned artists; their likenesses were also reproduced in less expensive popular prints. Descriptions of their characteristics appeared in Harris's *List of Covent Garden Ladies*, a guide to London brothels. Similarly, information about actresses reached the public through an expanding print culture in the form of reviews, satire, encomiums, biographies and autobiographies. Publications like *The Secret History of the Green Room* (1792) offered brief accounts of performers and gossip about their personal lives. Some actor/actress narratives functioned as scandal sheets, but others, especially toward the end of the century, became nearly hagiographic. Like some actresses, prostitutes such as Margaret Leeson, Ann Sheldon and Teresia Constantia Phillips published the stories of their own careers. Phillips's *Apology* for her life seems deliberately to echo the famous *Apology* of the actor-manager Colley Cibber. Other high-profile prostitutes, such as Fanny Murray, Kitty Fisher, Sally Salisbury and Fanny Davies, attracted unauthorised biographies. These two genres – the actress narrative and the prostitute narrative – become intertwined and sometimes even indistinguishable. Certain women, such as Ann Catley, Lavinia Fenton and Mrs Clarke, it seems, graduated from prostitution to the stage. Some of these narratives even represent the stage as a less profitable choice than prostitution. The elite courtesan Sally Salisbury was reportedly encouraged to translate her popularity into a stage career, but apparently felt that acting would be beneath her. According to her unauthorised *Juvenile Adventures* (1759), the high-profile courtesan Kitty Fisher, painted by Joshua Reynolds most famously and theatrically as Cleopatra, tried to make this shift, but concluded that a stage career would not support her in the style to which she had become accustomed. Her theatrical training, however, did not go to waste: when she later ran out of money and had to hide from her creditors, she posed successfully as an Italian castrato. The intersecting cultural position of certain eighteenth-century actresses and prostitutes, then, was not necessarily a degraded one.

Actress and prostitute memoirs commonly make similar claims on the reader's sympathies. In her memoirs, the actress George Anne Bellamy represents herself as a sentimental heroine and victim of male perfidy. This account strongly resembles that of the prostitute Ann Sheldon, who published her own life story five years after Bellamy's appeared (although the authorship of these accounts is not confirmed). According to this narrative, Bellamy fell into disrepute after having been abducted by an Earl. Rescued by her brother, she nevertheless lost her reputation, although this loss does not seem to have damaged her theatrical career. Such narratives offer surprisingly little discussion of actual performances. Instead, Bellamy recounts the highs and lows of her economic fortunes: her debts, earnings from the stage and her exploitation by men. Ann Sheldon's story offers some of the same attractions as Bellamy's: gossip about elite society, stories of female suffering and male perfidy, mild forms of erotic and voyeuristic pleasure. In particular, it takes up the problem of the economic survival of a woman without, or with insufficient, spousal or familial support. Like Bellamy, Sheldon claims her own innocence but narrates her scandals. Both memoirs constantly remind readers of financial exigency; both express a desire for virtue (Bellamy often returns with great pleasure to the convent in which she was educated; Sheldon reports her numerous small charitable acts); both record their falls into disrepute as partly tragic. In each case, pathos and triumph provide a combination of sentimental and scandalous entertainment.

Thus while moralists in the period may have divided women sharply between the virtuous and the disreputable, the theatre offered a third

11. *Dora Jordan in the character of Hypolita* by John Jones after J. Hoppner.

possibility of glamorous, independent woman with a mixed sexual reputation. This possibility inevitably became associated with other women who crossed the boundaries of gendered expectations. One such woman, in fact, dominated comic acting at the end of the century. Dora Jordan, who openly carried on an affair with Prince William (and other men before him), endured ridicule for her sexual behaviour, her Irish origins and her illegitimacy, but nevertheless triumphed on the stage and travelled in the most elite circles. Her career offers an informative comparison with that of Nell Gwyn in the Restoration. From her humble origins, Jordan became successful on stage and then attracted the love of a prince. Unlike Gwyn, who left the stage when she took up with Charles, Jordan continued acting during her affair with Prince William, later to become King William IV. According to her modern biographer, Jordan did so at least in part because she needed the money, supporting herself, her thirteen children and sometimes the prince as well.[11] Audiences loved to watch Jordan, but they also loved to watch William watching Jordan; their relationship, then, became incorporated into the evening's entertainment. During the same years, the incomparable Sarah Siddons emerged as a different kind of actress: serious, virtuous and maternal. Much contemporary praise of Siddons links the emotional power of her performance to her sexual virtue and maternal devotion. The end of the century thus offered to audiences both the scandalous comic energy of Dora Jordan and the tragic power of Sarah Siddons.

The cultural authority of the actress

The example of Sarah Siddons reminds us that drama belonged to a highly respectable literary and cultural tradition that held force in tandem with its scandalous elements. Certain actors, Joseph Roach has demonstrated, acquired the aura of dignity, power and authority from the roles they played, radiating the importance they imitated on stage.[12] David Garrick gained an unprecedented level of cultural capital not only by playing Shakespearean tragic heroes, but also through his revival of 'authentic' productions (as opposed to the adaptations more commonly performed) and his success in presenting himself as the public preserver of Shakespeare's memory.[13] Playing Hamlet associated Garrick with the crisis of an heir facing dispossession; playing Lear associated him with the burden of royalty. But did this authorising effect extend to women? Women, of course, rarely became involved in the management of theatres, an activity which brought Garrick much of his reputation and helped him to construct his public persona. On stage, as Roach explains, this dignifying effect depended on performing figures of crucial importance to the nation, usually kings or heirs to the throne. Women tended to hold less exalted positions in contemporary tragedies. The popular 'she-tragedies', while placing women in roles of key importance, often represented a woman's downfall in part through her sexual transgression. Some eighteenth-century tragedies feature women as heads of state, but often as evil, destructive ones who must be replaced by proper male leaders. Many tell stories of socially important women wrestling with a private dilemma rather than a crisis of state or succession or explore the private woes engendered by such conflicts, as in the case of Sarah Siddons's celebrated expression of maternal agonies in the role of Lady Randolph in Home's *Douglas*. Other tragedies, such as George Lillo's popular *The London Merchant*, divide women sharply into nefarious seductresses and virtuous maidens. Thus in general, the kind of cultural authority that male tragic actors acquired by playing heads of state did not consistently become available to women in the same way. Lisa Freeman, in fact, has argued that the eighteenth century defined tragedy, the genre traditionally devoted to expressing national identity, specifically through its marginalisation of the feminine.[14]

But while Roach's observations about the careers of actors might not fully extend to actresses, they still carry significance. All actresses regularly portrayed figures from high life, even though they themselves came from a range of social classes. Any successful actress therefore had to absorb and reproduce the complex manners of the elite, or at least of the highly respectable. Manners themselves became one of the great objects of interest in comedy, the genre in which women arguably made the greatest impact and which sometimes challenged, or at least troubled, contemporary gender ideologies. Margaret Woffington, for example, had been selling vegetables in the streets when the manager of a children's troupe offered her a position; she soon became a favourite of Dublin audiences. Her breakthrough into celebrity, however, came with the role of Sir Harry Wildair in George Farquhar's play *The Constant Couple*, which she chose as her London debut in 1738 and long continued to play: if Woffington should die, one critic declared, 'the play must die with her'.[15] There must have been something wickedly exciting, irreverent and even subversive about watching Woffington appropriate and perhaps ironise the swagger and bravado of this rake, destabilising gender identities in performance just as celebrity actresses challenged dominant assumptions about gender in eighteenth-century culture. A wealthy heir and avowed man of pleasure, Harry courts the disreputable Lady Lurewell and the virtuous Angellica, whom he comically mistakes for a prostitute. One popular anecdote captures the conflicts of gender Woffington produced in the role:

> Upon her coming off the stage, in the character of Sir Harry Wildair, [Woffington] said, with no little triumph, 'Lord, I believe the whole house think I am a man.' – 'By G-d, Madam,' says [James Quin], 'half the house knows the contrary.'[16]

William Hogarth later painted her in this role. Perhaps inspired by her success as Wildair, Woffington went on to play Lothario in *The Fair Penitent*.

Woffington became enormously powerful, negotiating between the two patent theatres for the best salary, supporting her mother in style and providing her younger sister with a genteel education. Tate Wilkinson called her 'the queen bee of the hive'.[17] She attracted admirers from the highest ranks of society and cohabited for a while with David Garrick, but never married. Contemporaries praised her wit and skill, remarking that 'she was an excellent actress in genteel comedy, and even in tragedy';[18] another declared that 'this lady's conversation was no less anxiously courted by men of wit and genius, than by men of pleasure'.[19] But hard as she worked for this kind of praise, she did not escape contempt for her origins. One writer reported that Woffington, after 'some theatrical squabbles ... set out for Dublin, where her beauty alone was an adequate certificate of her abilities. This actress had strong parts, but a low education. Her wit and spirits were formed on gross vulgarity.'[20] Similarly, Tate Wilkinson insisted that, though 'beautiful to a degree', Woffington had 'a most unpleasant squeaking voice'. Wilkinson, however, also praised her for always keeping her feet on the ground in spite of her celebrity. He found 'not the least defect in her duty to the public as a performer' noting that she often performed six nights a week, and willingly took on minor parts when called upon to do so.[21]

Elizabeth Farren, who took over many of Woffington's parts a generation later, forms an instructive contrast. Also of Irish extraction, Farren came from a respectable family that had fallen on hard times. While Woffington seems to have taken lovers freely and openly, Farren assiduously retained her reputation for virtue. She always travelled and attended social events in the company of her mother to ward off rumour. Many men courted her, but Lord Derby, estranged from his wife, remained her constant admirer. When Derby's wife died, Farren left the stage to become the Countess of Derby. Her spectacular upward mobility was not unprecedented: Lavinia Fenton, the original Polly Peachum in *The Beggar's Opera*, married the Duke of Bolton. Both women 'had the good fortune to be transferred from the mimic grandeur of the Stage to the real splendors of a Court'. But even before her marriage Farren was socialising with the elite, overseeing private theatricals in aristocratic households and being 'caressed, by a very long list of Fashionables'.[22]

Comparisons between Woffington and Farren regularly noted the difference between their sexual reputations and social origins. Tate Wilkinson praised Woffington and Farren as equally beautiful, elegant, well bred and witty. But while Farren had a 'musical and bewitching' voice, Woffington's was considered harsh, broken and discordant; Woffington could be 'rude and vulgar', Farren, 'never'.[23] Horace Walpole greatly admired Farren because he believed that only persons of genteel extraction could convincingly portray genteel figures on stage: 'when people of quality can act, they must act their own parts so much better than others can mimic them'. Another critic similarly praised Farren's Lady Teazle: 'It was Miss Farren's perfect intimacy with the better born that made her the accomplished woman of fashion she represented.'[24] Farren seems to have embodied the ideal of refined womanhood, a capacity variously associated with her birth and her blood. She possessed

> irresistible graces of her address and manner, the polished beauties of action and gait, and all the indescribable little charms which give fascination to the woman of birth and fashion.[25]

Some critics, then, tried to insist on genteel manners as ultimately inimitable: only women of proper virtue and proper extraction could possess them. Yet the fact that this case had to be made, and that actresses from humbler origins sometimes succeeded, pointed to class identity itself as conditional and performative. Beauty alone was never enough to qualify a woman for the stage: Woffington's sister, who apparently possessed equal attractions and benefited from her genteel education, failed in her attempt at a stage career. Hannah Pritchard, by contrast, succeeded in spite of her lack of conventional beauty: 'her manner and person were clumsy', recalls Tate Wilkinson, 'her face not delicate, but open and agreeable; yet with that large figure, she in comedy, nay, even in the Fine Ladies, threw all competitors at a distance'.[26] Pritchard created what became known as the signature gesture of Lady Macbeth when she decided to put down the candle to rub the imaginary blood spots off her hands, an innovation which attracted considerable discussion. She also remained popular in the title role of Jane Shore, even though some critics complained that her bulk rendered unconvincing Jane's starvation at the end of the play. Like their male counterparts, many actresses continued performing as they aged, sometimes taking more matronly parts but also sometimes continuing to play young girls. In general, actresses do not seem to have taken time off during their pregnancies and continued to portray virgins in spite of their gravid states. While alluring female bodies on stage certainly could become fetishised, actresses were successful in establishing their value through the stage effects they were able to produce.

The kind of living a woman could make from acting varied tremendously depending on her ability to draw in audiences. Performers such as Sarah Siddons who reliably packed the house earned spectacular salaries: contemporaries reported how fans fainted away from 'Siddons fever'. Any company that hired Siddons knew that it would get a return on its investment: audiences did not simply go to see *Macbeth*, but to see Siddons in *Macbeth*. Her wealth became as legendary as her genius and virtue. Most actresses, however, never reached anywhere near this level. As a result, some turned to support from wealthy male patrons, some accepted lesser forms of compensation and others supplemented their incomes with writing or other careers. Elizabeth Inchbald, Susanna Centlivre and Eliza Haywood, for example,

12. David Garrick as Macbeth and Hannah Pritchard as Lady Macbeth in *Macbeth* by Johann Zoffany.

acted on stage and also wrote plays. The actress Charlotte Charke's autobiography offers a long list of the author's strategies for making ends meet, including work as a sausage seller, a pastry cook, a waiter and a farmer. In addition to her successful stage career, Hannah Pritchard also ran Pritchard's Warehouse in Tavistock Street, where she sold fashionable attire for use on stage and off. In this dual capacity, she could advertise her company's clothes by wearing them on stage; the Warehouse, in turn, sold tickets for her benefits.[27]

Actresses in the plays

Playwrights took full advantage of the gender and class instability performed by eighteenth-century actresses, particularly in comedies. Like the earlier *Constant Couple* in which Woffington starred, several plays towards the end of the century include plots in which prostitutes and ladies become mistaken for each other. In Oliver Goldsmith's *She Stoops to Conquer: or, The Mistakes of a Night* (1773), for example, the plot turns on whether

Marlowe recognises Kate as a virtuous maiden or a whorish barmaid. Elizabeth Farren played this role in her London debut, and surely her own virtuous reputation, obscure origin and refined manners shaped the reception of her performance. Goldsmith's play, written partly in response to criticism of his earlier work for allowing 'low' manners on the stage, gently challenges the norms of respectability becoming prevalent in domestic fiction and in the dominant culture. In Act V, Kate realises that Marlowe has been disabused of Tony Lumpkin's trick and deftly switches to the new persona of a virtuous poor relation. But in Acts I–IV, she is only able to attract Marlowe's attention by deciding to resemble 'one of the dutchesses of Drury Lane' (Act II, scene i, p. 131) – that is, a prostitute and the kind of woman to whom Marlowe is capable of directing his sexual interest. This image of the 'dutchess of Drury Lane' suggests the eroticism of pairing the high and the low. Kate's disguise may have reminded spectators of reports about the inverse of Kate Hardcastle's efforts in which Drury Lane prostitutes impersonated particular elite ladies. When Hastings objects that Marlowe might rob an innocent barmaid of her honour, Marlowe responds, 'I don't intend to rob her . . . there's nothing in this house I shan't honestly pay for' (Act IV, scene i, pp. 59–61).

At a moment when performers were often suspected of selling their favours off-stage, the difference between paying and not paying becomes the comic point on which the entire play precariously balances. The brilliance of Goldsmith's dark humour lies in our double response to Marlowe's treatment of both Kate and her father. When Marlowe, for example, imperiously demands to see the menu, the joke lies first in Mr Hardcastle's comic outrage and our own squirming sense of Marlowe's faux pas. Beyond that, however, such scenes also raise the issue of how commercial relations transform human relations as they are expressed through manners. Marlowe's condescension toward Hardcastle is painfully comic, but also bitingly suggests that the young cosmopolitan had probably become accustomed to treating many kinds of people with similar arrogance. At the centre of these points of confusion lies the question of whether Kate's sexuality is available or not. Kate does not so much 'cure' Marlowe, as is often argued, as accurately assess his fetish, indicating that she can both indulge it and protect his outward respectability. While her deception may humiliate Marlowe, she wins him as a husband by demonstrating her ability to give a convincing performance as a whore. On stage, the audience sees an actress of relatively obscure origins master elite manners convincingly to play a respectable daughter; the respectable daughter, in turn, figures out that she must master the manners of a whore and a humbly-born maid in order to capture – and maintain – the desirable husband. With little money herself, Kate must rely on a good marriage. Though in domestic novels of the period such proximity to prostitution would cause unredeemable scandal, actresses and the characters they played teasingly explored this grey area between the extreme possibilities of female reputation.

We find this kind of exploration in plays written by women as well as by men. Hannah Cowley's *The Belle's Stratagem* (CG, 1780) offers a version of this plot that explicitly begs comparison to similar Restoration plots. The play's title, of course, echoes *The Beaux' Stratagem* (Queen's Theatre, Haymarket, 1707) by George Farquhar. Letitia and Doricourt have grown up together and their families long ago agreed to their marriage. Doricourt, however, has become thoroughly cosmopolitan after taking the grand tour, and he now loves French elegance and sophistication. He becomes convinced that the homespun Letitia will no longer hold his attention. Letitia responds by disguising herself as a mysterious, sophisticated lady, rumoured to be the mistress of a wealthy man. In another plot, Saville foils Courtall's attempt to seduce Lady Touchwood by replacing her with a prostitute named Kitty Willis at the key moment. Both of these plots, then, turn on substitutions between proper ladies and disreputable ones.

In her character names and in her title, Cowley evokes Restoration comedy; her plots recall Restoration strategic confusions between ladies and prostitutes, especially in Aphra Behn. In *The Feigned Courtesans* (1679), for example, three respectable women disguise themselves as prostitutes in order to escape unappealing marriages and attract the attention of different men. Similarly in *The Rover* (performed at court, 1677), Hellena disguises herself as a gypsy in order to escape her destiny as a nun. In this play, Behn portrays the prostitute Angellica Bianca, with whom Hellena competes for the affections of Willmore, with unusual sympathy. Nevertheless, we also see a stark distinction between respectable ladies and prostitutes which becomes less absolute in Cowley's hands. In Behn's plays, women disguise themselves as prostitutes in order to gain freedom – in particular, a kind of sexual freedom that would not be available otherwise. As a prostitute Angellica simply seduces Willmore; as an heiress, Hellena can only do so in disguise. Further, the ability to distinguish a prostitute from a respectable lady consistently reveals the difference between the savvy men and the buffoons. The prostitute Lucetta seduces the foolish Blunt by presenting herself to him as a respectable lady. Willmore reveals his own foolishness when he actually tries to rape the romantic heroine Florinda, who is engaged to his friend Belville. Blunt, however, becomes the play's laughing-stock because of his complete inability to distinguish between these kinds of women.

Cowley at first appears to be doing something similar with Courtall and Lady Touchwood. Courtall disguises himself as Lord Touchwood to take his 'wife' home, but just when she is about to step into the coach, at which point, presumably, she would have had no recourse, Saville replaces her with Kitty Willis in the same dress and mask. Thus later in the play when Courtall emerges proudly from his bedroom after seducing 'Lady Touchwood,' he becomes, like Blunt, the laughing-stock of his friends when Kitty Willis shows herself. There are, however, key differences between the two scenes. First, Kitty Willis is clearly a figure for a famous prostitute, such as Fanny Murray or Kitty Fisher, whom everyone recognises; Lucetta, by contrast is an anonymous streetwalker who complains to her pimp that he didn't even let her sleep with Blunt. Further, unlike Lucetta or Angellica Bianca, Kitty Willis has no erotic stake in the dramatic action: she merely plays a role here like any other prostitute or actress. Courtall, however, makes his mistake because in disguise these women truly are identical, and neither has any desire to sleep with him; by contrast, sexuality drives both Lucetta and Angellica Bianca to some extent. In Behn, then, prostitution becomes a figure for female desire; in Cowley, prostitution appears consistently as a kind of performance.

The difference becomes even more clear in the main plot. Letitia, unlike Behn's heroines, is not in conflict with her father over her marital choice: she only wishes to reinstate herself in Doricourt's affections. A plain, sexually innocent girl, however, has insufficient attraction for him. Letitia, then, disguises herself as a 'demi-rep' (a fashionable lady with a equivocal sexual reputation) not in order to rebel against her father's wishes or to fulfil her own erotic desires, but instead to prove that she can be sexually interesting enough to hold Doricourt's attention. Her impersonation of a prostitute does not undermine her reputation because it is not an expression of sexual desire; rather, it only proves, as Kate does for Marlowe in *She Stoops to Conquer*, her willingness and ability to act in a way which appeals to the man her father wants her to marry. Letitia, then, demonstrates her ability to master a particular kind of performance which has nothing to do with her truly 'virtuous' character. Behn often reveals the extent to which fathers and brothers can treat daughters and sisters as prostitutes or as tokens of exchange. The women in her plays, however, often enjoy impersonating prostitutes for the opportunity it provides to express or even fulfil their sexual desires. Letitia and Kate, by contrast, have more practical goals: they are interested in securing advantageous marriages by making themselves attractive to wayward suitors. For each of these characters, proving that she can act a bit like a whore makes her a better potential wife. For Letitia and Kate, then, becoming an actress and becoming a 'prostitute' constitute more or less the same kind of project. While in Behn such a disguise represented a way for oppressed women to express their sexuality, these later eighteenth-century plays represent actresses and prostitutes less as embodiments of transgressive female desire than as experts in pleasing performance. Eighteenth-century theatre thus confronts certain issues which fiction tends to mystify, representing acting, prostitution and securing a husband as different ways for a woman to make a living in an increasingly commercialised culture.

NOTES

1. Kristina Straub, *Sexual Suspects: Eighteenth-Century Players and Sexual Ideology*, Princeton, NJ: Princeton University Press, 1992.
2. See further Cheryl Wanko, *Roles of Authority: Thesbian Biography and Celebrity in Eighteenth-Century Britain*, Lubbock, TX: Texas Tech. University Press, 2003, p. 56.
3. Compare the viewpoints of Kimberly Crouch, 'The Public Life of Actresses: Prostitutes or Ladies?', in *Gender in Eighteenth-Century England: Roles, Representations, and Responsibilities*, eds. Hannah Barker and Elaine Chalus, London: Longman, 1997, pp. 58–100 and Deborah C. Payne, 'Reified Object or Emergent Professional? Retheorizing the Restoration Actress', in *Cultural Readings of Restoration and Eighteenth-Century English Theater*, eds. Douglas J. Canfield and Deborah C. Payne, Athens, GA: University of Georgia Press, 1995, pp. 24–38.
4. On the eighteenth century's media culture, see William B. Warner, *Licensing Entertainment: the Elevation of Novel Reading in Britain, 1684–1750*, Berkeley, CA: University of California Press, 1998.
5. See further Straub, *Sexual Suspects* and Elin Diamond, 'Gestus and Signature in Aphra Behn's *The Rover*', *English Literary History* 56:3 (1989), pp. 519–41.
6. Felicity Nussbaum, 'Actresses and the Economics of Celebrity, 1700–1800', in *Theatre and Celebrity in Britain, 1660–2000*, eds. Mary Luckhurst and Jane Moody, Basingstoke and New York: Palgrave, 2005, pp. 148–68, 155.
7. Lynn Hunt, 'Introduction', in *The Invention of Pornography: Obscenity and the Origins of Modernity, 1500–1800*, ed. Lynn Hunt, New York: Zone Books, 1993.
8. James Boswell, *Boswell's London Journal, 1762–1763*, second edn., ed. Frederick Pottle, New Haven, CT: Yale University Press, 2004, p. 94.
9. Joseph Roach, 'Patina: Mrs Siddons and the Depth of Surfaces', in *Notorious Muse: the Actress in British Art and Culture, 1776–1812*, ed. Robyn Asleson, New Haven, CT: Yale University Press, 2003, pp. 195–209.
10. See further Laura J. Rosenthal, *Infamous Commerce: Prostitution in Eighteenth-Century British Literature and Culture*, Ithaca, NY: Cornell University Press, 2006.
11. Claire Tomalin, *Mrs Jordan's Profession: the Actress and the Prince*, New York: Knopf, 1995, pp. 193–203.
12. Joseph Roach, *Cities of the Dead: Circum-Atlantic Performance*, New York: Columbia University Press, 1996, pp. 73–118.
13. On this point, see Michael Dobson, *The Making of the National Poet: Shakespeare, Adaptation and Authorship, 1660–1769*, Oxford: Clarendon Press, 1992, pp. 164–84.

14. Lisa A. Freeman, *Character's Theater: Genre and Identity on the Eighteenth-Century English Stage*, Philadelphia, PA: University of Pennsylvania Press, 2002, pp. 87–144.
15. John Jackson, *The History of the Scottish Stage, from its First Establishment to the Present Time*, Edinburgh: Peter Hill and G. G. J. and J. Robinson, 1793, pp. 335–6.
16. *The Life of Mr. James Quin, Comedian*, London: S. Bladon, 1766, p. 68.
17. Tate Wilkinson, *Memoirs of His Own Life*, 4 vols., York: Wilson, Spence and Mawman, 1790, vol. I, p. 104.
18. *Life of Mr. James Quin*, p. 67.
19. Robert Bisset, *The Life of Edmund Burke*, London: G. Cawthorn, 1798, p. 26.
20. [Gentleman of Covent Garden Theatre], *Memoirs of George Anne Bellamy, Including All her Intrigues; with Genuine Anecdotes of All her Public and Private Connections*, London: L. Walker and J. Debrett, 1785, pp. 63–4.
21. Wilkinson, *Memoirs*, vol. I, pp. 25, 108.
22. *Memoirs of the Present Countess of Derby (Late Miss Farren)*, London: H. D. Symonds, n.d., p. 20.
23. Wilkinson, *Memoirs*, vol. I, p. 122.
24. Quoted by Suzanne Bloxam, *Walpole's Queen of Comedy: Elizabeth Farren, Countess of Derby*, Worcester: Billing & Sons, 1988, pp. 91, 150.
25. Quoted by Bloxam, *Walpole's Queen of Comedy*, p. 76.
26. Wilkinson, *Memoirs*, vol. I, p. 140.
27. Anthony Vaughan, *Born to Please: Hannah Pritchard, Actress, 1711–1768*, London: Society for Theatre Research, 1979, p. 65.

12

JULIE A. CARLSON

Race and profit in English theatre

1. In the black

Ripe for analysis is the startling fact that from the 1770s to the 1830s London patent theatre managers stood a good chance – often, their best chance – of being in the black by staging plays including black characters, topics or settings. Isaac Bickerstaffe's comic opera *The Padlock* (DL, 1768), famous for introducing the first blackface comic figure on the London stage, received fifty-four performances in its first season, 142 in its first nine years and instituted Mungo, the character's name, as a byword in late eighteenth-century cultural discourse. George Colman the Younger's version of *Inkle and Yarico* was not only the most popular new play in the 1787–88 season, but ultimately became the sixth most popular London mainpiece during the years 1776–1800. John Fawcett's pantomime *Obi; or, Three Finger'd Jack* (HM, 1800), featuring the rebellious activity of the escaped Jamaican slave, Jack Mansong, ran for thirty-nine nights in a single summer, the longest single season run for any play at the Haymarket between 1777 and 1811. In 1807 Drury Lane mounted a Christmas pantomime entitled *Furibond; or, Harlequin Negro* which enjoyed twenty-eight performances. Then there is the remarkable series of adaptations of Aphra Behn's *Oroonoko* that together comprise the second most frequently produced drama in the eight-eenth century, beginning with Thomas Southerne's *Oroonoko* (DL, 1695) and including plays by John Hawkesworth (DL, 1759), Francis Gentleman (Edinburgh, 1760; DL, 1769) and an unstaged adaptation by Dr John Ferriar entitled *The Prince of Angola* (1788). Isaac Bickerstaffe's *Love in the City* (CG, 1767) and Archibald McLaren's *The Negro Slaves; or, The Blackman and the Blackbird* (Edinburgh, 1799) both deal with African slavery. Other plays featuring 'Negroes' arguably introduced for what Herbert Marshall and Mildred Stock call their 'box-office appeal' include Matthew Lewis's hit, *The Castle Spectre* (DL, 1797), Hannah Cowley's *A Day in Turkey* (CG, 1791), William Macready's *The Irishman in London; or, the Happy African*

(CG, 1792) and Frederic Reynolds's *Laugh When You Can* (CG, 1798).[1] As Jeffrey Cox comments, a 'regular London theatregoer would have seen depictions of African characters or of slavery during perhaps every season of the eighteenth and early nineteenth century'.[2]

What are we to make of this 'box-office appeal' of 'Negroes' during the height of Britain's participation in the slave trade, when only a decade or so earlier London newspapers openly advertised 'Negro boys' for sale at English coffeehouses and published hue-and-cry advertisements for run-away slaves or servants?[3] Should we endorse the connection between 'box-office appeal' and 'intense Abolitionist activity' made by Marshall and Stock and conclude that the popularity of these black subjects helped set the stage for the emancipation of slaves in Britain and its colonies (1833)?[4] Does this popularity prefigure the entertainment industry's position as almost the only arena of financial success and cultural visibility for black people?[5] And is this phenomenon an example of the paradoxes that, according to Aranye Fradenburg, compose the phrase 'entertainment value' in its contradictory assertions that a) entertainment does have *some* kind of value, b) something that has entertainment value is not very valuable otherwise and c) this very lack of value is what gives entertainment its ability to enchant and manipulate both groups and individuals?[6] The phrase 'in the black' – one of the very few wholly positive associations ascribed to 'black' or 'blackness' in any period of Anglo-European culture – helps to open up an important and neglected area of theatrical history in the long eighteenth century.[7]

This chapter explores the questions raised above by analysing two arenas of black theatrical practice. One concerns stage representations of Othello, the best-known black character in British theatre, and his eighteenth-century incarnation in *Oroonoko*. The second concerns aspects of the career of George Colman the Younger, one of the period's most prolific managers and playwrights, whose penchant for turning a profit prompted him to stage two of the most popular plays featuring black characters: the comic opera, *Inkle and Yarico*, and a melodrama entitled *The Africans; or, War, Love, and Duty*. Exploring these two arenas together foregrounds generic changes in British theatre – from tragedy to comedy and farce, from 'pure' to hybrid forms – and the theatre's commentary on subjects foreign to England. Underlying what critics condemned as the 'decline of the drama', I want to argue, is the status of sympathy. To what extent does the embodiment of others elicit sympathy for them, and of what value is this sympathy? For an analysis of the in-the-blackness of London theatre reveals the tension between moral and entertainment value which William Hazlitt ascribes to the experience of going to the theatre, whereby spectators come to identify with characters, feelings and experiences which are foreign to them and, at the same time, satisfy their curiosity, voyeurism and delight in novelty.[8]

2. *Othello*, an enduring tragedy for black men

The trial of O. J. Simpson is the most spectacular recent example of *Othello*'s persistence as the paradigm for understanding black male and white female sexual relations, but the habit was already thriving in eighteenth-century Britain. Outside the theatre, several prominent free blacks living in Britain, especially Ignatius Sancho and Julius Soubise, are discussed widely and typecast as Othello in their amatory dealings with white women. Inside the theatre, stage representations of *Othello* display the play's leading role in negotiating attitudes toward blackness and particularly black masculinity in the wake of debates regarding British nationalism, identity and participation in slavery.

Cedric Robinson sets the context for this dynamic in his claim that *Othello* is the key text in 'the inventions of the Negro'.[9] *Othello* not only reflects British anxieties regarding blackness, whether in the period of its composition or at any moment in its stage history, but also analyses how and to what ends the invention of 'the Negro' manages such anxieties. For a consciousness still alive to the waning reality of Moorish dominance in sixteenth-century Europe, there is nothing incredible about Othello's initial characterisation as commander of the Venetian troops in Cyprus and the lover of Desdemona. The work of the play entails forgetting that history and installing another in which 'black' no longer connotes nobility, dignity or artistry, but inferiority, bestiality or servility – work that is performed by Iago in his conscious manipulation of lies regarding Desdemona's sexual infidelity and Othello's 'sub-humanity'. Once in circulation, as Robinson shows, these lies prove performative. Neither the inventor nor their target can fully disentangle these falsehoods from realities and the ensuing tragedy is history. Part of that tragic history involves ascribing sexual misconduct to black men.

This reformulation of black as 'Negro' is inseparable from, though not identical to, the history of Britain's participation in the African slave trade.[10] Robinson points out that the word 'Negro' was manufactured during the Atlantic slave trade: traders appropriated the term in the seventeenth century to 'signify "Black Africans, the Indians of India, Native Americans, Japanese, and slaves of whatever ancestry."'[11] The broad range of national and ethnic types that 'Negro' comes to designate paradoxically indicates the precision of its signifying function: to elevate whiteness so that it can appear distinguishable from the host of gradations that not only complicate the binary of black and white but also display their prior mergers. *Othello* in its day thus constituted 'very likely the first, and for a long time the only, direct challenge to the emergent negrophobia' in Elizabethan England and delineated 'the trajectory of racism for the next three centuries'.[12]

Sweeping generalisations are risky especially in a medium such as theatre which prizes novelty, variety and the striking contrast, and whose audiences are neither predictable nor homogeneous. Still, it is hardly oversimplifying matters to see eighteenth-century London patent stages performing the reduction of 'African' to 'slave' and/or 'black' to 'negro' underway in British culture. In *Othello*, the separation of nobility from blackness takes two general forms. First, Othello's blackness is disregarded, anglicised or lightened. Class trumps the representation of race throughout the late seventeenth and early eighteenth centuries, and the pleasant distractions of tall, good-looking actors like Spranger Barry aid in the apparent disregard of Othello's colour.[13] Changes to Othello's costume and the depiction of his skin colour also manifest this 'white-washing' in a process that spans the early eighteenth-century practice of blackening the actor's skin with burnt cork but dressing him in an English general's uniform (sometimes even sporting a white-powdered wig), an unsuccessful attempt by David Garrick to adopt a turban and the later convention, initiated by Edmund Kean, of using light brown facial paint to depict a 'tawny' rather than a black Othello.[14] Theatrical commentary on Othello's race moves from seeing his blackness as accidental, contingent, no deeper than skin-paint, to the critical inability to see anything but his blackness. By the Romantic period, some critics are rejecting the staging of *Othello* altogether. Indeed, *Othello* is *the* play that proves the necessity to closet Shakespeare in order to preserve his genius at representing English national identity. Charles Lamb 'appeal[s] to everyone that has seen Othello played whether he did not sink ... Othello's mind in his colour'.[15] S. T. Coleridge is convinced that Shakespeare's Othello must be a Moor, not 'a barbarous *Negro* plead[ing] royal birth'.[16]

The second manoeuvre proves equally useful in debasing blackness by activating a pornographic imagination that associates blackness with hypersexuality. Iago not only promotes such a linkage but goads white fathers into envisioning their daughters copulating with the black beast. This anxiety over black male sexuality is also legible in the stage history of *Othello* in which the need to affirm the nobility of the love between Othello and Desdemona involves progressively censoring the sexual nature of that relationship. As Julie Hankey and Michael Neill show, Iago's 'talk about the blood being "made dull with the act of sport"' and the need for certain 'conveniences' to freshen the appetite is gone by 1755. In 1773 John Bell excises the 'topped' in 'Behold her –' and also underlines several passages which William Macready later eradicates, from 'Happiness to their sheets' (now 'Happiness to them') to Desdemona's 'Will you come to bed, my lord?'[17] Such excisions anticipate the closeting of *Othello* during the Romantic period on the grounds that 'there is something extremely revolting in the courtship and wedded caresses of Othello and Desdemona', and 'monstrous' in conceiving 'this beautiful Venetian girl falling in love with a veritable Negro'.[18] Play illustrations or frontispieces manage the anxiety by reducing the entire play to the bedroom murder scene. The one exception noted by Paul H. D. Kaplan (an Italian painting, c. 1760, ascribed to Francesco Capella and identified as *Geography Lesson*) proves the rule. This scene showcases Desdemona's attraction to the stories Othello tells of other peoples and climes.[19] In other words, the painting presents their attraction as dependent on, but not reduced to, or degraded by, a difference in skin colour. Here, Othello's blackness represents his knowledge of other worlds and experiences about which his difference authorises him to speak.

The multiple stage renditions of *Oroonoko*, the tragic successor to *Othello*, further enact the process of making black men inferior. The story concerns the captured Angolan prince, Oroonoko, who is taken to Surinam as a slave, where he discovers his beloved Imoinda, now also a slave, and leads an unsuccessful slave rebellion. As his act of surrender, Oroonoko kills Imoinda at her own prompting in order to prevent her ravishment by the Governor before stabbing the Governor and himself. Behn's novella already initiates the first demotion by affixing 'noble' no longer to Moor or commander but to the 'royal slave' connoted by Behn's subtitle, a denomination which every subsequent stage version takes up to varying degrees of protest (see the opposition to slavery in Ferrier's *Prince of Angola*).[20] But all stage versions stress the parallel to *Othello* in portraying Imoinda not as the African woman presented in Behn's novella but as a white European. Felicity Nussbaum presents this change as evidence of the differential sexual logic of theatrical representation, whereby, given the relatively recent phenomenon of women playing female characters, feminine virtue is regarded as credible only in white females, a point especially relevant to the whitening of Imoinda in Southerne's version. Moreover, since female performance is seen as retaining what Nussbaum calls a 'smudge' of darkness, the application of a black face only heightens her debasement.[21] But this change also spotlights the second mechanism involved in the 'Negro erasure of the Moor'.[22] Not only is the royal slave presented as an exception to that majority of 'inferior Negro slaves hardly worth saving' (a distinction identified by Wylie Sypher as the 'Oroonoko legend'), but the worthiness of his love also demands that his partner must be a white European.[23] Strikingly, no tragedy written or performed in the eighteenth century features a black hero in love with a black heroine. The need to maintain the nobility of the black–white love relation perhaps explains why later versions of *Oroonoko* by Hawkesworth, Gentleman and an anonymous playwright all eliminate the comic subplot invented by Southerne which had foregrounded the sexual connivings of white British women.

New plays and roles devised for black characters in the eighteenth century heighten this operation. Tied to the general decline of tragedy and the rise of hybrid comic forms, new black roles are invariably low in terms of social status (slave, servant) and 'white-washed' in their eroticism. The model black male shifts from Othello to Mungo, the comic, and frequently intoxicated servant in Bickerstaffe's *The Padlock* who became a 'popular obsession, celebrated in prints, silver tea caddies' and masquerades by persons of fashion.[24] Even granting his spirited challenges to white mastery (Mungo's name would become a 'synonym for any rude and forward black man in England'), he serves his master's interests by voicing his critique from a decidedly menial position.[25] In addition, neither male nor female black characters are allowed to have love interests directed at each other. Black comic males, like Hassan in *The Castle Spectre* and Cymbalo in John C. Cross's *The Surrender of Trinidad* (CG, 1797), assist in the intrigues of their masters. Sentimental or tragicomic black males, like the black slave Caesar in Mariana Starke's *The Sword of Peace* (HM, 1788) or the escaped slave, Jack, in *Obi; or, Three Finger'd Jack*, do not have any love interests. Early nineteenth-century black heroes, like Gambia in Thomas Morton's *The Slave* (CG, 1816), complicate the picture only slightly. An African slave in love with Zelinda, a quadroon slave, Gambia proves his nobility by making possible Zelinda's union with a white man, Captain Clifton. Even the first black slave to turn Harlequin (*Harlequin Mungo*) is paired with a white planter's daughter turned Columbine. Black female roles do not alter the pattern. The witty serving-girl Cubba in Macready's farce, *The Irishman in London; or the Happy African*, is so devoted to her mistress Louisa that she refuses the chance to be her own mistress. Wowski, Yarico's maid in *Inkle and Yarico*, is unabashed in her sexual desire for Trudge, Inkle's white servant.[26] Claims that the paucity of roles for black women mirror the relative scarcity of black women living in England during this time do not adequately address the reality being enjoined by this representation.[27]

3. Market trends

No theatre career better exemplifies the compromises and possibilities of being in the black on the late Georgian stage than that of George Colman the Younger. Famous for catering to popular trends, heightening the rage for music and spectacle and excelling in comic forms, Colman's management of the Haymarket Theatre from 1789 to 1817 demonstrated a keen eye for profit.[28] In 1787, Colman staged the most heart-rending story of the century, Inkle and Yarico, as a comic opera and 'musical extravaganza'.[29] His version accentuates the story's sentimentality as an explicit marketing ploy, offering a perfect opportunity to probe the politics of sentiment. In *The Africans; or, War, Love, and Duty* (1808) Colman went on to explore the connection between slavery, capitalism and British identity, offering the most systemic dramatic account of Britain's investment in slavery. It seems likely, then, that Colman's interest in the black was driven by more than just the theatrical market.

Both *Inkle and Yarico* and *The Africans* foreground the capacity of sentiment to arouse concern over the plight of marginalised subjects. *Inkle and Yarico* tells the story of the aspiring white English trader, Thomas Inkle, cast ashore in the wilds of America, who is rescued from the natives and lovingly tended by the beautiful Indian maiden, Yarico, only to attempt to sell her as a slave once they arrive at Barbardos. The plot of *The Africans* turns on reuniting Selico and Berissa, whose wedding is interrupted by an attack by neighbouring Mandingo warriors, by the very Mandingo king (Demba) who had engineered the massacre of the Foulah people and the intended rape of Berissa in the first place. Believing Berissa to be dead, Selico devotes himself to acquiring sustenance for his mother by having his brother attempt to sell him as a slave and, when this proves unsuccessful, to offer him up to Demba as the intruder who invaded the tent of his intended paramour (the imprisoned Berissa), the punishment for which crime is death. Both plays, then, situate their analysis of slavery within a love/marriage plot, a common device of abolitionist literature that ostensibly humanises slaves for British audiences by showing that, beneath differences of skin, good human hearts are all the same. Moreover, by stressing parallels between the predicaments of British wives and African slaves, these productions are said to broaden sympathy for slaves by comparing their situation to a form of subjection more familiar to English audiences.[30]

Already an acknowledged tear-jerker, *Inkle and Yarico* plays up the sentimental plot and pathos by tripling the love pairings (Colman invents the couples, Trudge and Wowski [the companions and servants to Inkle and Yarico] and Narcissa and Captain Campley) and changing the ending, so that, for the first time, Inkle repents of his betrayal and is reunited with Yarico.[31] The unsurpassed pathos of Yarico's loyalty and Inkle's eventual change of heart are deemed essential to the abolitionist message of the play as articulated by Sir Christopher Curry who declares that 'I can't help thinking the only excuse for buying our fellow creatures, is to rescue 'em from the hands of those who are unfeeling enough to bring 'em to market.'[32] In her preface to the play, Elizabeth Inchbald celebrates *Inkle and Yarico* for being 'popular before the subject of abolition of the slave trade was popular'.[33] But even if the play protests against a mercantilist mentality which thrives off markets in women and slaves, it leaves slavery essentially unchallenged in its conclusion that 'true' British subjects know the difference between love and profit.

The Africans questions the contingency of Inkle's heartlessness by suggesting that those schooled in British sentiment cannot separate love from interest precisely because they have been raised in a capitalist system driven by the profit motive. While wholly sentimental in its depictions of filial self-sacrifice and mother-love as the means by which to resolve disputes between brothers, *The Africans* pointedly ascribes these sentiments only to the African characters. The play's sentimental humanism neither endorses white/British supremacy nor inverts the Britain-African hierarchy. For *The Africans* acknowledges intertribal division and participation by some Africans in enslavement but nonetheless asserts that only British characters are capable of assigning a price to a human life because of their internalisation of capitalist principles. As Demba asks, pointing at Selico:

> Then pr'yee, merchant, tell me – you
> Of wisdom and experience – you, who boast
> A country, as they say, more civilized
> By far, than mine – at how much would you rate
> A man like this?[34]

The play's depiction of Mug, a character invented by Colman, along with the African slave, Sutta – otherwise the playwright relies on the cast in Jean-Pierre De Florian's tale, *Selico, Nouvelle Africaine* of 1784 – deepens this suggestion. Enslaved while on a trip to Africa to import ivory to England, Mug is the only voice of English liberty and superiority in the play, a position, like his character, deliberately portrayed as opportunistic. Mug's opportunism is linked explicitly to his ability to work the system, an ability presented not as any sign of talent or integrity but simply as the consequence of being British. A comic figure, even in his underlying goodness, Mug is shown to have no feelings that are free from the quest for profit. Moreover, his chief function, manifested both in his grudging attraction to Sutta and his frequent comparisons of Foulah customs to British ones, is to articulate the cultural relativism which the entire play works to envision. This perspective underpins the comic description of interracial attraction in which both Mug and Sutta find the colour of the other a liability but not a total impediment, and the more serious admission of intra- and inter-ethnic colour prejudice: 'We Foulahs are the prettiest of the Negroes – / The same sun that dyes our neighbours black, / Feloops, Mandingoes, Jaloops, and the rest, / Hath tinged us Foulahs lighter by ten shades' (*The Africans*, Act I, scene i, p. 228). Yet that lightness fetches a lower price on the market. To a quite unusual extent, then, *The Africans* enlists sentimental humanism in the service of difference, but a difference that remains plural and relative, rather than one of binary oppositions. This difference is accentuated by featuring a black hero and black heroine whose love remains noble and self-sacrificial right through to its happy ending.

The contrasting reception of these two plays highlights the compromises required when critiquing values deeply held by the very audience whose applause one must garner in order to attempt their reformation through performance. As we have seen, *Inkle and Yarico* was phenomenally success-ful: the role of Yarico all but made the career of Sarah Kemble whose poignant representation of suffering femininity obscured both her ethnicity (in contrast to that of Wowski) and the broader issue of British complicity in the systematic enslavement of others.[35] Despite its position as the most popular new play for 1808, *The Africans* had a more mixed reception. The first two acts were 'very well received', but the third 'went off very heavily', owing to the 'perpetual recurrence of a kind of dialogue which is neither diverting nor pathetic'.[36] The third act *is* all talk and no action because it strives to depict Demba's conversion as grounded in something other than British sentiment – that is, in something which is less intuitive and which therefore requires a rational explication of the relative merits of justice and mercy in leadership, the origins of slavery, distinctions between friendship and war and between British capitalism and Colman's version of African humanism. Oddly, all this takes place in a play which commemorates Britain for finally moving beyond talk to action by passing the 1807 bill abolishing the slave trade. As Fetterwell declares, '[T]his will be our last venture; for, when I left London, a bill was passing that will kick our business to the devil' (*The Africans*, Act II, scene iv, p. 262). Performance is bound to flag when the aim of instruction is felt to conflict with its entertainment value, a structural condition which courts conventionality. To the extent that a play ventures into foreign territory, then, it generally errs on the side of familiarity in order literally not to alienate audiences. About the best one can hope for on the level of rational understanding is to leave spectators curious to learn more about subjects which are foreign to them.

Satisfying (indeed, arousing) curiosity during performance is understood as the province of spectacle, the domain most vilified by defenders of legitimate drama in this period for leaving minds empty or stupefied by increasing the craving for novelty and sensationalism. Yet accounts of *The Africans* suggest that spectacle can serve less diversionary functions, especially in plays striving to introduce non-British subjects to British audiences. The play's setting, described in the stage directions as '[t]he town of Fatteconda, in Bondou, a district of Africa, inhabited by the Foulahs, and situate between the rivers Senegal and Gambia', is itself an innovation. The costuming and careful re-enactment of Foulah wedding rituals is entertainment which doubles as protoethnography. Playbills for plays featuring black characters or settings often advertised scenic novelties as if they were the main attraction of the play. A playbill for *The Revolt of Surinam, or A Slave's Revenge* (CG, 1825), an adaptation of Southerne's *Oroonoko*, announces that 'The Piece will exhibit a Variety of Characteristic West Indian Scenery.' Another bill, advertising *The Ethiopian* (C, 1825) boasts 'new local and picturesque scenery, painted expressly for this occasion', depicting 'a view of a Sea Port in the West Indies, with Fortifications ... to quell a Revolt of the Negro Slaves', a 'Bridal Procession of African Slaves', a 'Prison' and an 'apartment of a West Indian Villa'.[37] In other words, satisfying the rage for spectacle helped to bring a larger world home to London viewers. The experience of viewing scenic wonders like the Incan Temple of the Sun in Sheridan's *Pizarro* (DL, 1799), a site pitted in the play against the weaker splendours of Catholicism, and often deemed by press reports as the chief reason for the play's enormous popularity, may have encouraged some spectators to question the provincialism of England and its concepts of legitimacy (*Pizarro* became famous for its message of resistance to colonialism).

But scenic transports just as often get spectators nowhere in terms of truly valuing difference, for curiosity easily turns voyeuristic and exploitative. The ready slide from advertising the novelty of exotic set designs to advertising the novelty of viewing black characters encapsulates the theatre's profit in blackness. Monk Lewis justifies the 'anachronism' of having black servants attend Osmond in *The Castle Spectre* by stating, 'I thought it would give a pleasing variety to the characters and dresses if I made my servants black; and could I have produced the same effect by making my heroine blue, blue I should have made her.'[38] The rhetoric of novelty is constantly reiterated in playbills for and reviews of Ira Aldridge, the first black actor to perform on the English stage. In 1825, Aldridge migrated from the US after actors at the African Theatre in New York were prohibited from playing Shakespeare.[39] In these accounts, Aldridge's name changes intriguingly from 'Mr. Keene, Tragedian of Colour' (1825) and 'F. W. Keene Aldridge, the African Roscius' (1831) to 'Mr. Aldridge (A Native of Senegal) known by the appellation of The African Roscius' (1833). Thereafter, he was represented either as 'The Celebrated African Roscius, Mr. Ira Aldridge' or as 'The Celebrated African Tragedian' always with explicit reference to his colour.[40] Reviews are split between celebrating the heightened sympathy and credibility obtained by having a black person play a black character and the novelty or curiosity of seeing a 'real' African on stage.

This craze for the spectacle of blackness aligns theatre with the nascent ethnographic show business initiated in London in 1810 with the display of Sara Baartman, the 'Hottentot Venus'.[41] More halting and ambiguously, the craze makes way for more black actors to appear on the British stage, albeit in a very limited range of roles. Aldridge's career in England mirrors ongoing difficulties for marginalised subjects seeking to gain the cultural spotlight. The positive reception of his acting stands in inverse proportion to his proximity to England's cultural centre: Aldridge is lauded in the provinces and tolerated in the minor theatres but driven from the Covent Garden stage after only two performances in April 1833. Even before this performance, Aldridge's friends circulate a handbill publicising 'base and unmanly attempts' by the pro-slavery lobby to 'prevent MR. ALDRIDGE, commonly designated the "AFRICAN ROSCIUS", from making his appearance as OTHELLO, on Wednesday next'. Reviews complete the dirty work. 'Such an exhibition is well enough at Sadler's Wells, or at Bartholomew Fair, but it certainly is not very creditable to a great national establishment' (*Times*), for his 'enunciation is far from correct or pleasing; it is frequently broad and strikingly un-English' (*Morning Post*). Reviewers cannot even agree that Aldridge's 'fitness' for the role resides in his being able to play 'without the aid of lampblack or pomatum' (*Times*), for the *Spectator* contends that '[t]he property-man can furnish as good' or even a 'better' skin tone than 'Dame Nature herself'. And 'English audiences have a prejudice in favour of European features, which more than counterbalance the recommendations of a flat nose and thick lips'.[42]

But one reviewer, in linking *The Africans* to Sheridan's *Pizarro*, inadvertently raises a more liberating path for the interpretation of these plays. The writer means to criticise both playwrights for cashing in on their reputations by foisting 'trash' on their patrons and relying solely on scenic interest, but his mention of *Pizarro* also brings into orbit the period's most popular play of colonial resistance.[43] The fact that subsequent plays protesting against slavery advertise the presence of a famous scene borrowed from *Pizarro* gives us reason to surmise the existence of an anti-colonial visual underground. The playbill for *The Ethiopian* foregrounds a scene, also described in a review of *The Slave*, which features a 'Picturesque Landscape, with waterfall and hanging bridge', at which 'the Child about to be plunged into the Torrent by the Pursuers [is] wonderfully rescued by Gambia, & restored to his Mother's arms' – a visual allusion to the most famous scene in *Pizarro*, where the hero restores Cora's baby to her arms from a hanging bridge.[44] This visual cross-referencing of scenes in plays critical of colonial power encourages sympathetic viewers to read – that is, preview – the new play from a position of resistance, a particularly shrewd strategy in an age of theatrical censorship. The capacity to put more pressure on the binary opposition inaugurated during the Romantic period between viewing and reading, spectacle and poetry, may be one belated benefit of considering the ways in which late eighteenth-century theatres went into the black.

NOTES

1. Herbert Marshall and Mildred Stock, *Ira Aldridge, the Negro Tragedian*, Carbondale: Southern Illinois University Press, 1958, p. 85.
2. Jeffrey Cox, 'Introduction', in *Slavery, Abolition, and Emancipation*, eds. Peter J. Kitson and Debbie Lee, 8 vols., London: Pickering and Chatto, 1999; vol. V, p. ix.
3. Folarin Shyllon, *Black People in Britain 1555–1833*, London: Oxford University Press, 1977, pp. 16–29.
4. J. R. Oldfield, 'The "Ties of Soft Humanity": Slavery and Race in British Drama, 1760–1800', *Huntington Library Quarterly* 56 (1993), pp. 1–14.
5. See Greg Tate, (ed.), *Everything but the Burden: What White People are Taking from Black Culture*, New York: Harlem Moon, 2003, pp. 1–15, especially p. 3.
6. L. O. Aranye Fradenburg, 'Entertainment Value', unpublished paper given at the conference 'Entertainment Value' at the University of California at Santa Barbara, 3–4 May 2002.
7. Oxford English Dictionary: Black 1.d. to be in the black: to show a profit; to have a credit balance (from the practice of recording credit items and balances in black).
8. *Hazlitt on Theatre*, eds. William Archer and Robert Lowe, New York: Hill and Wang, 1958, p. 38.
9. Cedric J. Robinson, 'The Inventions of the Negro', *Social Identities* 7:3 (2001), pp. 329–61.
10. Robinson, 'Inventions of the Negro', pp. 330–1.
11. Robinson, 'Inventions of the Negro', p. 332.
12. Robinson, 'Inventions of the Negro', p. 339.
13. Virginia Mason Vaughan, *Othello: a Contextual History*, Cambridge: Cambridge University Press, 1994, pp. 112, 119–22.
14. Julie Hankey, (ed.), *Othello. Plays in Performance Series*, Bristol: Bristol Classical Press, 1987, pp. 22, 37; Kris Collins, 'White-Washing the Black-a-Moor: *Othello*, Negro Minstrelsy and Parodies of Blackness', *Journal of American Culture* 19:3 (1996), pp. 87–101, 91–2.
15. Charles Lamb, 'On the Tragedies of Shakespeare, considered with reference to their fitness for stage representation', in *The Works of Charles and Mary Lamb*, ed. E. V. Lucas, 7 vols., London: Methuen, 1903–05, vol. I, p. 102.
16. *Coleridge on Shakespeare*, ed. Terence Hawkes, New York: Penguin, 1969, p. 187.
17. Michael Neill, 'Unproper Beds: Race, Adultery, and the Hideous in *Othello*', *Shakespeare Quarterly* 40: 4 (Winter 1989), pp. 383–412, 385; Hankey, *Othello*, pp. 45–8, 65.
18. Lamb, 'On the Tragedies of Shakespeare', p. 108 and Coleridge in *Coleridge on Shakespeare*, p. 188.

19. Paul H. D. Kaplan, 'The Earliest Images of Othello', *Shakespeare Quarterly* 39:2 (Summer 1988), pp. 171–86, 172–3.

20. See Jane Spencer, *The Afterlife of Aphra Behn*, Oxford: Oxford University Press, 2000, pp. 225–30; Mita Choudhury, *Interculturalism and Resistance in the London Theater, 1660–1800: Identity, Performance, Empire*, Lewisburg, PA: Bucknell University Press, 2000, pp. 161–75.

21. Felicity Nussbaum, *The Limits of the Human: Fictions of Anomaly, Race, and Gender in the Long Eighteenth Century*, Cambridge: Cambridge University Press, 2003, pp. 157–77, 160.

22. Robinson, 'Inventions of the Negro', p. 338.

23. Wylie Sypher, *Guinea's Captive Kings*, Chapel Hill, NC: University of North Carolina Press, 1942, pp. 108–15. Cited in 'Introduction' to *Thomas Southerne: Oroonoko*, eds. Maximillian E. Novak and David Stuart Ross, Lincoln, NE: University of Nebraska Press, 1976, p. xxix.

24. Oldfield, 'The "Ties of Soft Humanity"', p. 9.

25. Gretchen Gerzina, *Black England: Life before Emancipation*, London: John Murray, 1995, p. 10.

26. On Wowski's eroticism, see Daniel O'Quinn, 'Mercantile Deformities: George Colman's *Inkle and Yarico* and the Racialization of Class Relations', *Theatre Journal* 54:3 (2002), pp. 389–409, 402–6.

27. Gerzina, *Black England*, pp. 68–89.

28. On Colman's opportunism, see Julia Swindells, *Glorious Causes: the Grand Theatre of Political Change, 1789–1833*, Oxford: Oxford University Press, 2001, pp. 1–12. On the importance of theatrical profit, see William J. Burling, *Summer Theatre in London, 1661–1820, and the Rise of the Haymarket Theatre*, Madison, NJ: Fairleigh Dickinson University Press, 2000, p. 9.

29. Frank Felsenstein, (ed.), *English Trader, Indian Maid: Representing Gender, Race, and Slavery in the New World: an Inkle and Yarico Reader*, Baltimore, MD: Johns Hopkins University Press, 1999, pp. xi, 18–27.

30. Joseph Roach, *Cities of the Dead: Circum-Atlantic Performance*, New York: Columbia University Press, 1996, pp. 152–60.

31. Barry Sutcliffe, 'Introduction', in *Plays by George Colman the Younger and Thomas Morton*, Cambridge: Cambridge University Press, 1983, p. 20.

32. *Inkle and Yarico* in Ibid., Act III, scene iii, p. 104.

33. Elizabeth Inchbald, *The British Theatre; or, A Collection of Plays which are acted at the Theatres Royal, Drury Lane, Covent Garden, and the Haymarket*, 25 vols., London: Longman, Hurst, Rees and Orme, 1808, vol. XX, p. 3.

34. *The Africans* reprinted in *Slavery, Abolition, and Emancipation*, vol. V, Act III, scene iii, p. 279.

35. See O'Quinn, 'Mercantile Deformities', pp. 398–402.

36. *Times*, 30 July 1808; *Morning Chronicle*, 30 July 1808; see also Jeremy Bagster-Collins, *George Colman the Younger*, Morningside Heights: King's Crown Press, 1946, pp. 207–10.

37. The playbills are cited in Marshall and Stock, *Ira Aldridge*, pp. 57–9.

38. Marshall and Stock, *Ira Aldridge*, p. 85.

39. Joyce Green MacDonald, 'Acting Black: *Othello, Othello* Burlesques, and the Performance of Blackness', *Theatre Journal* 46 (1994), pp. 231–49, 234–7.

40. Marshall and Stock, *Ira Aldridge*, p. 55.

41. Z. S. Strother, 'Display of the Body Hottentot', in *Africans on Stage: Studies in Ethnological Show Business*, ed. Bernth Lindfors, Bloomington, IN: Indiana University Press, 1999, pp. 1–62.
42. Marshall and Stock, *Ira Aldridge*, pp. 118–25.
43. Cited in Bagster-Collins, *George Colman*, p. 208.
44. Marshall and Stock, *Ira Aldridge*, p. 60.

PART IV

Places of Performance

13

GILLIAN RUSSELL

Private theatricals

Probably the best-known example of a private theatrical in the Georgian period is a fictional one: the scheme to stage *Lovers' Vows* in Jane Austen's *Mansfield Park* (1814). Literary critics have tended to focus on the moral and philosophical dimensions of Austen's representation of acting in the novel, taking its apparent antitheatricalism for granted, and it is only comparatively recently that the complexity of her engagement with private theatricals, and indeed with the theatre in general, has been properly acknowledged.[1] *Mansfield Park* not only reveals Austen's familiarity with the practicalities of getting up a play in a country house in the early nineteenth century; it also demonstrates her awareness of how the fashion for private theatricals could illuminate some central concerns of Georgian society and culture, such as the relationship between public and private spheres, the changing meanings of family and issues of gender, sexuality, class and national identity. Insofar as *Lovers' Vows* is never actually staged in the novel (Austen instead focusing on preparations for a performance abandoned after the unexpected arrival of Sir Thomas Bertram) *Mansfield Park* illustrates the way in which the sociable rituals associated with private theatricals became at least as important as the performance itself. For the Georgians, the play was never entirely the thing: they were equally fascinated with the sociable, spatial and material contexts in which play-making took place. Because it was invested in such contexts, commemorated in ephemeral literature such as tickets and playbills, the phenomenon of private theatricals is especially revealing of this aspect of eighteenth-century theatrical culture as a whole. Private theatricals enabled men and women not only to play at being actors and actresses but also to participate in theatre as a key social ritual which in many respects defined what it meant to be a subject in Georgian Britain and its empire. This chapter will survey the obsession with amateur acting in this period, ranging from the glittering performances of the aristocracy to the tavern theatricals or spouting clubs of shop-workers and artisans.

Print culture, publicity and the private theatrical

To begin with, what was private about a private theatrical? Insofar as it related to an entertainment or event, the term private was understood to mean an occasion that was not open to the paying general public and therefore outside forms of regulation such as licensing and censorship that governed the commercial theatre. Some private theatricals of the gentry, such as those attended by Jane Austen and Fanny Burney, were private in that they were limited to particular families and their circles. We only know about such occasions because they were described in letters and journals that came to notice because of the later fame of these writers. But private theatricals could be very public indeed. In July 1799, for example, Edward Hartopp staged a theatrical at the family seat of Dalby Hall in Leicestershire which attracted three earls, a lord, baronet, at least one MP and a 'long train of fashionables'. Publicity for the event commended a Mr Bilsborrow who had designed 'very elegant' tickets, as well as the scenery and stage machinery. Also involved were the volunteer band of the Melton infantry and professional actors from the Nottingham theatre: Mr Sharpe of Grantham composed the music while the costumes were courtesy of Johnson of London.[2] The Dalby Hall theatricals were therefore much more than a private family affair but an important event in the calendar of the east-Midlands elite, which involved a diverse range of people, including theatre professionals, as well as attracting attention in the national media. This latter factor – print publicity – is highly significant in the development of the private theatrical after 1750. The staging of plays in private households was a long-standing tradition in British culture, going back to the early modern period at least. The prevalence of the custom in the early eighteenth century is suggested by William Hogarth's painting of 1732–35, *A Scene from 'The Indian Emperor'*, which depicts the children of John Conduitt performing in a private production of Dryden's play. But it was in the second half of the century that the fashion for private theatricals really took off, closely linked with the expansion of the print media – newspapers and journals, books in general and associated forms of visual art such as graphic satire. The period after the accession of George III in 1760 witnessed a development in all forms of leisure, stimulated by a booming economy that followed the end of the Seven Years' War (1756–63). Not only were new venues and modes of entertainment developed, but the elite and gentry household also featured significantly as a venue for sociability in the form of balls, masquerades, concerts, card parties and private theatricals. Women were prominent in such entertaining because of the authority they traditionally exercised as managers of households. The fashionable sociability that characterised the early decades of George III's reign therefore represented an opportunity for women to assert themselves in public culture as a whole, largely because of the way that the print media disseminated news of such activities, thereby blurring the boundaries between private and public spheres. Intelligence about private balls, masquerades and theatricals developed as a distinctive subgenre of journalism in this period: it served the interests of the print media by attracting readers intrigued by the affairs of the fashionable world, while for the subjects of such reports it offered fame without the stigma of performing for financial gain. The importance of print as a means of amplifying the social and political meaning of private theatricals is noted by Austen in her description of the Hon. John Yates's disappointment at the postponement of theatricals in Cornwall: 'To be so near happiness, so near fame, so near the long paragraph in praise of the private theatricals at Ecclesford, the seat of the Right Hon. Lord Ravenshaw ... was an injury to be keenly felt.'[3]

Such 'long paragraphs' in newspapers and magazines form the main evidence for the private theatricals craze of the late eighteenth century.[4] In the 1770s the press noted the thespian activities of gentlemen such as Sir Watkin Williams Wynn at Wynnstay in Denbighshire, Stephen Fox at Winterslow House in Wiltshire, William Hanbury at Kelmarsh in Northamptonshire, and the Earl of Essex at Cassiobury Park in Hertfordshire. A number of these occasions took place during the Christmas and New Year period, highlighting one enduring reason for country-house theatricals – the need to amuse family and guests during a period when travel was difficult and days were short. As a character in Maria Edgeworth's 1814 novel *Patronage* remarks, apropos of theatrical amusements, 'the only possible way to make the country supportable was to have a large party of town friends in your house'.[5] But country-house theatricals did much more than merely alleviate boredom. For elite families whose attention was otherwise focused on London, they served the useful purpose of advertising a return to the country, renewing ties with local families through sociability, and offering an opportunity to patronise local businesses, including, in some cases, provincial theatres. The dramatist Richard Cumberland commended the paternalism of private theatricals in a prologue to a performance at Kelmarsh in 1774: 'In this voluptuous dissipated age, / Sure there's some merit in our rural stage, / Happy the call, nor wholly vain the play, / Which weds you to your acres for a day.'[6]

However, such entertaining was often as much for the benefit of a metropolitan and national audience as it was for the local community. Lacking an interest in parliamentary politics, the young Sir Watkin Williams Wynn turned to theatricals in the 1770s as a means of making a name for himself. He was a frequenter of London masquerades and a well-known macaroni, a precursor

13. Ticket for Wynnstay theatricals from the *European Magazine*, November 1787.

of the nineteenth-century dandy. In 1770 he famously appeared as a Welsh druid at one of Teresa Cornelys's masquerades at Carlisle House in London. Sir Watkin used his private theatricals at Wynnstay – a tradition lasting seventeen years for which he built his own theatre – as a means of integrating his local pre-eminence with his metropolitan fashionability. He invited men of the theatre such as David Garrick, Richard Brinsley Sheridan and George Colman to witness and sometimes act in his productions and ensured that his theatre received regular 'long paragraphs' in the press.[7] Another metropolitan visitor, the gentleman caricaturist William Henry Bunbury, commemorated the theatricals at Wynnstay in the form of drawings and ticket designs. One such design, reproduced in the *European Magazine*, encourages guests to participate in a scene of pastoral sociability under the protection of the Welsh oak.[8] It suggests the importance of the theatricals to Sir Watkin's cultivation of a distinctively British public identity, a performative Welshness that brought the metropolis to the provinces and vice versa.

The Wynnstay theatricals are also notable for the involvement of Sir Watkin's servants, particularly his butler Samuel Sidebotham who acted in some productions with other members of his family. Sidebotham was also given prominence in the Wynnstay playbills as the person to whom visitors should apply for tickets, thereby making an analogy between his status as an upper servant and the box-keeper of the public theatre. This indicates another important dimension of private theatricals – their relationship to dynamics of power between master and servant in the Georgian household. A traditional definition of family, which was undergoing change in this period, was that it included all the dependents within a household which meant that ideologically, if sometimes not practically, servants had an implicit role to play as part of the family in elite and gentry theatricals.[9] Jane Austen draws attention to this in *Mansfield Park* by describing the disruptive effects on the servants, ranging from the housemaids who have to make curtains from an 'enormous roll of green baize' to five under-servants, rendered 'idle and dissatisfied' by the presence of a scene-painter from Northampton.[10] Private theatricals had the potential to highlight the way in which gentlemen such as Sir Watkin Williams Wynn were always performing before an audience of their dependents, both within the household and without. Such a context explains the popularity within elite theatricals of plays such as *High Life below Stairs*. James Townley's 1759 farce was a satire on the pretensions of a group of servants who ape the manners and dress of their masters and mistresses. The play drew attention to the potential for fashion and luxury to dissolve social distinctions while also disclosing the more subversive message that hierarchy was not natural but a matter of how well one played one's part. However, as performed at Wynnstay and other houses with actual members of the elite playing servants pretending to be lords and ladies before an audience of their own servants, *High Life Below Stairs* was capable of assuming another meaning, one which reinforced the boundaries of class which, in the public theatre, may have seemed more fluid.

One aristocrat who used private theatricals as a laboratory through which to explore the theatricality of class relations was the eccentric Richard Barry, the seventh Earl of Barrymore. A crony of the Prince of Wales, the young Earl was a gambler, a notable patron of the turf and a stage fanatic. In the late 1780s, he built a lavish private theatre at his seat at Wargrave in Berkshire at a phenomenal cost of £60,000. Later enlarged in 1792, the theatre included a special box for the Prince of Wales with its own drawing room and private staircase. Nearly as lavish provision was made for the theatre's servants: there was a carpenter's room with a bed, dresser and the considerable luxury of a sink. At Wargrave Barrymore entertained his friends and associates including a number of theatre professionals such as the comedian John Edwin. His secretary or publicist was the notorious hack John Williams, better known as Anthony Pasquin, who organised a steady stream of 'Wargrave intelligence' for the press and wrote a life of the Earl. The audience for the theatricals included not only the London 'fast set' but also local farmers and servants. Pasquin claimed that the Earl would sometimes disguise himself as a ticket collector, on one occasion refusing to admit a farmer whose ticket was for the previous evening's entertainment. Unaware of the ticket collector's identity, the farmer bribed Barrymore with a shilling. The Earl later regaled his guests in the green room with the adventure, asking them 'if he was not liable to be carried before Mr. Justice Chace of Reading, for taking money at his booth without a licence from the county magistrates!'[11] Pasquin also claimed that he would accompany his patron in incognito visits to the country in order to eavesdrop on local people's view of the theatricals, comments which Barrymore would then relay to his upper-class friends. This suggests that the thrill that Barrymore got from his theatre was derived not only from the opportunity to entertain royalty and mix with theatrical 'low-lifes' but also from the exercise in privilege his entertainments made possible. His glee in the transgressive implications of the bribe was a marker of his ability to act outside the laws governing public entertainment in the provinces: it was precisely the fact that he did not need a licence to use his theatre which so amused the Earl and his friends. An audience of the lower orders was essential for this aspect of the theatricals to be realised, hence the Earl's invitation to the local people to be (unsuspecting) elements of the overall entertainment. What Barrymore was staging at Wargrave was therefore not simply a series of lavishly produced plays but theatre's capacity to mimic and realise the conditions of the eighteenth-century social order itself.

The literature of the private theatrical: playbills, prologues and epilogues

The Wargrave experiment illustrates the importance of the extra- or para-theatrical to the social phenomenon of private theatricals – spaces such as the green room, the Prince of Wales's private staircase and the entrance in which Barrymore acted out his cross-class masquerade with the farmer. The textual equivalents of these spaces were the playbill, prologues and epilogues, and tickets. These texts were also significant in the public theatres, but they were of even more importance to private theatricals because they drew attention to factors of place, personnel and time as defining contexts for performance. Press reports of theatricals often commented on the elegance of the tickets which functioned as souvenirs of the event, denoting privilege as an invitee, and distinguishing private theatricals from other forms of entertainment in which money changed hands. Of similar value as a currency of sociability was the playbill. Either handwritten or printed, as in the case of the Wynnstay theatricals (by a local bookseller), playbills form the main record for private theatricals, as they do for the theatre as a whole in this period. A performance was not a performance and a theatre not a theatre without the legitimation of a playbill: phrases such as 'as acted at', 'tickets to be had', 'Theatre —— ' were preconditions for this normative ritual of Georgian cultural life. The prologue and epilogue performed a similar role in both the public and private theatres. These verse monologues which framed the mainpiece comedy or tragedy represented a zone of mediation between on the one hand, the performance event, the performer and the theatre institution itself and on the other, the audience both within the auditorium and in the wider world. In the case of private theatricals, they were particularly important in defining the specificity of the event and in making claims for its value. Outsiders such as gentlemen literati and dramatists composed prologues and epilogues which were often published in newspapers to the mutual fame of the author and the event, blurring even further the distinction between private and public. The poet laureate William Whitehead, for example, wrote a prologue for the opening of the theatre of an Oxfordshire gentleman, Oldfield Bowles, at North Aston, later published in the *Universal Magazine*. Whitehead adapts Prospero's fare-well to his art in *The Tempest* and references *King Lear* and *Othello* to suggest the inevitable evanescence of all pomp and show:

> ... time may come when all this glittering show
> Of canvas, paint, and plaister, shall lie low;
> These gorgeous palaces, yon cloud capt scene,
> This barn itself, may be a barn again;
> The spirit stirring drum may cease to roar,
> The prompter's whistle may be heard no more,
> But echoing sounds of rustic toil prevail,
> The winnowing hiss, and clapping of the flail.
> Hither once more may unhous'd vagrants fly
> To shun the inclement blast and pelting sky;
> On Lear's own straw may gypsies rest their head,
> And trulls lie snug in Desdemona's bed.[12]

Taking place at the very limit of Oldfield Bowles's domain, both literally and metaphorically, the theatricals are a sign of the precariousness of that authority. Whitehead's reference to 'unhous'd vagrants' resuming occupa-tion of a place that the elite have temporarily made their home figuratively looks out from the 'glittering show' of privilege to contemplate a surrounding darkness. The prologue illustrates how the literature of private theatricals, as exemplified by the prologue and epilogue, could adumbrate a social context for the eighteenth-century theatre as a whole.

The capacity of texts such as the prologue and epilogue, the playbill and the ticket to register the specificity of a performance as an occasion drawing people together in a gesture of sociality, and, most significantly, as a mode of transformation, was particularly important in the case of military and naval theatricals. As I have outlined elsewhere, soldiers and sailors were thoroughly absorbed with theatricals, taking over public stages to perform plays, or constructing their own theatres in battle zones or on board ship.[13] The capacity of the private theatrical to register nuances of power within the household could be extrapolated to equally complex hierarchies of the naval 'family' or the military company. The manager and actor Tate Wilkinson witnessed one such occasion in 1791 when he was invited on board HMS Bedford, anchored off Portsmouth for a performance of Nicholas Rowe's *The Fair Penitent* and the farce of *Who's the Dupe?* by Hannah Cowley. Military and naval men also collaborated in amateur theatricals with civilian servants of the empire in places as far afield as Kingston in Jamaica, the Cape of Good Hope and Calcutta. The prologue and epilogue were important in legitimising these occasions and, implicitly, the imperial enterprise as a whole. The designation of a mud-walled hut as a 'theatre royal' as in the case of the performance of *The Recruiting Officer* at Port Jackson, Australia, in 1789, marked both what was alien about the imperial experience and the enduring capacity of Britons to recreate the rituals of 'home'. However mean the context, whether it be a barn in Oxfordshire or a swamp on the Gulf of Mexico, getting up a play signalled the mobility of privilege as a political and cultural category. The private theatre of the British empire was capable of embracing the globe.

Private theatricals reached their glittering apogee in the late 1780s when occasions such as the theatricals in Richmond House caused a sitting of the House of Commons to be postponed so that MPs could attend. This event marked a development in the thespian mania in that it took place not in the country but at the very centre of the metropolis at the height of the social season. It was notable for the dominance of women of fashion, particularly Anne Seymour Damer (the niece of Horace Walpole), who spoke several epilogues and took various roles. Damer was well known as a sculptor and her busts of Lady Aylesbury and Lady Melbourne featured prominently in the design of the apartments for Lady Lovemore, the character Damer played in a performance of Arthur Murphy's *The Way to Keep Him*.[14] The actress Elizabeth Farren supervised the Richmond House theatricals as manager, leading to rumours of a sapphic connection between her and Damer.[15] In spite of gossip, Damer persisted in her career as an amateur thespian, organising performances at her house at Strawberry Hill in 1800. Damer was joined in her passion for acting by a number of elite women, including Elizabeth Craven, the Margravine of Anspach, who built a theatre at Brandenburgh House in London for which she wrote her own plays, and Albinia Hobart, later Countess of Buckinghamshire, an enthusiastic thespian, socialite and gambler.

Private theatricals enabled women of the elite to define a public role for themselves without the stigma of involvement in the professional stage. Such activity was not confined to the upper classes: a number of middling-class women emulated Damer and Anspach by establishing their own theatres and in some cases writing plays. As Catherine B. Burroughs has argued, 'the British private theatrical gave those who would otherwise have had no theatrical experience a mode of exploring the theatre arts'.[16] The self-styled grocer's daughter, Mariana Starke, had her first play, *The Sword of Peace*, staged at the private theatre of Lady Mary Champion de Crespigny in Camberwell in 1789. At Norwich Anne and Annabella Plumptre organised private theatricals with their brother James, for which Amelia Alderson, later Opie, wrote a tragedy, *Adelaide*, in 1791. Anne Plumptre would go on to translate the plays of the German dramatist August von Kotzebue, while Opie achieved fame as a novelist. The Plumptre family theatricals resembled many such occasions in gentry and middling-order homes throughout the country, such as the Austen theatricals at Steventon and performances at Burney family gatherings. In her journal, Fanny Burney described acting as a nerve-wracking ordeal in which she was subjected to the the scrutiny of male members of her family and some of their friends, suggesting that family theatricals could function as a kind of initiation for both girls and boys in the gendered roles they would have to perform as adults.[17] The educational value of acting had long been recognised in British schools and universities: the performance of Greek and Latin plays was a tradition at the major public schools and was publicised in the press on the same terms as other elite theatricals. Acting for boys, particularly young gentlemen, instructed them in the arts of oratory and performance that would fit them for a public career. Private theatricals were also encouraged at some girls' boarding schools with the aim of preparing them not for recognised public careers, but for the performance of a regulated femininity necessary for success as proper wives and mothers.

Gender and class in private theatricals

Another important school of drama was the spouting club, an assembly consisting mostly of young men of the lower-middle and artisanal classes who would gather together to stage performances and assay particular roles.

Spouting clubs were located in venues such as taverns and were an integral element of the homosociality of the male lower orders. Strictly speaking spouting clubs were not private, insofar that their members would pay a fee to perform and their activities came under the licence of a tavern. Nonetheless, they can be identified as part of the craze for private theatricals, the spouter serving as the lower-class counterpart of elite performers such as Barrymore or Sir Watkin Williams Wynn. Spouting clubs were controversial because they were felt to encourage idleness and dissipation in tradesmen and apprentices. In Arthur Murphy's 1760 comedy *The Apprentice*, Dick Wingate defies his merchant father to join a spouting club, described in the play as 'a meeting of prentices and clerks, and giddy young men, all intoxicated with plays! and so they meet at public houses, and there they repeat speeches and alarm the neighbourhood with their noise, and neglect their business, and despise the advice of their friends, and think of nothing but becoming actors'.[18] In 1771 the *Oxford Magazine* echoed Murphy, claiming that the contagion of acting among the lower orders needed government intervention: the 'ignorance and want of education' of the youths who frequented spouting clubs 'can only be equalled by the mad ambition they have to become actors'.[19] This 'mad ambition' was capable of signifying much more than an urge to strut about the stage like Garrick or Kemble: it suggested a desire for other kinds of self-transformation, to step out of one's place and identity. In the context of the French Revolution and its aftermath, the prospect of little men strutting as kings and princes roused even greater alarm and spouting clubs, like debating societies, became regarded as venues of promiscuous association and metamorphosis that were profoundly threatening to social stability. They continued to thrive, however, when the more elite theatricals became unfashionable. Charles Dickens gives a characteristically vivid account of one such private theatre in *Sketches by Boz* (1836), indicating that the spouting club endured as an institution of metropolitan sociability well into the nineteenth century.

Plays such as *The Apprentice* suggest that the public theatres were all too well aware of the enthusiasm for acting in society as a whole. One of the most interesting plays to tackle the subject of private theatricals is Isaac Jackman's *All the World's a Stage* (DL, 1777). The farce depicts the household of a country squire, Sir Gilbert Pumpkin, which has been turned upside down by theatricals. Sir Gilbert's servants are obsessed with heroic tragedy and his ward, Kitty Sprightly, has been encouraging them in their histrionics. Worth £30,000, she is being pursued by Sir Gilbert's nephew Charles Stanley who, with his friend Harry Stukely, arrive as outsiders to be entertained by the servants' theatricals. The naive Kitty describes to Charles how she had encouraged the servant Cymon, playing Othello, to rehearse the murder scene in Shakespeare's play with her as Desdemona – 'I only desired him … to go into the barn and get by heart the speech, where the blackamoor smothers his wife, and I had not been in bed ten minutes, when he came into the room, and repeated every word of it!' Black with soot and goose dripping, Cymon demands a kiss, leaving a mark on Kitty's face that compels her to tell the 'whole story' to the company the next morning – 'And, do you know, that I am locked in my room every night since.'[20] Kitty is later clandestinely married to Charles Stanley, under the cover of the theatricals, but the real transgression is her role-play with Cymon which suggests the possibility of a class as well as a racial miscegenation. The blacked-up servant, using Shakespeare to invade his mistress's bedroom, and possibly her body, signifies the capacity of theatre as a whole to overturn hierarchies of class, race and genre. Private theatricals are therefore used in Jackman's play, as the spouting club is in *The Apprentice*, as a means for the public theatre to reflect on itself. In both cases private theatricals are a kind of Hyde to the public theatre's Jekyll – an undisciplined, licentious playhouse as opposed to the commercial theatre's capacity to regulate itself, suggested in Jackman's play by the resolution which secures Kitty's money and her status for the right man. But, as the farce also highlights, the servants' enthusiasm for theatre is something to be embraced through laughter rather than rejected: sometimes being Hyde can be sheer fun.

In *All the World's a Stage* the threat represented by private theatricals is synonymous with the threat to Kitty Sprightly's sexual honour. Throughout the eighteenth century, these entertainments were persistently associated with adultery. As I have suggested, private theatricals explored the external and internal politics of family, both in terms of how the family presented itself to the wider world and also as occasions which articulated the structures of power within the household. Such exposure carried an inherent risk: as Austen suggests in *Mansfield Park*, the introduction of the outsider Mr Yates with his theatrical scheme is the catalyst for a series of events which causes the Mansfield family to fracture before it eventually coalesces around the marriage of Fanny Price and her cousin Edmund. The sign of this profound disruption to the family, which the novel identifies as the outcome of the theatricals, is the adultery between Maria Rushworth and Henry Crawford. In making this connection Austen was reflecting an association between private theatricals and adultery that was an eighteenth-century commonplace. A number of high-profile divorce cases in the 1780s and 90s were linked to the vice of private acting: Major Arabin, a prominent associate of the Earl of Barrymore, was involved in a notorious case in 1786, while Lord Chief Justice Kenyon, who led a public campaign in the courts against adultery in the 1790s, nominated the rage for theatricals as one of its chief causes. Adultery, like private theatricals, blurred distinctions between the intimate sphere of the family and the social and political realm: both phenomena revealed profound anxieties about the stability of the domestic order – and the control of women in particular – which were increasingly regarded as necessary to the wellbeing of the nation as a whole.

These anxieties came to a head in 1798 in an adultery case involving a theatre-mad young couple, Thomas Twistleton, heir of Lord Say and Sele and his wife Charlotte, née Wattell.[21] They had met at a private theatre at Adlestrop, the home of Twistleton's sister, and married in 1788. Their interest in acting was such that they continued to perform after their marriage and in 1793 they ventured onto the professional stage by appearing at the Liverpool Theatre. The couple was subsequently engaged by Thomas Harris for Covent Garden but Twistleton's family persuaded him not to accept the offer. Charlotte Twistleton defied their advice, however, and made her debut as Belvidera at Covent Garden in February 1794. The Twistletons separated by private agreement soon afterwards and in 1798 Thomas petitioned for a parliamentary divorce which would allow him to remarry and secure the legitimacy of the family line. He gave evidence in the divorce case at the House of Lords which, rather than focusing on Mrs Twistleton's alleged adultery with a Mr Stein, instead concentrated on her seduction by the theatre as the cause of the couple's initial separation. Reports of the case noted Twistleton's assertion that their disagreements were due to his wife's 'Extravagance, and her ill-temper ... but chiefly on Account of the acting'.[22] After the divorce Charlotte Twistleton persisted in her career as a professional performer, falling on increasingly harder times. She disappears into obscurity in the early 1800s, eking out a living on the provincial stages of North America.

Charlotte Twistleton's story, with which Jane Austen was probably familiar – she was a remote cousin of the Twistletons – was a wilful embrace of downward mobility which began at a private theatrical. It represents a very different trajectory from the career of Elizabeth Farren, manageress of the Richmond House theatricals, who became a woman of fashion in earnest when she married the Earl of Derby in 1797. The Twistleton affair exemplifies the power of theatre as a crossing point in eighteenth-century culture and society, a zone in which the tectonic plates of rank, race and gender were in productive interaction. Rather than being of marginal significance, private theatricals are capable of revealing what generated most energy at that contact zone – the possibility that the categories of gender, rank and nation, and indeed private and public could be re-imagined through performance. A private theatrical initiated Charlotte Wattell not in the proper rituals of femininity but in the correlative of such a performance – the embrace of another self. It was the first and probably the most important of the stages on which she was to perform for the rest of her life and as such exemplifies the risk inherent in transformation which was at the heart of the attraction of private theatricals and the eighteenth-century theatre as a whole.

NOTES

1. See Paula Byrne, *Jane Austen and the Theatre*, London: Hambledon, 2002; Penny Gay, *Jane Austen and the Theatre*, Cambridge: Cambridge University Press, 2002.
2. *Monthly Mirror*, 8 July 1799, p. 57.
3. Jane Austen, *Mansfield Park*, ed. James Kinsley, Oxford: Oxford University Press, 1990, p. 109.
4. The standard history of the phenomenon is Sybil Rosenfeld, *Temples of Thespis: Some Private Theatres and Theatricals in England and Wales, 1700–1820*, London: Society for Theatre Research, 1978.
5. Maria Edgeworth, *Patronage*, London: Whitaker and Co, 1845, p. 305.
6. Joseph Cradock, *Literary and Miscellaneous Memoirs*, 4 vols., London: J. B. Nichols, 1828, vol. IV, p. 262.
7. See George Colman the Younger's account of the theatricals in his *Random Records*, 2 vols., London: Henry Colburn and Richard Bentley, 1830, vol. II, pp. 40–56.
8. *European Magazine*, November 1787, p. 362.
9. See Naomi Tadmor, *Family and Friends in Eighteenth-Century England: Household, Kinship, and Patronage*, Cambridge: Cambridge University Press, 2001.
10. Austen, *Mansfield Park*, pp. 117, 172.
11. Anthony Pasquin, *The Life of the Late Earl of Barrymore*, third edn., London: H. D. Symonds, 1793, p. 17.
12. *Universal Magazine*, November 1777, p. 270.
13. Gillian Russell, *The Theatres of War: Performance, Politics and Society, 1793–1815*, Oxford: Clarendon Press, 1995.
14. *The World*, 18 May 1787.
15. Emma Donoghue, *Passions Between Women: British Lesbian Culture 1668–1801*, New York: Harper Collins, 1993, pp. 145–6.
16. Catherine B. Burroughs, *Closet Stages: Joanna Baillie and the Theater Theory of British Romantic Women Writers*, Philadelphia, PA: Pennsylvania University Press, 1997, p. 148.
17. See Russell, *Theatres of War*, pp. 130–1.
18. Arthur Murphy, *The Plays of Arthur Murphy*, ed. Richard B. Schwartz, 4 vols., New York and London: Garland Publishing, 1979, vol. II, p. 15.
19. *Oxford Magazine* 6 (1771), p. 215.
20. [Isaac Jackman], *All the World's a Stage*, third edn., London: J. Wilkie, 1777, pp. 27–8.
21. See Rosenfeld, *Temples of Thespis*, pp. 128–32.
22. *Journal of the House of Lords* 41 (1798), p. 542.

14

MICHAEL BURDEN

Opera in the London theatres

To say that the greater part of the English audience was suspicious of continental opera is an understatement. They found an entirely sung 'play' difficult to accept, disliked recitative, thought the plots ludicrous and treated opera with suspicion because it was 'foreign'. To such an audience, a genre with spoken dialogue called 'English Opera' (as opposed to opera in English) was decidedly preferable. Nevertheless, the arrival of Italian opera early in the eighteenth century was welcomed by that part of the public keen for something exotic and prepared to be charmed by the music, captivated by the stagings and scandalised by the singers. That these types of opera were used for different types of critical discourse emphasises the fact that Italian opera remained a separate and distinct force and indeed came to delineate a binary opposition in eighteenth-century culture.[1]

This binary opposition manifested itself most obviously in the division of the repertoire between the London theatres. On the one hand, Drury Lane and Covent Garden put on mainly spoken plays; the all-sung operas staged there were usually afterpieces in English, though operas with spoken dialogue also appeared among the mainpieces in various guises, including ballad opera and burletta. There were three other venues for opera in English. The oldest of these was the Little Theatre in the Haymarket. Opened in 1720, it was an occasional venue for opera performances, including those in the summer under Samuel Foote from 1747 and George Colman the Elder's seasons from 1777. The English Opera House, later the Lyceum, which opened in 1772 and was first able to function as a proper theatre in 1809, was restricted to performing opera; not until the Licensing Act of 1843 was it allowed to present spoken drama. There was, lastly, the Olympic Theatre, which, for a short period in the 1830s under Eliza Vestris, was licensed to produce 'entertainments of music, dancing, burlettas, spectacle, pantomime, and horsemanship': the meaning of the term 'burletta' came to encompass almost any musical entertainment other than all-sung opera.

To respond to this binary opposition by lumping playhouse entertainments in a group labelled with the catch-all phrase 'plays with music', however, is not only misleading, but incorrectly suggests that the word 'opera' (and therefore an operatic approach) was abandoned in works employing spoken dialogue. Nothing could be further from the truth. Indeed, in an effort to catch the public's attention, authors began to add a variety of descriptive titles, which by the nineteenth century had expanded to include comic opera, grand opera, grand heroic opera, grand serious opera, heroic opera, heroic-comic opera, lyric comedy, melodramatic opera, musical comedy, musical drama, musical entertainment, musical farce, opera, *opéra comique*, operatic drama, romantic opera, serio-comic opera, serious opera, semi-serious opera, tragic opera and more. As far as opera at the playhouses is concerned, it is important to acknowledge that promoters, authors and composers had at their disposal a large range of genres that were thought to be operatic, and an even greater number of choices for the employment of music in spoken drama. Indeed, the texts of such works were often supplied by the same authors who were providing entirely spoken dramas such as Arthur Murphy, Isaac Bickerstaffe and the Colmans. In both situations, the employment of music was often used as a draw for an audience which might be attracted by sound rather than sense.

There is no difficulty at all about defining what opera was at London's fifth venue, one known colloquially as the Opera, and more formally as the King's Theatre; under annual licence, it put on all-sung affairs in Italian, works recognisable to us today as operas.[2] Under impresari with varied rates of artistic success – and equally varied financial results[3] – it remained the principal seat of Italian opera well into the nineteenth century, becoming Her Majesty's Theatre and the home of the Royal Italian Opera Company on the accession of Queen Victoria in 1837. Financial struggles finally caused the Company to disperse in the 1840s, the last of its seasons seeing the manager Benjamin Lumley mounting the first stagings in London of operas by Verdi.[4] There was some short-lived competition in the 1790s from the Pantheon Opera enterprise which ended in bankruptcy and arson,[5] but the repertoire of the house did not differ significantly in style from that of the King's.[6]

The opera house and the playhouses were not only marked out by a division in repertory, but also in staging and performing conventions. In essence, while the 'foreign' performers were held to be stylised and to strike attitudes (and were expected to do so), the English singers were required to be 'natural'.[7] Quite what this term meant at any one particular point in the period was variable, but there is no doubt that the placing in opposition of the 'naturalness' of the English theatre singer and the 'artifice' of the Italian opera singer had to do not only with language and acting, but with differences in vocal technique and repertoire.[8] On one hand, there was the singer-actor, who was an actor who could sing, for better or for worse as the case may be. The performer may not have been very talented vocally, and may well have used characterisation to carry the music but could at least make a fair fist of it. The theatre singer was a more highly trained individual, with more set pieces of greater technical difficulty to sing. By contrast, the Italian singers' vocal skills were novel and fascinating but their acting was often regarded as stilted and uncommunicative.

The process of writing, preparing and staging of opera was not organised in the way we would expect today, that is, with the same clear and consistent line of interpretative control. The composer, resident librettist, singers, costume-makers and scene-painters went about their business separately. Rehearsals were used to revamp and rework the piece, and appear to have been run by whoever had the greatest authority in the company at the time. Sometimes, this was the music director, as in the case of Pietro Guglielmi at the King's Theatre in the 1760s, or the lead performers, as in the case of the English opera *The Iron Chest*, which the actor-manager J. P. Kemble rehearsed until he became ill; then the prompter took over, making, as George Colman pointed out, 'a very curious march of it'. Whatever routines were in use, the results clearly satisfied the performers, the critics and the audience alike.

English opera at the playhouses

For much of the eighteenth century, Drury Lane and Covent Garden – like the King's Theatre – had a multifaceted bill which included a mainpiece, one or two afterpieces, and interval music and dancing. On the whole, the main-piece slot was usually reserved for a spoken play, with the shorter afterpieces containing the operatic interest. Sometimes, however, the mainpiece took the form of a major operatic or all-sung work such as Thomas Arne's 1738 setting of Dalton's adaptation of Milton's *Comus*, J. C. Smith's version of *A Midsummer Night's Dream* (1755), or Prince Hoare's opera seria, *Dido, Queen of Carthage* (1792). As mentioned above, the predilection for opera with spoken dialogue mitigated against the notion of an English composer developing an all-sung tradition, though composers such as Thomas Arne, William Shield, Stephen Storace, Thomas Linley Senior and Junior and Charles Dibdin all had the capacity to write such pieces.[9] And there was no compromise when commissioning a major foreign composer. In 1824, the manager Charles Kemble asked for a new opera from the German composer, Carl Maria von Weber. Weber was offered the subjects of *Faust* or *Oberon* and chose *Oberon*, but even with the German singspiel tradition behind him, Weber found it a matter for concern that many of the principals did not sing and that music was omitted 'in the most important moments'. As Weber's commission suggests, and *Comus* and *Dido* exemplify, the repertoire did not consist entirely of new stories but included a large number of adaptations and reworkings of old tales.[10] The music for such works occupied the middle ground: the grandest numbers emulated Italian forms, while simple and affecting sentiments inspired an infinite variety of music to match.

Afterpieces – often known as 'the farce' regardless of content – used spoken dialogue and were frequently comedies. Typical of these afterpieces was Storace's Drury Lane opera, *No Song, No Supper* (1790), one of the few English scores to survive intact from the later eighteenth century.[11] The music was not all by Storace – the tunes are drawn from a variety of sources including Grétry, Giordani and Pleyel – and, in common with many afterpieces, the tunes are simple and accessible. By the early years of the nineteenth century, the number of afterpieces had increased to two, and the playhouse programmes – which by now included much more English opera – also contained numerous musical fillers. When Arnold at the English Opera House increased the total number of pieces to four, Leigh Hunt declared that the bills ought to carry the note 'Night-caps and breakfast in the lobbies'.[12] Some sense was brought into this situation by the actress and opera singer Madame Vestris who tried to restrict performances to between four and five hours. By 1840, the programmes had shortened slightly but an evening listening to English opera was bound still to be long, involved and spectacular.

Foreign opera was 'English'd' through translation and adaptation, although not always successfully. As Edward Pigott commented: 'one of the comic operas was the Deserter translated from the French; the music tho very preety in French is very bad in English, Sung without taste and altered, as also the plot, very much to the worst'.[13] The contrasting stagings of André Grétry's popular escape opera, *Richard Coeur de Lion* (1786) not only illustrate this practice, but also provide an insight into the musical competition between the patent houses. Grétry had become very popular in Paris during the 1770s, and *Richard Coeur de Lion*, premiered by the Comédie Italienne in 1784, was produced at the height of his fame. An opera on an English subject was bound to appeal to London audiences, so Sheridan asked John Burgoyne to prepare a translation for Drury Lane, while Thomas Harris at Covent Garden invited Leonard MacNally to do the same. MacNally's version leaves the story broadly intact, whereas the Drury Lane version replaces Richard's Queen Berengaria with a mistress called Matilda. Conversely, the music for Drury Lane, overseen by Thomas Linley Senior, used most of Grétry's music; Covent Garden's, compiled by William Shield, drew on the work of composers including Grétry, Anfossi, Bertoni, Hayes, Wilson, Carolan and Shield. The two productions were staged within a fortnight of each other in 1786, and their afterlife gives some clues about their relative success. McNally's version survives only in the 1786 edition, whereas Burgoyne's translation went through numerous London editions.[14]

This process – typical of the adaptation of Continental works – continued well into the nineteenth century. Other adaptations included Covent Garden's 1819 staging of Mozart's *The Marriage of Figaro* (described by one appalled German as being full of 'the most tasteless and shocking alterations');[15] the English Opera House's 1828 version of Mozart's *Così fan tutte*, renamed *Tit for Tat, or, the Tables Turn'd*; Rossini's *Guillaume Tell* now called *Hofer, the Tell of the Tyrol* (DL, 1830); and Auber's *Le Dieu et la Bayadère* which appeared as a ballet-opera entitled *The Maid of Cashmere* (DL, 1833), with the story adapted from Eugène Scribe by Edward Fitzball. The music for these last two pieces was the work of Henry Bishop, whose compositional efforts almost single-handedly kept the flame of English opera alight until his death in 1855. Often in conjunction with the playwright and librettist James Robinson Planché, Bishop produced many new works and adaptations in almost every musical-dramatic genre conceivable.[16]

Also present in the playhouse repertory were a number of ballad operas, which were the fruit of the genre's brief flowering in the 1730s following the astonishing success of *The Beggar's Opera* (1728). A comic and often satirical form, ballad opera had spoken dialogue with songs – either new tunes or old tunes with new words fitted – worked closely into the action. Although a number of works continued to be performed until the end of the century, new works were scarce after 1740, and the form's satirical functions were usurped by the burletta. Making its appearance in the 1760s, the burletta satirised classical myths and, like ballad opera, the musical scores consisted largely of well-known tunes including folk-songs, music borrowed from the opera house, and old favourites by composers such as Purcell and Handel. Eighteenth-century burletta also produced a runaway success: *Midas*, a burletta by the Irishman Kane O'Hara, first performed in 1760 and still being played in New York during the nineteenth century. Other works in a similar vein included O'Hara's *The Golden Pippin* and James Hook's setting of Thomas Bridges's *Dido*, in which the unfortunate Queen of Carthage hangs herself with her own garters.[17]

The performance of *Midas* in New York (rather than, say, Paris or Vienna) points to a disappointing truth, namely that English opera was an export of interest only to English-speaking countries: none of its conventions had any influence on the course of Continental opera. Musically, English operas remained what they had always been: collections of elegantly written tunes in both high and low styles which never developed into an identifiable and consistent national tradition. This is not to say that Britain did not have a profound effect on Continental opera, but it was through the narratives of Walter Scott's fashionable Waverley novels such as *The Bride of Lammermoor* that such influence would be exerted.[18]

Italian opera at the King's Theatre

Until the 1760s, a London season at the Opera consisted of some seven or eight opera seria, usually labelled 'dramma per musica'. Thereafter, audiences demanded a balanced diet of opera seria and opera buffa, albeit with a distinct leaning towards the buffo type, although a season with too many comedies could expect – and did receive – negative criticism. Proper subjects for opera seria remained heroic deeds drawn from ancient history and medieval romance. Indeed, London continued to support opera seria long after the form had been largely abandoned on the continent. Each year's repertoire was largely new, with only one or two works appearing in consecutive seasons, and pasticcio represented a staple element.[19]

No single composer or librettist dominated London's Italian opera scene, with the exception of the poet Metastasio: settings of his libretti received nearly 1,000 performances between 1727 and 1843. Indeed, there were two seasons when Metastasian opera was about all that was on offer: the first (1756–57), under the impresario Regina Mingotti, consisted of five operas featuring three Metastasio libretti – *Alessandro nell'Indie*, *Antigono*, and *Il Re Pastore* – while the second (1764–65) consisted of eight operas, six of which were by Metastasio: *Ezio*, *Adriano*, *Demofoonte*, *Il Re Pastore*, *Antigono* and *L'Olimpiade*.

Though the texts of these operas were originally by Metastasio, they were nearly all subject to alteration. Indeed, almost no opera imported from the Continent was performed without adaptation to the London scene, whether at the desire of the music director, to meet the requirements of the cast, or to answer the needs of a London audience. Italian opera arrived in London in a number of forms. There were the settings performed elsewhere and then imported and adapted; there were settings written in London of previously existing libretti; there were libretti which were specifically prepared for London composers and then set; and there were pasticci – operas with music drawn from works by a number of composers – usually prepared in London, which used aria settings from other contexts to compile a 'new' opera.

Even when the opera was 'completed', further alteration could take place, for singers would frequently introduce their own songs during the rehearsal process. Though an anathema to modern concepts of 'the work', the practice was widespread in London and was not confined to old operas; of the all-new *L'usurpator innocente* (1790), it was dryly remarked that the music was by Vincenzo Federici 'except the songs of Madam Mara', who appears to have replaced many of those for her character of Dircea with her own 'suitcase' arias.[20] The practice was assisted by the structure of opera seria. For much of the period, opera seria consisted of works in three acts which had as their staple structural unit the da capo aria. This tripartite form – in which the third section was a repeated, ornamented version of the first – was not necessarily opera-specific; the text tended to reflect in general on the dramatic content of the preceding recitative, so as long as the sentiment of the aria was appropriate to its context, all was well. Libretti were arranged so that, at the end, a singer would almost always exit from the stage (naturally to applause!). There were few ensembles: a duet could usually be found, and the opera always closed with a chorus sung by the soloists, but that was about all. As the century wore on, composers tried to soften this rigid recitative-aria-exit pattern, using accompanied recitative, and gradually, ensembles were added in increasing numbers. Finally, towards the end of the century, the da capo (and its variant, the dal segno) arias began to be outnumbered by a range of through-composed forms and the number of acts was reduced to two, shortening the text but reflecting an expanded musical structure.

The more flexible employment of musical form had much to do with the popularity of opera buffa, a genre new to eighteenth-century London and only recently contrived in Italy. As in other centres, London audiences immediately took the form to their hearts. Early works included Leo's *La finta frascatana* (1749), Cocchi's *Gli amanti gelosi* (1753) and performances of Galuppi's *Il mondo della luna*. However, it was not until the arrival in 1761 of Goldoni and Galuppi's *Il filosofo di campagna* that the genre became a staple in almost every season. Subjects for opera buffa were satirical and contemporary, and unlike most serious operas, their popularity kept them in the repertory, year in, year out. Between its premiere and the end of the century, for example, Piccini's setting of *La buona figliuola* played in every season apart from one. While it would be tempting to attribute this popularity to the familiarity of its source – Samuel Richardson's *Pamela* – the novel's adaptation by Goldoni, first as the play *Pamela nubile* and then for the libretto, left little or nothing of the original.[21] Other popular opera buffe include Piccini's *La schiava*, Guglielmi's *I viaggiatori ridicoli* and Paisiello's *La frascatana*.

As the turn of the century approached, the division of the genres, musically at least, became less obvious, as opera seria adopted the more fluid musical forms of, or at least very similar to, those of its comic counterpart. Opera seria subjects began to be taken less from the ancient world and more from contemporary literature and recent history. The growth of interest in new subjects and styles was largely responsible for the first serious challenge faced by Italian opera in London when, in 1832, a German opera season was staged at the King's Theatre. This was something of a revelation. Consisting of works such as Weber's *Der Freischütz* (a work already popular in London through English adaptations) and Beethoven's *Leonore*, the company gave solid solo performances and used chorus work that was powerful and well organised, a style way beyond the 'rueful shabby people who used to shout their easy Italian tunes out of tune, in a meagre, motionless semi-circle'.[22]

The end of the eighteenth century saw a number of fundamental changes taking place in the opera house. Opera began to enter what might be described as 'the age of the single composer', an attitude already in place when the first opera by Mozart was produced in London in 1806. The advertisement for *La Clemenza di Tito* emphasised that the opera was 'entirely composed' by the master; it was the music of the composer that was being emphasised, not simply another version of Metastasio's story.[23] Extended musical forms now adopted by opera seria involved more complex and distinctive structures, making the deployment of numbers from one opera to another difficult if not impossible. By 1840, many of those foreign operas performed in their original language were being staged, if not quite in their original form, then without the extensive aria substitution characteristic of previous decades.

Opera on the London bill

To see how this overview of the repertoire of both groups of theatres might work in practice, let us examine one evening's entertainment: 1 May 1770. At the King's, an audience would have enjoyed (we hope) a performance of the ever popular comedy *Il Signor Dottore*, a 1758 setting of Goldoni's story by Domenico Fischietti. The score was rather dated but had a superficial attraction which prompted sporadic revivals. On the same evening, Drury Lane was advertising Arthur Murphy's play *Zenobia* and David Garrick's musical extravaganza, *The Jubilee; or, Shakespeare's Garland* as the after-piece. Murphy's *Zenobia* was his adaptation of Crebillion's heroic tragedy, *Rhadamisthe et Zenobie*. This work illustrates the requirements for music in spoken plays: the text asks for four flourishes of trumpets as well as grand, warlike music and soft music. *The Jubilee*, on the other hand, was a musical event, consisting of songs and other material culled from Garrick's Shakespeare jubilee at Stratford upon Avon in 1769.[24] The music by Charles Dibdin consisted of songs, mostly in strophic form, and music for a pageant or procession including a 'Tambourins dance' and a 'Dance of the Graces'. Such musically extravagant processions were included in theatrical events more and more frequently after this date, and were the subject of much complaint towards the end of the eighteenth century.

Meanwhile, Covent Garden staged Joseph Reed's comic opera *Tom Jones* with Thomas Otway's comedy *The Cheats of Scapin* (1676) as the afterpiece. *Tom Jones* was not based directly on Henry Fielding's novel, but on the French adaptation undertaken by Alexandre Poinsinet for François-André Danican Philidor's opera of 1765. The score is a pasticcio, with music drawn from a long list of composers: an overture taken from Piccini, a finale set to the last movement of Corelli's 'Concerto Grosso no. 2 in F', tunes by Abel, Arne, Arnold, J. C. Bach, Baildon, Bates, Boyce, Galuppi, Granom, Handel, Hasse, Holcombe, Pergolesi and Van Maldere, and with the well-known tunes of 'Old King Cole' and 'Roger de Coverley' thrown in for good measure. Like Murphy's *Zenobia*, Otway's play was an adaptation from the French, this time of Molière's *Les Fourberies de Scapin*, a work originally performed with Otway's adaptation of Racine's *Bérénice*. The text has no cues for music, suggesting that the band may have gone home before the afterpiece began. The bill that night also included dancing between the acts of the opera – a minuet, 'by desire' and a new dance called 'The Tambourine' – and at the end, which featured a new pantomime dance entitled *The old grown young*, together with an allemande, also 'by particular desire'. The month of May fell in the benefit season and the exact choice of works in all the theatres was governed by factors such as the piece's popularity, or the desire of the beneficiary to play a lead role, or to represent a new piece. Nevertheless, this cross-section of works, with the attendant music played by an orchestra of some thirty players, can be found in a similar format for much of the eighteenth century.

By the nineteenth century, although the offerings of opera and musical drama were still much the same, the rest of the bill was much altered. On 15 February 1817, for example, the King's Theatre was staging Mozart's all-sung *Le Nozze di Figaro* in Italian, but with 'an incidental divertissement' in the course of the opera. After the opera, audiences saw a three-act ballet, *Le Prince Troubadour* by Armand Vestris, with music by F. Venua. Drury Lane was presenting George Farquhar's old comedy, *The Inconstant* and the pantomime, *Harlequin Horner; or the Christmas Pie*. The former required no music, but the latter had a number of musical inserts as well as a turn by Signor Verani who was billed to 'exhibit his wonderful performance of six instruments at the same time'. At Covent Garden, the bill featured Frederic Reynolds's version of Shakespeare's *A Midsummer Night's Dream*, with music written and arranged by Bishop including tunes by Arne, Cooke, Handel, Smith and Stevens. The play included new speeches and an additional scene as well as a recitative, twenty-one songs, ensembles and choruses, and incidental music including two flourishes, a hunting-horn call, a bird symphony, an invocation, a procession and a closing pageant. After this came Bishop's ballet divertissement, *Aurora; or the Flight of the Zephyr* and Isaac Pocock's ludicrous banditti melodrama, *The Miller and his Men*, which not only required some four vocal pieces and seven different cues for music, but contains the priceless request for 'appropriate music' to cover the action as 'Frederick draws his sword, Wolf draws pistols in each hand from side-pockets, his hat falling off at the same instant.' By this time, the playhouses were maintaining larger orchestras than the Opera – some seventy odd players to the King's Theatre's fifty or so – and the orchestral effects were clearly as extravagant in realisation as the printed stage directions suggest they were in conception.[25]

Artaxerxes

All these strands of operatic writing and performance can be found in what would ultimately be the greatest operatic achievement of any composer in eighteenth- and early nineteenth-century London, Arne's *Artaxerxes*. A setting of an English translation of Metastasio's *Artaserse*, the work premiered at Covent Garden on 2 February 1762, with a star-studded cast including Niccolo Peretti as Artaxerxes, John Beard as Artabanes and Giusto Ferdinando Tenducci as Arbaces. The work, steadily popular for at least sixty years, would go on to have some 450 performances and circulated widely well into the nineteenth century. Arne had achieved a most remarkable feat: as Charles Burney pointed out, 'the *Artaxerxes* of the late Dr. Arne . . . found an English audience that could tolerate even recitative'.[26]

The season of 1833–34 illustrates *Artaxerxes*' enduring popularity. The bills included twelve performances at the Haymarket, one at Covent Garden, one at Drury Lane and one at the English Opera, as well as those at other London venues. *Artaxerxes* was also a frequent choice for royal command performances such as the one at Drury Lane in 1821, with Madame Vestris in the title role, John Braham as Arbaces and Miss Wilson as Mandane. It was reported that the King was seen retiring 'a few minutes after eleven, the performance being over': the idea of George IV sitting through to the end of a mid eighteenth-century opera seria is not what one would have expected. Performances outside Britain included Charles Edward Horn's arrangement which opened in New York in 1828.

Artaxerxes also gained a certain monumentality, for the role of Mandane achieved iconic status. This part came to exemplify the reputation of certain singers and they often chose to have themselves engraved as Mandane.[27] The singer to create the role, Charlotte Brent, was Arne's pupil – and reputedly more – and her behaviour during the rehearsal period is the stuff of legend. She was so annoyed that the tenor Tenducci had been given what she considered to be the 'best air' that Arne sat down and wrote her a new number called 'Let not rage thy bosom firing', which both appeased and amused her. The popularity of *Artaxerxes* was such that each house had their own Mandane; in the 1780s, Cecilia Arne was Mandane for Drury Lane, and the great Elizabeth Billington sang the role for Covent Garden; by the 1820s, Drury Lane had Miss Paton (in 1825 playing opposite Madame Vestris in the title role) while Elizabeth Hughes sang for Covent Garden.

The reaction of the other theatres to this success was typical of the way in which one playhouse responded to another in moments of operatic competition. David Garrick attempted to cash in on Arne's ideas at Drury Lane by staging three operas of a similar style: *The Royal Shepherd*, a reworking of Metastasio's *Il Re Pastore* by Richard Rolt, set by George Rush, later reworked by Tenducci for the rival house under the title of *Amintas*; *Almena*, also with a libretto by Rolt; and *Pharnaces*, based on Lucchini's libretto, *Farnace*.

Why should *Artaxerxes* have been so popular? It cannot have been the plot, for there were four settings of the text before Arne's and six after his, none of which managed more than about thirty performances. Certainly some of Arne's songs had a 'national' flavour, but do not appear to have caught the zeitgeist in a distinctive way. The composer did, however, provide a score which employed simple English-style tunes with grander Italian flourishes, supported by an orchestration of unusual complexity and flair. The result is a musically weightier work than the lighter Italian operas, in a language that the playhouse audience could understand, but requiring singers skilled enough to appeal to those who patronised the Opera.

Arne's *Artaxerxes* stands as a monument to the process of preparing opera for performance in London: an adaptation and a translation into English of a work by an Italian librettist living in Vienna, set to music by an English composer who was barred from official and Court jobs by his Catholic faith and whose style represented an amalgam of Italian and English elements. It has not, however, been my purpose to argue that works such as *Artaxerxes* – and the others I have described above – are in some way inferior because they do not answer to our notions of all-sung opera or ideas of authorship; it has been to emphasise that the key words for any opera composer, promoter, prompter and singer in eighteenth- and early nineteenth-century London were adaptation, re-interpretation and competition, and that the city was a melting pot for works of all operatic genres and musical styles.

NOTES

1. Suzanne Aspden, '"An Infinity of Factions": Opera in Eighteenth-Century Britain and the Undoing of Society', *Cambridge Opera Journal* 9:1 (1997), pp. 1–19.

2. W. C. Smith, *The Italian Opera and Contemporary Ballet in London, 1789–1820*, London: Society for Theatre Research, 1955.

3. See, for example, the tale of Felice Giardini as recounted in Curtis Price, Judith Milhous and Robert D. Hume, *The Impresario's Ten Commandments: Continental Recruitment for Italian Opera in London 1763–64*, London: Royal Musical Association, 1992, pp. 18–29.

4. Frederick C. Petty, *Italian Opera in London 1760–1800*, Ann Arbor, MI: University of Michigan Press, 1980; Curtis Price, Judith Milhous and Robert D. Hume, *Italian Opera in Late Eighteenth-Century London*, 2 vols., Oxford: Clarendon, 1995, vol. I and Theodore Fenner, *Opera in London: Views of the Press, 1785–1830*, Carbondale, IL: Southern Illinois University Press, 1995.

5. Curtis Price, 'Opera and Arson in Eighteenth-Century London', *Journal of the American Musicological Society* 42 (1989), pp. 55–107.

6. Judith Milhous, Gabriella Dideriksen and Robert D. Hume, *Italian Opera in Late Eighteenth-Century London*, 2 vols., Oxford: Clarendon, 2001: vol. II.

7. Pier Francesco Tosi, *Observations on the florid song; or, sentiments on the ancient and modern singers*, trans. J. E. Galliard, London: J. Wilcox, 1743, pp. 140–73.

8. Robert Toft, *Heart to Heart: Expressive Singing in England, 1780–1830*, Oxford and New York: Oxford University Press, 2000, pp. 147–81.

9. Roger Fiske, *English Theatre Music in the Eighteenth Century*, London: Oxford University Press, 1973, pp. 179–98, 302–318, 413–80.

10. A. Fischler, '*Oberon* and Odium: the Career and Crucifixion of J. R. Planché', *Opera Quarterly* 12:1 (1995), pp. 292–9.

11. Stephen Storace, *No Song, No Supper*, ed. Roger Fiske, *Musica Britannica* XVI, London: Stainer and Bell, 1958.

12. Leigh Hunt, *Leigh Hunt's Dramatic Criticism 1808–1859*, eds. Lawrence H. Houtchens and Carolyn W. Houtchens, New York: Columbia University Press, 1949, p. 281.

13. Edward Pigott, MS diary in the Beinecke Library, Yale University, quoted in Elizabeth Gibson, 'Edward Pigott: Eighteenth-Century Theatre Chronicler', *Theatre Notebook* 42:2 (1988), pp. 62–72, 67.

14. David Charlton, *Grétry and the Growth of Opéra-Comique*, Cambridge: Cambridge University Press, 1986, pp. 226–51.

15. [Ludwig H. von Pückler-Muskau], *A Tour in Germany, Holland and England in the Years 1826, 1827, and 1828*, London: Effingham Wilson, Royal Exchange, 1832, pp. 147–8.

16. Eric Walter White, *A History of English Opera*, London: Faber and Faber, 1983, pp. 243–94.

17. Joseph W. Donohue, Jr, 'Burletta and the Early Nineteenth-Century English Theatre', *Nineteenth-Century Theatre Research* 1 (1973), pp. 29–51, and Phyllis T. Dircks, *The Eighteenth-Century English Burletta*, Victoria, BC: English Literary Studies, University of Victoria, 1999, pp. 55–57ff.

18. J. Mitchell, *The Walter Scott Operas: an Analysis of Operas based on the Works of Walter Scott*, Birmingham, AL: University of Alabama Press, 1977.

19. Curtis Price, 'Unity, Originality and the London Pasticcio', *Harvard Library Bulletin* 2:4 (1991), pp. 421–44 and Michael Burden, 'Metastasio's "London pasties": Curate's Egg or Pudding's Proof?', in *Pietro Metastasio (1698–1782), 'uomo universal'*, eds. Elisabeth Theresia Hilscher and Andrea Sommer-Mathis, Vienna: Verlag der Österreichischen Akademie der Wissenschaften, 2000, pp. 293–309.

20. *Morning Herald*, 7 April 1790, p. 2.

21. William C. Holmes, 'Pamela Transformed', *Musical Quarterly* 38:1 (1952), pp. 581–94.

22. Henry F. Chorley, *Thirty Years' Musical Recollections*, London: Hunt and Blackett, 1862, p. 74.

23. Emanuele Senici, '"Adapted to the Modern Stage": *La Clemenza di Tito* in London', *Cambridge Opera Journal* 7:1 (1997), pp. 1–22.

24. John A. Parkinson, 'Garrick's Folly; or the Great Stratford Jubilee', *Musical Times* 110 (1969), pp. 922–6 and *Shakespeare's Garland; songs, choruses, [&c] which are introduced in the new entertainment of the Jubilee*, London: T. Becket and P. A. de Hondt, 1769.

25. See, for example, Edward Brayley, *Historical and Descriptive Accounts of the Various Theatres of London*, London: J. Taylor, 1826, p. 32.

26. Charles Burney, *A General History of Music*, ed. Frank Mercer, 2 vols., London: G. T. Foulis, 1935, vol.II, p. 643.

27. Maria Ines Aliverti, 'Major Portraits and Minor Series in Eighteenth-Century Theatrical Portraiture', *Theatre Research International* 22:3 (1983), pp. 234–54.

15

HELEN BURKE

Acting in the periphery: the Irish theatre

Shortly after he took up the position of Deputy Manager and Treasurer at Smock Alley, the Irish Theatre Royal, in 1746, Benjamin Victor, an English newcomer to Ireland, approached the manager, Thomas Sheridan, with a number of suggestions that he felt would result in a better regulated theatre in that location. However, as he later reported in his *History of the Theatres of London and Dublin* (1761), Sheridan always rejected his proposals as too dangerous, saying '*You forget yourself, you think you are on English Ground.*'[1] Theatre historians who have followed Victor in writing on the eighteenth-century Irish stage have generally been guilty of a similar kind of forgetting when it comes to this institution. Focusing on the similarities between the Dublin and London stages, they have concluded that the Irish theatre of this period was either a provincial theatre or a British colonial institution.[2]

In this essay, however, I will suggest that the Irish theatre is better char-acterised as a subaltern site in the sense that the post-colonial critic, David Lloyd, uses the term; a space in the Irish colonial past which was capable of bringing into being new, non-'English' states of culture and practice.[3] In Ireland, as in other imperial sites, the forces of colonialism and modernity generated more politically ambiguous hybrids than properly reformed colonial subjects. As these improper subjects made their way into the Irish theatre – as writers, actors and audience members – they produced forms and practices that resisted British colonial culture while also gesturing at alternative Irish cultural logics. The subversive play of these unorthodox 'actors' is not easy to recover and requires us to shift our historiographic gaze from centre stage to the theatrical peripheries – to the 'shadow play' that was always being staged around the edges of the British colonial theatre and within the interstices of the British dramatic text.[4] What at first looked like imitative acts were, in effect, acts of colonial mimicry which subverted and estranged the dominant cultural script.[5]

In its origins, the professional theatre in Ireland was a colonial institution.[6] Successive viceroys tried to retain their control over the Irish stage through direct and indirect forms of patronage. In the early decades of the eighteenth century, they began a tradition of paying the manager of the Theatre Royal – then Smock Alley – a yearly sum so that the boxes would be free to the 'Ladies' on a number of important official holidays such as royal birthdays and anniversaries. These 'government nights' were some of the most glittering, as well as most manifestly English, nights of the theatrical season. The Dublin Castle administration – that is, the viceroy and his court – and the Anglo-Irish Protestant gentry would turn up at the playhouse in all their finery, creating a spectacle of ruling class power and solidarity. Viceroys also 'commanded' performances on numerous other occasions, thereby ensuring their continued influence over the Theatre Royal.

But not all the Anglo-Irish were enamoured of the English administration at Dublin Castle, and it is with this internal difference in the colonial ruling class that the narrative of an Irish counter-theatre begins. Early in the eighteenth century, a small number of Anglo-Irish, then the theatre's principal patrons, became resentful of England's political and cultural dominance of Ireland, and began to demand a theatre that was more locally controlled and more reflective of their concerns. One of the first playwrights to articulate these patriotic sentiments was Matthew Concanen who called for a more 'native Note' in the drama and denounced what he saw as the 'second Hand' nature of the Irish theatre:

> Long had our Stage, on foreign Refuse fed,
> To a proud Mistress bow'd her servile Head;
> Her Leavings treasur'd up, and curs'd the Land
> With broken Scraps of Wit at second Hand [...][7]

In the 1720s, too, Concanen and other Anglo-Irish writers began incorporating Irish settings and Irish matter into their plays for Smock Alley. In some cases at least these plays had a critical political edge.[8] Charles Coffey's *The Beggar's Wedding* (SA, 1729), is an Irish rewriting of Gay's ballad opera which critiques the corruption of Dublin city officials.

More commonly, Anglo-Irish writers staged their political difference in what could be called the margins of the drama proper – in the prologues, epilogues and entr'acte performances that filled out an evening's entertainment. For a Smock Alley production of *Hamlet* in 1721, Jonathan Swift and Thomas Sheridan wrote a prologue and an epilogue protesting about the impoverished state of the Dublin weavers and urging the audience to wear clothes of Irish manufacture. The actor playing Hamlet also wore Irish wool for that production. By the early 1730s, patriots were interjecting this kind of critical Irish note into the 'government night'. On the occasion of George II's birthday in 1731, Nancy Sterling (better known in Dublin as the 'Irish Polly

Peachum') spoke a prologue, written by her dramatist husband, which criticised the 'Ladies and Beaux' for not supporting the Irish wool trade.[9]

Pressure for change, however, also came from less elite sources. In the 1730s, new entertainment venues began to spring up all over the city, and the demands of the audiences in these marginal sites led to the creation of more localised and more Irish theatrical entertainments. One of the first to meet these populist demands was Madame Violante, an Italian rope-dancer who in 1730 opened a wooden theatrical 'Booth' in Dame Street. In her booth, three young Irish actors who later became famous – Peg Woffington, Isaac Sparks and John Barrington – made their debut as part of a children's performing group. With Woffington as Polly, this 'Lilliputian' company of children players reportedly performed *The Beggar's Opera* in an 'Irish manner' to crowded houses in 1731.[10]

The theatrical company that emerged from this unlikely site led to a spurt of theatre building, renovation and competition in the city. In 1733, three of Violante's young actors formed a company and, under the patronage of the Earl of Meath, built a new theatre in Rainsford Street, just outside the city limits. Two years later, 'noblemen and gentlemen of the first rank and consequence' built a new, larger, and more ornate playhouse for the Theatre Royal company in the fashionable area of Aungier Street.[11] In order to compete with this bigger theatre, the Rainsford Street company moved back into the city, took over, and rebuilt Smock Alley.

This new Smock Alley was also a more middle-class and local venture than its Aungier Street competitor. When the rebuilt house opened for the 1736–37 season, Louis Duval listed his company as playing 'By Permission of the Lord Mayor'. Smock Alley was thus, for the first time, a city rather than a 'royal' theatre. This playhouse was more engaged in the social concerns of the city than the Theatre Royal. During the terrible famine year of 1741 (known in Irish as *bliahhain an air* or 'the year of the slaughter'), Aungier Street only sponsored one charity benefit, while Smock Alley sponsored six.[12]

The theatre's connection with the Charitable Musical Society for the Relief of Imprisoned Debtors also had the effect of bringing more native Irish patrons and performers into the playhouse. The entr'acte entertainment for the 'Distressed Prisoners in the Several Marshalseas' at Smock Alley on February 1738, for instance, featured 'the famous Mr. Murphy' who performed on 'the Irish Harp', and, on other occasions, Lawrence Whyte, a schoolteacher who came from the rural Catholic gentry, wrote special prologues for these benefits.[13] Native Irish writers and musicians were undoubtedly in the Smock Alley audience on these nights both to show their support for their friends and for the 'distressed Prisoners', many of whom would have come from the poorer, native Irish population.

The violent conflicts that erupted at Smock Alley during Thomas Sheridan's reign as manager also revealed how much the Irish stage had changed by mid-century. In 1743, harsh conditions forced the Smock Alley and Aungier Street companies to unite, and in 1745, Sheridan, a popular young Dublin actor, took over the management of the united company at Smock Alley, now again the Theatre Royal. In a play that he had written in the early 1740s – *The Brave Irishman* (or *Captain O'Blunder*, as it was first called) – Sheridan also showed a keen awareness of the sensibilities of an Irish audience. This two-act farce, which deals with an Irishman's encounters in London, is one of the first significant rewritings of the debased stage Irishman type. Though Captain O'Blunder, the play's Irish hero, has many of the typical characteristics of this type – he is naïve, makes verbal blunders and is quick to fight – he also emerges as a brave and generous lover. The tacit message is that the English negative stereotype about the Irish is wrong. With Dublin actor Isaac Sparks in the role of O'Blunder this play was a great favourite with Dublin audiences.[14]

Sheridan showed no such sensitivity to his audience, however, in his managerial capacity. He believed that the Irish stage was being 'destroyed at the Will and Pleasure of the People', and, he later explained, he was determined to regulate it so that Dublin theatre might 'vie' with, or surpass that of London.[15] To Irish ears, this reform mission sounded suspiciously like the English civilising mission, and it sparked resistance from all but the most loyalist element in his audience. His first confrontation, perhaps not surprisingly, was with some native Irishmen, and it occurred in 1747 after Sheridan beat a Galway man named Kelly for going behind the scenes during a play and (reportedly) accosting a woman player. Because Kelly came from an Irish Catholic background,[16] he and his supporters read this beating as Sheridan's refusal to recognise Kelly's status as a gentleman – for a mere player to beat a gentleman was otherwise unimaginable, they reasoned – and when the manager refused to apologise for this affront, they rioted in the playhouse. The uproar that followed was so intense that the authorities ordered the closing of the theatre for six weeks. Kelly and some of his supporters were subsequently found guilty of assault, while Sheridan was acquitted.

A number of patriot-minded Protestant gentlemen then took offence about Sheridan's refusal to consider the work of aspiring Irish playwrights. Edmund Burke and two other Trinity College undergraduates berated Sheridan for encouraging the 'wretched productions' of a 'neighbouring isle' while ignoring 'such Productions of our own as promise Genius'.[17] At the same time, Paul Hiffernan, a playwright friend of Burke and a supporter of the Kelly faction, rented a little theatre at Capel Street. With a small company which at one point included Samuel Foote and the Irish writer,

Letitia Pilkington, he began ridiculing Sheridan and the Theatre Royal from that stage. Hiffernan's satirical mock-puppet play, *The Election* (CS, 1749), represents Sheridan as Fustian, a self-important actor who alters plays to suit his powerful patrons and who threatens to call anyone who insults him before '*my Lord Chief Justice*'.[18]

The enforced closure of Henry Brooke's new ballad opera, *Jack the Giant Queller*, in 1749 also had the effect of highlighting the manager's dependence on government, thus activating yet another more plebian kind of patriot opposition. There was no equivalent to the English Stage Licensing Act in Ireland because the government thought it could depend on the loyalty of the Theatre Royal managers. Brooke took advantage of this loophole in 1744 to bring *Gustavus Vasa, the Deliverer of his Country*, a play of his which had been banned in London, to the Smock Alley stage. Performed under the title *The Patriot*, this play was 'loudly called for' in Dublin.[19]

In 1749, Brooke tried to repeat this act of political daring with *Jack the Giant Queller*. Brooke wrote this ballad opera in support of Charles Lucas, a fiery Dublin apothecary who, that year, was campaigning on a populist patriot platform against a government-backed candidate for a seat in the Irish parliament. Jack Good, the peasant-hero who leads an uprising against tyrannical Giants in this opera, was a figure for Lucas who was then leading Dublin's lower orders in a battle against the oligarchy at Dublin Castle. The government evidently saw through the political allegory because on the morning after *Jack's* first performance, the Lord Justices sent word to Sheridan that they wanted the play shut down.[20] Without hesitation, the manager complied, and shortly afterwards, Lucas's supporters began to satirise Sheridan in their pamphlets, portraying him as an obedient lackey of government.[21]

On 2 March 1754 these disparate strands of Irish opposition came together. As they did so, they generated one of the more spectacular pieces of anti-colonial theatre, a staging otherwise known as the *Mahomet* riot. The immediate context for this 'memorable Night of the Subversion of the Theatre' was a dispute about the allocation of Irish monies.[22] But by the early months of 1754, the dispute was being cast in Irish versus English terms, and anti-government passions ran high throughout Ireland. Sheridan had also became the focus of new hostility because of his recently established Beefsteak club at which, it was rumoured, toasts were drunk praising the viceroy and mocking the patriots and their supporters.

The events that unfolded at the playhouse demonstrated the subversive power of colonial mimicry in such a context. When the leaders of the parliamentary opposition heard that James Miller and John Hoadly's *Mahomet the Imposter* was being staged at Smock Alley, they showed up in the pit and transformed this very British Whiggish play into a vehicle for expressing Irish patriot resentments. One of the speeches that was repeatedly encored, for instance, was Alcanor's prayer to the gods to 'crush these Vipers' who sell out the rights of their community 'for a grasp of [ore] / Or paltry Office'. This speech was an innocuous enough expression of republican civic virtue in its original context. Once dislodged from this context, it functioned as a pointed criticism of Sheridan and the court faction in the Irish parliament. Both, in the eyes of the patriots, had sold out Irish interests for money and office.

The publicity given this subversive patriot performance ensured that an even larger crowd arrived for the next announced performance of *Mahomet*. On that occasion, however, the actor playing Alcanor refused to comply with the audience's request for an encore of one of his defiant speeches. Gentlemen patriots rose up and attacked the stage, and with the assistance of the galleries and a crowd who broke in from outside, they demolished the playhouse interior. But perhaps this 'incensed Multitude' were simply completing the patriot gentlemen's subversive dramatic mimicry. In Act IV of *Mahomet*, we hear that the 'Citizens are rous'd, and all in Arms' and in a climatic moment of Act V, these enraged citizens come on the stage to confront the tyrant Mahomet.[23] As one writer sardonically noted, the theatrical monarch – and by extension, the colonial administration that he had come to figure – was 'forced to retire with as much Precipitation as *Mahomet* . . . from the blood-thirsty Citizens of *Mecca*'.[24]

After Sheridan's forced retirement, some of his erstwhile opponents invited Spranger Barry, an Irish actor then managing Covent Garden, to build a new Theatre Royal on the site of an old music hall at Crow Street. This new Crow Street theatre opened in 1758 and from then, there were always at least two public playhouses operating in Dublin until the final closure of Smock Alley in 1787. The title of Theatre Royal also floated between these various playhouses as they and the patent changed hands. This competition helped to regenerate popular interest in the Irish theatre: even the lowliest Dubliners were drawn into the rivalry. As George Stayley noted in the prologue to his farce, *The Rival Theatres: or, a Play-house to be lett* (1759), 'There's scarce a 'Prentice, *but neglects his Trade,* / *To talk how* This, *and* That, *and* Th'other Actor *play'd.*' As he observed, most working-class Dubliners favoured the new house over the old: '*mincing* Chamber-Maids, *throughout the Town,* / *Are all agreed,* – Smock Alley *must go down*'.[25] Many of these stage-struck Dubliners came from a Catholic background. When these men and women went on to become actors and playwrights, which they did in ever larger numbers, they helped to transform the Irish stage.

John O'Keeffe, who recalled, as a boy, jumping over the foundations of Crow Street as this playhouse was being erected, was one of the most important of this new generation of native Irish writers and actors.[26] O'Keeffe made his debut at Smock Alley in 1765–66, and from then until he emigrated to London in 1781, he played in Dublin playhouses and in the various regional theatres that had sprung up around the country.[27] During his time as an actor and strolling player, he wrote comic plays and entertainments which incorporated local situations and Irish matter including *Harlequin in Waterford; or, The Dutchman Outwitted* (performed in Waterford and Kilkenny, 1767–78); *The Giant's Causeway; or, A Trip to the Dargle* (Belfast, 1770) and *Tony Lumpkin's Rambles thro' Cork* (Cork, 1773). This last 'histrionic interlocution' was then adapted to suit Dublin and other locations. In each town that he visited, O'Keeffe used the persona of the country bumpkin, Tony Lumpkin, to deliver a long satirical monologue on local manners and customs which 'kept the Theatre in an uproar of applause'.[28]

O'Keeffe's dramatic writing reflected the aspirations of Irish Catholics who were then petitioning to have their political rights restored. *The Shamrock; or St. Patrick's Day* (Crow Street, 1777), a pastoral musical comedy written for his actress wife's benefit, concluded with a 'grand emblematical ... Pageant' which gestured at the Irish nation to which Catholics aspired. In this spectacle, the different ethnic groups and cultures which had historically opposed each other in Ireland – Native Irish, Anglo-Normans, Danes and Hibernians – all marched together in a show of unity, and joined in a final grand chorus, led by an actor in the role of 'Carolan, the ancient Irish Bard'.[29]

When O'Keeffe later reworked this piece for Covent Garden in 1783 as *The Poor Soldier*, he built this message of intercultural harmony into the play itself. At the end, Patrick, an Irish Catholic who is returning from military service overseas is revealed to be the 'poor soldier' who has saved the life of his Anglo-Irish rival, Captain Fitzroy, during the American revolutionary war. As a reward for his loyalty, this poor soldier is granted a commission and the hand of his sweetheart, Norah. The play's implicit argument is that Irish Catholics should be similarly recognised and rewarded for their service to the British state: Patrick's recovery of his Irish sweetheart stands for the Irish Catholic's longed-for recovery of his place in the Irish political nation.

Native Irish actors and writers who had made their name in London also began to return to Ireland on a regular basis. As the case of Charles Macklin illustrates, these individuals transformed the Irish stage through their reworking of received scripts and plots. Macklin (or Cathal Mac Loughlin, to give him his original Irish name) was recognised in his own day as one of the greatest actors on the London stage, and his two-act farce, *Love à la Mode* (1759), remained in the London repertory until the nineteenth century. But he was also one of Dublin's most celebrated actors and playwrights, often performing with the young O'Keeffe.

In *The True-Born Irishman; or, The Irish Fine Lady*, Macklin reworked the English sentimental comic genre so that it became a vehicle for expressing the desires of dispossessed native Irish families like his own. This two-act farce, first performed at Crow Street in 1761, ends with the reform of a rakish character, Mrs Diggerty, 'the Irish Fine Lady' of the play's subtitle. But, in a daring variation on the typical 'reform of the rake' theme, this lady's rehabilitation also requires that she abandon her affected 'London English' in favour of 'good, plain, old Irish English', and that she change her anglicised name (Diggerty) back to her husband's 'fine sounding Milesian' [or native Irish] name, O'Dogherty. In persuading his wife to make these changes, Murrough O'Dogherty, the 'true born Irishman' of the play's title, also defends the antiquity of native Irish names like his own. His hopes for their restoration evoke, by implication, the restoration of the Irish Catholic nation. Native Irish names, he tells his wife, are 'as old and as stout as the oak at the bottom of the bog of Allen', and 'though they have been dispossessed by upstarts and foreigners, buddoughs and sassanoughs [churls and Englishmen]', he hopes that 'they will flourish in the Island of Saints, while grass grows or water runs'.[30]

The True-Born Irishman was greeted with 'thunders of applause' when it was first produced in Dublin,[31] and it continued to be enormously popular with Irish audiences for the rest of the century. However, when Macklin brought this farce to London in 1767, 'John Bull, pit, box, and gallery, said No!' as John O'Keeffe dryly noted.[32] Indeed, the reaction was so negative that Macklin felt it necessary to go before the audience and apologise for his work. After that first unsuccessful night, the piece was withdrawn.[33] This difference in reception can also be attributed to the different level of tolerance for Irish nationalistic discourse in the two capitals at this point. '[T]hough it abounds with great humour and observation' wrote one anonymous English commentator in 1773, 'the ridicule is *local*, and the dialogue, for the most part, *national*'.[34]

Robert Owenson's rise to prominence in the 1770s and 1780s even more clearly points to an Irish stage that was becoming more 'local' and more 'national' during this period. Like Macklin, Owenson (or Mac Eoghan, to give him his 'true-born' Irish name) was a native Irishman who had gone to try his luck on the London stage. Unlike Macklin, though, this Irish actor could not lose his Irish 'brogue' – he was apparently ridiculed by English critics for his accent when he played the lead role in Rowe's *Tamerlane* – and this failure led him to return to Ireland in the mid 1770s.[35] The very linguistic and cultural differences that caused him to be rejected by London audiences, however, endeared him to Dublin and particularly to the galleries. When he played the role of Major O'Flaherty in Richard Cumberland's *The West*

Indian for his first appearance at Crow Street in 1776, for instance, he inserted Gaelic words and Irish music into this part. Though one Dublin paper chastised him for these interpolations, these bilingual performances made him a great favourite in Irish playhouses.[36]

Such interpolations also worked to undermine the stage Irishman. If played according to script, the role of Philim O'Flaherty in George Colman's prelude *New Brooms* would have reinforced the view that the Irishman was an uncultured buffoon. Philim's linguistic incompetence and 'howling' are meant to demonstrate the foolishness of his declared ambition to go on the English stage: 'Voice! oh, by my sowle, voice enough to be heard across the channel, from the Gate or the Hid, to ould Dublin: – and then I can sing, *Arrah my Judy, Arrah my Judy*! and the Irish howl! – *Hubbub-o-boo*! (*howling*) – oh, it would do your heart good to hear it.'[37] But when Owenson took this role at Crow Street in 1777, he gave a bilingual performance that displayed his mastery of several different musical traditions including 'some favourite Italian and Irish songs, particularly Carolan's "Receipt for Drinking" in Irish, and "Ple Raca na Ruarka" in English and Irish, the Irish by Carolan, the translation by Dean Swift'.[38]

The increased politicisation of the Irish theatre during the later 1770s and early 80s, however, also produced a backlash. For the first time, the government passed legislation 'regulating' the Irish stage. The politicisation that led to this crackdown, ironically, was, at first loyalist in nature. When the American revolutionary war broke out, Volunteer militia sprung up all over Ireland to defend the country against French invasion, and Dublin theatres began to display their support for these militia by incorporating Volunteer prologues, epilogues, interludes, songs and dances into the nightly dramatic entertainments. Smock Alley and Crow Street even staged a new comic opera with an Irish Volunteer theme – *The Contract* – in 1782 and 1783.[39]

By the 1780s, however, the Volunteer militias were also backing the patriots in their increasingly strident demands for free trade and a more autonomous Irish parliament. As the street theatre and gatherings of these military corps took on a more subversive edge, so did the Volunteer productions. At Smock Alley in 1780, for instance, Owenson (who was himself a Volunteer) sang a 'Song in the Character of a Volunteer' against the backdrop of a 'Grand Emblematical Transparency ... representing *Britannia, Hibernia, and America, on the Subject of the Free Trade of Ireland*'.[40] In autumn 1784, Owenson opened and began managing Fishamble Street Theatre. This little theatre also lent its support to the Volunteers and their increasingly radicalised political allies.

By the summer of 1784, the upper galleries of Smock Alley were openly voicing their support for democratic reform at home and abroad. Before the play on 9 July, for instance, there were cheers from the gallery for the 'Thirteen United States of America' and claps for 'Independence to Ireland'.[41] This agitation came to a head at a command performance by Sarah Siddons. Three days before this performance was announced, the viceroy had offended the patriot leaders at city hall by expressing his public disapproval of a reform petition that they had presented. When the Duke appeared in the viceregal box on the night of the command performance, then, there was an immediate uproar. To show their disapproval, the audience called for 'The Volunteers' March' in place of the usual 'God Save the King'. Even after the curtain went up, the 'choruses of groaning, hissing, and shouting with whistles, cat-call, horse-legs and geld-horns ... made the drama a complete farce'. When the viceroy and his attendants made a hurried retreat, they were followed by the enraged crowd.[42] As one Dublin paper put it; 'the people ... directed their fury against the hated object in the stage-box, and pursued him even out of the house, to the gates of the castle, with their groans and hisses – 'till the horse-guards rushing out, protected him from the further reproaches of a justly irritated people'.[43] Sarah Siddons 'came away in a terrible fright'; and with the routing of this British cultural icon, the Irish audience also dramatically enacted its refusal to bow to that *proud Mistress* (to use Concanen's phrase from the 1720s) who had, for so many years, dominated the Irish stage.[44]

To end these kinds of scandalous displays and to put an end to Fishamble Street's political activities, the Irish Parliament passed the 'Act for Regulating the Stage in the City and County of Dublin' (26 Geo. III, 1786), a piece of legislation that restricted the staging of drama to the patent holder while also emphasising the government's right to grant other licences if it saw fit. This was not the first time that the idea of using legislative action to ensure a monopoly for the Theatre Royal had been broached. But the fact that the 1786 Stage bill passed while earlier attempts had failed was evidence of how conditions had changed. The Irish theatre had become a dangerous site of dissent, the government and its supporters believed, and they could hope to control it only by restricting its expansion and buying the loyalty of its sole manager. The patent holder – in this case, Richard Daly – knew that if he did not comply with the desires of government, the authorities could easily license other playhouses and put him out of business.

In the short term, the Act did curtail the growth of theatre in Dublin. Bowing to the inevitable, Owenson sold out his interest in Fishamble Street to Daly in 1785, and in 1787, Daly moved the Theatre Royal company from Smock Alley to Crow Street and closed down the older theatre. The long era of Smock Alley was finally over. But by the end of the 1780s, the upper galleries at Crow Street were again in an uproar as Daly engaged in a drawn-out conflict with James Magee, the owner of the city's most popular opposition paper. In the late 1790s, the gallery spectators at the Amphitheatre Royal in Peter Street – a circus operated by the famous (and ultra-loyalist) London equestrian, Philip Astley – were using that site to show their support for the revolutionary republican group, the United Irishmen. As these new oppositions revealed, the Stage Act could slow down but ultimately could not stop the struggle to create a free Irish stage and a free Irish state.

The history of the eighteenth-century Irish stage is obviously important to a broader Irish theatrical and national history. But it is also important to British theatrical history because it provides a striking reminder of the performativity – and therefore the capacity for acting otherwise – which was at the core of this theatrical tradition. Eighteenth-century British theatre, the Irish case shows, was an unstable and dynamic export that could always be reworked to tell the stories of other peoples and other cultures. There was almost always a subaltern sideshow to the colonial stage.

NOTES

1. Benjamin Victor, *The History of the Theatres of London and Dublin*, 2 vols., London: T. Becket, 1761, vol. I, p. 95.
2. Notable exceptions are Christopher Morash, *A History of the Irish Theatre, 1601–2000*, Cambridge: Cambridge University Press, 2002 and Christopher Wheatley, *'Beneath Ierne's Banners': Irish Protestant Drama of the Restoration and Eighteenth Century*, Notre Dame, IN: University of Notre Dame Press, 1999.
3. See David Lloyd, *Ireland after History*, Notre Dame, IN: University of Notre Dame Press, 1991, pp. 77–8.
4. Lloyd, *Ireland after History*, p. 77.
5. See Homi Bhabha's influential essay, 'Of Mimicry and Man: the Ambivalence of Colonial Discourse', *October* 28 (1984), pp. 125–33.
6. See William Smith Clark, *The Early Irish Stage: the Beginnings to 1720*, Oxford: Clarendon Press, 1955, pp. 26–42 and Morash, *History of the Irish Theatre*, pp. 4–12.
7. Matthew Concanen, 'To the Author of the Rival Generals', in *The Rival Generals*, London: A. Bettesworth, 1722, p. viii.
8. Concanen wrote a comedy (not extant) called *Wexford Wells* (1720).
9. *The Poetical Works of the Rev. James Sterling*, Dublin: G. Faulkner, 1734, p. 28.
10. John C. Greene and Gladys L. H. Clark, *The Dublin Stage, 1720–1745*, Bethlehem, PA: Lehigh University Press, 1993, pp. 135–6.
11. Robert Hitchcock, *An Historical View of the Irish Stage*, 2 vols., Dublin: R. Marchbank & W. Folds, 1788–94, vol. I, p. 87.
12. Greene and Clark, *The Dublin Stage*, pp. 30, 191, 278–9.
13. Greene and Clark, *The Dublin Stage*, pp. 218, 197.
14. See Esther Sheldon, *Thomas Sheridan of Smock-Alley*, Princeton, NJ: Princeton University Press, 1967, pp. 20–7.

15. Thomas Sheridan, *An Humble Appeal to the Publick, Together with Some Considerations on the Present Critical and Dangerous State of the Stage in Ireland*, Dublin: G. Faulkner, 1758, pp. 13, 19.

16. For a full account, see my *Riotous Performances: the Struggle for Hegemony in the Irish Theatre, 1712–1784*, Notre Dame, IN: University of Notre Dame Press, 2003, pp. 117–48 and Susan Cannon Harris, 'Outside the Box: the Female Spectator, *The Fair Penitent*, and the Kelly Riots of 1747', *Theatre Journal* 57 (2005), pp. 33–55.

17. *The Reformer* 1 (28 January 1748), pp. 1–2.

18. *The Election: A Comedy of Three Acts. As it is now acting in London with Great Applause* (1749), p. 44. There is no record of the play ever having been acted in London. For Hiffernan's authorship of this play, see *Riotous Performances*, pp. 200–8.

19. Cited in Greene and Clarke, *The Dublin Stage*, p. 387.

20. Hitchcock, *Historical View of the Irish Stage*, vol. I, p. 197.

21. See *A Full and True Account of the Woefull and Wonderfull Apparition of Hurloe Harrington* [*Late Prompter to the Theatre-Royal in Dublin ... in a Letter from the Reverend Parson Fitz-Henery to his G – e the A. B. of C – y*], London: R. Watkins, 1750, p. 27.

22. Thomas Sheridan, *Humble Appeal to the Publick*, p. 34.

23. James Miller, *Mahomet the Imposter: A Tragedy*, London: J. Watts, 1744, pp. 59, 65.

24. *An Epistle from Th-s Sh-n, Esq; to the Universal Advertiser*, Dublin, 1754, p. 4.

25. George Stayley, *The Rival Theatres: or, a Play-house to be lett*, Dublin: J. Hamilton, 1759.

26. John O'Keeffe, *Recollections of the Life of John O'Keeffe*, 2 vols., London: H. Colburn, 1826; reprinted New York and London: Benjamin Blom, 1969, vol. I, p. 29.

27. On the provincial Irish theatre, see William Smith Clark, *The Irish Stage in the County Towns, 1720–1800*, Oxford: Clarendon Press, 1965.

28. For an account of O'Keeffe's performance, see the *Hibernian Chronicle*, 24–28 August 1780.

29. *Freeman's Journal*, 10–12 April 1777.

30. *The True-born Irishman; or, The Irish Fine Lady* in *Four Comedies by Charles Macklin*, ed. J. O. Bartley, London and Hamden, CT: Archon Books, 1968, pp. 111–12.

31. *Gentleman's and London Magazine* (June 1762), cited in William J. Lawrence, *Notebooks on the History of the Dublin Stage 1909–34*, 99 vols., Cincinnati: University of Cincinnati Library, vol. XIX, pp. 51–52.

32. O'Keeffe, *Recollections*, vol. I, p. 62.

33. James Thomas Kirkman, *Memoirs of the Life of Charles Macklin*, 2 vols., London: Lackington, Allen & Co., 1799, vol. II, pp. 2–3.

34. 'An Account of the Life and Genius of Mr. Charles Macklin, Comedian', in *An Apology for the Conduct of Mr. Charles Macklin, Comedian*, London: T. Axtell, 1773, p. 37.

35. See Sidney Owenson, *Lady Morgan's Memoirs: Autobiography, Diaries and Correspondence*, London: W.H. Allen & Co., 1862, p. 56.

36. *Freeman's Journal*, 26–29 October 1776.

37. George Colman, *New Brooms*, in *The Plays of George Colman the Elder*, ed. Kalman A. Burnim, 6 vols., New York and London: Garland, 1983, vol. IV, p. 20.
38. William John Fitzpatrick, *Lady Morgan: Her Career, Literary and Personal*, London: Charles J. Skeet, 1860, p. 23.
39. This opera was first performed at Smock Alley on 14 May 1782. It opened at Crow Street the following year, and played at least five times during that season.
40. *Freeman's Journal*, 21–23 March 1780.
41. *Hibernian Journal*, 7 July 1784.
42. *Gentleman's Magazine* 54 (1784), p. 550.
43. *Volunteers Journal*, 12 July 1784.
44. Joshua Reynolds to the Duke of Rutland, 24 September 1784, H.M.C., Rutland MS, cited in Jim Smyth, *The Men of No Property: Irish Radicals and Popular Politics in the Late Eighteenth Century*, New York: St. Martin's Press, 1992, pp. 135, 215.

16

DANIEL O'QUINN

Theatre and empire

When we put the words empire and theatre together, two key questions emerge: what happened to British theatre as it migrated to Britain's colonies? And how did global domination inflect theatrical production in Britain? At the close of the Seven Years' War, Britain possessed a burgeoning colonial empire in the Atlantic and was emerging as the dominant power in the Asian subcontinent. Bringing these two very different imperial economies into some form of governable structure was exceedingly complex. Soon after the Peace of Paris, the Atlantic empire was in tatters and British imperial attention turned resolutely eastward. The vicissitudes of triumphalism and defeat in the 1760s and 1770s are the crucial backdrop for many orientalist plays; indeed, symptoms of imperial anxiety lasted well into the 1780s. This period is marked by complex scrutiny of the economic instability generated by the East India Company both at home and abroad, and by a remarkable silence on the catastrophic loss of the American colonies. One can hypothesise that the trauma of the American war was handled indirectly through orientalist fantasies but proving such a proposition is beyond the scope of this essay. However, a transition in theatrical representations of the east took place which corresponds to alterations in the governance of colonial affairs and the economics of empire. The complexity of this transition is intimately tied to significant developments in the representation of race, class and the sex/gender system.

The late 1780s and early 1790s witness a fundamental change not only in imperial policy but also in theatrical imperialism. The intense sexualisation of oriental subject matter and the desire to provide ethnographic and topographic information about distant lands undergo changes both in form and in function. From the 1790s onwards, the military becomes an important player, both on the stage of colonial history, and on imperial stages from London to Cape Town and Calcutta. Imperial theatre focused attention on the regulation of despotism and constructed representations of masculinity appropriate to the military and bureaucratic rule of Britain's colonial holdings. Spectacle was being mobilised in remarkably sophisticated ways, not only to reap profits at the box-office, but also to secure volatile notions of imperial supremacy and national election.

Sexuality and imperial governance

Let's start with a seemingly trivial document from *Hickey's Bengal Gazette*, an early and often muck-raking newspaper published in Calcutta:

> The Managers of the Theatre having generously offer'd to give a Benefit play, to Mr. Soubise, toward the Completion of his *Menage*, Mr. Soubise will appear on that night in the Character of *Othello*. And afterwards perform the part of *Mungo* in the Entertainment. Monsieur B – vere is preparing a new Dance, which, in compliment to the occasion, is to be called the African Fandango – the part of *Iago* will be attempted by the Author of the *Monitor*, and *Desdemona* by Mr. H – , a gentleman of the *doubtful Gender*.[1]

If this notice refers to a genuine performance by Julius Soubise in Isaac Bickerstaffe's *The Padlock* (DL, 1768) and *Othello*, then it is arguably the earliest appearance by an African on an English-language stage. Soubise, a formerly enslaved African known at different times in his life as 'Mungo' and 'Othello' (and reputed to have been the lover of the Duchess of Queensbury) had fled to India after a rape charge and then found a niche in Calcutta society teaching riding and fencing. The text's tone and rhetoric suggest that this advertisement is a clever satirical hoax, but what are we to make of the possibility that it refers to an actual performance?

As Felicity Nussbaum has argued, these roles are inextricably linked to fantasies about the sexual prowess of black men.[2] In *The Padlock*, Mungo is the much-abused slave of Don Diego, an impotent old man who jealously locks up his young wife in what amounts to a harem of one. The plot is essentially that of an eastern tale with Mungo in the part of the Eunuch who helps his mistress to break out of the harem. Like many similar plays including Bickerstaffe's *The Sultan* (DL, 1775), the despot is ultimately humiliated and a more just sexual regime established. According to the advertisement, Soubise appears in the mainpiece as the embodiment of masculinity and dangerous possibility; in the afterpiece he performs as the eunuch. The theatrical evening seems to produce and simultaneously contain Soubise as a sexual threat. The anxiety indicated by this doubling is exemplified by Hickey's satire on the colonial administrator Nathaniel Halhed, who is presented here as a man of doubtful gender, playing Desdemona to Soubise's Othello. The advertisement suggests that British officials in India have forsaken the precincts of conventional masculinity, thereby opening up a space for a character such as Soubise to operate. And the internal link is one well-worn in orientalist discourse, namely, that the despot is feminised by his power. Suspect sexuality and suspect governance are thus combined into one overarching critique of the East India Company.

Regardless of whether Hickey is discussing an actual performance, the advertisement highlights the ideological stakes of many theatrical productions both at home and abroad. Whether the play is set in the harem or in the divan of the despotic ruler, questions of sexual desire and appropriate governance are necessarily intertwined. Plays dealing with imperial matters often activate anxieties about national character and imperial decline in order to generate narratives of supremacy over subject peoples. In *The Padlock*, the concatenation of racial otherness, sexual impotence and master/slave relations serves to define interracial and intergenerational liaisons as foreign to the realms of love. With the dissolution of Don Diego's household and its implied slave economy, Mungo becomes a residual container for anxieties regarding black potency. *The Sultan* moves in precisely the opposite direction but with much the same result. Roxalana, the captive English coquette famously played at Drury Lane by Fanny Abington, forces the Sultan to break with Islamic mores and eventually marries him in order to gain control of the state. In this case, Turkish despotism is found to be no match for pert English femininity and the pleasure afforded by the shaming of the Sultan is magnified by the thrill of witnessing Roxalana's sexual agency.

In the hands of women playwrights, representations of empire could be turned inside out to ridicule the theatrical taste which produces and consumes such fare or could be used to allegorise metropolitan political concerns. Elizabeth Inchbald recognised these possibilities and five of her plays directly engage with the politics of India. The farcical afterpiece, *The Mogul Tale* (HM, 1784) directly parodies *The Sultan* and also satirises the defeat of Fox's India Bill in 1783. The play opens with a spectacular contravention of the harem walls by the descent of a runaway balloon. This balloon allegorises the fate of Fox's Bill, for as Bolton and others have recognised, Fox's doomed Indian policy was frequently caricatured as an economic balloon ready to burst.[3] But in Inchbald's play the balloon deposits three English characters who seem to evoke the principal figures from *The Sultan* – Isaac Bickerstaffe, Fanny Abington and Thomas Dibdin – in the court of the Great Mogul. The Great Mogul decides to exploit his captives' fears by playing the part of the despot. When he releases the English captives, he explains that 'your countrymen's cruelty to the poor Gentoos has shown me tyranny in so foul a light, that I was determined henceforward to be only mild, just and merciful'.[4]

The sophistication of this intervention is typical of Inchbald and also informs her five-act comedy *Such Things Are* (CG, 1787) which opened on the eve of Warren Hastings's impeachment for high crimes and misdemeanours. At the same time that Edmund Burke, Charles James Fox and Richard Brinsley Sheridan used highly sexualised language in their attempts to prove the despotism of Hastings's governance in Bengal, Inchbald wove together the discourses of sexuality and despotism to generate a comedy which critiques the nature of governance not only in the colonies but also at home.

The island of Sumatra, a clear allegory for Britain, is ruled by a despotic Sultan who turns out to be a closet Christian and whose intense grief for the loss of his beloved Arabella has resulted in the promulgation of absolute terror among his subjects. Ruling by intimidation, the Sultan has turned the island into one vast prison; his European subjects play out all the roles prescribed by Montesquieu in his influential description of despotic governance in *The Spirit of the Laws* (1748). The principal British residents are either incapacitated by fear, like Sir Luke and Lady Tremor, or aspire to power through tactics usually associated with the Sultan's vizier. Lord Flint and Mr Twineall, for example, are marked by contrasting forms of sexual and political deviance. Lord Flint is a predatory and politically dangerous man who affects to forget all conversation; Mr Twineall is an excessively effeminate character whose telegraphic utterances are literally without substance.

The characters in *Such Things Are* seem to have been corrupted by what amounts to a constitutive blindness on the part of the Sultan. The entire state has fallen into despotism not because the Sultan is inherently evil, but rather because his love has been focused exclusively on Arabella. This pathology is uncovered and rectified by Mr Haswell (a character modelled on the prison reformer John Howard), who discovers that the supposedly dead Arabella is actually alive and sequestered in the Sultan's prison. On the eve of the Hastings trial, Inchbald is arguing that politicians such as Burke, Fox and Sheridan and functionaries in the colonies are failing to attend to the spirit of the laws because they are mired in defective forms of masculinity. The Sultan's excessive and exclusive desire, Lord Flint's aggression and Mr Twineall's effeminacy are all symptoms of a type of masculine behaviour which fails to remember or feigns to forget the full extent of civil sociability.[5]

Representing imperial economies

This concern with the relationship between private domestic concerns and questions of public statesmanship suffuses Inchbald's comedies. Later plays such as *Wives as They Were, Maids as They Are* (CG, 1797) and *The Wise Man of the East* (CG, 1799) turn their lens on the economic vicissitudes of

British imperialism. Both dramas are part of a long line of plays starting with Samuel Foote's three-act comedy *The Nabob* (HM, 1772) and Sheridan's *The School for Scandal* (DL, 1777) and concluding with Frederic Reynolds's *Speculation* (CG, 1795) and Fanny Burney's five-act comedy *A Busy Day*. These plays analyse the effect of the infusion (or non-infusion) of vast amounts of wealth from India into British society. The incursion of newly monied merchants into precincts of privilege and power formerly reserved for the gentry threatened not only to undermine the fundamental link in the British constitution between landed property and liberty but also to replace it with potentially less stable forms of property and class relations.

The Nabob set the terms in which later plays represented transitions in class identity during the early phases of the second British empire. Foote's play was first staged in 1772, following the near catastrophic collapse in public and private credit in which the volatility of East India stock played a conspicuous role. The complexity of *The Nabob*'s economic argument indicates the degree to which financial issues surrounding India policy preoccupied London audiences. The first and third acts focus on the nabob Sir Matthew Mite's extortion of Lord and Lady Oldham, a couple whose embarrassed finances make them easy targets for his unscrupulous bid to enter the ranks of the aristocracy. Through a series of legal but unethical credit arrangements, Lord Oldham finds himself in debt to Sir Matthew. Sir Matthew, a former East India Company official, is looking for a way to rise up the social ladder and demands the hand of the Oldhams' daughter and thus an alliance with a prominent landed family. The demand comes with a threat, for if the family refuses he will recall his loans and acquire their property including their estate.

Foote is ruthless not only in his portrait of Mite, but also in his account of the Oldhams' failure to confront the dissipation of their class. The play suggests that they fail to recognise their economic obsolescence in the emerging imperial economy. The critique is subtle and once again figured in sexual terms: Lord Oldham is a largely passive character and his wife has distinctly amazonian qualities. It is left to Lord Oldham's brother Thomas, a merchant from the City, to rescue his landed relations, but that rescue leaves the play's critique of the landed gentry intact. When Sir Matthew attempts to recall his loans, Thomas immediately pays them down and becomes Lord Oldham's new creditor. But his credit comes with an eerily similar security: Thomas demands the hand of Lord Oldham's daughter for his own son. Such a marriage between the landed and middling ranks maintains the Oldhams as the titular embodiment of landed liberty but clearly locates the models of productive and, most importantly, reproductive prosperity in styles of living associated with commercial enterprise and conjugal love.

Foote's critique of class relations is accompanied by a much more blunt caricature of the nabob. In the second act, Sir Matthew's appearance as a foppish gambler establishes a link between effeminacy and suspect forms of accumulation. Mite is also terrified that his jaundiced skin will be interpreted either as a sign of illness or of Indianisation. Foote emphasises the theme of suspect sexuality by connecting Sir Matthew's attempts to prey on financially embarrassed aristocratic women to his interest in establishing a seraglio in London. All these characteristics fuse stereotypes of fearsome yet feminised Eastern masculinity with similar notions of errant aristocratic behaviour to crystallise the nabob's threat to social and political relations in Britain. Thomas, by contrast, who advocates slow and steady accumulation, national purity and conjugal love, has the capacity to counteract this threat. He – no less than the nabob himself – becomes an enduringly popular character in subsequent representations of imperial relations.

Like Sir Matthew Mite, Sir Oliver Surface in Sheridan's *The School for Scandal* (DL, 1777) returns from India having made a fortune. Unlike Sir Matthew, however, he becomes the play's moral arbiter. It is not often remarked that Sir Oliver's ability to reward Charles Surface for his moral worth depends upon his prior Indian service. In both plays, aristocratic society is seen to be in a state of decadence akin to that which characterised the late Roman empire. But in the political climate of the mid 1770s, during a period of widespread suspicion that imperial activity was destabilising the British nation and corrupting its morals, Sheridan's gesture substantially refines Foote's critique. In particular, *The School for Scandal* is part of the continuing debate about Britons' capacity to withstand the potential corruption of their newfound imperial power.

Mita Choudhury has recently explored the staging of *The School for Scandal* in the new Theatre at Calcutta in 1782 and has speculated upon the tight theatrical network connecting London and this colonial stage.[6] So how might audiences have interpreted this play in Calcutta? At Drury Lane, Sir Oliver's Eastern fortune comes to be bestowed on a young man who will manage it to the credit of society. Because Sir Oliver's colonial past has not destroyed his character, he and the audience are able to imagine a just future. In Calcutta, Sir Oliver may stand as a contrast to East India Company officials, such as Lord Clive, whose characters had been called into question. But he may also act as a theatrical representative of current Company employees amassing fortunes in India. When defending his actions before the House of Commons in 1772, Clive had argued that corruption of character represented a British problem which, when exported to the colonies, had become truly malignant. Sheridan's careful scrutiny of British society perhaps allowed British audience members in Calcutta to distance themselves from accusations of corruption in Britain. In this context, spectators could applaud the play as an effective counter to the widespread attacks on the East India Company.

The new Calcutta Theatre had opened in 1775 although private performances of English plays were being staged in India from mid-century onwards. There is little evidence that the audience included residents of the 'Black Town', and the theatre's primary function, like much of the print media, was to immerse the audience in British culture. According to the Bengal papers for 1781, the first productions of the year were Goldsmith's *She Stoops to Conquer* and Otway's *Venice Preserv'd* and all the parts were played by men. If the lack of actresses made the performances a historical throwback by comparison with theatrical production in Britain, the reviews displayed some familar conventions of metropolitan dramatic criticism:

> Last Thursday the Tragedy of Venice Preserv'd, and the Musical Lady was performed here. Capt. Coll play'd Jaffier admirably well, and may be justly stiled the Garrick of the East.
> When the Tragedy King entered in Pierre a universal Skitt ran thro' the House and when he describ'd himself, 'a fine gay, bold-faced Villain' – a general concurrence of whispers seemed to pronounce – 'A V_____ he truly is' ...
> Mr. Norford played Belvidera with such an Amorous glow of features, and utterance – and was so characteristic in the description of Madness, – as to procure him (as usual) universal applause.[7]

The review suggests that some of the Calcutta spectators – like those in London – had allegorised the political elements of Otway's tragedy.[8] The Tragedy King referred to here is Hickey's enemy, Barnard Messinck, who managed the Calcutta Theatre and also published a rival Gazette. Although not of the same import as John Thelwall's attempt to appropriate the democratic scenes of *Venice Preserv'd* by raucously drawing attention to their political topicality in the early 1790s, it is notable that audiences seem to be aligning theatrical situations with specific historical characters and conflicts.[9]

After a considerable hiatus, Cumberland's *The West Indian* was staged in June followed by *The Provok'd Wife* in September together with *The Recruiting Sergeant*. Congreve's comedy, *The Way of the World,* was staged in December along with another comic opera, *Two Misers*. The new year saw productions of *Macbeth* with *Three Weeks After Marriage* in January, and the production of *The School for Scandal* discussed earlier, together with a revival of *The Recruiting Sergeant*, in February. The schedule is ambitious and frequent discussions take place in the newspapers about how reverses in the Second Mysore War were draining the 'White Town' of potential actors and funds for the theatre.

By 1791–92, women had begun to take female parts in the Calcutta Theatre, topical prologues were being written for plays such as Colman's *Inkle and Yarico*, musical entertainment was expanding and local panto-mimes including *Mungo in Freedom, or Harlequin Fortunate* had begun to emerge.[10] The calendar includes serious tragedy such as *The Grecian Daughter*, comic operas such as *The Flitch of Bacon*, farces and pantomimes. The repertoire closely followed that of the London theatres. In part, this is because Calcutta newspapers reprinted reviews of plays from the metropo-litan papers (so residents would have been familiar with Siddons's fame in the role of Euphrasia in *The Grecian Daughter*); in part because plays and performers were arriving in India on the same ships which brought soldiers, arms and supplies for the company. Audiences in Calcutta were consolidat-ing a sense of British identity through contact with metropolitan plays and through participation in the culture of spectatorship associated with London productions. At the same time, however, reviews indicate that plays were presented and interpreted according to the political and social imperatives of British society in Calcutta.

In London meanwhile, the scrutiny being given to the East India Company's activities was matched by a proliferation of defective colonial administrators on the London stage. James Cobb's play *Love in the East; or, Adventures of Twelve Hours* (DL, 1788) is set in Calcutta and many of its set designs were based on William Hodges's drawings of the city.[11] The comic opera features Mr and Mrs Mushroom, residents of Calcutta, who torment each other by continually threatening to engage in adultery. Act II includes a disguise scene in which Mrs Mushroom is forced to conceal the libertine, Colonel Baton, from her husband. The Frenchman Colonel Baton has arrived fresh from his nation's defeat at Pondicherry and hopes to compen-sate for the loss of the colony with a series of sexual conquests. His actions associate French foppish effeminacy with inept colonial policy and failed military action, implying that the decline of the French colonial project in India is the result of a deformation of character.

Baton is forced to masquerade as Twist the Tailor – the very embodiment of lower-class English identity – and Twist, in turn, masquerades as the sexually voracious Frenchman and proceeds to give offence to everyone involved. The fascination of the scene lies in the success and failure of the disguise. Mr Mushroom who, as his name suggests, thrives in 'dark' places, is unable to see through the masquerade being played out in front of him. Cobb insinuates that the British residents of India are unable to recognise Britishness in a manner that serves to confirm his metropolitan audience's ability to do so.

Similarly, Mariana Starke's *The Sword of Peace* (HM, 1788) caricatures Indianised British men and women from the lower ranks in order to represent the threat of Eastern corruption to the British body politic. But unlike *Love in the East*, Starke presents contrasting examples of men and women successfully navigating the dangers supposedly inherent in colonial service. Starke's heroines are ultimately married to respectable military men and their commander, David Northcote, a character clearly modelled on Lord Cornwallis, is the epitome of military restraint. In the 1790s such examples become connected to the military and are recognisably middling in their social relations. The character of Captain Campley in Colman's popular comic opera *Inkle and Yarico* (HM, 1787), for example, is explicitly contrasted to Inkle, whose excessive investment in trade is satirised as a constitutional defect which must be overcome as Britain enters an era of colonisation based on territorial domination rather than on mercantilism. And the terms of Campley and Inkle's contrasting fates are revealing. Whereas Campley marries Narcissa, the Governor of the Bahamas's daughter, Inkle's partnership with Yarico is one in which erotic and economic desires are at cross purposes. Interracial sexuality, the play seems to suggest, is suitable only for the lower orders and, in the theatre, for low comedy.[12]

Metropolitan theatre also capitalised on the increasing militarisation of colonial relations. This was nowhere more evident than at minor theatres such as Astley's Amphitheatre and Sadler's Wells. Astley was a former cavalry officer and his forte was the spectacular simulation of warfare with a combination of trained horses, machines and rigorously trained soldier-like performers. *Tippoo Saib, or British Valour in India* (1791), *Tippoo Sultan, or The Siege of Bangalore* (1792), *Tippoo Saib, or, East India Campaigning* (1792) and *Tippoo Saib's Two Sons* (1792) literally dramatised the incoming news from each of Cornwallis's campaigns against Tipu Sultan in the Third Mysore War. These productions evoked the anxieties about captivity and defeat which had attended earlier setbacks in British military operations in India and also generated intense fantasies of imperial supremacy through the enactment of military discipline in an enclosed viewing space. Astley's distinct innovation lay in the meticulous choreography of British military discipline in the face of Mysorean disorder. In Astley's last Tipu play, *The Siege and Storming of Seringapatam* (1800), celebrating the final defeat of Tipu in the Fourth Mysore War, the chaotic movement of antiquated Eastern arms is literally subsumed by exhibitions of European technological and logistical supremacy. As the play moves through a series of 'blow-ups' and demonstrates the action of a tightly drilled artillery battery, the audience is left contemplating the spectacle of Tipu's *zenana* (the residence of his wives) on fire and modernity's overwhelming superiority.

Ethnographic spectacle

The impact of such productions had a profound impact on the legitimate stage as well. Explorations of Eastern despotism such as Colman's *Blue-Beard* (DL, 1798) and Matthew Lewis's *Timour the Tartar* (CG, 1811) brought many of Astley's dramaturgical innovations to the patent houses, but these plays also built their plots and their chief effects on a long history of Eastern tales and stage spectacles. What changed was the function of spectacle and protoethnography in this new theatrical economy. With the defeat of Tipu Sultan of Mysore in the early 1790s, Britain entered a new phase of colonial activity. The East India Company was progressively militarised and by the end of the century an entire host of practices associated with the bureaucratic regulation of Indian peoples was being set in motion. As Sudipta Sen has argued, the East India Company's ethnographic activities were aimed at demonstrating that neither Hindu nor Moslem peoples were capable of effectively governing themselves.[13]

A similar imperative suffused even the lowest and most spurious forms of entertainment. Plays often combined ostensibly accurate depictions of people, places and customs with entirely fanciful and often racist representations. By looking at a series of spectacular productions it is possible to discern a number of key transitions in the politics of colonial display. James Messinck's *A Choice of Harlequin* (CG, 1782) offers a useful starting point in part because his son Barnard was active both as a manager and as a player on the Calcutta stage (he performed in the productions of *Venice Preserv'd* and *The School for Scandal*) and in part because Messinck's pantomime incorporates a critique of Indian affairs into a conventional harlequinade. Like *The Nabob*, the pantomime attacks East India Company employees and stockholders as little more than gamesters. The play's Eastern dramaturgy takes the form of an elaborate procession of 'Hircarrers with painted sticks, Nishamburdars with flags, Ticktaws with fire pots ... and Ramjanneees or dancing girls'.[14] The emphasis here is on the sheer number of eroticised bodies traipsing across the stage. The fact that Harlequin, Virtue and Pleasure are incorporated into the list suggests that the entire panoply is presumed to be similarly bizarre.

The same desire to specify and yet eroticise animates the extraordinary procession which closes Philippe Jacques de Loutherbourg's and John O'Keeffe's pantomime, *Omai; or, A Trip Round the World* (CG, 1785), but in this case the effect is entirely different. What distinguishes this production is the participation of John Webber, the chief illustrator on Captain Cook's final voyage. Webber assisted Loutherbourg in the design and execution of the sets and costumes. Loutherbourg also consulted actual artifacts

14. Philippe Jacques de Loutherbourg, costume designs for the Prophet's dress in *Omai*, watercolour, 1785.

from the Cook voyages on display at the Holophusicon, Sir Ashton Lever's museum in Leicester Square. This was pantomime as enlightenment and most London papers recommended the play for its capacity to educate audiences in the culture and topography of the South Seas and in the heroism of Cook's mission. In spite of glowing praise for the accuracy of its views, costumes and stage effects, reviewers expressed disappointment about the lack of tricks and songs in the harlequinade. Loutherbourg and O'Keeffe responded to these criticisms by steadily altering the pantomime to bring it in line with public taste, both by inventing a strange character, referred to only as a 'Travelled native of Tongataboo' [Tongatapu] whose costume was a patchwork of Pacific cultures, and by introducing a number of racist songs which emphasised the sexual profligacy of the South Seas. In its final version, *Omai* became a strange hybrid of Enlightenment observation and ethnocentric fantasy.[15]

Reviews of plays with Asian settings, situations or implications invariably remark upon the accuracy of the customs and cultural artifacts presented. Although one account of Mariana Starke's *The Widow of Malabar* (CG, 1791) challenged the playwright's knowledge of suttee, another suggested that Starke had gleaned her information about the practice from a family member working for the East India Company. As reviews attest, the reception of imperial theatre was embedded in a wider practice of cultural consumption including travel narratives, engravings and botanical and historical books. For this reason, a great deal of attention was paid to scene design. Reviews of James Cobb's *Ramah Droog* (CG, 1798) dutifully encapsulate the plot but pay much more attention to scene-painting, costumes and the procession with its mechanical elephant. John Inigo Richards's set designs for this production were explicitly based on Thomas and William Daniells's famous watercolours and engravings of India and the papers made a great deal of their authenticity. Indeed, the set designs encode a history of colonial representation extending back through William Hodges's images of hillside fortresses to widely circulated images of the fortresses overrun by Clive during his successful campaigns in the 1750s. Set painters and costume designers could draw on such visual memories to remind the audience of earlier military victories, while the plays themselves disparaged subjugated peoples either through overt sexualisation or through insinuations of gender insubordination.

This shift in scenography and critical practice is evident in William Thomas Moncrieff's melodrama, *The Cataract of the Ganges! or, The Rajah's Daughter* (DL, 1823). Moncrieff's play, featuring real horses, was by all accounts an extraordinary spectacle:

> To the scenery, show, and music, the Manager has looked for triumph, and to these we will turn our attention. The opening scene is beautiful: it is by far the handsomest scene in the whole piece, and does the painter, STANFIELD, infinite credit. It is a field of battle by moonlight, viewed after a conflict. There are a number of figures in the foreground, and distributed over the stage, which are grouped with admirable taste and effect: the landscape also and distance are finely executed, and the light which is cast upon the whole is wonderfully true to nature.[16]

Stanfield is one of the most important scene-painters in the early nineteenth century and the scene for which he is being lauded here is instructive.

Moncrieff's *Cataract* opens on a scene of military carnage which raises the spectre of past military unrest in the Asian subcontinent. Following the defeat of Tipu Sultan in 1799 and the suppression of the Maratha insurgency in 1805, British rule in India had focused primarily on the bureaucratic management of the subject populations. This policy resulted in a massive collection of ethnographic knowledge for political ends and issues such as suttee in Bengal and female infanticide in the Rajput became significant flashpoints for imperial policy. Female infanticide was the object of much attention at this time and Moncrieff's play demonstrates a thorough knowledge of contemporary discussions.[17] The elaborate marriage procession at the end of Act I evokes the political problems posed by excessive expenditure among the Rajput lineage, but more importantly realises the potential for crowd-pleasing spectacle. The melodrama is punctuated with increasingly spectacular scenes including an elaborate piece of action in the Temple of Juggernaut and a denouement in which the heroine rides a horse up what the *New Times* described as 'a prodigious cataract'. The review continued, 'The water was real, and it tumbled with headlong fury and in great quantities from the height of the proscenium to the level of the stage.'[18]

As the plot unfolds, Mordaunt, the middle-class British officer, persuades the Rajah to renounce female infanticide and helps the Rajah to defeat his enemies and to rescue his endangered daughter, Zamine. Mordaunt's actions thus conjoin military prowess, moral rectitude and Christian benevolence in one overwhelming fantasy of imperial paternalism. This was an image that the British attempted to promulgate not only to the Indian population but also to British spectators. However, the recourse to ever more breathtaking spectacle perhaps indicates that this image of imperial benevolence was itself improbable and in need of continual reiteration and/or obfuscation. In many ways, Moncrieff's melodrama encapsulates the theatrical engagement with questions of empire in the preceding sixty years.

NOTES

1. *Hickey's Bengal Gazette*, 23–30 December 1780.
2. See Felicity Nussbaum, *The Limits of the Human: Fictions of Anomaly, Race, and Gender in the Long Eighteenth Century*, Cambridge: Cambridge University Press, 2003, pp. 151–212.
3. See Betsy Bolton, *Women, Nationalism and the Romantic Stage: Theatre and Politics in Britain, 1780–1800*, Cambridge: Cambridge University Press, 2001, pp. 204–6.

4. Elizabeth Inchbald, *The Mogul Tale*, in *The Plays of Elizabeth Inchbald*, ed. Paula Backscheider, New York: Garland Publishing, 1980, pp. 19–20.

5. For an extended discussion of Inchbald's political intervention in *Such Things Are* see my *Staging Governance: Theatrical Imperialism in London, 1770–1800*, Baltimore, MD: Johns Hopkins University Press, 2005, pp. 124–63.

6. See Mita Choudhury, *Interculturalism and Resistance in the London Theatre, 1660–1800: Identity, Performance, Empire*, Lewisburg, PA: Bucknell University Press, 2000, pp. 87–108.

7. *Hickey's Bengal Gazette*, 27 January–3 February 1781.

8. Gillian Russell, 'Burke's Dagger: Theatricality, Politics and Print Culture in the 1790s', *British Journal for Eighteenth-Century Studies* 20 (1997), pp. 1–16, p. 8.

9. For a discussion of Thelwall's attempt to 'steal' *Venice Preserv'd* see John Barrell, '"An Entire Change of Performances?" The Politicisation of Theatre and the Theatricalisation of Politics in the mid 1790s', *Lumen* 17 (1998), pp. 11–50.

10. This play was performed on 9 February 1792 and there is evidence that it was published in Calcutta.

11. For a very useful reading of Cobb's relation to colonial fantasy see Nandini Bhattacharya, 'James Cobb, Colonial Cacophony, and the Enlightenment', *Studies in English Literature, 1500–1900* 41:3 (2001), pp. 583–603.

12. See Daniel O'Quinn, 'Mercantile Deformities: George Colman's *Inkle and Yarico* and the Racialization of Class Relations', *Theatre Journal* 54:3 (October 2002), pp. 389–410.

13. Sudipta Sen, *Distant Sovereignty: National Imperialism and the Origins of British India*, New York: Routledge, 2002, pp. 12–26.

14. *The Choice of Harlequin; or, The Indian Chief*, London: Riley, 1782, p. 6.

15. For an extended discussion of the pantomime see Kathleen Wilson, *The Island Race: Englishness, Empire and Gender in the Eighteenth Century*, London: Routledge, 2003, pp. 63–70; Greg Dening, *Mr. Bligh's Bad Language: Passion, Power and Theatre on the Bounty*, Cambridge: Cambridge University Press, 1992, pp. 9–76 and my own *Staging Governance*, pp. 74–114.

16. *The New Times*, 28 October 1823.

17. The plot of the play may be derived from reviews of Edward Moor's *Hindu Infanticide, An account of the measures adopted for suppressing the practice of the systematic murder by their parents of female infants*, London: J. Johnson & Co., 1811.

18. *The New Times*, 28 October 1823.

PART V

Further Reading

17

JONATHAN MULROONEY

Reading theatre, 1730–1830

Over the past two decades, scholars of British theatre in the long eighteenth century have produced some of the most imaginative and exciting work in contemporary cultural studies. Just as radical changes in the nature and scale of Britain's print culture spurred theatre's growing importance as a public experience in this period, so in our own historical moment the changing exigencies of the academy have transformed how we think about the period's theatre. Divergent approaches to studying or even defining theatre have long hindered conversation between scholars in different disciplines. While twentieth-century theatre historians maintained an interest in acting styles, repertories and production techniques, literary scholars – inheriting a Romantic fascination with the lyric imagination – neglected theatre's 'claims of the body, the institution, and the market' (Moody 2000). As Jacky Bratton (2003) has argued, this theoretical and institutional divide cut off the study of theatre *as literature* from the study of theatre *as performance*. Because they relied on a critical apparatus which placed elite dramatic 'art' in opposition to popular theatrical 'entertainment', literary critics tended to overlook the myriad ways that text and acting, production and reception, authorship and spectatorship intersected in British theatre.

Influenced by new historicism and by the emergence of interdisciplinary approaches to cultural history, a new generation has addressed these oversights by exploring more fully the material, social and political conditions of theatrical production. Scholars in fields as diverse as art history, literary and performance studies, women's studies, economics, sociology and anthropology have contributed to a bold reassessment of how theatre shaped the social, political, cultural and institutional life of eighteenth- and nineteenth-century Britain. Concepts such as elite, popular, theatrical, performance, even Britishness itself have come under new kinds of scrutiny. This *Companion* – which crosses boundaries between text and performance and between traditional literary periods – exemplifies the range of historical, theoretical and textual methodologies which characterise scholarly debate in the field. With an eye toward that fruitful heterogeneity, I provide here suggestions for further reading, offering in the process an outline of the developments described above.

Reference works and bibliographic tools

The empirical and bibliographical work produced in the mid twentieth century continues to inform recent reassessments. Chief among such resources are the final three parts of *The London Stage, 1660–1800* edited by Scouten, Stone, and Hogan, respectively, as well as the volumes of Nicoll's *History* which cover the late eighteenth and early nineteenth centuries. These works contain detailed information on performances at London's major theatres and, in the case of Nicoll, a short-title list of plays and an invaluable index of playwrights (1959). Other significant reference resources include Mander and Mitchenson's volumes describing London's playhouses (1961, 1968), Stratman's comprehensive bibliography of theatrical periodicals, Langhans's bibliography of eighteenth-century promptbooks, and Highfill's dictionary of London theatre personnel, which includes useful short biographies of performers and managers. Loftis (1960) is a brief but valuable sample of eighteenth-century theatrical criticism. Sybil Rosenfeld's hugely important body of work includes an analysis of Georgian scene design (1981), as well as monographs on topics often neglected by later scholars: private theatrical performances (1978) and strolling players in the provinces (1970). Thomas's useful volume, *Restoration and Georgian England 1660–1788* in the Cambridge series, *Theatre in Europe: A Documentary History*, reprints licences, contracts, playhouse designs, theatrical reviews and other public records, while John Brewer explains theatre's position in the wider context of leisure and entertainment during the period which saw the rise of the professional theatre manager and the birth of the modern mass audience. Most recently, Donohue's volume in the *Cambridge History of British Theatre* (2004) offers helpful essays by Robert Hume on the development of the repertory and Joseph Donohue on nineteenth-century theatre architecture. In addition to an extensive commentary on the politics of theatre production between 1789 and 1860, Roy reprints and annotates over four hundred documents about company organisation, repertoire, production design, acting and playhouse architecture.

Recent editions and anthologies

For some years, Paula Backscheider's series of eighteenth-century playtexts and Michael Booth's five-volume *English Nineteenth-Century Plays* provided standard, if not readily available, editions of plays. In the last decade, a variety of new editions have begun to appear. Notably, many of these focus on women playwrights. Franceschina's edition of gothic melodramas by women complements Cox's earlier *Seven Gothic Dramas* (1992). Broadview Press has taken the lead in offering inexpensive texts that break new editorial ground, including Wolfson and Fay's parallel text edition of *The Siege of Valencia*, Duthie's edition of Baillie's *Plays* and two important anthologies: Cox and Gamer's *Broadview Anthology of Romantic Drama* and Crochunis and Eberle-Sinatra's *Broadview Anthology of British Women Playwrights, 1777–1843*. Finberg provides a sample of eighteenth-century dramas by women and Scullion's volume offers a nineteenth-century counterpart. Volumes 4–6 of Hughes are devoted to the plays of Elizabeth Griffith, Hannah Cowley and Elizabeth Inchbald. Recent work has also transformed ideas about the relationship between text and performance: see the work of Bratton (2002) and Bush-Bailey on the Sans Pareil playwright, Jane Scott, in Burroughs (2000) and in *Nineteenth Century Theatre and Film* and Charles Rzepka's work on *Obi* (Rzepka 2000). Among the most important web-based publishing initiatives are the *Chadwyck-Healey Online Database* (though the source texts for the plays included here can sometimes be questionable) and Crochunis and Eberle-Sinatra's *British Women Playwrights around 1800* website, now a model for collaborative electronic publishing (Crochunis 1998, Crochunis and Eberle-Sinatra 2003).

Genres

For a variety of reasons, genre became an important political and cultural battleground in the eighteenth-century theatre. Many critics perceived the rise of melodrama and pantomime as a threat to legitimate drama: debate raged among critics, managers, actors and authors about the moral and aesthetic value of particular genres. By the Romantic period, some authors even began to withdraw from writing for the stage altogether, imagining their plays would be read in the solitude of the private space or 'closet'. These plays – what Byron called 'mental theatre' – represent a significant intervention in theatrical history and remain a major interest for scholars. Recent criticism has viewed the Romantics' seeming disengagement with the theatre of the day as a complicated response to changes in theatrical production and in the market for literary works. In turn, dramatic genres have come to be treated more fully as products of the historical conditions from which they emerged and to which they responded.

Bevis (1988) offers a good introduction to eighteenth-century drama, highlighting the many kinds of generic experimentation taking place.

Kavenik contextualises the work of major playwrights in a detailed chronology of political and theatrical events from the Restoration to 1780. Ever since Oliver Goldsmith's 1773 'An Essay on the Theatre; or, A Comparison between Laughing and Sentimental Comedy', theatre historians have debated the question of what constitutes eighteenth-century 'comedy'. Against conventional wisdom emphasising the domination of sentiment in the decades before Goldsmith and Sheridan, Sherbo's *English Sentimental Drama* (1957) argues for the coexistence of a variety of comic genres throughout the eighteenth century. Bevis (1980) argues even more forcefully for the persistence of 'laughing comedy' in illegitimate forms such as pantomime. In a valuable collection which includes essays on satire and on sentimental and laughing comedy, Hume (1983) emphasises the generic variety of eighteenth-century performance. More recently, Kinservik offers a fruitful analysis of the Licensing Act's effects on theatrical satire, with particular reference to the work of Samuel Foote and Charles Macklin. Smith and Lawhon's book, *Plays about the Theatre in England* reveals the range of plays which make playwrights, performers and critics objects of laughter. Laura Brown's rich generic history argues that eighteenth-century tragedies and comedies display drama's growing inability to imagine states of psychological interiority, even as the novel becomes increasingly adept at such imaginings. Though their conclusions diverge from Brown's, other scholars have also presented the instability of dramatic genres in this period as a sign of the culture's shifting ideas about individual and group identities. Lisa Freeman (2002) sees eighteenth-century theatre as an important venue for representing human experiences that do not fit into the typical narrative of self-development associated with novels. Displaying a similar concern with theatre's power to question and challenge social and political institutions, Anderson describes how playwrights such as Aphra Behn, Susanna Centlivre, Hannah Cowley and Elizabeth Inchbald addressed women's growing social freedom by developing new comic forms that complicated the conventional marriage plot.

With the notable exception of Curran (1970), little scholarly attention was paid before the 1980s to plays written in the Romantic period. This changed, however, with the advent of new historicism, which was driven not only by the desire to recover forgotten texts, but also by a determination to challenge assumptions about conflicts between 'theatre' and 'drama'. Cave (1986) offers several essays attentive to historical connections between Romantic writers and the stage, including the editor's own review of 'Romantic Drama in Performance'. Richardson (1988) was the first major study of plays by Romantic poets such as Wordsworth and Byron which treated those dramas as worthy in their own generic terms rather than simply as orphans of lyric. Hoagwood and Watkins (1998) includes chapters – by Kucich on the vexed relation between Romantic drama and performances of Shakespeare, and by Kenneth Johnston and Joseph Nicholes on Wordsworth's *The Borderers* as a meditation on Revolutionary France – which valuably explore Romantic tragedy's complex engagements with history. Watkins (1993) argues that many Romantic writers rejected traditional dramatic forms because of their inability to portray realities commensurate with the experiences of a newly ascendant middle class. Purinton, however, sees Romantic verse drama as a unique site of social disruption, occupying a liminal space between performance and the solitude of the lyric voice. Following studies by Parker (1987, 1994) which examine the relationship between rhetoric and action in Wordsworth's and Coleridge's plays, Jewett (1997) suggests that Romantic tragedy explores, in a way that could not be accomplished on the public stage, how individuals act in politically volatile situations. More recently, Simpson (1998) contends that the dramas composed by Byron and Shelley constitute an attempt to intervene in contemporary history. By presenting themselves as 'closet dramas' – conspicuously refusing performance, but also conspicuously incomplete without it – Simpson suggests that these plays provide a purposely 'insufficient' reading experience which invites audiences to desire compensatory public action.

The 1960s saw the publication of two groundbreaking books on popular theatrical forms. Booth's *English Melodrama* (1965) recounts the emergence of the genre throughout the nineteenth century and devotes chapters to gothic, eastern, military and domestic melodramas. Mayer offers a similarly rich analysis of early nineteenth-century English pantomime. With its extensive discussions of pantomime's performance styles, scene designs, technologies of representation and generic borrowings, Mayer's analysis still influences much of the best work currently taking place in theatre history. Following Mayer, Marilyn Gaull emphasised the thematic and formal connections between Romantic writing and pantomime: her article heralded a growing interest in theatre's influence on other aspects of public life. Hadley (1995) examines a range of textual and visual culture to argue for the presence of a 'melodramatic mode' informing various kinds of public behaviour in nineteenth-century Britain. Such melodramatic imaginings became more frequent, Hadley contends, in the face of a crisis of individual identity brought on by England's emerging mass culture. Published within a year of Hadley's study, Hays and Nikolopoulou's volume contains several essays exploring the politics of melodramatic production including Nikolopoulou on adaptations of Walter Scott, Jeffrey Cox on nautical melodrama and Hartmut Ilsemann on the radicalism of early nineteenth-century melodrama. More recently, Swindells argues that playwrights such as George Colman the Younger and Douglas Jerrold catered to audiences who recognised in melodrama's rhetoric and spectacle models for their own political action, O'Brien explores the origins of English pantomime, contending that its popularity reveals the 'permeation' of spectacular entertainment into the eighteenth-century public sphere, and Taylor suggests that English melodrama's metaphorical plots and archetypal characters repeatedly evoke the revolutionary historical events occurring in France. Backscheider (1993) describes how technical innovation and the power of metaphor enabled late eighteenth-century gothic dramas to stage a contemporary crisis in class and gender roles. More broadly, Gamer (1997, 1999, 2000) presents gothic theatre as a powerful social and aesthetic force shaping Romantic literature. In the background of texts as canonical as *Lyrical Ballads*, Gamer finds a deep and ambivalent engagement with those anxieties about privacy, publicity, religion and the nation which gothic plays exhibited on the stage. Beginning with *In the Shadows of Romance* (1987), which explores the relations between English and Continental Romantic tragedy, Cox's rich body of work also imagines an alternative genealogy of Romanticism. With detailed accounts of the period's antirevolutionary drama (1991) and the rise of gothic drama (2002), Cox challenges critical assumptions about the relation between elite and popular culture, textual drama and performed theatre, private writing and public experience.

Readers interested in theatre's many points of contact with the musical world can turn to several excellent resources. Fiske's work discusses pantomime, burlesque, ballad opera and other generic hybrids, attributing many innovations in those forms to the management of David Garrick at Drury Lane. More recently, Girdham presents Stephen Storace, house composer at Drury Lane in the 1780s and 1790s, as a case study in the production of English theatrical music, Woodfield provides a strong analysis of opera as a cultural business and Dircks traces the history of English burletta. The two volumes of *Italian Opera in Late Eighteenth-Century London* by Curtis Price et al analyse many aspects of opera production – managerial structure, repertoire, performers, costumes – at London's two great opera houses: the King's Theatre in the Haymarket and the Pantheon. Two recent online publications are also worth mentioning: an issue of *Romantic Praxis* on 'Romanticism and Opera' edited by Wood and a special issue of *Romanticism on the Net* entitled 'Opera and Nineteenth-Century Literature', edited by Halmi.

Performers and playwrights

The prominence of the performer in theatre history evinces what recent scholarship has made explicit: that our modern ideas about theatrical celebrity were born in the late eighteenth and early nineteenth centuries. Stone and Kahrl's massive biography (1979) presented a new account of Garrick's life based on the publication of previously unavailable archival material and MacIntyre's even more readable *Garrick* is a worthy successor to that still impressive achievement. According to Woods (1984), Garrick represents a new kind of public self, eliciting from his audiences unprecedented forms of sympathetic identification. Benedetti focuses on both Garrick's 'natural' acting style and his professionalisation of the theatre. Wanko describes how biography and autobiography played a crucial role in the fame of Lavinia Fenton, Charlotte Charke, Barton Booth, Colley Cibber and David Garrick and altered the balance of cultural power between stage and print. Price (1973) provides a wide-ranging view of mid eighteenth-century theatre culture including chapters on acting, costumes and provincial theatres. Nicoll's *The Garrick Stage* (1980) is more concerned with the technical aspects of production and contains an extensive illustrated discussion of playhouse architecture.

Kelly's *The Kemble Era* (1980) incorporates letters, reviews and actors' diaries into a cogent account of the lives and careers of Sarah Siddons and John Philip Kemble, while Roach's important study (1985) charts the long-standing debate between the 'nature' and 'science' of acting, with excellent discussions of major figures such as Garrick, Kemble, Siddons and Kean. Baker and Manvell remain informative biographies of John Philip Kemble and Sarah Siddons respectively. Booth (1996) focuses especially on Siddons's innovative physical poses and her presentation of Shakespearean characters. Though Playfair, Hillebrand and Fitzsimons are significant accounts of Edmund Kean's life, the definitive biography of Kean remains to be written. Woods (1994), however, presents a cogent account the biographical 'myth-making' surrounding Kean. Donohue (1975) discusses the technical and stylistic advances in production which accompanied Kean's career, Bratton (2005) examines the print controversy surrounding Kean's sexual transgression and Tracy Davis (1995), Mulrooney (2003) and Kahan (2006) consider the impact of the actor's celebrity on literary culture.

Luckhurst and Moody's collection of essays explores theatrical celebrity from the Restoration to the present and contains essays by leading scholars from several fields, including Shearer West on theatrical portraiture and Peter Thompson on the professional rivalry between David Garrick and James Quin. In her compelling study *The Image of the Actor* (1991), West elucidates theatre's complex position at the intersection of verbal, textual and visual cultures. Essays by West, Shelley Bennett, and Mark Leonard in Asleson (1999) present a comprehensive account of Sarah Siddons's presence as a subject of Romantic-period portraiture and Asleson's later collection *Notorious Muse* (2003) is a lavishly illustrated study of the influence of actresses on fashion, art and women's social roles in Georgian Britain.

Because changes in acting style and production values affected the reception of traditional English playwrights, Shakespearean performance and adaptation occupies an important corner of the period's theatre history. Jacobus, George, Mahoney, Moody (2002) and Page all provide article-length studies of Shakespearean performances and their political implications. Michael Dobson's book, *The Making of the National Poet* (1992), is an invaluable tool for understanding the ongoing attempt in the mid eighteenth-century to mould Shakespeare, via print and stage, to fit a nationalist ideology, and Jonathan Bate provides the most comprehensive account of the popular battle to appropriate the image and idea of Shakespeare for various political ends in the Romantic period. Claiming that Shakespeare's contemporaries also influence Romantic-period performance, Donohue (1970) argues for an historical continuity between 'the affective drama of situation' characteristic of playwrights such as Beaumont and Fletcher and Romantic drama's relentless interest in the actor's emotional states. The connection Donohue emphasises between the literary and theatrical aspects of these dramas anticipated the work of the next three decades.

Danzinger and, more recently, Worth provide concise introductions to the two major playwrights of the eighteenth century, Oliver Goldsmith and Richard Brinsley Sheridan. Among a host of Sheridan biographies (Glasgow, Gibbs, Bingham, Morwood, Kelly 1997), O'Toole stands out as a thoroughly researched account of the political and social challenges faced by a public Irishman achieving fame in London. The 1970s and 80s saw a major rehabilitation of Sheridan's scholarly reputation. Durant's work (1975, 1983, 1987) attends in valuable ways to both formal and historical aspects of the plays and his scrupulously annotated bibliography (1981) encompasses Sheridan studies from 1816 to 1979. Loftis (1976) presents Sheridan as 'a propagandist for humanitarian causes' whose plays respond to similar concerns present in the drama of George Colman the Elder, Richard Cumberland and Hugh Kelly. Though limited by capitulations to social decorum, Auburn argues, Sheridan's comedies represent the height of eighteenth-century plot construction and characterisation. Morwood and Crane is a major revaluation of Sheridan's career as artist, manager and politician, with a particular emphasis on rhetoric. This collection includes essays by Richard Taylor on Sheridan's reviewers and Marc Baer on Sheridan's reformist politics. Carlson (1996) on *Pizarro* and Jones on *The Camp* and *The Critic* stand out among more recent explorations of Sheridan as a political dramatist.

Goldsmith has received less attention from biographers, though accounts by Gwynn, William Freeman (1952), Wardle and Ginger are useful points of departure, and Rousseau's *Oliver Goldsmith: The Critical Heritage* remains a valuable review of criticism. Both Quintana and Kirk provide overviews of

Goldsmith's multifarious career. Swarbrick's collection offers essays which consider Goldsmith from a variety of formal and historical perspectives, including Davie on Goldsmith's politics and Bernard Harris on the playwright's changing critical reputation.

Gender has played a crucial role in the last two decades' reconceptualisation of the theatrical field. A new wave of scholarship has brought explorations of women's creative responses to the social and institutional challenges of writing for and acting in the theatre. Donkin links the careers of women playwrights such as Frances Brooke, Sophia Lee, Elizabeth Inchbald and Frances Burney to David Garrick's innovative management of Drury Lane and argues that their success also occasioned a critical and institutional backlash. Baruth explores the ways in which Charlotte Charke's authorship and performances challenged traditional gender roles. Bolton argues that the public theatrical lives of Hannah Cowley, Elizabeth Inchbald, Emma Hamilton and Mary Robinson shaped the construction of Britain's 'national romance'. Burroughs's study of Baillie (1997) rejects the notion that Romantic 'closet drama' necessarily involves a withdrawal from the concerns that accompany public performance. Rather than being the imaginative space to which the Romantic poets repaired in the face of their disgust with contemporary theatre, Burroughs argues, the closet served as a site for the development of experimental 'theatre theory', especially by women. Crochunis's article (2004) provides a concise but thorough overview of working female playwrights from Joanna Baillie to Jane Scott and in the collection of essays, *Joanna Baillie: Romantic Dramatist* (2004), he and his contributors further reclaim that playwright's career by examining – from economic, aesthetic and philosophical perspectives – Baillie's position within the cultural field of dramatic authorship.

Two essay collections have greatly advanced our understanding of women's importance in the theatrical world, as well as our awareness of the ways that their contributions have been consistently erased from historical memory. Davis and Donkin (1999) includes essays by Gay Gibson Cima on female dramatists and the cultural marketplace, Bratton on Jane Scott as a 'writer-manager' and Moody on gender and the nature of dramatic authorship. In Burroughs (2000), Cox traces Sarah Siddons's and Joanna Baillie's success in negotiating theatrical institutions, Greg Kucich discusses the contemporary critical reception of women playwrights and Kate Newey examines how Hannah More, Ann Yearsley, Frances Burney and Mary Russell Mitford imported history into their tragedies to bolster their cultural authority. Straub (1992) explores eighteenth-century fears over the power of players – particularly women – both on stage and as public figures in English society, and in a later essay (1995) she charts the association of eighteenth-century actors with the sexually 'deviant' effeminate male. Nussbaum (2005) describes the ways in which eighteenth-century actresses reshaped public notions of femininity. For Carlson (1994), the desire to preserve masculine high culture against the threat of female bodies underpins the Romantic attempt to 'closet' Shakespeare by defining his plays as objects of solitary readerly contemplation. Carlson's discussion of Coleridge's growing ambivalence about the stage represents a forceful demonstration of how the literary and the theatrical were bound up with questions of gender, identity and politics. Her article on 'Master Betty' (1996), a child sensation on the Regency stage, further explores spectators' fascination with the performance of androgyny.

Theatre as institution

There are a number of useful introductions to the nature of the theatrical public in the eighteenth century. Lynch provides a wide-ranging review of eighteenth-century production and reception, with chapters on theatrical repertory, management, acting and audience fashions while Pedicord focuses more squarely on the rising consumerism behind aesthetic and technological changes in play production and includes appendices containing a statistical survey of repertoire at the London patent theatres and a chart of box-office receipts. Gray's history of theatrical criticism between 1720 and 1795 explores in detail periodical debates about theatre's moral and aesthetic value.

Barker (1971) called for greater attention to the material conditions of theatre's reception. Altick (1978) challenged academic prejudices against the popular through a comprehensive analysis of London's varied metropolitan amusements: his magisterial volume includes chapters on panoramas, dioramas, the Eidophusikon and the Crystal Palace. Hume (1980) remains an important work, containing essays on eighteenth-century company management, scenic design, performing styles, censorship, music and the development of theatrical repertoires. Anticipating later theatre historians who decried the conceptual separation of theatrical performance from print culture, Stone (1981) demonstrates the importance of music and dance in reconstructing eighteenth-century performance. Government regulation and censorship of play production, an area of continuing interest today, became a new focus of scholarship in an article by Ganzel. Conolly and Stephens, recently followed by Worrall (2006), offer detailed histories of theatrical censorship in the period. Peters's important study of the relationship between theatre and print culture concentrates on the publication and circulation of play texts and the operation of intellectual property.

New historicist criticism helped to stimulate interest in the politics of theatre in this period. Writing in 'Romantic Performances' (a special issue of *Texas Studies in Literature and Language* edited by Theresa Kelley),

Jane Moody (1996) argued that a nearly exclusive focus on the 'legitimate' entertainments of the major playhouses had long hindered our understanding of theatre's relationship to state power. The essays in the *TSLL* volume, along with those of its 1999 companion, 'Romantic Drama in Place', edited by Michael Simpson, evince a clear methodological shift in theatrical historiography. Increasingly, scholars have emphasised theatre's material dimensions: playbills, cast-lists, production documents, reviews, theatre design. Tracy Davis's meticulously detailed inquiry (2000) follows the flow of money along the institutional channels of British theatre, from consumers to managers to actors and theatrical labourers, analysing the intimate connections between theatre's economic, political and aesthetic power. Milhous and Hume also draw attention to the economics of theatre by charting the complex system of payments and benefits by which playwrights earned their living in eighteenth-century London. Canfield and Payne contains several important essays on the eighteenth century, especially James Thompson on the representation of money in plays. With discussions of city comedians, spectacular melodramas and unlicensed Shakespearean adaptations, Moody (1996, 2000) opens up the wide world of illegitimate theatrical production in London's minor playhouses and reclaims a vital institutional context for the study of the Romantic period and its literature. Like Moody, Bratton's 'new overview' of the London theatre scene (2003) includes 'a much wider variety of venues in and around London than is usually surveyed', and her chapter 'Claiming Kin' uses family genealogies to shape a novel account of nineteenth-century acting. Eberle-Sinatra's study of Leigh Hunt's career as a theatrical critic also emphasises the importance of institutional contexts.

Beginning with Kruger, the last fifteen years have produced numerous investigations into theatre's representations of class, gender and the British nation, notably Russell (1990) and Baer (1992). Burke argues that rioting in Dublin theatres between 1712 and 1784 manifested an increasingly self-conscious Irish nationalism. Terence Freeman (1995) and Russell (1995) both draw convincing connections between Britain's theatrical and military cultures. Freeman explores representations of military figures on stage as well as references to soldiers in theatrical speeches and songs, contending that theatre managers employed the 'poor soldier' figure to elicit audience sympathy. Russell presents theatre as a powerful imaginative force in shaping Britons' ideas about citizenry, patriotism and national history, giving specific attention to the military's presence in Britain's theatrical spaces, to dramatic performances in camps and on ships and to the theatricality of military spectacle during the Napoleonic wars.

Recent accounts also consider the period's extensive representations of national, international and colonial cultures. Exotic characters and faraway scenes fascinated audiences who were becoming aware of their country's growing political and economic power. Much of the work in this area explores how representations of gender and race intersect on stage. The arguments of Wilson (2003, 2004) exemplify a theoretical and methodological shift which is radically altering our understanding of theatre's function in the imperial state. Nussbaum's wide-ranging discussion of blackness on the British stage (2004) explores the functions of race in the cultural imagination of eighteenth-century Britain. Roach (1996) provides an illuminating analysis of how the public representation of ethnic figures in London and New Orleans shaped historical consciousness of the Black Atlantic. In many ways, this deeply influential book represents the extraordinary potential of historically located performance studies. Choudhury also challenges colonial/post-colonial oppositions in her presentation of theatre's complex depictions of 'intercultural contact'. Seemingly disparate controversies over the importation of Italian operas or performances of Sheridan's *The School for Scandal* in colonial India, she argues, reveal the social anxieties accompanying British imperialist expansion. Bhattacharya's discussion of the portrayal of Indian women by eighteenth-century British writers includes an important chapter on the drama of the female nabob. Similarly, O'Quinn's interdisciplinary work (2002, 2005) not only describes how figures such as the native American and African transformed communal ideas of domesticity and the nation, but also considers how theatricality impinged on and in turn was shaped by British colonial policy in India. Hadley (1999) also charts melodrama's projection of domestic concerns onto orientalist locales, while Pratt argues that the stage figure of the North American Indian challenged audiences' prejudices about the limits of the human.

Theatre's changing position in the period's culture also transformed individual and communal practices of self-representation. Scholars such as Pascoe (1997) and Tracy Davis (2003) have invited us to think in new ways about concepts such as theatricality and sociability. Russell and Tuite's volume, *Romantic Sociability*, gives a glimpse of where the future may lead by asking how collective experiences such as theatregoing – and the conversations these experiences produced – may have altered Britons' ways of thinking about themselves as citizens of a larger world. As we develop new approaches to reading theatre between 1730 and 1830, so new possibilities emerge for fashioning ourselves as the inheritors, and interrogators, of the world which theatre helped create.

BIBLIOGRAPHY

Altick, Richard. *The Shows of London*. Cambridge: Belknap, 1978.

Anderson, Misty G. *Female Playwrights and Eighteenth-Century Comedy: Negotiating Marriage on the London Stage*. New York: Palgrave, 2002.

Asleson, Robyn, ed. *A Passion for Performance: Sarah Siddons and Her Portraitists*. Los Angeles, CA: Getty Museum, 1999.

Asleson, Robyn, ed. *Notorious Muse: the Actress in British Art and Culture, 1776–1812*. New Haven, CT: Yale University Press, 2003.

Auburn, Mark S. *Sheridan's Comedies, their Contexts and Achievements*. Lincoln, NE: University of Nebraska Press, 1977.

Backscheider, Paula, ed. *Eighteenth-Century Drama*, 69 vols. New York: Garland, completed 1983.

Spectacular Politics: Theatrical Power and Mass Culture in Early Modern England. Baltimore, MD: Johns Hopkins University Press, 1993.

Baer, Marc. *Theatre and Disorder in Late Georgian London*. Oxford: Clarendon, 1992.

Baillie, Joanna. *Plays on the Passions*. Ed. Peter Duthie. Peterborough: Broadview Press, 2001.

Baker, Herschel. *John Philip Kemble: the Actor in His Theatre*. Cambridge, MA: Harvard University Press, 1942.

Barish, Jonas. *The Antitheatrical Prejudice*. Berkeley, CA: University of California Press, 1981.

Barker, Clive. 'A Theatre for the People'. In *Essays on Nineteenth Century British Theatre: the Proceedings of a Symposium Sponsored by the Manchester University Department of Drama*. Ed. Kenneth Richards and Peter Thomson. London: Methuen, 1971.

Barrell, John. *The Political Theory of Painting from Reynolds to Hazlitt: 'The Body of the Public'*. New Haven, CT and London: Yale University Press, 1986.

'"An Entire Change of Performances?" The Politicisation of Theatre and the Theatricalisation of Politics in the mid 1790s'. *Lumen* 17 (1998): 11–50.

Baruth, Philip, ed. *Introducing Charlotte Charke: Actress, Author, Enigma*. Chicago, IL: University of Illinois Press, 1998.

Bate, Jonathan. *Shakespearean Constitutions: Politics, Theatre, Criticism 1730–1830*. Oxford: Clarendon, 1989.

Baugh, Christopher. 'Philippe James de Loutherbourg and the Early Pictorial Theatre: Some Aspects of its Social Context'. In *Themes in Drama, Volume 9, The Theatrical Space*. Ed. James Redmond. Cambridge: Cambridge University Press, 1987.

Garrick and Loutherbourg. Cambridge: Chadwyck-Healey, 1990.

Benedetti, Jean. *David Garrick and the Birth of Modern Theatre.* London: Methuen, 2001.

Bevis, Richard. *The Laughing Tradition: Stage Comedy in Garrick's Day.* Athens, GA: University of Georgia Press, 1980.

English Drama: Restoration and Eighteenth Century, 1660–1789. New York: Longman, 1988.

Bhattacharya, Nandini. *Reading the Splendid Body: Gender and Consumerism in Eighteenth-Century British Writing on India.* London: Associated University Presses, 1998.

Bingham, Madeleine. *Sheridan: The Track of a Comet.* London: Allen and Unwin, 1972.

Bolton, Betsy. *Women, Nationalism, and the Romantic Stage: Theatre and Politics in Britain, 1780–1800.* Cambridge: Cambridge University Press, 2001.

Booth, Michael R. *English Melodrama.* London: Herbert Jenkins Ltd, 1965.

Booth, Michael R., ed. *Eighteenth-Century Tragedy.* London: Oxford University Press, 1965.

English Plays of the Nineteenth Century. 5 vols. Oxford: Clarendon, 1969–1976.

Booth, Michael R. 'Sarah Siddons'. In *Three Tragic Actresses: Siddons, Rachel, Ristori.* Ed. Michael R. Booth, John Stokes and Susan Bassnett. Cambridge: Cambridge University Press, 1996.

et al., eds. *The Revels History of Drama in English, Volume 6: 1750–1880.* London: Methuen, 1975.

Bratton, Jacky. 'Theatre of War: the Crimea on the London Stage'. In *Performance and Politics in Popular Drama.* Ed. David Bradby, Louis James and Bernard Sharratt. Cambridge: Cambridge University Press, 1980.

'Jane Scott the writer-manager'. In *Women and Playwriting in Nineteenth-Century Britain.* Ed. Tracy C. Davis and Ellen Donkin. Cambridge: Cambridge University Press, 1999.

'Introduction'. *Nineteenth-Century Theatre and Film* 29:2 (2002): 6–22.

New Readings in Theatre History. Cambridge: Cambridge University Press, 2003.

'The Celebrity of Edmund Kean: an Institutional Story'. In *Theatre and Celebrity in Britain, 1660–2000.* Ed. Mary Luckhurst and Jane Moody. Basingstoke: Palgrave, 2006.

Brewer, John. *The Pleasures of the Imagination: English Culture in the Eighteenth Century.* New York: Farrar, Straus and Giroux, 1997.

Brooks, Peter. *The Melodramatic Imagination: Balzac, Henry James, and the Mode of Excess.* New Haven, CT: Yale University Press, 1976.

Brown, Frederick. *Theater and Revolution: The Culture of the French Stage.* New York: Viking Press, 1980.

Brown, Laura. *English Dramatic Form, 1660–1760: an Essay in Generic History.* New Haven, CT: Yale University Press, 1981.

Burke, Helen M. *Riotous Performances: the Struggle for Hegemony in the Irish Theatre, 1712–1784.* Notre Dame, IN: University of Notre Dame Press, 2003.

Burnim, Kalman A. *David Garrick, Director.* Pittsburgh, PA: University of Pittsburgh Press, 1961.

Burroughs, Catherine B. *Closet Stages: Joanna Baillie and the Theater Theory of British Romantic Women Writers*. Philadelphia, PA: University of Pennsylvania Press, 1997.

Burroughs, Catherine B., ed. *Women in British Romantic Theatre: Drama, Performance, and Society, 1790–1840*. Cambridge: Cambridge University Press, 2000.

Bush-Bailey, Gilli. 'Still Working it Out: an Account of the Practical Workshop Rediscovery of Company Practice and Romantic Performance Styles via Jane Scott's Plays'. *Nineteenth-Century Theatre and Film* 29:2 (2002): 6–22.

Byrne, Paula. *Jane Austen and the Theatre*. London: Hambledon, 2002.

Canfield, J. Douglas and Deborah Payne, eds. *Cultural Readings of Restoration and Eighteenth-Century English Theater*. Athens, GA: University of Georgia Press, 1995.

Carlson, Julie A. *In the Theatre of Romanticism: Coleridge, Nationalism, Women*. Cambridge: Cambridge University Press, 1994.

'Forever Young: Master Betty and the Queer Stage of Youth in English Romanticism'. *South Atlantic Quarterly* 95:3 (1996): 575–602.

'Trying Sheridan's *Pizarro*'. *Texas Studies in Literature and Language* 38:3/4 (1996): 359–78.

'Hazlitt and the Sociability of Theatre'. In *Romantic Sociability*. Ed. Gillian Russell and Clara Tuite. Cambridge: Cambridge University Press, 2002.

Carlson, Marvin. *Places of Performance: The Semiotics of Theatre Architecture*. Ithaca, NY: Cornell University Press, 1989.

Cave, Richard Allen, ed. *The Romantic Theatre: an International Symposium*. Totowa, NJ: Barnes & Noble, 1987.

Choudhury, Mita. *Interculturalism and Resistance in London Theater, 1660–1800: Identity, Performance, Empire*. Lewisburg, PA: Bucknell University Press, 2000.

Cima, Gay Gibson. '"To be public as a genius and private as a woman": the Critical Framing of Nineteenth-Century British Playwrights'. In *Women in British Romantic Theatre: Drama, Performance, and Society, 1790–1840*. Ed. Catherine B. Burroughs. Cambridge: Cambridge University Press, 2000.

Clark, William Smith. *The Early Irish Stage: The Beginnings to 1720*. Oxford: Clarendon Press, 1955.

The Irish Stage in the County Towns, 1720–1800. Oxford: Clarendon Press, 1965.

Conolly, L. W. *The Censorship of English Drama, 1737–1824*. San Marino, CA: Henry E. Huntington Library and Art Gallery, 1976.

Corman, Brian. 'Comedy'. In *The Cambridge Companion to English Restoration Theatre*. Ed. Deborah Payne Fisk. Cambridge: Cambridge University Press, 2000.

Cox, Jeffrey N. 'Ideology and Genre in British Antirevolutionary Drama in the 1790s'. *ELH* 58 (1992): 579–610.

ed. *Seven Gothic Dramas 1789–1825*. Athens, OH: Ohio University Press, 1992.

Cox, Jeffrey N. 'Baillie, Siddons, Larpent: Gender, Power, and Politics in the Theatre of Romanticism'. In *Women in British Romantic Theatre: Drama, Performance, and Society, 1790–1840*. Ed. Catherine B. Burroughs. Cambridge: Cambridge University Press, 2000.

'English Gothic Theatre'. In *The Cambridge Companion to Gothic Fiction*. Ed. Jerrold E. Hogle. Cambridge: Cambridge University Press, 2002.

Cox, Jeffrey N. and Michael Gamer, eds. *The Broadview Anthology of Romantic Drama*. Peterborough: Broadview, 2003.

Crochunis, Thomas C. 'British Women Playwrights Around 1800: New Paradigms and Recoveries'. Introduction to special issue of *Romanticism on the Net* 12 (1998): www.erudit.org/revue/ron/1998/v/n12/index.html.

'Women and Dramatic Writing in the British Romantic Era'. *Literature Compass* 1 (2004): 1–14 www.literature-compass.com/view point.asp.

Crochunis, Thomas C., ed. *Joanna Baillie, Romantic Dramatist: Critical Essays*. London: Routledge, 2004.

Crochunis, Thomas and Michael Eberle-Sinatra. 'Putting Plays (and More) in Cyberspace: An Overview of the British Women Playwrights Around 1800 Project'. *European Romantic Review* 14:1 (2003): 117–31.

eds. *The Broadview Anthology of British Women Playwrights, 1777–1843*. Peterborough: Broadview, forthcoming.

Crochunis, Thomas and Michael Eberle-Sinatra. *British Women Playwrights Around 1800*: www.etang.umontreal.ca/bwp1800/.

Crouch, Kimberly. 'The Public Life of Actresses: Prostitutes or Ladies?'. In *Gender in Eighteenth-Century England: Roles, Representations, and Responsibilities*. Ed. Hannah Barker and Elaine Chalus. London: Longman, 1997.

Curran, Stuart. *Shelley's Cenci: Scorpions Ringed with Fire*. Princeton, NJ: Princeton University Press, 1970.

Danzinger, Marlies. *Oliver Goldsmith and Richard Brinsley Sheridan*. New York: Ungar, 1978.

Darby, Barbara. *Frances Burney, Dramatist: Gender, Performance, and the Late Eighteenth-Century Stage*. Lexington, KY: University Press of Kentucky, 1997.

Davie, Donald. 'Notes on Goldsmith's Politics'. In *The Art of Oliver Goldsmith*. Ed. Andrew Swarbrick. London: Vision, 1984.

Davis, Jim. 'Self-Portraiture On and Off the Stage: The Low Comedian as Iconographer'. *Theatre Survey* 3:2 (November 2002): 189–97.

Davis, Jim and Victor Emeljanow. *Reflecting the Audience: London Theatre Audiences, 1840–1880*. Iowa, IA: University of Iowa Press, 2001.

Davis, Tracy C. '"Reading Shakespeare by Flashes of Lightning": Challenging the Foundations of Romantic Acting Theory'. *ELH* 62 (1995): 933–54.

The Economics of the British Stage, 1800–1914. Cambridge: Cambridge University Press, 2000.

Davis, Tracy C. and Thomas Postlewait, eds. *Theatricality*. Cambridge: Cambridge University Press, 2004.

Davis, Tracy C. and Ellen Donkin, eds. *Women and Playwriting in Nineteenth-Century Britain*. Cambridge: Cambridge University Press, 1999.

Dircks, Phyllis. *Eighteenth-Century English Burletta*. Victoria, BC: University of Victoria Press, 1999.

Dobson, Michael. *The Making of the National Poet: Shakespeare, Adaptation and Authorship, 1660–1769*. Oxford: Clarendon, 1992.

Donkin, Ellen. *Getting into the Act: Women Playwrights in London, 1776–1840*. Cambridge: Cambridge University Press, 2000.

Donohue, Joseph W. Jr. *Dramatic Character in the English Romantic Age*. Princeton, NJ: Princeton University Press, 1970.

Theatre in the Age of Kean. Totowa, NJ: Rowan & Littlefield, 1975.

Donohue, Joseph W., Jr, ed. *The Cambridge History of British Theatre, Volume 2: 1660–1895*. Cambridge: Cambridge University Press, 2004.

Durant, Jack D. *Richard Brinsley Sheridan*. Boston: Twayne, 1975.

Richard Brinsley Sheridan: A Reference Guide. Boston, MA: G. K. Hall, 1981.

'Sheridan, Burke, and Revolution'. *Eighteenth-Century Life* 6:2/3 (1981): 103–113.

'Sheridan's Grotesques'. *Theatre Annual: A Journal of Performance Studies* 38 (1983): 13–30.

'Sheridan's Picture-Action Scene: A Study in Contexts'. *Eighteenth-Century Life* 11:3 (1987): 34–47.

Eberle-Sinatra, Michael. 'Introducing *Critical Essays*: Leigh Hunt and Theatrical Criticism in the Early Nineteenth Century'. *Keats-Shelley Journal* 50 (2001): 100–23.

Elsaesser, Thomas. 'Tales of Sound and Fury: Observations on the Family Melodrama'. In *Home Is Where the Heart Is: Studies in Melodrama and the Woman's Film*. Ed. Christine Gledhill. London: British Film Institute, 1987.

Felsenstein, Frank. *English Trader, Indian Maid: Representing Gender, Race, and Slavery in the New World*. Baltimore, MA: Johns Hopkins University Press, 1999.

Finberg, Melinda, ed. *Eighteenth-Century Women Dramatists*. Oxford: Oxford University Press, 2001.

Fiske, Roger. *English Theatre Music in the Eighteenth Century*. Oxford: Oxford University Press, 1986.

Fitzsimmons, Linda and Arthur W. McDonald. *The Yorkshire Stage, 1766–1803: A Calendar of Plays*. London: The Scarecrow Press, 1989.

Fitzsimons, Raymund. *Edmund Kean: Fire from Heaven*. London: Hamish Hamilton, 1976.

Franceschina, John. *Sisters of Gore: Seven Gothic Melodramas by British Women, 1790–1843*. New York: Garland, 1997.

Freeman, Lisa A. *Character's Theater: Genre and Identity on the Eighteenth-Century English Stage*. Philadelphia, PA: University of Pennsylvania Press, 2002.

Freeman, Terence M. *Dramatic Representations of British Soldiers and Sailors on the London Stage, 1660–1800: Britons Strike Home*. Lewiston, NY: Edwin Mellen, 1995.

Freeman, William. *Oliver Goldsmith*. New York: Philosophical Library, 1952.

Gamer, Michael. 'National Supernaturalism: Joanna Baillie, Germany, and the Gothic Drama'. *Theatre Survey* 38:2 (1997): 49–88.

'Authors in Effect: Lewis, Scott, and the Gothic Drama'. *ELH* 66:4 (1999): 831–61.

Romanticism and the Gothic: Genre, Reception and Canon Formation. Cambridge: Cambridge University Press, 2000.

Ganzel, Dewey. 'Patent Wrongs and Patent Theatres: Drama and the Law in the Early Nineteenth Century'. *PMLA* 76 (1961): 384–96.

Gaull, Marilyn. 'Romantic Theater'. *The Wordsworth Circle* 14:4 (1983): 255–63.

Gay, Penny. *Jane Austen and the Theatre*. Cambridge: Cambridge University Press, 2002.

George, David. 'Restoring Shakespeare's *Coriolanus*: Kean versus Macready'. *Theatre Notebook* 44:3 (1990): 101–18.

Gibbs, Lewis. *Sheridan: His Life and His Times*. New York: William Morrow, 1948.

Ginger, John. *The Notable Man: The Life and Times of Oliver Goldsmith*. London: Hamish Hamilton, 1977.

Girdham, Jane. *English Opera in Late Eighteenth-Century London: Stephen Storace at Drury Lane*. Oxford: Clarendon, 1997.

Glasgow, Alice. *Sheridan of Drury Lane*. New York: Frederick Stokes, 1940.

Gray, Charles Harold. *Theatrical Criticism in London to 1795*. New York: Columbia University Press, 1931.

Greene, John C. and Gladys L. H. Clark. *The Dublin Stage, 1720–1745*. Bethlehem, PA: Lehigh University Press, 1993.

Gwynn, Stephen. *Oliver Goldsmith*. New York: Holt, 1935.

Hadley, Elaine. *Melodramatic Tactics: Theatricalized Dissent in the English Marketplace, 1800–1885*. Stanford, CA: Stanford University Press, 1995.

'Home as Abroad: Orientalism and Occidentalism in Early English Stage Melodrama'. *Texas Studies in Literature and Language* 41:4 (1999): 330–50.

Halmi, Nicholas, ed. 'Opera and Nineteenth-Century Literature'. *Romanticism on the Net* 34–35 (2004): www.erudit.org/revue/ron/2004/v/n34-35/index.html.

Harris, Bernard. 'Goldsmith in the Theatre'. In *The Art of Oliver Goldsmith*. Ed. Andrew Swarbrick. London: Vision, 1984.

Harris, Susan Cannon. 'Outside the Box: The Female Spectator, *The Fair Penitent*, and the Kelly Riots of 1747'. *Theatre Journal* 57.1 (2005): 33–55.

Hays, Michael and Anastasia Nikolopoulou, eds. *Melodrama: The Cultural Emergence of a Genre*. New York: St. Martin's, 1996.

Heilman, Robert B. *Tragedy and Melodrama: Versions of Experience*. Seattle, WA and London: University of Washington Press, 1968.

Hemans, Felicia. *The Siege of Valencia: A Parallel Text Edition*. Ed. Susan Wolfson and Elizabeth Fay. Peterborough: Broadview Press, 2002.

Highfill, Philip H. Jr, Kalman A. Burnim and Edward A. Langhans. *A Biographical Dictionary of Actors, Actresses, Musicians, Dancers, Managers, and other Stage Personnel in London, 1660–1800*. 16 vols. Carbondale, IL: University of Southern Illinois Press, 1975.

Hillebrand, Harold Newcomb. *Edmund Kean*. New York: Columbia University Press, 1933.

Hoagwood, Terence Allan and Daniel P. Watkins, eds. *British Romantic Drama: Historical and Critical Essays*. London: Associated University Presses, 1998.

Hogan, Charles Beecher, ed. *The London Stage 1660–1800: A Calendar of Plays, Entertainments and Afterpieces, Part 5: 1776–1800*. 3 vols. Carbondale, IL: Southern Illinois University Press, 1968.

Howe, Elizabeth. *The First English Actresses: Women and Drama, 1660–1700*. Cambridge: Cambridge University Press, 1992.

Hughes, Derek, ed. *Eighteenth-Century Women Playwrights*. 6 vols. London: Pickering and Chatto, 2001.

Hughes, Leo. *The Drama's Patrons: A Study of the Eighteenth-Century London Audience*. Austin, TX and London: University of Texas Press, 1971.

Hume, Robert D. 'Goldsmith and Sheridan and the Supposed Revolution in "Laughing" Against "Sentimental" Comedy'. In *Studies in Change and Revolution: Aspects of English Intellectual History, 1640–1800*. Ed. Paul J. Korshin. Menston: Scolar Press, 1972.

Hume, Robert D., ed. *The London Theatre World, 1660–1800*. Carbondale, IL: Southern Illinois University Press, 1980.

Hume, Robert D. *The Rakish Stage: Studies in English Drama, 1660–1800*. Carbondale, IL: Southern Illinois University Press, 1983.

'Theatres and Repertory'. In *The Cambridge History of British Theatre, Volume 2: 1660–1985*. Ed. Joseph W. Donohue, Jr. Cambridge: Cambridge University Press, 2004.

Hyde, Ralph. *Panoramania! The Art and Entertainment of the 'All-Embracing' View*. London: Trefoil in association with the Barbican Art Gallery, 1988.

Ilsemann, Hartmut. 'Radicalism in the Melodrama of the Early Nineteenth Century'. In *Melodrama: The Cultural Emergence of a Genre*. Ed. Michael Hays and Anastasia Nikolopoulou. New York: St Martin's, 1996.

Jacobus, Mary. '"That Great Stage Where Senators Perform": *Macbeth* and the Politics of Romantic Theatre'. In *Romanticism, Writing, and Sexual Difference: Essays on The Prelude*. Oxford: Clarendon, 1989.

Jewett, William. *Fatal Autonomy: Romantic Drama and the Rhetoric of Agency*. Ithaca, NY: Cornell University Press, 1997.

Johnston, Kenneth R. and Joseph Nicholes. 'Transitory Actions, Men Betrayed: The French Revolution in the English Revolution in Romantic Drama'. In *British Romantic Drama: Historical and Critical Essays*. Ed. Terence Allan Hoagwood and Daniel P. Watkins. London: Associated University Presses, 1998.

Jones, Robert W. 'Sheridan and the Theatre of Patriotism: Staging Dissent during the War for America'. *Eighteenth-Century Life* 26:1 (2002): 24–45.

Kahan, Jeffrey. *The Cult of Kean*. Aldershot: Ashgate, 2006.

Kavenik, Frances M. *British Drama, 1660–1779: A Critical History*. New York: Twayne, 1995.

Kelley, Theresa M., ed. 'Romantic Performances'. Special issue of *Texas Studies in Literature and Language* 38:3/4 (1996).

Kelly, Linda. *The Kemble Era: John Philip Kemble, Sarah Siddons, and the London Stage*. London: Bodley Head, 1980.

Richard Brinsley Sheridan: A Life. London: Sinclair-Stevenson, 1997.

Kenny, Shirley Strum, 'Humane Comedy'. *Modern Philology* 75:1 (August 1977): 29–43.

Kinservik, Matthew J. *Disciplining Satire: the Censorship of Satiric Comedy on the Eighteenth-Century London Stage*. Lewisberg, KY: Bucknell University Press, 2002.

Kirk, Claire M. *Oliver Goldsmith*. New York: Twayne, 1967.

Kruger, Loren. *The National Stage: Theatre and Cultural Legitimation in England, France, and America*. Chicago, IL and London: University of Chicago Press, 1992.

Kucich, Greg. '"A Haunted Ruin": Romantic Drama, Renaissance Tradition, and the Critical Establishment'. In *British Romantic Drama: Historical and Critical Essays*. Ed. Terence Allan Hoagwood and Daniel P. Watkins. London: Associated University Presses, 1998.

'Reviewing Women in British Romantic Theatre'. In *Women in British Romantic Theatre: Drama, Performance, and Society, 1790–1840*. Ed. Catherine B. Burroughs. Cambridge: Cambridge University Press, 2000.

'Joanna Baillie and the Re-Staging of History and Gender'. In *Joanna Baillie, Romantic Dramatist*. Ed. Thomas C. Crochunis. London: Routledge, 2004.

Langhans, Edward A. *Eighteenth-Century British and Irish Promptbooks: a Descriptive Bibliography*. New York: Greenwood, 1987.

Loftis, John. *Essays on the Theatre from Eighteenth-Century Periodicals*. Los Angeles, CA: Clark Memorial Library, 1960.

Loftis, John, ed. *Restoration Drama: Modern Essays in Criticism*. New York: Oxford University Press, 1966.

Loftis, John. *Sheridan and the Drama of Georgian England*. Oxford: Blackwell, 1976.

Loftis, John, Richard Southern, Marion Jones and A. H. Scouten, eds. *The Revels History of Drama in English, Vol 5: 1660–1750*. London: Methuen, 1976.

Luckhurst, Mary and Jane Moody, eds. *Theatre and Celebrity in Britain, 1660–2000*. Basingstoke: Palgrave, 2006.

Lynch, James J. *Box, Pit and Gallery: Stage and Society in Johnson's London*. Berkeley and Los Angeles, CA: University of California Press, 1953.

MacDonald, Jan. 'Acting and the Austere Joys of Motherhood: Sarah Siddons Performs Maternity'. In *Extraordinary Actors: Essays on Popular Performers – Studies in Honour of Peter Thomson*. Ed. Jane Milling and Martin Banham. Exeter: University of Exeter Press, 2004.

MacIntyre, Ian. *Garrick*. New York: Penguin, 1999.

Mahoney, Charles. 'Upstaging the Fall: Coriolanus and the Spectacle of Romantic Apostasy'. *Studies in Romanticism* 38:1 (1999): 29–50.

Mander, Raymond and Joe Mitchenson. *The Theatres of London*. Illus. Timothy Birdsall. London: Rupert Hart Davis, 1961.

The Lost Theatres of London. New York: Taplinger, 1968.

Mann, David D. and Susan Garland Mann, with Camille Garnier. *Women Playwrights in England, Ireland, and Scotland, 1660–1823*. Bloomington and Indianapolis, IN: Indiana University Press, 1996.

Manvell, Roger. *Sarah Siddons: Portrait of an Actress*. New York: Putnam, 1970.

Marshall, Herbert and Mildred Stock. *Ira Aldridge, the Negro Tragedian*. Carbondale and Edwardsville, IL: Southern Illinois University Press, 1958.

Mayer, David. *Harlequin in His Element: The English Pantomime, 1806–1836*. Cambridge, MA: Harvard University Press, 1969.

Meisel, Martin. *Realizations: Narrative, Pictorial and Theatrical Arts in Nineteenth-Century England*. Princeton, NJ: Princeton University Press, 1983.

Mellor, Anne K. 'Joanna Baillie and the Counter-Public Sphere'. *Studies in Romanticism* 33.4 (1994): 559–67.

Milhous, Judith and Robert Hume. 'Playwrights' Remuneration in Eighteenth-Century London'. *Harvard Library Bulletin* 10:2/3 (1999): 3–90.

Milhous, Judith, Gabriella Dideriksen and Robert D. Hume. *Italian Opera in Late Eighteenth-Century London, Vol. 2: The Pantheon Opera and its Aftermath 1789–1795*. Oxford: Clarendon, 2001.

Milling, Jane and Martin Banham, eds. *Extraordinary Actors: Essays on Popular Performers – Studies in Honour of Peter Thomson*. Exeter: University of Exeter Press, 2004.

Moody, Jane '"Fine Word, Legitimate!" Towards a Theatrical History of Romanticism'. *Texas Studies in Literature and Language* 38:3/4 (1996): 223–44.

'The Silence of New Historicism: A Mutinous Echo from 1830'. *Nineteenth Century Theatre* 22:2 (1996): 61–89.

'Illusions of Authorship'. In *Women and Playwriting in Nineteenth-Century Britain*. Ed. Tracy C. Davis and Ellen Donkin. Cambridge: Cambridge University Press, 1999.

Illegitimate Theatre in London, 1770–1840. Cambridge: Cambridge University Press, 2000.

'Romantic Shakespeare'. In *The Cambridge Companion to Shakespeare on Stage*. Ed. Stanley Wells and Sarah Stanton. Cambridge: Cambridge University Press, 2002.

Morash, Christopher. *A History of the Irish Theatre, 1601–2000*. Cambridge: Cambridge University Press, 2002.

Morwood, James. *The Life and Works of Richard Brinsley Sheridan*. Edinburgh: Scottish Academic Press, 1985.

Morwood, James and David Crane, eds. *Sheridan Studies*. Cambridge: Cambridge University Press, 1995.

Mulrooney, Jonathan. 'Keats in the Company of Kean'. *Studies in Romanticism* 42:2 (2003): 227–50.

Newey, Katherine. 'Women and History on the Romantic Stage: More, Yearsley, Burney and Mitford'. In *Women in British Romantic Theatre: Drama, Performance, and Society, 1790–1840*. Ed. Catherine B. Burroughs. Cambridge: Cambridge University Press, 2000.

Women's Theatrical Writing in Britain. Basingstoke: Palgrave, 2005.

Nicoll, Allardyce. *A History of English Drama, 1660–1900, Vol 6: A Short Title Alphabetical Catalogue of Plays produced or printed in England from 1600–1900*. Cambridge: Cambridge University Press, 1959.

A History of English Drama, 1660–1900, Vol 3: Late Eighteenth Century Drama, 1750–1800. Cambridge: Cambridge University Press, 1963.

A History of English Drama, 1660–1900, Vol 4: Early Nineteenth Century Drama, 1750–1800. Cambridge: Cambridge University Press, 1966.

The Garrick Stage: Theatres and Audiences in the Eighteenth Century. Manchester: Manchester University Press, 1980.

Nikolopoulou, Anastasia. 'Historical Disruptions: the Walter Scott Melodramas'. In *Melodrama: The Cultural Emergence of a Genre*. Ed. Michael Hays and Anastasia Nikolopoulou. New York: St Martin's, 1996.

Nussbaum, Felicity. *The Limits of the Human: Fictions of Anomaly, Race, and Gender in the Long Eighteenth Century*. Cambridge: Cambridge University Press, 2003.

'The Theatre of Empire: Racial Counterfeit, Racial Realism'. In *A New Imperial History: Culture, Identity, and Modernity in Britain and the Empire, 1660–1840*. Ed. Kathleen Wilson. Cambridge: Cambridge University Press, 2004.

'Actresses and the Economics of Celebrity, 1700–1800'. In *Theatre and Celebrity in Britain, 1660–2000*. Ed. Mary Luckhurst and Jane Moody. Basingstoke: Palgrave, 2005.

O'Brien, John. *Harlequin Britain: Pantomime and Entertainment, 1690–1760*. Baltimore, MA: Johns Hopkins University Press, 2004.

O'Quinn, Daniel J. 'Inchbald's Indies: Domestic and Dramatic Re-Orientations'. *European Romantic Review* 9:2 (1998): 217–30.

'Scissors and Needles: Inchbald's *Wives as They Were, Maids as They Are* and the Governance of Sexual Exchange'. *Theatre Journal* 51:2 (1999): 105–25.

'Mercantile Deformities: George Colman's *Inkle and Yarico* and the Racialization of Class Relations'. *Theatre Journal* 54:3 (2002): 389–409.

Staging Governance: Theatrical Imperialism in London, 1770–1800. Baltimore, MA: The Johns Hopkins University Press, 2005.

O'Toole, Fintan. *A Traitor's Kiss: The Life of Richard Brinsley Sheridan*. New York: Farrar, Straus and Giroux, 1997.

Page, Judith. '"Hath not a Jew Eyes?": Edmund Kean and the Sympathetic Shylock'. *Wordsworth Circle* 34:2 (2003): 116–19.

Parker, Reeve. 'Reading Wordsworth's Power: Narrative and Usurpation in *The Borderers*'. *ELH* 54:2 (1987): 299–331.

'*Osorio's* Dark Employments: Tricking Out Coleridgean Tragedy'. *Studies in Romanticism* 33:1 (1994): 119–60.

Parsons, Florence Mary. *Garrick and His Circle*. London: Methuen, 1906.

Pascoe, Judith. *Romantic Theatricality: Gender, Poetry, and Spectatorship*. Ithaca, NY: Cornell University Press, 1997.

Payne, Deborah C. 'Reified Object or Emergent Professional? Retheorizing the Restoration Actress'. In *Cultural Readings of Restoration and Eighteenth-Century English Theater*. Ed. Douglas J. Canfield and Deborah C. Payne. Athens, GA: University of Georgia Press, 1995.

Pedicord, Harry William. *The Theatrical Public in the Time of Garrick*. New York: King's Crown Press, 1954.

'The Changing Audience'. In *The London Theatre World, 1660–1800*. Ed. Robert D. Hume. Carbondale and Edwardsville, IL: Southern Illinois University Press, 1980.

Peters, Julie Stone. *Theatre of the Book, 1480–1880: Print, Text, and Performance in Europe*. Oxford: Oxford University Press, 2000.

Playfair, Giles. *Kean: The Life and Paradox of a Great Actor*. London: Reinhardt and Evans, 1939.

Postlewait, Thomas. 'From Melodrama to Realism: The Suspect History of American Drama'. In *Melodrama: The Cultural Emergence of a Genre*. Ed. Michael Hays and Anastasia Nikolopoulou. New York: St Martin's Press, 1996.

Pratt, Kathryn. '"Dark Catastrophe of Passion": The "Indian" as Human Commodity in Nineteenth-Century British Theatrical Culture'. *Studies in Romanticism* 41:4 (2002): 605–26.

Price, Cecil. *Theatre in the Age of Garrick*. Oxford: Blackwell, 1973.

Price, Curtis, Judith Milhous and Robert D. Hume. *Italian Opera in Late Eighteenth-Century London, Vol 1: The King's Theatre, Haymarket, 1778–1791*. Oxford: Clarendon, 1995.

Pullen, Kristen. *Actresses and Whores: On Stage and In Society*. Cambridge: Cambridge University Press, 2005.

Purinton, Marjean. *Romantic Ideology Unmasked: The Mentally Constructed Tyrannies in Dramas of William Wordsworth, Lord Byron, Percy Shelley, and Joanna Baillie*. Newark, DE: University of Delaware Press, 1994.

Quintana, Ricardo. *Oliver Goldsmith: A Georgian Study*. London: Weidenfeld and Nicolson, 1967.

Richards, Jeffrey. *Drama, Theatre, and Identity in the American New Republic*. Cambridge: Cambridge University Press, 2005.

Richards, Kenneth and Peter Thomson, eds. *Nineteenth Century British Theatre: The Proceedings of a Symposium Sponsored by the Manchester University Department of Drama*. London: Methuen, 1971.

Richardson, Alan. *A Mental Theater: Poetic Drama and Consciousness in the Romantic Age*. University Park, PA: Pennsylvania State University Press, 1988.

Roach, Joseph. *The Player's Passion: Studies in the Science of Acting*. London: Associated University Presses, 1985.

  Cities of the Dead: Circum-Atlantic Performance. New York: Columbia University Press, 1996.

  'Patina: Mrs Siddons and the Depth of Surfaces'. In *Notorious Muse: The Actress in British Art and Culture, 1776–1812*. Ed. Robyn Asleson. New Haven, CT: Yale University Press, 2003.

Rosenfeld, Sybil. *Strolling Players and Drama in the Provinces 1660–1765*. New York: Octagon, 1970.

  Temples of Thespis: Some Private Theatres and Theatricals in England and Wales, 1700–1820. London: Society for Theatre Research, 1978.

  Georgian Scene Painters and Scene Painting. Cambridge: Cambridge University Press, 1981.

Rosenthal, Laura J. 'The Sublime, The Beautiful, The Siddons'. In *The Clothes that Wear Us: Essays on Dressing and Transgressing in Eighteenth-Century Culture*. Ed. Jessica Munns and Penny Richards. Newark, DE: University of Delaware Press, 1999.

  Infamous Commerce: Prostitution in Eighteenth-Century British Literature and Culture. Ithaca, NY: Cornell University Press, 2006.

Rousseau, G. S. *Oliver Goldsmith: The Critical Heritage*. London: Routledge, 1974.

Roy, Donald, ed. *Romantic and Revolutionary Theatre, 1789–1860*. Cambridge: Cambridge University Press, 2003.

Russell, Gillian. 'Playing at Revolution: The Politics of the O.P. Riots of 1809'. *Theatre Notebook* 44 (1990): 16–26.

  The Theatres of War: Performance, Politics and Society, 1793–1815. Oxford: Clarendon, 1995.

  'Burke's Dagger: Theatricality, Politics and Print Culture in the 1790s'. *British Journal for Eighteenth-Century Studies* 20 (1997): 1–16.

Russell, Gillian and Clara Tuite, eds. *Romantic Sociability: Social Networks and Literary Culture in Britian, 1770–1840*. Cambridge: Cambridge University Press, 2002.

Rzepka, Charles, ed. *Obi. Romantic Praxis* (August 2002) www.rc.umd.edu/praxis/obi/about.html

Saglia, Diego. 'Mediterranean cenresh: 1820s Verse Tragedies and Revolutions in the South'. *Romanticism* 11:1 (2005): 99–113.

Schofield, Mary Anne and Cecilia Macheski, eds. *Curtain Calls: British and American Women and the Theater, 1660–1820*. Athens, OH: Ohio University Press, 1991.

Scouten, Arthur H., ed. *The London Stage, 1660–1800: A Calendar of Plays, Entertainments and Afterpieces, Part 3: 1729–1747*. 2 vols. Carbondale, IL: Southern Illinois University Presss, 1961.

Scullion, Adrienne. *Female Playwrights of the Nineteenth Century*. London: J. M. Dent, 1996.

Sherbo, Arthur. *English Sentimental Drama*. East Lansing, MI: Michigan State University Press, 1957.

Simpson, Michael. *Closet Performances: Political Exhibition and Prohibition in the Dramas of Byron and Shelley*. Stanford, CA: Stanford University Press, 1998.

ed. 'Romantic Drama in Place'. Special issue of *Texas Studies in Literature and Language* 41.4 (1999).

Smallwood, Angela J. 'Women in the Theatre'. In *Women and Literature in Britain, 1700–1800*. Ed. Vivien Jones. Cambridge: Cambridge University Press, 2000.

Smith, Dane Farnsworth and M. L. Lawhon. *Plays About the Theatre in England; or, The Self Conscious Stage from Foote to Sheridan*. Lewisburg, KY: Bucknell University Press, 1979.

Steiner, George. *The Death of Tragedy*. London: Faber and Faber, 1961.

Stephens, J. R. *The Censorship of English Drama, 1824–1901*. Cambridge: Cambridge University Press, 1980.

Stone, George Winchester, Jr, ed. *The London Stage, 1660–1800: A Calendar of Plays, Entertainments and Afterpieces, Part 4: 1747–1776*. 2 vols. Carbondale, IL: Southern Illinois University Press, 1962.

Stone, George Winchester, Jr. *The Stage and the Page: London's 'Whole Show' in the Eighteenth-Century Theatre*. Berkeley and Los Angeles, CA: University of California Press, 1981.

Stone, George Winchester, Jr. and George M. Kahrl. *David Garrick: A Critical Biography*. Carbondale, IL: Southern Illinois University Press, 1979.

Stratman, Carl J. *Britain's Theatrical Periodicals, 1720–1967*. New York: New York Public Library, 1972.

Straub, Kristina. *Sexual Suspects: Eighteenth-Century Players and Sexual Ideology*. Princeton, NJ: Princeton University Press, 1992.

Straub, Kristina. 'Actors and Homophobia'. In *Cultural Readings of Restoration and Eighteenth-Century English Theater*. Ed. J. Douglas Canfield and Deborah C. Payne. Athens, GA: University of Georgia Press, 1995.

Swarbrick, Andrew, ed. *The Art of Oliver Goldsmith*. London: Vision, 1984.

Swindells, Julia. *Glorious Causes: The Grand Theatre of Political Change, 1789–1833*. Oxford: Oxford University Press, 2001.

Taylor, George. '"The Just Delineation of the Passions": Theories of Acting in the Age of Garrick'. In *Essays on the Eighteenth-Century English Stage*. Ed. Kenneth Richards and Peter Thomson. London: Methuen, 1972.

The French Revolution and the London Stage, 1789–1805. Cambridge: Cambridge University Press, 2000.

Thomas, David, ed. *Restoration and Georgian England, 1660–1788*. Cambridge: Cambridge University Press, 1989.

Thompson, James. *Models of Value: Eighteenth-Century Political Economy and the Novel*. Durham, NC: Duke University Press, 1996.

Thomson, Peter. *On Actors and Acting*. Exeter: University of Exeter Press, 2000.

Tomalin, Claire. *Mrs Jordan's Profession: The Actress and the Prince*. New York: Knopf, 1995.

Wanko, Cheryl. *Roles of Authority: Thespian Biography and Celebrity in Eighteenth-Century Britain*. Lubbock, TX: Texas Tech University Press, 2003.

Wardle, Ralph, M. *Oliver Goldsmith*. Lawrence, KS: University of Kansas Press, 1957.

Watkins, Daniel. *A Materialist Critique of English Romantic Drama*. Gainesville, FL: University of Florida Press, 1993.

Watson, Ernest Bradlee. *Sheridan to Robertson: A Study of the Nineteenth-Century Stage*. New York: Benjamin Bloom, 1926.

West, Shearer. *The Image of the Actor: Verbal and Visual Representations in the Age of Garrick and Kemble*. New York: St. Martin's, 1991.

West, Shearer. 'The Public and Private Roles of Sarah Siddons'. In *A Passion for Performance: Sarah Siddons and Her Portraitists*. Ed. Robyn Asleson. Los Angeles, CA: Getty Museum, 1999.

'Body Conoisseurship'. In *Notorious Muse: the Actress in British Art and Culture, 1776–1812*. Ed. Robyn Asleson. New Haven, CT: Yale University Press, 2003.

Wheatley, Christopher. '*Beneath Ierne's Banners': Irish Protestant Drama of the Restoration and Eighteenth Century*. Notre Dame, IN: University of Notre Dame Press, 1999.

White, Shane. *Stories of Freedom in Black New York*. Cambridge, MA: Harvard University Press, 2002.

Wilson, Kathleen. 'Pacific Modernity: Theater, Englishness, and the Arts of Discovery'. In *The Age of Cultural Revolutions: Britain and France, 1750–1820*. Ed. Colin Jones and Dror Wahrman. Berkeley, CA: University of California Press, 2002.

The Island Race: Englishness, Empire and Gender in the Eighteenth Century. London and New York: Routledge, 2003.

Wilson, Kathleen, ed. *A New Imperial History: Culture, Identity, and Modernity in Britain and the Empire, 1660–1840*. Cambridge: Cambridge University Press, 2004.

Wood, Gillen D'Arcy, ed. 'Romanticism and Opera'. *Romantic Praxis* (May 2005): www.rc.umd.edu/praxis/opera/toc.html.

Woodfield, Ian. *Opera and Drama in Eighteenth-Century London: The King's Theatre, Garrick, and the Business of Performance*. Cambridge: Cambridge University Press, 2001.

Woods, Leigh. *Garrick Claims the Stage: Acting as Social Emblem in Eighteenth-Century England*. New York: Greenwood, 1984.

Worrall, David. 'Artisan Melodrama and the Plebeian Public Sphere: The Political Culture of Drury Lane and its Environs, 1797–1830'. *Studies in Romanticism* 39:2 (2000): 213–27.

Theatric Revolution: Drama, Censorship and Romantic Period Subcultures, 1773–1832. Oxford: Oxford University Press, 2006.

Worth, Katharine. *Sheridan and Goldsmith*. London: Macmillan, 1992.

Worthen, William B. *The Idea of the Actor: Drama and the Ethics of Performance*. Princeton, NJ: Princeton University Press, 1984.

Ziter, Edward. *The Orient on the Victorian Stage*. Cambridge: Cambridge University Press, 2003.

INDEX

Cambridge Companions to . . .

AUTHORS